HARVARD ECONOMIC STUDIES

VOLUME XCVII

The studies in this series are published by the Department of Economics of Harvard University, which, however, assumes no responsibility for the views expressed

THE ENFORCEMENT OF ENGLISH APPRENTICESHIP

A Study in Applied Mercantilism

1563 — 1642

By

Margaret Gay Davies

HARVARD UNIVERSITY PRESS

Cambridge, Massachusetts

1956

Distributed in Great Britain by
Geoffrey Cumberlege
Oxford University Press
London

Library of Congress Catalog Card Number 55–10967
Printed in the United States of America

PREFACE

The present study was begun under the guidance of the late Edwin Francis Gay as an inquiry into the operation of the Statute of Artificers in the eighteenth century, with the hope of isolating some factors in the rise of *laissez faire*. The investigation was to be concerned principally with the Act's most important apprenticeship clause, that requiring the seven-year term. But in spite of works of major value and importance on the subject of English mercantilism, the actual means of enforcement of mercantilist regulations in the sixteenth and seventeenth centuries is virtually unexplored territory, and the Act of 1563 is no exception. Separate treatment, therefore, of the apprenticeship law before 1642 appeared to be advisable. The one full-length study heretofore published rests mainly on municipal records; in the present book, the history of regulation in borough and corporate town was disregarded, as being already better documented and more fully known than in the county jurisdictions.

Prosecutions in central and local courts, and inquiries and orders by central and local authorities, have been utilized as basic objective evidence of attempted enforcement of the law. Essential manuscript materials were the court records. Those of two central courts were selected for examination: the Memoranda Rolls of the King's Remembrancer's Department of the Exchequer and the Coram Rege Rolls of the King's Bench, Crown Side. Time was lacking to search those of the Court of Common Pleas, where it is known that apprenticeship prosecutions were brought. Surviving records of the circuit courts were utilized, but a continuous series from 1563 is extant only for Essex out of the fifteen counties to which the study was intentionally limited. These counties were selected, their number and identity varying in the different periods according to the availability of their quarter sessions records, to represent the woolen industry of the southwest, the mixed textile industries of the north, the agricultural and metalworking midlands, and the industrial and commercial east. London and adjacent shires, Essex excepted, were omitted from consideration as presenting special problems. The fifteen (arranged by regional groups) are: Devonshire, Somersetshire, Wiltshire, Worcestershire, Essex, Norfolk, the West and North Ridings of Yorkshire, Lancashire, Cheshire, Staffordshire, Warwickshire, Nottinghamshire, Northamptonshire, Leicestershire.

In this group, the only county for which manuscript records were not utilized was the North Riding. For the others, examination of the archives was necessary either to supplement published material or because of the lack of it. So far as time permitted, both sessions rolls and sessions minute books (the memoranda of sessions business) were searched, and order books (the record of judicial and administrative orders issued at quarter sessions) were sampled. It was occasionally possible also to examine some of the files of petitions, depositions, and recognizances, but not as fully as would have been desirable. Search was continuous through each reign, except where indicated in the text below or in the Bibliography. The sessions rolls, in which all the original documents for each sessions were usually filed, were found to be the most satisfactory class of record wherever they are reasonably intact, for the purpose of accumulating a total of prosecutions and orders, although minute books may be an indispensable record of the results of prosecution. Because of the long and relatively continuous series of sessions rolls in Essex, preserved from pre-Elizabethan days with fewer serious gaps than in the other selected counties, the Essex quarter sessions supplied most of the evidence of local procedures and practice in apprenticeship enforcement in the sixteenth and earlier seventeenth centuries. But this would not have been possible had publication of the present study not been delayed many years — an undeserved reward for procrastination, since in the interval the policy of the Essex county authorities underwent a complete change. Whereas in former days a fee was charged for the use of the county's archives sufficient to limit research to only a sampling for discontinuous periods, recently the Essex county authorities have put historians greatly in their debt by preparing a full typescript calendar of the sessions rolls down to 1660 and by allowing it to be filmed.

In two other counties of the group, Staffordshire and Wiltshire, publication in full of sessions records of the Elizabethan period has added, since the days when research in England for this study was completed, to the growing body of valuable printed sources for the history of local government. It has therefore been possible, for these counties and for Essex, to check the writer's notes taken from manuscript with the records now available in print or typescript. While it is not vital to the conclusions of the present work that the number of apprenticeship cases originally tabulated from manuscript should have been found to be exact, it is a satisfaction to be able to state that in the three counties no major discrepancies were seen and only three certain additions discovered to the original count of apprenticeship cases. The comparison suggested, however, the possibility that in other counties an occasional case may have escaped the writer's observation if the sole record of it is among the files of recognizances from defendants: lack of time prevented more than brief sampling of this class of document.

For the sake of brevity, several shortcuts in phrasing have been adopted throughout the following pages. When reference is made to quantity of prosecutions in quarter sessions records, this will be understood to mean, unless otherwise specified, the records of the group of selected counties as listed herein, with the necessary variations from one reign to the next according to the survival of sessions material. These variations, however, did not affect the tabulation of prosecutions in the Westminster courts, which were traced for twelve counties throughout, as shown in the Tables in Appendix II. When reference is made to the Westminster courts, this will mean the two departments in the Exchequer and the King's Bench mentioned above. Violations of the seven-year term of apprenticeship, the Section 24 of the Act of 1563 which is the subject of this work, will usually be referred to as "apprenticeship offenses" or "apprenticeship prosecutions"; when violations of any other of the apprenticeship provisions of the Act are intended, they will be specifically designated.

The lapse of time since I first began to gather the materials for this monograph has made it difficult to acknowledge my obligations in full. Some of those to whom my gratitude is due are no longer alive.

During the initial period of research in England in 1927–1930, and again in the summer of 1933, I received the aid always so freely given to the visiting American scholar by the custodians of central and local archives. To the officials then at the Public Record Office, at the British Museum, at shire hall and town hall, my obligations are many. I must add a special word of thanks for friendly help in the use of county sessions records in Norfolk, Northamptonshire, Lancashire, and Wiltshire. In the last county in particular, no pains were spared to solve a problem in logistics for my attack on the archives, presented by the fact that the latter were housed at Devizes while a comfortable room in which to work — with a fire, if I remember correctly — was put at my disposal in the county offices at Trowbridge. I have grateful memories also of opportunities to read in various libraries in England: that of the Institute for Historical Research then so conveniently accessible in hours after the Record Office and the British Museum had closed, and in city or town libraries whose staffs were uniformly welcoming.

To several individuals in England I owe my thanks for advice and encouragement. I can mention here only the names of the late Hubert Hall whose kindly assistance benefited so many scholars, both beginners like myself and the experienced; Sir Hilary Jenkinson; Professor R. H. Tawney, who allowed me to attend one of his seminars; the late Walter Rye of Norfolk, for an interview in which his commonsense approach to Tudor local government offered valuable hints; Mr. A. P. Wadsworth and the late James Tait for useful suggestions about local sources and treatment of the subject; and not least, Miss Joan Wake, for helpful references to material and for sympathetic interest.

For continuing work in this country, chiefly in secondary materials, I had the privilege of access in earlier years to the rich collections of local history in Harvard University's Widener Library, and in more recent years to those of the Huntington Library. Here I must especially speak not only of the microfilms obtained by the Huntington Library of manuscript material essential for the study of local government — *Libri Pacis* of the Elizabethan and early Stuart periods and the typescript Calendar of Essex sessions rolls — but of the atmosphere of friendliness created by the library staff and of their unfailing willingness and ability to assist readers.

My list of debts to American teachers and scholars should begin with those of my undergraduate and graduate student days who stimulated my interest in historical studies: the late Wilbur C. Abbott and the late Charles H. Haskins; Professor Charles F. McIlwain; Professor Abbott P. Usher in whose course a term paper on English mercantilism initiated me into the difficulties of that topic.

In direct connection with the making of this book, I am grateful to Miss Bertha H. Putnam both for her works as exemplars of scholarship and for the spoken word of encouragement in the early days of my research. I am grateful also to Professor N. S. B. Gras for his encouragement, particularly in giving me an opportunity to contribute a paper on my subject to a *Festschrift* though I was yet untried.

For encouragement and advice in revising my doctoral dissertation, I am deeply grateful to Professor Herbert Heaton. I have endeavored to turn his valuable suggestions to account. I owe thanks also to Professor Helen M. Cam and to Sir George Clark for their stimulating criticism, and to Professor John H. Gleason for helpful comment on the pages dealing with the justices of the peace. My thanks go to Mrs. Jane Carroll for her care and patience in typing the manuscript.

To Radcliffe College I owe not only my training but the financial aid which made possible two of the years in England necessary for this study. Its publication was facilitated by the kind interest of Professor Arthur H. Cole, Chairman of the Committee on Research in Economic History, in submitting the manuscript for approval. I wish to express my gratitude to the Department of Economics of Harvard University for making publication possible.

To my parents, the late Edwin Francis Gay and Louise Randolph Gay, I owe a constant support both material and spiritual and an intellectual debt which spans my life. Those who were students under my father knew what riches of knowledge and wisdom were theirs for the taking. For the many defects of this book his memory bears no blame. The first draft of most of it had been put entirely aside during and immediately after the war years 1941–1945. When I began once more the task of writing, I was without his guidance. Of the manuscript as read and criticized by him, only a little remains — some sections of Chapters II, III, and VII to IX. My attention was originally directed to the problems of business fluctuations in the sixteenth and seventeenth centuries by a collection he was making of business annals of these periods. But the analysis of relationships between apprenticeship enforcement and business fluctuations, in Chapter V of the present book, was undertaken when he could no longer approve or direct. His pioneer use of Exchequer sources for his study of the inclosure movement not only prompted him to set me at work on them but also provided, later on, supplementary material on the informer from the storehouse of his notes.

To my husband Godfrey Davies my debt is of shorter duration but equally impossible to express. He has underwritten my slow labors with his unflagging support and interest, and few pages of the book have not benefited from his gift for lucid statement.

May 28, 1955 M. G. D.

CONTENTS

THE ENFORCEMENT OF ENGLISH APPRENTICESHIP

A STUDY IN APPLIED MERCANTILISM

1563–1642

ABBREVIATIONS USED IN THE NOTES

Acts P.C.	*Acts of the Privy Council of England*
C.J.	*Journals of the House of Commons*
Cal. Q.S.	Calendar of Quarter Sessions Rolls (Essex Record Office)
Cal. S.P.D.	*Calendar of State Papers Domestic*
K.B.C.R.	King's Bench Coram Rege
K.R.M.R.	King's Remembrancer Memoranda Rolls
N.R.R.S.	North Riding Record Society
P.C.R.	Privy Council Register
P.R.O.	Public Record Office
Q.B.C.R.	Queen's Bench Coram Rege
Q.R.M.R.	Queen's Remembrancer Memoranda Rolls
Q.S.R.	Quarter Sessions Records
S.P.D.	State Papers Domestic

GENERAL INTRODUCTION

The Statute of Artificers of 1563 declared itself to be, and was, with two very important exceptions, a codification of previous legislation. Its provisions have been too often described for all of them to need review, especially since of the three main parts of the Act — regulation of the contract of service for all hired labor, wage assessment by the justices of the peace, and the regulation of apprenticeship — the present study deals only with the third.[1]

The regulation of apprenticeship was one of the important new departures of the Act, the other being the periodic assessment of wages.[2] The novelty of the apprenticeship clauses attached chiefly to Section 24. The seven-year term of apprenticeship which this required for entry into "every craft, mystery, or occupation" then used in the realm was not a new practice in industrial life. But its removal from the sphere of municipal and craft control and its uniform application without distinction of place were new. Two other features of the apprenticeship policy created by the Act were new in detail if not in principle. One was an elaborate definition of eligibility to take

[1] The fullest outline of the provisions of the Act (*Statutes of the Realm*, IV, Pt. 1, 5 Eliz., c. 4) with emphasis on its character as uniform national legislation will be found in W. Cunningham, *The Growth of English Industry and Commerce*, 6th ed., II, 25ff; discussion of the apprenticeship clauses in O. J. Dunlop and R. D. Denman, *English Apprenticeship and Child Labour*, 64–71, with emphasis on the Act's relation to the problem of vagrancy; the most modern and in some points more illuminating review, in Eli Heckscher, *Mercantilism*, tr. M. Shapiro, I, 224–32. A valuable unpublished study appears to be that of T. K. Derry, "The Enforcement of a Seven Years' Apprenticeship under the Statute of Artificers," known to the present writer only in summary in *Abstracts of Dissertations for the Degree of Doctor of Philosophy*, Oxford University, IV, 9–17.

[2] In practice, this had been anticipated by wage assessments in 1560–61; see B. H. Putnam, "Northamptonshire Wage Assessments of 1560 and 1667," *The Economic History Review*, I, No. 1, 124–134; *Tudor Economic Documents*, ed. R. H. Tawney and E. Power, I, 334–338.

apprentices or be apprenticed, according to residence, income level, and occupation, which, in contrast to Section 24, was selective between town and country. The other was the institution of compulsory apprenticeship up to the age of twenty-one at the discretion of the justices of the peace, a provision which seems to be modeled on the parallel compulsion to enter hired service which was imposed on all meeting certain conditions of age and status.[3] The final item in the Act's series of rules for apprenticeship was a limitation on the proportion of apprentices to journeymen imposed on employers in textile occupations, shoemaking, and tailoring, a replica of a clause in a statute of 1549/50.[4]

The present study will be centered on the requirement for a seven-year term, the most durable of all the provisions. This comprised several objectives, though it cannot be known whether all were consciously intended. For industry, compulsory training in the occupation later to be followed as a livelihood was applied regardless of location.[5] Ostensibly at least, the similar requirement imposed earlier for the woolen industry [6] had been welcomed by mercantile and established craft interests as a means of improving the quality of the product.[7] For the national economy, a standard of occupational immobility was established, which if effective would tend to retard all expansion in industrial output. This restrictionism was probably even more acceptable than the required industrial training to the monopolizing merchants and craftsmen who had urged it eleven years before for the woolen industry. For social policy, the apprenticeship clauses as a whole reveal the intention that the seven-year term must not release the apprentice before the minimum age of twenty-one anywhere, and twenty-four in corporate towns. This was probably directed against a too rapid increase of poor households, and has a parallel in a rule for London seven years before in which increased poverty was ascribed to "over-hasty marriages and over-soon setting

[3] The pertinent clauses of the Act are transcribed in Appendix I, except for Section 18 which merely defines the right of a householder tilling half an acre or more to take apprentices in husbandry.

[4] Sect. 26 of 5 Eliz., c. 4, repeating Sect. 3 of 3 & 4 Ed. VI, c. 22. See App. I.

[5] With two exceptions: the Act expressly left intact the pre-existing "custom of London" permitting entry into *any* occupation by a freeman of the city, i.e. one who had been admitted by apprenticeship, patrimony, or redemption to make his living therein; and the similar "custom of Norwich" (Sect. 33).

[6] By a series of statutes in the 1550's; see below, Chap. V, n. 6.

[7] G. Unwin, *Studies in Economic History*, 148.

up of households by young folk."[8] The same association reappears forty years later, when a set of orders drawn up in quarter sessions at the request of Wiltshire weavers included, for the same purpose, a prohibition on apprentices coming out of their covenants before twenty-four years of age.[9]

The particular objectives of the Act are dominated by the necessary preoccupation of the period with the dangers of social unrest and disorder. These were at the root of the "pro-agrarian" character of English economic policy,[10] of which the Statute of Artificers is the most comprehensive expression. As a theoretical matter, agrarianism was grounded on belief in stability; as a matter of policy for the realm, on greater independence of foreign markets and food supply. The men who legislated agrarian measures faced the practical problem of a sufficient supply of docile labor in fields and rural crafts as one of daily importance, and recognized in the existence of bands of roving vagabonds a dangerous threat to the security of life and property.

An often quoted expression of the responsibility of industry in sowing the seed of rebellion is that of John Hales early in the reign of Edward VI, in the words of the knight in his dialogue who is thought to represent the views of the country gentry: "all these insurrections do stir by occasion of all these clothiers; for when our clothiers lack vent over sea, there is great multitude . . . idle; and when they be idle, then they assemble in companies and murmur for lack of living. . ."[11] Fifteen years later, Sir William Cecil, already the leading statesman of the age, who had seen since 1549 further alternations of "vent over sea," favored continued nonintercourse with Antwerp on the ground that "the diminution of clothing in this realm were profitable" since the industry caused the decay of tillage and import of foreign grain, created a class of people "of worse condition to be quietly governed than the husbandmen," and was the reason for the lack of artificers in corporate towns and of "laborers for all common

[8] Dunlop and Denman, *English Apprenticeship*, 69–70.

[9] Wiltshire MS. Sessions Rolls, Michaelmas Sessions, 1 Jas. I. The contemporary acceptance of the utility of apprenticeship on these grounds is mentioned by R. H. Tawney, *The Agrarian Problem in the Sixteenth Century*, 106n. He cites the London rule, and the Wiltshire weavers' petition which closely resembled the final order.

[10] The term is applied by Heckscher, in *Mercantilism*, I, 231.

[11] [John Hales], *A Discourse of the Common Weal of This Realm of England* [1549], ed. E. Lamond, 88; see Unwin, *Studies*, 187–188.

works."[12] The framers of the Act of 1563 would also, like Cecil, have remembered the depressions and discontents of the years since the still recent insurrection in 1549. What they feared from such a decline of cloth exports as had occurred since 1561[13] is illustrated by the muttering of a credulous unemployed weaver of Colchester in 1566. He was accused of inciting to rebellion, with speeches such as "weavers occupation is a dead science nowadays and it will never be better before we make a rising" and with plans to ride through the clothing villages crying "they are up" to Colchester where the church bells would be rung, and all this in midsummer "for at that time began the last commotion."[14]

Attempts to cure the complex of evils described by Cecil had produced since 1549 a series of legislative proposals to halt the extension of country industry. Their chief outcome was the group of statutes known as the Cloth Acts, which by 1557 had enunciated a policy of restricting entry into textile occupations by requiring apprenticeship and of checking growth of the industry outside the towns by direct prohibition as well as by limitations on the size of the individual craft unit.[15] By 1559 the problem of wages was giving rise to adjustments locally in the statutory rates, and to debate in Elizabeth's first Parliament.[16] Other proposals submitted at this time included the revival of the harsh act of 1547 condemning vagabonds to slavery, tighter control of the hiring of servants and laborers, property restrictions on the choice of occupations by intending apprentices, as well as suggestions for education, regulation of imports, enforcement of laws for the maintenance of tillage, and various other matters of economic and social policy.[17] Some of the existing legislation on these

[12] *Tudor Economic Documents*, II, 45.

[13] F. J. Fisher, "Commercial Trends and Policy in Sixteenth-Century England," *The Economic History Review*, X, No. 2, 96–105.

[14] P.R.O., Assizes Records, Southeastern Circuit, Essex, Indictments Bundles, No. 8.

[15] For a review of some of the bills brought in the Commons, see Cunningham, *Growth of English Industry*, II, 26n. For the Cloth Acts (those restricting entry and expansion) see below, Chap. V, n. 6.

[16] See above, n. 2; *Journals of the House of Commons* (hereafter to be cited as *C.J.*), I, April 21 and April 25, 1559. The national wage levels set by the well-known Ordinances of Laborers of 1349 and the Statute of Laborers of 1351 had been altered from time to time by successive statutes, the most recent of which prior to 1563 was that of 1514/15 (6 Hen. VIII., c. 3, modified the next year for London building trades).

[17] *Tudor Economic Documents*, I, 325–330.

subjects was embodied in proclamations of 1561 and 1562, and committed to the justices of the peace in the counties to enforce. If this was in any sense a trial balloon to test the reception of new legislation, the results cannot have been encouraging, for a report sent to Cecil from Buckinghamshire in 1561 warned him that men were murmuring abroad against the doings of "master secretary Cecil." The justices were described as indifferent to executing the laws, or themselves offenders, or afraid of the rich and great men involved.[18] This resistance demonstrated the power of passive obstruction possessed by the local authorities to whom enforcement of the Statute of Artificers as of other economic regulation was committed. But local resentment was not apparently directed toward that part of the government's exhortations to better administration which concerned the regulation of service, apprenticeship, or wages. These three matters, and also the enforcement of the statutes of apparel, were dealt with by the Buckinghamshire justices of the peace in 1561. They issued a wage assessment for agricultural labor and rural craftsmen which was accompanied by a series of orders applying in part the legislative "program" of 1559 and thus also in part foreshadowing the Act of 1563. The chief anticipation of the latter's apprenticeship clauses was in the order prohibiting husbandmen of less than a specified minimum estate to apprentice their sons to any craft.[19]

The growth of industry, the uncertainties of the market, unemployment and idleness, discontent and vagabondage, violence and rebellion — this was the fatal sequence which must be prevented. Nearly all the steps in it were attacked by some one or more sections of the compendious statute enacted in 1563. The objective of attaining a stable agricultural society stands out prominently: the preamble to the Act of 1563 is devoted chiefly to the problem of adjusting wages to rising costs of living, and concludes with the aspiration that the Act will "banish idleness, advance husbandry, and yield unto the hired person . . . a convenient proportion of wages."

Characteristically, little attention was devoted to the administrative and police machinery which was to effectuate the huge design.

[18] *A Collection of the Substance of Certain Necessary Statutes* . . . (London, 1561); *Tudor Economic Documents*, I, 330–334.

[19] *Tudor Economic Documents*, I, 334–338. The minimum estate was set in these orders at 20/– a year freehold, a more stringent restriction, especially since it applied to all crafts everywhere, than the restrictions of the Act of 1563 (see App. I below).

General competence to hear and determine offenses under the Act was assigned to any of the queen's courts of record, to the justices of oyer and terminer, to "any other justices," to the presidents and councils of the North and of Wales, and to the head officers of corporate jurisdictions.[20] The further special duties of inquiry and of administration which the Act committed to the justices of the peace of every shire are discussed below, so far as they concerned apprenticeship. These indispensable officials, whose early powers derived in considerable measure from the fourteenth-century ancestors of the Act, collectively formed in voluntary association unique and enduring structures of county government. Already the lawmakers — most of whom had some experience as justices — took for granted that these bodies were the natural executives of their multiplying and expanding pronouncements. Still more did the legislators assume without examination the collaboration in this work of the several levels of local officialdom inferior to the justices of the peace. Of these the police and administrative arms concerned in enforcing the Statute of Artificers were the high constables of the chief traditional county subdivisions, and the petty constables of the parishes. Essential to the processes of hearing and determining by the justices of the peace in their courts of quarter sessions were the local juries of presentment as well as the petty juries of trial. Part II of the present work deals with the actual contribution each of these branches of county government made to upholding the apprenticeship law.

The service clauses of the Act, and in essence the regulation of wages, were familiar, almost customary, matters of local enforcement, with the old procedures of the fourteenth and fifteenth centuries still in active use in at least some districts. But outside the incorporated towns, in which compulsory apprenticeship was no novelty, no official means existed to supervise the making and enrolment of apprenticeship contracts or to examine the credentials of new entrants into crafts and trades. None was created by the Act itself. The influence of this lack of administrative machinery and of the absence of customary procedures will be reviewed in connection with the enforcement of the seven-year term. But the virtually complete neglect of the other provisions for apprenticeship requires comment here, since these will not be considered elsewhere in detail.

The vagrancy in Tudor England, which it was the object of a

[20] Sect. 32 of 5 Eliz., c. 4; see App. I

long series of statutes to check [21] and which was perhaps part of a European phenomenon,[22] inspired much of the Act of 1563; in particular the provision of Section 28 for the compulsory apprenticeship of those under twenty-one years of age. In England in the sixteenth and seventeenth centuries little distinction was made in either theory or practice between vagabondage and the mobility of labor. The extent of the latter has not been investigated. But modern hypotheses of the mobility of the Tudor population, based on studies of muster rolls and parish registers, are confirmed to some extent by the Statute of Artificers itself with its stress on a yearly-service contract and its restrictions on the laborer's liberty of movement; by continuing local efforts to enforce these provisions, and by the frequency of presentments of offenders; and by the need to control squatters, resulting at the close of the century in new legislation.[23] The restlessness of labor, which could be documented to advantage from examinations and depositions in county sessions records, may have been partly a characteristic of conditions still those of regional economic frontiers, partly the result of rising prices and rents, and partly, in certain areas, the outcome of inclosures and depopulation. It seems likely that it caused much of the complaint of labor shortages and of "idleness." To the settled householder the migrant craftsman or laborer who would not be content with regular service at the prevailing wage embodied the worst dangers of vagabondage and disorder.[24] The clauses of the Act directly applicable to such irregular labor would probably have been implemented even if the means of doing so had not already been created by early legislation. But Section 28 does not seem to have received an equivalent attention. This relative disregard, if it existed, may be connected with the difficulty apparently experienced after 1597 in finding masters willing to accept parish apprentices; the two

[21] On this, see E. M. Leonard, *The Early History of English Poor Relief*, 47–60, and *passim*.

[22] See the comment on its prevalence in Spain, in E. J. Hamilton, *American Treasure and the Price Revolution in Spain, 1501–1650*, 296.

[23] On mobility, see S. A. Peyton, "The Village Population in the Tudor Lay Subsidy Rolls," *The English Historical Review*, XXX, 234–250; C. Hill, "Professor Lavrovsky's Study of a Seventeenth-Century Manor," *The Economic History Review*, XVI, No. 2, 125–129; E. E. Rich, "The Population of Elizabethan England," *ibid.*, Second Series, II, No. 3, 247–265; A. L. Rowse, *The England of Elizabeth*, 220–225. On squatters, the Act of 1589 (31 Eliz., c. 7).

[24] For an illustration of the contemporary association between the failure of the service contract and vagrancy, see below, Chap. VIII, n. 22; see also the preamble to an act of 1549/50 (3 & 4 Ed. VI, c. 22).

together suggest that the demand in any one locality for child labor on the farm, in the household, and in the craft unit, was limited.[25]

Section 26 of the Act of 1563 restricted the number of apprentices to three for each journeyman employed in six designated occupations. The infrequency and the substance of prosecutions on this clause tend to confirm the impression of small-scale operation in these crafts, which presumably had shown the most marked tendency to increase the size of the shop unit by adding the cheapest labor. Outside London and the larger towns, the charge in the few recorded cases is rarely for more than the minimum illegal number of three apprentices employed without a journeyman. The analogous offense in the textile industry of keeping too many looms likewise is of rare occurrence: cases are numerous in only one area, and even there the number of excess looms per offender is small.[26]

Obscurity conceals the fate of the clauses in the Act of 1563 which set up property and occupational qualifications for apprenticing, distinguishing therein between country and town and among classes of towns.[27] Instances of the enrolment of the required certificate are to be found in some municipal archives, but the present study has made only occasional use of town records.[28] The forerunner of this

[25] Allowance has to be made in judging the enforcement of Sect. 28 for the possibility that unrecorded action under it was usually taken at the justices' "petty sessions" or by a single justice of the peace. By the Act of 1597 (39 Eliz., c. 3), refusals to accept as apprentices the children assigned by local authorities could be proceeded against at the quarter sessions. Presentments in the sessions records occur sufficiently often to justify the suggestion in the text, but there is room for further inquiry into local enforcement. Presumably the quality of the apprentice labor, supplied under the compulsion of the Acts of 1563 and 1597, would be lower than that freely available.

[26] See App. I for the six crafts enumerated in Sect. 26. Regulation of the number of looms was by the Act of 1555 (2 & 3 P. & M., c. 11, §§ 1 and 2). In the later 1570's, numerous prosecutions were brought in the Westminster courts under the Act of 1566 regulating the number of apprentices per journeyman employable in feltmaking, no doubt associated with the struggle of the feltmakers to protect their position, for which see George Unwin, *Industrial Organization in the Sixteenth and Seventeenth Centuries*, 131–135. For indications of the small scale of the ordinary craftsman's work-force, see below, Chap. VIII, n. 11.

[27] Sects. 19–23, 25. In a lawsuit in the reign of James I (involving an apprenticeship contract) the court reportedly commented that the statutory practice of certification by the justices was neglected; see below, Chap. X, n. 50.

[28] For example, enrolments of apprentices' indentures to drapers in the city of Chester are occasionally accompanied in the Elizabethan period by the certificate from the justices of the peace in the parent's county of the latter's estate (MS. Apprentice Indentures, Vol. 1550–1650, sampled for Elizabeth's reign).

type of regulation was a statute of 1405/06,[29] which was among those ordered enforced in the proclamation of 1561. The report made then to Cecil indicated past disregard of the qualification. But Cecil evidently firmly intended reviving a partial direction of the choice of occupations, for the proposals of 1559 laid before Parliament included a measure similar to the property clauses in the Act of 1563. The stated aim was to reduce entry into the occupation of merchant, which was termed "a cloak for vagabonds and thieves," and to remedy the shortage of agricultural labor. Nothing came of the measure proposed at the same time to limit landowning by merchants; the social mobility of the age was too strong a force. Though property qualifications for apprenticing in certain occupations were enacted in 1563, and only sons of townsmen, neither husbandmen nor laborers, could be apprenticed to townsmen, these restrictions belonged to the same futile effort to crystallize a changing social stratification.[30] In any event, the property requirement was set at levels which must have been obsolescent almost from the start, in view of the rising rents and land values. The occupations to which it applied, with the exception of rural weaving, were those which later were able to select apprentices from well-to-do families, as can be seen when the practice of paying a premium developed. A rough comparison can be made of the 40/– and £3 qualifications in the Act of 1563 with incomes of a social group which by no means averaged among the highest, the country clergy. Even by 1535, it has been shown for Leicestershire that the poorest living was worth 45/– a year, there were others from £3½ to £4½, and the most frequent was from £6 to £8. Scattered figures on average holdings and on land values suggest that the affected groups must have been primarily the smaller husbandmen, the cottagers, and the laborers.[31] Their sons might in any event have been

---

But a recent study of the Shrewsbury drapers' organization finds it "hard to imagine" that Sect. 20 of the Act was observed, although the evidence is considered not clear on the point. (T. C. Mendenhall, *The Shrewsbury Drapers and the Welsh Wool Trade in the 16th and 17th Centuries*, 99–100.)

[29] 7 Hen. IV, c. 17, requiring a 20/– landed property on the part of the parents for apprenticeship within a city or borough.

[30] For the comment on the proposal to restrict landowning, see the discussion of social mobility in the Introduction to T. Wilson, *A Discourse upon Usury*, ed. R. H. Tawney, 41.

[31] The parsons' livings, in W. G. Hoskins, *Essays in Leicestershire History*, 1–2. Comparisons taken from different places have very little utility in view of the probably wide disparities in movement of rents and size of holding. In

discouraged from apprenticeships in corporate towns by the enrolment fees. The clause that might have been in practice a real obstruction if enforced was Section 25, the £3 estate qualification for the parents of an apprentice to a country weaver, but on present evidence it must be supposed that this was largely disregarded.

There can be little doubt that the most original provision of the Act, the requirement of a seven-year term of apprenticeship for entry to all occupations, was, alone among the apprenticeship clauses, already widely applied on a voluntary basis. The long continued vitality of the institution of apprenticeship cannot be understood without appreciating that the Act of 1563 did not legislate this into being, not even in the narrower sense of the precise length of term and not even in country places. The adoption of a seven-year term, compulsory in some municipalities for generations and in others a recent requirement,[32] is found in too many scattered rural localities too soon after the passage of the Act, for this to have been the cause. An already widespread practice of a long apprenticeship appears the most reasonable explanation of the statute's peculiar distinction from continental legislation, its freedom from the rigidities of local privilege.[33] In imposing no requirement that the place where the term of apprenticeship was served must be that of residence for the later exercise of the occupation, the Act may have recognized that apprenticeship had already ceased to be the prerogative of the town craftsman and had become a characteristic feature of the intermingled agricultural-industrial life of the countryside. This is not to say that the Act in itself increased local mobility, since it conferred no *right*

Leicestershire an average husbandman, in one group sampled, by 1530 held about 36 acres of arable land alone (*ibid.*, 147–148); but elsewhere the most frequent size of holding might be under 10 acres (Tawney, *The Agrarian Problem*, 64–65). Values in 1563 might have ranged from 6d. per acre to 2/– (quoting at random rents cited in M. Campbell, *The English Yeoman*, 84; Tawney, 256; and E. Kerridge, "The Movement of Rent, 1540–1640," *The Economic History Review*, Second Series, VI, No. 1, 24–25, 30–31).

[32] A review of municipal usage in regard to the seven-year term is provided in Dunlop and Denman, *English Apprenticeship*, Chap. I. Mendenhall finds no evidence that the Shrewsbury Drapers' Company had adopted formal requirements for apprenticeship before 1563 (*The Shrewsbury Drapers*, 99).

[33] This difference is emphasized by Heckscher, *Mercantilism*, I, 230, and was suggested, though not in detail, by Cunningham, *Growth of English Industry*, II, 27. The latter, however, assumes that there was much initial difficulty in enforcing the seven-year term and credits the Act with its later diffusion; the former writer does not discuss this question.

on the duly-qualified craftsman to ply his craft wherever he pleased. He was thus as much subject as before to the prescriptions of borough and corporate custom or local ordinance which required "foreigners" (those neither born nor apprenticed within the jurisdiction) to buy their freedom to trade within the town.[34]

An incidental implication of the Act's lack of restrictiveness on the location of the craftsman, and one which again suggests the need of further inquiry into the nature of labor mobility in the sixteenth century, is the apparent difference in attitude thus revealed toward the movement of the skilled workman from place to place and that of the hired servant or laborer. This difference may have been only the result of an implicit assumption that the former, released from apprenticeship when sufficiently mature to establish a household, would normally settle where his years of training had been spent.

Actual evidence of the prevalence of apprenticeship outside corporate limits, other than the occurrence of prosecutions for lack of the legal term, is not available for the first decade after the passage of the Act, owing to the severe losses in early sessions records. By the 1570's, the quarter sessions in two counties, Essex and Norfolk, yield sufficient casual mention of seven-year apprenticeships to give assurance of considerable diffusion. In succeeding years, such casual mention is so frequently to be found in various counties that apprenticeship, of some form, must be assumed to have been solidly established for village as well as town crafts. The explanation of the institution's wide acceptance belongs to a far wider subject than that of the present inquiry. It must have fitted integrally into the social life of the period. The nearest analogy in the modern world is the institution and practice of compulsory formal education, but apprenticeship in the sixteenth and seventeenth centuries involved also economic conveniences for both the master and the apprentice's parents which gave it a firm place within the social structure.

No matter how general a practice the binding of children and young people to learn a "trade" may have been, little can be affirmed

[34] Here the principle of statute interpretation would apply, that special acts and local custom or law are not abrogated or affected by later general acts except by explicit application or clear intention (see P. B. Maxwell, *The Interpretation of Statutes,* Chap. VII, Sect. 3). In two well-known cases of the seventeenth century in which the apprenticeship requirement of the Act of 1563 conflicted with borough exclusiveness, the local ordinance was apparently of later date than the Act (see below, Chap. X, n. 46, n. 49).

about the formality with which this was done or the laxity that may have existed in regard to the length of term, though the casual evidences of apprenticeship already cited testify frequently to a term of seven years. But sometimes the term mentioned even in an official enrolment of an indenture in town records or among the hirings at statute sessions [35] is for less than seven years. There is usually nothing to show whether this is a setting-over of an apprentice from one master to another to complete the full legal term or whether such instances illustrate that tolerance of individual departures from strict legality which was typical and seemingly expected in Elizabethan and Stuart enforcement of mercantilist regulation.

The extent to which the prevalence of the family as a working unit in the economic structure may have helped or hindered the maintenance of apprenticeship is impossible to judge, in the entire absence of statistics as to the training of sons at home in their fathers' occupations through formal or informal contracts of service. The acceptance of patrimony as a qualification equivalent to formal apprenticeship for admission to the freedom of the guild or the corporate town obviously weakened the rigid enforcement of the statutory term even in these strongholds of restrictionism. (And so did the allowance of redemption — the purchase of the freedom — which was one of the many forms of the flourishing practice of compounding for illegalities.) But in a broader sense a pattern of life such that the adolescent worked in the home, under supervision as a matter of course, would have facilitated the spread of apprenticeship as the normal means of training a boy or girl in a new craft by substituting one family unit for another.

The subject of parochial apprenticeship, as required and regulated by the Acts of 1597 and 1601, has been omitted from consideration as having only an indirect bearing on the enforcement of the seven-year term according to the Act of 1563. The relation between compulsory apprenticeship for all entering into a craft or trade, and apprenticeship at parish expense as a means of employing the children of paupers, is an interesting question but one not perhaps capable of much illumination from the sources. The use of apprenticeship in the reign of Henry VIII as part of the attack on the problem of controlling vagrancy [36] may help to explain why it assumed so central a

[35] See below, Chap. VIII.

[36] Leonard, *English Poor Relief*, 55–57.

place in the efforts of the 1550's and in 1563 to stabilize the pattern of economic life. Much later than the period to which the present study is restricted, the growing abuses of parish apprenticeship may have contributed to the decline of the whole institution. In the long interval between, no evident connection between the two kinds of apprenticeship has been perceived by the present writer. The apparent improvement, for example, in the attention given by local authorities to apprenticing pauper children in the 1630's is not paralleled by increased enforcement by these agencies of the apprenticeship provisions of the Statute of Artificers.[37]

Violations of the apprenticeship law in any occupation had some relation to the numbers engaged in it in a given place or to the area of the market for the product or service involved. In discussing the degree of enforcement, a measure of relative size for the economic world of the day would be helpful. Here and there can be found figures on the population of individual places which have some reliability, at least in the order of magnitude they reveal. The county of Somerset in the last quarter of the eighteenth century furnishes a standard of comparison. There, out of 118 parishes and villages described by a contemporary, including some of the county's most populous, over 60 per cent had not more than 100 houses, and most of these under 75; a quarter of the total had under 50 houses.[38] This agrees with census returns for all England and Wales a little more than a generation later, when "four-fifths of all the townships had fewer than 200 families each."[39] In Essex in 1575, a list of the market towns, and of the "great towns" ranking with them though without markets, includes two for which there is also later information on size. One of the second class, the "clothing town" of Dedham, in 1597 was described as having 200 households, and the market town of Chelmsford in 1591 as having 300.[40] Prosecutions during the reign of Elizabeth in the Westminster courts and in Essex quarter

[37] See below, Chapters VIII and IX; and for the enforcement of parish apprenticeship, see Chapter V, n. 131, a reference to the Privy Council's Orders of 1631 in which the apprenticing of poor children was included.

[38] J. Collinson, *The History and Antiquities of the County of Somerset*, I–III, *passim*.

[39] S. and B. Webb, *English Local Government: English Poor Law History: Part I, The Old Poor Law*, 156n.

[40] Essex, Typescript Calendar of Quarter Sessions Rolls, VI, 170–172, S.R. 55/3; *Acts of the Privy Council*, ed. J. H. Dasent, Eliz., XXVIII, 69; *The Victoria History of the County of Essex*, II, 331.

sessions, on charges of using crafts or trades without qualifying by apprenticeship, numbered about a dozen against Chelmsford residents and one against a Dedham baker,[41] a difference probably due to the former town's more active role as a market. Even more exceptional than to be able to compare, however inexactly, all cases of this type with the size of the community in which the offenders lived, is to be able to relate prosecutions for apprenticeship offenses directly to even an approximate contemporary number in the occupation concerned. But in rare instances this can be done. A report to the Privy Council in 1577 of Essex clothiers buying wool lists twenty-seven clothiers in the "town" of Coggeshall as buyers. Even if this is not equivalent to the total of resident clothiers, at least it must represent the majority, so that the occurrence in 1565 of two prosecutions against unapprenticed clothmakers and in 1583 of one against an unapprenticed weaver — all within the near neighborhood of Coggeshall — can be judged with a little more perspective than the tiny figure of three such cases taken by itself.[42] The scale of the economic environment thus illustrated at Chelmsford, Dedham, and Coggeshall must be remembered in following the analysis of apprenticeship prosecutions.

[41] The totals are taken from the Exchequer Queen's Remembrancer Memoranda Rolls and the Queen's Bench Coram Rege Rolls, as well as from the Essex MS. Sessions Rolls (checked against the Typescript Calendar already cited) and include three prosecutions brought under the Act of 1557 (4 & 5 P. & M., c. 5, §22, the seven-year term of apprenticeship required for clothmaking) of unapprenticed kersey-makers at Chelmsford. The apprenticeship cases at this town under the Act of 1563 were of retailers.

[42] *Victoria History of Essex*, II, 391; Exchequer Queen's Remembrancer Memoranda Rolls, Hilary 7 Eliz., m. 88d., 171, 171d., and Trinity 25 Eliz., m. 132d. See below, Chap. IV, n. 29, for reference to the scale of the tilemaking industry in late Elizabethan Essex.

Part I

ENFORCEMENT BY PRIVATE INTERESTS

INTRODUCTION

In the eighty years from the passing of the Statute of Artificers to the outbreak of the Civil War, private interests took an overwhelmingly larger part than public agencies in the enforcement of a statutory seven-year term of apprenticeship, in so far as enforcement can be measured by prosecutions in the law courts. For the representative sample of counties included in the present study, the percentage of recorded prosecutions by public agencies, through the entire period, is so small that over 95 per cent of the apprenticeship cases must be attributed to private persons. The true proportion of private to public prosecutions, making a generous allowance for the extensive losses suffered by local archives, must have been at least three to one and was probably nearer four to one.[1]

The private prosecutions fall into two main classes: those of professional informers seeking a share of the penalty by legal or illegal means and without a greater interest in a particular offense than in any other from which they could hope for equal financial return; and those of other individuals, who can rarely be identified but who must be assumed to have had some business or personal animus against the alleged offenders. To the latter category belong prosecutors representing a trade group (where it has been possible to determine or suppose the presence of this element). The first class of prosecutions assume the technical form of the information "qui tam," the rise and nature of which will be discussed. This is, at any rate, their common characteristic during the eighty years under discussion, though after the Restoration and in the eighteenth century the professional prosecutor seems sometimes to have employed the indictment. The second class of private prosecutions may appear in the guise either of the

[1] The same preponderance of private interests must have characterized enforcement within corporate jurisdictions. The statement in the text applies to county areas.

information "qui tam" or of the indictment, the latter form being generally more frequent throughout in proceedings before quarter sessions and later superseding the information entirely.

To distinguish between the two classes of prosecution necessarily involves some arbitrary classifications and a wide margin of error. In analyzing the apprenticeship cases, the test has been the appearance of the prosecutor in suits under other statutes or in apprenticeship suits against more than one craft or trade. Since prosecutions for offenses not under the Statute of Artificers could not be systematically noted, identification of prosecutors rests chiefly on the apprenticeship cases. Prosecutors may thus be classified here as nonprofessional merely because their operations on other statutes were unknown to the present observer; but this bias will only increase the conservatism applied to estimating the professionals' share in enforcing the Act of 1563.

The professional prosecutor was indispensable for the enforcement of all statutes carrying a money penalty, from the middle of the sixteenth century into the later seventeenth century. Had it not been for "sundry varlets that go about the country as promoters,"[2] most of sixteenth- and seventeenth-century economic regulation would have had few guardians. Their activities have been recognized by economic historians. George Unwin remarked upon "that new species — half common informer, half amateur inspector — which the exigencies of Tudor policy had called into existence"; Alfred P. Wadsworth referred to "the numerous tribe of professional informers who played so curious a part in Stuart administration"; and Eli F. Heckscher pointed out that the ubiquity of informers and holders of dispensing patents imposed an indirect tax on business enterprises.[3] But in the absence of quantitative analysis of prosecutions their predominant role has not perhaps been fully appreciated. In prosecutions for nonobservance of the statutory seven-year term of apprenticeship, professional informers were responsible in the reign of Elizabeth for

[2] William Harrison, *Description of Britaine and England*, 2nd and 3rd Books, Part I, The Second Book, ed. F. J. Furnivall, The New Shakspere Society, I, 206.

[3] Unwin, *Studies*, 189; A. P. Wadsworth and J. De L. Mann, *The Cotton Trade and Industrial Lancashire 1600–1780*, 61; Heckscher, *Mercantilism*, I, 253–254. A recent article on an early Tudor specimen is that of G. R. Elton, "Informing for Profit: A Sidelight on Tudor Methods of Law-Enforcement," *The Cambridge Historical Journal*, XI, No. 2, 149–167.

about three-quarters of all the cases, approximately 675 from the group of counties selected for study, in the higher courts and at quarter sessions; in the reign of James I, for over two-fifths of the known total of about 750; and in that of his successor for two-thirds or more of the 850–900 cases.[4] These proportions can be considered minimal, in view of the bias of error already mentioned. Incidental observation of prosecutions under other statutes, particularly those governing middlemen in commodity distribution and the prohibition of usury, for which the number of prosecutions in Westminster courts runs into several thousands, suggests that the share of professional prosecutors in these cases was probably even greater than in those for apprenticeship.

An inquiry which seeks to estimate the effectiveness of the enforcing agencies must put three questions aimed at appraising the degree of deterrence achieved: first, did they discover an adequate number of offenses; second, did they take action, by reporting or by prosecuting, against an adequate number of the discovered offenders; third, was this action carried through to an adequate conclusion. Throughout Part I, these will be the chief questions applied to the

[4] For the aggregate figures see App. II, Tables I–III. The order of the counties in all tables will be regional: southwestern, eastern, northern, and midland. Of the Westminster courts' records, the Exchequer K.R. Memoranda Rolls were searched, by means of the Agenda Books' index, throughout 1563–1642 (and later); the K.B. Coram Rege Rolls were searched for sample periods as follows: 1563–1588 inclusive, Easter term 1603 to Hilary 1607, Easter 1616 to Hilary 1617, Easter 1625 to Hilary 1628, Easter 1635 to Hilary 1637, Hilary 1647 to Hilary 1648 (and for similar sample periods through 1670).

For the reign of Elizabeth, the counties with quarter sessions records (mostly for only the last years of the period) are: Devon, Somerset, Wiltshire, Worcestershire, Essex, Norfolk, the West Riding of Yorkshire, Cheshire, Staffordshire; for the reign of James, the foregoing, minus the West Riding, and plus the North Riding, Lancashire, and Nottinghamshire; for the period 1625–1642, the same list, plus the West Riding, Warwickshire, and Northamptonshire (the last county to the extent only of one year's records plus the entry in another year of a case removed by certiorari from the quarter sessions into the King's Bench).

Three doubtful entries (one in Essex, two in Wiltshire) have been excluded from the totals. The first may be under one of the statutes regulating leather crafts (a shoemaker charged in 1598 with "unlawful usage of his trade," Essex Cal.Q.S., XVII, 94, S.R. 143/62). The other two, tailors exercising their craft "contrary to the statute" in 1591, were probably bachelors who were working out of service though under thirty years of age, contrary to Sect. 3 of the Act of 1563, a frequent offense particularly in tailoring. This interpretation of the phrase is suggested by the reference of their cases to one justice of the peace to determine (*Minutes of Proceedings in Sessions, 1563, 1574–92*, ed. H. C. Johnson, Wiltshire County Records, IV, 145).

evidence, though they will not necessarily be taken up in the order here stated or explicitly mentioned. But obviously the answers cannot rest on knowledge of the actual amount of violations within a given period or place. They can be based only on probabilities which take into account both the frame of reference already described — the existing scale of economic life — and apparent correspondence between the distribution of apprenticeship cases and such variables as fluctuations in business activity or the growth of crafts and trades.

Chief attention among these agencies will be given in the present inquiry to the professional informer, in accordance with his major share of the ascertained prosecutions. Other private prosecutors will be noticed only so far as their operations represent certain business interests. But it is believed that the distinction between professional and nonprofessional prosecutors is of the first importance in interpreting the occurrence of the apprenticeship cases, because the two classes differed in their effectiveness and in the relation each bore to varying business conditions, this latter difference itself resulting in a probable dissimilarity in their coverage of offenses.

Since the professional prosecutor was trying to get his living, or at least to supplement another occupation, by his informing, he found his material wherever he could. This is demonstrated by the characteristic variety of statutes on which he laid informations and by the latter's usually considerable geographical diffusion. The assumption may also be made, and a later analysis of the distribution of apprenticeship cases will in part rest on it, that the professional informer was likely to look for offenders where business activity in a given occupation, place, or period, had been expanding, rather than where conditions were static or declining. But the nonprofessional private prosecutor was by definition concerned, for personal or business reasons, with particular individuals and offenses, so that his area of knowledge was a restricted one in contrast to the broad scope of the professional. Moreover, as was normally the case, if his interest in unapprenticed "intruders" was that of a business competitor, his need to attack such threats to his security was at least as great when business was poor as when it prospered and there seemed room for all.

But though he must have discovered far fewer offenses than the professional, and though his response to variations in economic conditions can be assumed to have been less consistent, his actual prosecution of offenders may have been more thorough. While the professional would gain from leaving his victims in a position to continue their illegal practices so that he might pluck them again, the other kind of prosecutor hoped to damage or actually suppress dangerous competitors. The aims of the professional were achieved as well or better through out-of-court settlements, those of the aggrieved businessman by forcing the defendants through every possible stage of expensive court procedure to the final goal of the statutory money penalty.[5] The efforts of the nonprofessional to enforce the law might even be hampered by the professional's arrangements to condone infractions, especially when these were generalized into a grant by letters patent to dispense with the penalties of a statute in return for an agreed payment from the offenders. No instance of this has been found in regard to apprenticeship cases, but what could happen is illustrated by the troubles of the Elizabethan shoemakers of Barnstaple. They complained in an influential quarter, to the Lord Lieutenant of the county, of the bad quality of leather supplied them by the tanners who were "animated to careless disregard of the laws" by having secured dispensations from the prescribed standards, which barred the petitioners from prosecuting them.[6]

The apparently unlimited scope of the professional informer was

[5] Statements of intention by prosecutors are naturally rare. But the class of sessions archives known as Petitions, Depositions, or Examinations, has occasionally survived, though the present writer seldom had time to sample such records adequately. These add a wealth of living detail to the dry outlines of the formal procedures. In 1710 a group of tanners in the Lancashire village of Tottington and its neighborhood undertook to prosecute some competitors whom they accused (under the regulations for dealing in raw leathers) of buying hides without having been apprenticed as tanners. One of the prosecutors was reported to have declared that since the costs of prosecution would be divided among the group they would be able to harass the defendants until the latter were ruined, as he remembered had been done in like manner by his father, whose enemy had been worth £300 or £400 when the court proceedings began but was "not worth a groat" when they were over. (Lancs. MS. Sessions Petitions Bundles, Manchester Sessions, 1710.)

[6] B.M. Lansdowne MS. 22, f. 37–38. The then Lord Lieutenant, the Earl of Bath, forwarded the petition to the Privy Council, recommending its bearer, a Thomas Lugg, as "experienced in the working and tanning of leather." From this mention of Lugg (possibly identical with a later informer, see below, Chap. II, n. 8) the petition can be dated about June 1597, since on June 28 the Council sent it on to the justices of assize, referring to Lugg in their letter (*Acts P.C.*, Eliz., XXVII, 260). Lugg's interest in the matter may have been that of the trade informer, employed by the craft group but himself of the craft, or he may have been a professional. The dispensing patent involved probably was that granted to Sir Edward Dyer in 1576 (W. H. Price, *The English Patents of Monopoly*, 148).

in fact narrowed by considerations affecting particular offenses. He could choose from among the many penal statutes or among the provisions of a single statute those whose violation would yield him the greatest profit. His estimate of this would in turn be affected not merely by the amount of the statutory penalty and the tendency of the courts to mitigate it, but by the frequency of violations, the financial and social status of offenders — whether sufficiently provided for to be worth squeezing without being so important as to be dangerous — and the reception his prosecution would receive either in the courts or from his victims in their readiness to agree with him out of court. The potential money return to an informer from apprenticeship offenses was much lower than that from other penal statutes, notably those controlling usury and middlemen.[7] This factor affecting the informer's choice of the subjects for prosecution, and the other factors suggested above, must be taken into account in interpreting the occurrence of professional informations under Section 24 of the Statute of Artificers. These may be less than the actual violations by the extent to which professionals preferred to ignore them in favor of bigger or more available game. Their distribution in place and time may be distorted by the accident of being only the secondary interests of an informer following the larger spoors but adding to his bag whatever small kills he could make on the way. Thus fluctuations in the volume of apprenticeship cases may reflect less the business conditions determining the entry of the unapprenticed into an occupation than those, not necessarily coincident, which influenced the commission of quite different offenses.

Yet despite these various limitations on the professional informer's free and full discovery and prosecution of offenses, the interpretations offered in the present work are based on the conclusion that the distribution of professional informations for a given offense tends to correspond sufficiently with the distribution of actual violations to give these informations utility not only as indicating the relative frequency of the offense in time and place, but also as suggesting the

[7] A professional informer was indicted in the Essex quarter sessions in 1623 for bringing a false information against a middleman with the intent, it was stated, of exacting from the defendant £200. Essex, Cal. Q.S., XIX, 509, S.R. 241/21, July 1623. The maximum claimed on informations for lack of apprenticeship was £22 or £24, i.e. at 40s. a month for 11 or 12 months (usually the former). The limitation to one year was made mandatory by a statute of 1589 (see below, Chap. III).

state of business activity. For apprenticeship offenses this conclusion must be modified to apply fully only to the period 1563–1589, for reasons to be discussed in the opening chapters. Thereafter it holds good only within certain counties.

The random elements in nonprofessional prosecutions and, for apprenticeship, their comparative scarcity, confine their value as indicators to particular situations, some of which will be considered.

I

INFORMATIONS AND PATENTS

By the middle of the sixteenth century the device of the information "qui tam" was well established in the central courts at Westminster as a method of initiating criminal prosecutions. Its basic difference from the other and in England the older form of criminal procedure, that of presentment and indictment, was that the latter required allowance by the Grand Jury, whereas process could issue on an information as soon as it was exhibited before those authorized to accept it. Sir William S. Holdsworth has suggested the element of inquisitorial rather than merely accusatory procedure latent here, a feature of the partial adoption in sixteenth-century England of the practices of Continental civil law.[1] But the essential superficiality of some of these adoptions is admirably illustrated by the history in England of procedure by information — a potential tool of absolutism virtually abandoned to private hands.

The history of the origins and growth of the common information fortunately does not require review here. The administrative dilemma

[1] W. S. Holdsworth, *A History of English Law*, V, 176–177. On by-passing the Grand Jury, IX, 243, though Holdsworth discusses only the procedures applicable to ex officio criminal informations in the King's Bench these appear to be identical in this respect for informations initiated by private persons. The statement has been made elsewhere that the information had the advantage that "the defendant in an indictment had a right to trial by jury" (Derry, "Enforcement of Apprenticeship," 10). But Holdsworth expressly states that the difference (for ex officio informations) from procedure by presentment and indictment was only in initiating the proceedings, and that "the same trial by jury was had" (IX, 245). Certainly proceedings observed by the present writer in the minority of apprenticeship informations adequately recorded, whether at Westminster or in local courts, involved trial by jury.

in sixteenth-century England is familiar, that of a complex and growing society with insufficient public agencies to handle the increasing burden of public affairs. Together with the application of town and guild policies to economic life on the national scale, methods applied in local and guild regulation were appropriated for national administration. One of these was the use of the informer. Public opinion and local knowledge expressed through the presentments of juries in manorial and hundred courts, in quarter sessions and at assizes, had served for centuries to bring to notice disturbances of the peace, local nuisances, or violations of the contemporary concept of fair trade. But the private individual, whether serving on a presentment jury or as an unpaid constable or other local officer, must often have found it simpler to close his eyes, for the sake of security or of comfortable relationships with his neighbors and his superiors. From an early time, therefore, he had been encouraged to keep them open by the offer of a share in the penalty. The developing economic and social policies of the Tudor period had similarly to rely, in the absence of paid public inspectors, on creating sufficient incentives for private interests to take part in enforcing the laws.[2]

Employment of the informer was well known to the medieval guild system in England and on the continent.[3] In England, at least as early as the fourteenth century, the central government offered part of the penalties under certain statutes to any who would sue, as in the Ordinance of Laborers and the Statute of Laborers.[4] The first express grant of power to justices of the peace to proceed by information on matters of economic regulation appears to have been by the Act of 1464 prescribing standards for woolen cloth, in which the clause enjoining payment of workers in money authorized the individual justice of the peace to determine and fine violations on information or complaint by a third person.[5] Until the reign of Henry VII no

[2] Continued resort to the informer in the twentieth century suggests that it was not alone the absence of a modern police organization which led to his employment in earlier times. On the need for the informer and the patentee, see Holdsworth, *English Law*, IV, 355.

[3] For example: *The Little Red Book of Bristol*, ed. F. B. Bickley, II, 7, ordinances of dyers in 1381; A. Doren, *Das Florentiner Zunftwesen*, 600–602; G. Espinas, *La Vie Urbaine de Douai*, II, Pt. 3, 62–64.

[4] 23 Ed. III, c. 1–5 and 25 Ed. III, c. 2. Holdsworth, on the origins of the popular action "qui tam" and information "qui tam," *English Law*, IX, 236–238, and on the extensive use of the procedure, IV, 356–357.

[5] 4 Ed. IV, c. 1. This had been preceded by at least one other statute

further reference in statutory social and economic regulations to procedure by the justices of the peace is to be found. Then it is mentioned in two statutes, and there was a general authorization in 1495 of justices of the peace equally with justices of assize to hear and determine upon informations for the king without indictment.[6] After the repeal of this act in 1509,[7] the justices of the peace received no other explicit power to proceed by information until 1532–33.[8] For the succeeding thirty years the usual formula for the recovery of penalties continued to provide only in general terms for suit in any of the king's courts of record.[9] The effect of the repeal of 1509 on the use of the common information before sessions of the peace is obscure. As late as 1564 there seems to have been official doubt regarding the competence of commissions of oyer and terminer to execute the increasing number of penal statutes. At an assembly of all the judges held that year at the Queen's order to confer on the better execution of nine of these statutes — the list of which includes the Statute of Artificers — all but three of the judges reportedly agreed that the phrase providing for the recovery of penalties in any of the courts of record by action of debt referred only to the four Westminster courts.[10] William Lambard, himself a justice, warned the justices of the peace in his famous book of instructions that they could award

(2 Hen. VI, c. 7, on tanning leather) which came very close to recognizing procedure before justices of the peace by common information. Neither statute is mentioned by writers on the subject of the information: I. S. Leadam refers only to the famous statute of 1468 against retainers to prove that the act of 1495 had been anticipated. *Select Cases before the King's Council in the Star Chamber, Selden Society* XVI, XXV, I, xcix.

[6] The act of 1495, 11 Hen. VII, c. 3; the others are 1 Hen. VII, c. 7 (hunting at night), 11 Hen. VII, c. 17 (to preserve game birds).

[7] By 1 Hen. VIII, c. 6.

[8] This was given in three statutes: 24 Hen. VIII, c. 1 and c. 4; 25 Hen. VIII, c. 13.

[9] Holdsworth distinguished between the common information brought by a private individual on behalf of the crown and himself, and the ex officio information brought in the King's Bench, nominally for the king alone (*English Law*, IX, 237); it is the latter which he discusses in connection with the acts of 1495 and 1509. Another writer refers merely to procedure by information without indictment, not defining the varieties of information, K. Pickthorn, *Early Tudor Government, Henry VII*, 149.

[10] J. Dyer, *Reports of Cases . . .* , II, 236. Sir James Dyer, then Chief Justice of the Common Pleas, must himself have been present at the assembly in Michaelmas Term of 1564. His note on the occasion is cited by R. R. Reid, *The King's Council in the North*, 293, who believes the question may have originated with this Council.

process on an information only when expressly empowered by the statute creating the specific offense.[11]

This authority is conferred by the Statute of Artificers in a detailed clause.[12] Yet the scanty Elizabethan sessions archives indicate that common informations under this act were brought before the justices of the peace only during the last decade of the century. Contributing to their absence must have been the unknown factors responsible for an apparent rarity, in much of the Elizabethan as compared with later periods, of all types of prosecutions before county quarter sessions on all economic regulations. With the exception of presentments by local officials and juries under the service clauses of the Statute of Artificers, which occur with some frequency,[13] or prosecutions for breaking the assizes of bread and ale, the sessions calendars are singularly empty of cases involving the steadily enlarging legislation for trade, industry, and agriculture. For procedure by information, however, an important cause may have been the probable nuisance value to the professional informer of suits brought at Westminster. An accused country craftsman or farmer, faced with the prospect of an expensive and time-consuming journey to London and an indefinite wait there for trial, would have been likely to submit promptly.[14]

The appearance of apprenticeship informations in sessions records in the 1590's can be accounted for largely by a statute of 1589, by which original informations on the Statute of Artificers were required to be brought in the local courts of the county where the offense was alleged to have been committed.[15] Though the act gave rise to conflicting judicial opinions on whether it altogether barred informations on the offenses specified in it from being exhibited in the Westminster courts, its effect on the whole seems to have been greatly to reduce their numbers in the Exchequer, and to cause some shifting

[11] William Lambard, *Eirenarcha* (1581), 405.

[12] See App. I, Sect. 32 of the Act.

[13] This can of course be affirmed only for the few counties for which this class of sessions record has survived in sufficient quantity. See below, Chap. VIII.

[14] See below, Chap. VI, for brief discussion of the importance of this element in prosecutions. Some confirmation of the difficulty of attending lawsuits in the metropolis may perhaps be seen in the fact that until the later seventeenth and the eighteenth centuries, it was rare for defendants in apprenticeship cases at quarter sessions to secure a writ of certiorari for removal of the suit to Westminster.

[15] 31 Eliz., c. 5, §6.

to the local arena.[16] The earliest observed professional informations before quarter sessions, under Section 24 of the Statute of Artificers, were four or five in 1591, in Cheshire, Essex, and Staffordshire; thereafter none can be identified as professional before 1602, when there is record of a Norfolk informer. The only other similar apprenticeship informations known are in 1598–1600, when four in Wiltshire and one in Worcestershire can be considered as the work of trade interests.[17]

A margin of error in this dating of the first appearances of informations in quarter sessions must be recognized. In part, it lies in possible omissions by the present writer when beginning research in sessions archives. But though pressure of time and initial ignorance may have led to overlooking some informations on statutes other than the Act of 1563, it is believed no considerable number of these, still less of apprenticeship informations, could have escaped notice. More important are the probable losses of the original papers. Practice varied among counties and among successive generations of clerks of the peace as to treatment of informations. Where and when pains was taken to enter a minute of cases before each sessions, loss of the original document would not affect the modern reader's knowledge of its existence. But the industry and system of the clerk of the peace only too often leave much to be desired in fullness of the record preserved. Probably because the information did not have to be reviewed by the Grand Jury, the informer's communication, sometimes a mere scribble, was by no means always engrossed on the parchment employed for the formal processes of the court or strung through with these on the rolled "file" for each sessions. The common information thus belongs to a class of sessions document peculiarly subject to loss. This is occasionally made evident. In Wiltshire, where despite a

[16] See below, Chap. III, n. 14, for the conflict of opinion and for the influence of the act on the effectiveness of the professional informer in apprenticeship cases.

[17] In Essex in 1591, the same informer who brought two apprenticeship charges informed also under other penal statutes, and this was true of the Norfolk informer in 1602 (one apprenticeship case, and some others). Documentation for these informations, where individual reference is appropriate, is provided in Chaps. IV and V; all are from MS. sessions rolls or minute books. A partial check on the selected group may be made from the printed extracts from the Middlesex sessions records, where the first information entered is in 1598; but since the editing of this series was selective, earlier examples may have been omitted. *Middlesex County Records*, ed. J. C. Jeaffreson, I, 246.

record available from 1575 only four apprenticeship informations are known by 1600, the justices of the peace in that year apparently thought it necessary to forbid the exhibition in court of any information for exercising trades without apprenticeship unless first approved by the justice living nearest the accused. It hardly seems possible that the two brought at the preceding sessions could have been sufficient to evoke this rather extreme extension of the potential authority of a single justice.[18] But such an order suggests that the occasion for it was new and so reinforces the other indications that apprenticeship informations had been infrequent. Another possible illustration of loss comes also from Wiltshire, an entry in 1601 of a charge against an informer for unlicensed composition, but without mention of the offense for which he had secured the payment.[19] A similar example occurs in Nottinghamshire, where there was a like charge in 1622 against an informer, without record of previous informations.[20]

Thus so far as is known at present, the professional informer made little use of local courts during Elizabeth's reign for suits against apprenticeship offenders.[21] Before 1603 his share was only one-fifth to one-fourth of all the observed cases of this sort before county quarter sessions. In the reign of James I, about two-fifths of the known apprenticeship prosecutions were brought by professional informers, their activity varying considerably from county to county. From 1625 through 1642 they were responsible for about two-thirds, though again their operations were concentrated in certain areas.[22] The professional informer on apprenticeship offenses came most fully into his own in the courts of quarter sessions — but it is believed from random observation that this applies almost equally to viola-

[18] Wiltshire MS. Sessions Minute Books, II, Mich. 42 Eliz. The informations mentioned in the text above were entered at the July Sessions against two men of the same surname for unapprenticed weaving. Nothing is known of their status, but if they were clothiers of some substance their complaint alone might have been effective with the justices.

[19] Wiltshire MS. Sessions Minute Books, II, April, 43 Eliz.

[20] Nottinghamshire MS. Sessions Minute Books, VI, Mich. 20 Jas. I (sessions at Nottingham and at Newark).

[21] Municipal records might tell a different story. In Norwich in the 1560's there were at least two informers operating before the city sessions (MS. Minute Books of Sessions Proceedings, IV, 1561–1570, and MS. Books of Depositions, 1563–1572). But in the few MS. borough and town archives examined briefly by the present writer, no other such evidence was seen.

[22] See App. II, Tables I–III.

tions of other economic controls — in the second quarter of the seventeenth century, an increase associated in part with the almost complete exclusion of original informations from the Westminster courts by the Act of 1624.[23]

Since the judges of assize, like the justices of the peace, were explicitly empowered to receive, and issue process upon, informations of offenses against the Statute of Artificers, the professional informer might be expected to busy himself in the circuit courts as in Westminster. Unfortunately, no satisfactory testing of this expectation can be hoped for. Assizes records for the sixteenth century survive only for the old southeastern circuit, which formerly included both Essex and Norfolk, and only one class of these records, the "Indictment Bundles." But though this series begins in 1563, there are no bundles for Norfolk until the later seventeenth century. The Essex bundles contain no apprenticeship cases of any type earlier than 1609 and no informations before 1626. Clearly there have been losses, and one cause of the slimness of these records is obvious from examination of the Essex Sessions Rolls, among which there occur a few rolls of proceedings at the assizes for the county. One such of 1573 yields a memorandum of fifty-six men who are to be charged with "exercising the art of a musician" without apprenticeship, but with no indication of the procedure by which they were accused.[24] But the presence of a few indictments under the service clauses of the Act of 1563 in the Essex Assizes bundles suggests that if there had been any considerable quantity of apprenticeship prosecution in this court, some trace would have survived.

In the Westminster courts, the great age for the professional informer in apprenticeship prosecution and possibly in prosecution of numerous other offenses against mercantilist regulations was in the reign of Elizabeth. Certainly professional informers in the Exchequer and the Star Chamber in the 1530's and 1540's[25] were prosecuting offending clothmakers, tanners of leather and exporters of grain. But in the 1550's, the calendar of informations on penal statutes in the

[23] See below, Chap. III. The effect of this Act on apprenticeship informations was noticed by Derry, "The Enforcement of Apprenticeship," 10.

[24] Cal.Q.S., IV, 205, S.R. 43/23, at Lent Assizes, 15 Eliz.; see App. II, Table I. See Bibliography for the Assizes records which were examined. The Essex prosecutions for apprenticeship after 1603 are included in Tables II and III, App. II.

[25] Elton, "Informing for Profit," *passim*. Leadam, *Select Cases*, II, xxvi, 219–221, 277, *passim*.

Exchequer grows heavier only from 1557, with a sharp acceleration in the early 1560's. In the Queen's Bench the Coram Rege Rolls show a somewhat later and smaller increase. This expanding activity was largely, perhaps even entirely on some statutes, exhibited by the professional informer: in the Exchequer and the Queen's Bench his ascertainable share of the apprenticeship cases of Elizabeth's reign was at least four-fifths.[26] Hugh Latimer's plea of 1550 was within a few years only too fully answered: "There lacketh one thing in this realm, that it hath need of; for God's sake make some promoters. There lack promoters, such as were in King Henry the Seventh's days . . . men to promote . . . all offenders. I think there is great need of such men of godly discretion, wisdom, and conscience, to promote transgressors, as rent-raisers, oppressors of the poor, extortioners, bribers, usurers." [27] That the character of the Elizabethan promoter hardly achieved this standard will appear in later pages.

In the Elizabethan age, the rise of procedure by information was accompanied by a growing practice of conferring, by royal grant, monopoly powers on private persons to collect statutory penalties, compound for them, or even dispense with them. These parasites on the unwieldy and growing body of penal statutes had ample reason to flourish. A high proportion of inconclusive prosecutions among the total recorded in the courts' calendars, no matter what the offense, suggests the attraction for the Crown that this device possessed as compared with the use of the informer. This was stated during James's reign as "to draw some reasonable benefit to his Majesty by composition for . . . penalties . . . whereof every common informer taking hold did prosecute them for his own advantage without regard of his Majesty's profit." [28] The anticipation of improved financial return did not always materialize,[29] and no return at all could be expected when a dispensing rather than a compounding patent was issued as a reward for service. But for some of these grants

[26] See App. II, Table I.

[27] Hugh Latimer, *Sermons*, ed. G. E. Corrie (Parker Society), 279: Sermon before Edward VI.

[28] Letter from the Privy Council to the justices within the jurisdictions of the Council of Wales and the Palatinate of Chester, justifying a grant to compound with recusants (*Acts of the Privy Council,* Jas. I, V, 275, 16 August 1620).

[29] The Council appears to have been surprised that the collectors for another patentee were compounding for less than the full fines, "seeking rather to nourish than abolish" the offense in question (*Acts P.C.*, Jas. I, 1623–1625, 152).

the pleasant jingle of ready money passing from the patentee to the Crown replaced the uncertainties of dependence on informers' honesty. For the grantee, such patents promised better than the contingent profits of mere informing. Since in any event the original patentees usually were of too high a social position [30] to be personally active as informers, they could profitably sell or lease their rights, in whole or piecemeal, in a market which seems, like that for public offices, to have been prevailingly bullish.[31] The actual user had two advantages: he could usually, and with a dispensing patent always, avoid resort to the courts; and if fortunate he might have his monopoly protected against competition from the ordinary informer.[32]

Among the numerous patents for forfeitures known to have been granted by Elizabeth and James I, none appears to have been issued specifically for any part of the Statute of Artificers before 1619.[33] A dispensing patent of generous scope, covering several unrelated but important economic regulations, was held in 1575 by two grantees, but even this did not include any offenses under the statute.[34] The

[30] Several are identifiable as men of consequence at Court or in the country; see notes on following pages.

[31] For the rising price of office, see H. R. Trevor-Roper, "The Gentry 1540–1640," *The Economic History Review*, Supplement 1, 28–29. No prices for patents on penal statutes have been collected; the text above is based only on the obvious activity of deputies under one or another patent, references to which are frequent in the State Papers, etc., and some of which are mentioned in the text above.

[32] For example, the courtier Simon Bowyer (a Wiltshire justice of the peace), patentee for compounding on the regulations for dealing in wool, was allowed to place his own attorney in the Queen's Bench to prevent the entry of any information or composition for such offenses (*Acts P.C.*, Eliz., XXI, 66–67, 25 April 1591; Holdsworth, *English Law*, IV, 358 n.1).

[33] See below for the 1619 grant. No complete list of patents has ever been compiled. W. H. Price's citation of contemporary lists, and his text, *English Patents*, 142–153 and *passim*, omit some patents for forfeitures known to have existed and mentioned in the text above. A commission applicable in a somewhat different way to the Statute of Artificers was granted in 1566 to Sir Nicholas Bacon, lord keeper, to compound with justices of the peace for the penalty imposed on them by the act for failure to execute the wage clauses. (Palmer, MS. Indexes to Chancery Patent Rolls, XX, 36).

[34] *Acts P.C.*, Eliz., VIII, 371, 25 April 1575, at which date this patent and several others were revoked, evidently during an interval of inquiry into patents on penal statutes; see also 280, 393, 396. The two holders were: Henry Mackwilliams, Gentleman Pensioner, justice of the peace of Essex and Suffolk, member of Parliament in four Parliaments, at some period keeper of Colchester Castle (see various Libri Pacis as listed in Bibliography, Essex MS. Sessions Rolls, J. E. Neale, *The Elizabethan House of Commons*, 312, *Calendar of State Papers Domestic*, Addenda 1580–1625, 426); and Robert Colshill, Gentleman Pen-

earliest recorded applicant for a patent for apprenticeship violations is anonymous, and the cause of the rejection of his suit — assuming that it was rejected — is unknown. The project has been assigned to the year 1573, and consisted of proposals to set up a registry of apprenticeships and to compound with the unapprenticed. A semblance of official supervision was given by the further suggestions that the lord chancellor should be authorized to license compounders to continue in their trades and with the lord treasurer should approve the agreed "fines." [35] In the next thirty years of the reign, during which so many patents of all sorts were distributed, touching nearly every side of economic life,[36] only two other applications for patents on the Act of 1563 are known. These also proposed both a registry for apprentices and dispensation for offenders.[37] But early in the succeeding reign, a number of projects were presented, all apparently abortive.[38]

sioner, a justice of the peace in 1580 of Devon and Somerset (Libri Pacis; *Cal. S.P.D.*, Eliz., 1547–1580, 391, 569). The statutes named in the grant were for "usury, the preservation of woods, the assize of fuel, the true making of leather, the export of corn, wood, and victuals, for keeping sheep, . . . exactions of sheriffs."

[35] State Papers Domestic, Eliz., XCIII, Nos. 26–36, of which the first is printed in *Tudor Economic Documents*, I, 353–363, and elsewhere. Various writers have cited it; see for example Unwin, *Industrial Organization*, 137. Its dating is based on its text.

[36] Some fifty patents were granted in the last eighteen years of the reign, twenty-three in 1593 alone. E. P. Cheyney, *A History of England from the Defeat of the Armada to the Death of Elizabeth*, II, 289–290. By 1572 an appreciable number of dispensing patents must already have been issued, since an Exchequer official in October of that year recorded a memorandum "to make a note . . . of all commissions for compounding upon penal statutes." (Exchequer Q.R. Entry Books of Decrees and Orders, Series I, VI, 1.)

[37] One application was from Sir William Russell, Sir Thomas Gorges, and Thomas Maria Wingfield; it is undated, but in October 1593 it was still pending after "great charges and long suit." There seems to have been a competing petition in 1593 and a registry office for London and its environs already established. (B.M. Lansdowne MS. 114, f. 5; Hist. MSS. Comm., *Hatfield House MSS.*, IV, 384.)

Two of the petitioners were justices of the peace: Sir William Russell (Lord Deputy of Ireland, 1594–1597) in Northamptonshire, at least from 1596; Sir Thomas Gorges (Gentleman Usher of the Privy Chamber, keeper of Hurst Castle) in Hampshire and Wiltshire. Sir Thomas, at any rate, was also a member of Parliament. Wingfield was related to the important Wingfields of Kimbolton in Huntingdonshire and to the Knollys family. (See Libri Pacis; Neale, *House of Commons*, 299; *Victoria History of Huntingdonshire*, III, 81.)

[38] See list in *Commons Debates, 1621*, ed. W. Notestein, F. Relf and H. Simpson, VII, Appendix B, 327–329; S.P.D., Jas. I, XXIV, Nos. 71, 72, 73. These were proposals either to collect forfeitures or to establish a registry, or both.

That of the Earl of Dunbar, about 1606, was different from most, in specifying that the forfeitures to be collected were those arising from presentments of apprenticeship offenders to be made by local juries specially summoned.[39] Its character suggests the existence of rival applications or of grants which would have precluded collecting forfeitures from informations. The first known patent for apprenticeship offenses was that of February 1619, to Sir James Spence and three others, allowing them to give dispensations to the unapprenticed without court actions.[40] Although its stated term was for seven years, the grant had short shrift, as it was among those revoked in 1621 after complaint in Parliament.[41] Projectors attempted in vain to revive this patent or others like it during the next reign.[42] Though a host of commissions to compound on various statutes had apparently been issued by 1638, contemporary references to the offenses covered by them do not include apprenticeship.[43]

Besides the type of patent applicable to one or more specific statutes, comprehensive grants were also sometimes sought and made, which purported to be for collecting penalties rather than dispensing with them. Obviously such grants might be exercised in reference to forfeitures on apprenticeship offenses, although there is nothing to show whether any were so used. An Elizabethan project to establish an office of "Surveyor of Informations" was the first of a series, but

[39] S.P.D., Jas. I, XXIV, Nos. 71, 72, 73.

[40] *Tudor and Stuart Proclamations*, ed. R. Steele, 1242; *Cal. S.P.D.*, Jas. I, 1619–1623, 242; *Commons Debates*, loc. cit., and 503. Sir James Spence was presumably a Scots knight; he had some part in the hated patent of Sir Francis Mitchell for licensing ale-houses (VI, 260ff). A second patentee was Archibald Primrose, probably another Scot and an ancestor of the Earls of Rosebery. A third was one Henry Goldsmith, who is credited with a knighthood in one version of the debates on the patent but not elsewhere; he was probably an attorney. The fourth was Robert More, identical (?) with an earlier unsuccessful petitioner: in 1607 a Robert More had applied to enrol apprentices, on behalf of his "lord and master" Lord Haddington (later Earl of Holderness); see n. 38 above.

[41] On the end of the Spence patent, see *Commons Debates*, II, 123, 250; Price, *English Patents*, 167; and below.

[42] Three of these were: the persistent More (S.P.D., Chas. I, XLIV, No. 29); Sir Alexander Gordon (*ibid.*, CCXXXI, No. 67, possibly also S.P.D., Jas. I, CV, No. 79, undated but endorsed with Gordon's name; see also Unwin, *Industrial Organization*, 141); and Sir Edmund Verney (S.P.D., Chas. I, CCCLXXVII, No. 1), somewhat exceptional among the applicants in the Stuart period in being of the English gentry.

[43] S.P.D., Chas. I, CCCLXII, No. 31; CCCLXXI, foll. No. 108; CCCXCVII, Nos. 71, 72; Price, *English Patents*, 171–175.

is not known to have ripened into a patent.[44] In 1606 and 1607 four patents of this kind had been assigned; thereafter no similar grants are known to have been made until 1620 and 1631,[45] the last of which was still in operation in 1638.[46]

One more patent deserves mention, a comprehensive grant whose terms, apparently unique, were applicable to the Statute of Artificers as to all other penal statutes. This was the appointment in 1560 of a John Martin, haberdasher of London, as "informer and prosecutor" for the Crown on all past or future penal laws, with unrestricted powers of entry and search, of seizure, arrest, and pleading; he was to take the informer's customary half of the forfeitures and, further to stimulate him to be "the more diligent and painful," an additional

[44] S.P.D., Eliz., CCLXXXVIII, No. 3 (undated).

[45] By 1606 Lord Danvers and Sir John Gilbert had been given a patent to collect the Crown's share of forfeitures on penal statutes, but this had already been attacked in the House of Commons and was revoked before the end of the year (*Cal. S.P.D.*, Jas. I, 1603–1610, 311; *The Parliamentary Diary of Robert Bowyer, 1606–1607*, ed. D. H. Willson, 112–113, 126–127, where there is also mention of other patents for forfeitures). In 1607 a courtier, Charles Chambers, received a patent to supervise the collection of the Crown's share of forfeitures from informers' compositions (Exch. Q.R.M.R., Mich. 5 Jas. I, m. 309; *Commons Debates*, VII, App. B, 420). This seems to have been duplicated by grants to Robert Bedoe, a well-established professional informer (B.M. Lansdowne MS. 167, f. 138, marginal note), and to Sir Stephen Proctor (f. 16, f. 23, f. 123), a newcomer in the mid-1590's to the circle of West Riding justices of the peace. The latter secured two more patents, one to collect fines left unlevied by sheriffs, and one of 1609 in which he was styled "Collector and Receiver of Fines on Penal Statutes" (f. 24; *Cal. S.P.D.,* Jas. I, 1603–1610, 533). But after a Commons inquiry in 1610, he was imprisoned (*Commons Debates*, loc. cit., 421; B.M. Lansdowne MS. 167, f. 94). In 1611, a petitioner who was undaunted by Proctor's fate was seeking a similar patent, and in 1613 one was being prepared for Lord Morley which was to apply to the Crown's share of forfeitures in the Exchequer and the King's Bench on penal statutes. (*Acts P.C.*, Jas. I, I, 231.) By 1620, it was thought that Proctor's patent could be "safely renewed," and it was assigned to Dr. James Chambers, later physician to Charles I, and a John Brooke (*Commons Debates*, loc. cit., 421), but only after competition from the informer Bedoe. The recipient of the 1631 grant was again Dr. Chambers. It was reinforced by proclamation in 1635 (*Cal. S.P.D.*, Chas. I, 1635, 369–370). Other proposals for like patents, *Commons Debates*, loc. cit.; Lansdowne MS. 172, f. 241, MS. 168, f. 70, 72, MS. 167, f. 138.

[46] Citation, in MS. Notes of Edwin F. Gay, from Exchequer Proceedings, K.R., Bundle 84, of "A schedule of such compositions . . . as have been . . . made by informers . . . in [the] Court of Exchequer since 16 Jacobi Regis, whereof his Majesty hath as yet received no satisfaction for his part, . . . as the same are certified into Doctor Chambers' office . . ." The list appears to have been made up mostly of recusancy cases, but the notes do not record definitely the presence or absence of apprenticeship informations.

shilling in the pound.[47] The relationship to this patent of some individual informers and of a marked concentration of apprenticeship informations in one area will be discussed in the next chapter.

In general, the relationship has not been found between patentees, and informers in apprenticeship prosecutions. The question remains open, whether some of the recorded informations against apprenticeship offenders represent work on behalf of a patentee's deputies or collectors, or in competition with them. But so few patents were actually issued which concern apprenticeship either specifically or as part of a comprehensive grant, and those issued were so soon revoked, that the question pertains to comparatively brief intervals except for the unknown duration of the Martin patent. Presumably, however, this operated in the same manner as the ordinary information. Thus it does not present the problem created by other patents for forfeitures, that unknown numbers of recorded court prosecutions might have been anticipated by composition and dispensation without entry of process in any court. Such distortion of the pattern of apprenticeship violations as it is traced by ordinary prosecutions need be taken into account only for the periods 1607–1609, 1619–1621, and 1631–1639, when there was some activity under the Proctor, Spence, and Chambers patents with perhaps one or two others concurrently. Proctor was accused shortly after the final grant of his patent in 1609 of "vexing and abusing many thousands" by taking bribes and compounding at his pleasure on penal statutes, and his patent was included among the "grievances of the subject" in a speech in the Commons.[48] Spence's patent of 1619 also aroused opposition, ex-

[47] The authorization does not seem to have included the right to compound or dispense without court action. No other similar grant is known to the present writer nor any reference in modern studies to this one. Contemporary mention of it had been found by the writer in the Exchequer Q.R. Agenda Books, Pasch. 2 Eliz., m. 8. Knowledge of its terms was derived later from the MS. Notes of Edwin F. Gay. His source was: Patent Roll, 2 Eliz., Pt. 3, m. 7, date of patent 26 April, 2 Eliz. In 1592 this or another patent was described as an authorization to inform for the Haberdashers' Company of London (*Cal. S.P.D.*, Eliz., 1591–1594, 187).

[48] The Commons sent to the Lords a bill against Proctor's patent, asking that he be excepted from a pending bill of pardon; in July 1610 his name was excepted. (B.M. Lansdowne MS. 167, f. 27, 94, 101; *C.J.*, I, 24 February 1610, speech of Sir Edwin Sandys; *Commons Debates*, VII, App. B, 421.) In August 1609 Proctor had said that he would "forbear for the present" to exercise his patent as Receiver of Fines "except where it be acceptable to the court" (*Cal. S.P.D.*, Jas. I, 1603–1610, 539).

pressed vividly in 1621 by a Devonshire member of Parliament and justice of the peace: "the abuse and vexation of these men is very great," Sir William Strode told the Commons, "for when they come to a town they warn 30 or 40 to come before them. If they sell anything, be it but a pound of candles besides the trade he [*sic!*] was bound apprentice unto, they must come to London or else give £4 or £5 for a composition." [49] But evidence is lacking on the duration or extent of the annoyance. The patentee Goldsmith explained to a Commons committee that he had compounded without prosecuting, as a preliminary experiment on a temporary warrant, with thirty or more persons "in the country" during 1616–17, not himself receiving more than £143 in compositions; then while awaiting the grant of the "grand patent," the applicants lost ground by the exclusion of "the trade of brewers" from its scope. The full grant was exercised, according to Goldsmith, less than a year before its surrender, and had before this been made ineffective by a Council inquiry so that Spence and Primrose reportedly secured compositions from only sixty persons.[50] As to the effects of the Chambers patent in the 1630's, still less can be said. Late in 1631, the Devonshire justices of the peace consulted the Privy Council about "a general outcry among the meaner people" caused by the extortions of "one Jones, an instrument in the execution of a patent, with title of forfeitures of penal laws." [51] With what kind of offenders Jones was compounding cannot be known, whether he was working under the Chambers patent or some other undiscovered grant, and no further trace of patentees' activities has been seen.

Thus the quantitative importance is uncertain of the patents for forfeitures, in taking potential prosecutions away from ordinary professional informers whose efforts might otherwise have been visible in the records of central or local courts. If in the comprehensive type of patents the proportion of apprenticeship offenses to all offenses therein included may be judged by their respective proportions in the Westminster courts, the interference of this type of patent with

[49] *Commons Debates*, II, 125; his speech differently reported, VI, 266 (as referring only to a "barber" forced into composition for selling candles).

[50] *Commons Debates*, VII, App. B, 503ff. Primrose and Goldsmith had been ordered to attend the general committee for grievances; on March 19 the patent was condemned in committee, two days later in the Commons, and the condemnation was confirmed by the king, after hesitation, in June (*ibid.*, 329).

[51] *Cal. S.P.D.*, Chas. I, 1631–1633, 161.

the regular course of prosecutions must have been slight, and apparently so also was that of the only known specific grant for apprenticeship, the Spence patent.

Interpretation of the lack of such patents during the preceding fifty-five years is equally difficult. A lower level of statutory penalties can hardly have been sufficient cause. The secret of success for the holder of a dispensing patent must have been in the volume of payments, based in some instances on the establishment of a regular tariff. This would presumably have been influenced much more directly by the character of the offense and the status of the majority of offenders than by the statutory penalty. For example, a low rate of composition was set by the patentees (or their deputies) for forfeitures under the Act of 1571 which enjoined wearing woolen caps.[52] If a patent for apprenticeship forfeitures was not expected to be as profitable as others — and two such anticipations are on record [53] — two reasons for this appear more probable than the level of the prescribed penalty. One is the likelihood of widespread resistance to a patent which, despite its limitation to a particular offense, necessarily concerned a great variety of occupations. Resistance developed quickly to the Spence patent after brief initial success,[54] and this result may have been foreseen in the more cautious and shrewder era of patent policy. Even as late as 1617, the Spence application was opposed by the lord keeper, the chief justice of the King's Bench, and the solicitor-general.[55] The second reason seems the more cogent, that

[52] The Chamberlains' Accounts for Stratford-on-Avon record for the fiscal year 1576: "Pd. . . . for the agreement with the informer having the benefit of the statutes for the wearing of caps, 10/8." *Minutes and Accounts of the Corporation of Stratford-upon-Avon*, ed. R. Savage and E. I. Fripp, Publications of the Dugdale Society, II, 117. In 1579 one of the two original grantees was accused of having made £900 while accounting for only £30 of the share which he was supposed to turn over to authorities for the relief of poor capmakers (*Acts P.C.*, Eliz., XI, 352).

[53] Sir Julius Caesar, as chancellor of the exchequer, said of one project to enrol apprentices and collect forfeitures: "the profit very uncertain and extreme small" (*Commons Debates*, VII, App. B, 327–328).

[54] Goldsmith stated that his first try-out, to see if offenders would compound, was a success (*ibid.*, 504).

[55] Certificate of October 25, 1617, from Sir Francis Bacon, Sir Henry Montagu, Sir Thomas Coventry. *The Works of Francis Bacon*, ed. J. Spedding, XIII, The Letters and the Life, VI, 269–270, cited in *Commons Debates*, VII, App. B, 329. The general reason assigned is the lack of ground in law for the patent, but two points made against it are that the Statute of Artificers itself provides for the enrolment of apprentices in cities and other corporations, by

there was in fact a very considerable self-enforcement of the apprenticeship requirement through traditional observance, and that with the exception of special conditions in certain occupations, a moderate rate of business expansion gave little inducement to flout the law.[56] The increase in the proposals for apprenticeship patents early in James I's reign was probably merely a part of a general multiplication of patent projects. It was accompanied by a change in the character of the applicants which merits further study, and is commented on again in later pages.[57]

---

the proper officers; and that as for country villages, "we cannot give the suitors hope that any profit will be there made, warrantable by law."

[56] For discussion of conditions in certain occupations, see below, Chaps. IV and V. The reader is reminded that the Act restricted the seven-year requirement to occupations in use in 1563. Therefore any growth situations which developed in new rather than established crafts and trades would lie outside a patentee's grasp.

[57] See below, Chaps. III and VII.

II

THE PROFESSIONAL INFORMER: METHODS AND REWARDS

The central role of the professional informer in enforcing mercantilist regulations compels study of the kind of man he was, his methods of operating, what he gained and how, and whether he himself had to submit to restraints. Much depends on the answer to these questions. His effectiveness in law enforcement was influenced by his economic and social status, and the social regard in which he and his calling were held. The last was itself affected by the informer's attributes, as well as by the methods he employed, which in turn depended in large part on his incentives to stay within the law or work outside it. All these elements in his performance interacted with whatever controls were imposed upon him from outside.

The personal characters and characteristics of individual informers can only be imagined. Since the great majority belonged to a class only dimly visible in the Elizabethan and Stuart worlds, the lower middle class of petty tradesmen and artisans, their lives were never important except to themselves and the few whom they directly touched. But some have left indistinct trails of their passage which supply hints of how they worked. Most of the examples presented here necessarily concern informers in apprenticeship cases in the Westminster courts of the sixteenth century.

Two professionals of Devonshire deserve first mention, not for the amount known about them but for their large share of the apprenticeship informations in the Exchequer and Queen's Bench. John Otterey of South Molton, weaver, and Andrew Holmer, Exeter tailor, together brought almost half of all the professional informations for apprenticeship from the two counties of Devon and Somerset in the reign of Elizabeth. Their sixty-three cases accounted for over one-eighth of all the professional apprenticeship informations from the selected counties entered in the two Westminster courts during forty years. Both of them confined their activities in these informations to the southwest, and both tended to specialize in textile occupations, being prime informers also under various clauses of the Cloth Acts.[1] This local and occupational specialization might make their classification as professionals dubious, were it not for the clear evidence that at least Otterey was busy informing in numerous other offenses as well, from 1563 through 1586.[2] But their prominent part in local informing, which does much to make up one of the two geographical concentrations of Elizabethan apprenticeship cases,[3] suggests that they may possibly represent the semimonopoly conferred by a patent for forfeitures. If so, they and perhaps one other informer would be the sole examples of professionals operating in apprenticeship offenses under a patent.[4] The grant was that to John Martin in 1560, already mentioned. The excuse for the speculation is the presence of, first, a John Martin, described as of Minehead, Somerset, informing against Devon and Somerset weavers in the early years of the reign; and, second, a later apprenticeship informer from the same area, Edward

[1] The offenses for which their prosecutions were chiefly observed were those of unapprenticed weaving (and to a less extent, unapprenticed clothmaking), making cloth outside a market town, and keeping too many looms. These were created by the following acts: 5 & 6 Ed. VI, c. 8; 2 & 3 P. & M., c. 11, §§1, 2, 7; and 4 & 5 P. & M., c. 5, §§21, 22.

[2] Otterey informed against inclosure (MS. Notes of Edwin F. Gay); usury (Q.B.C.R., Hil. 27 Eliz., a group of cases by informers whose names appear in apprenticeship suits); engrossing (*ibid.*, Trin. 25 Eliz., list of fines); illegal export (*ibid.*, Mich. 28/9 Eliz., and Exch. Q.R.M.R., Pasch. 11 Eliz., m. 13 and 21).

[3] See Table I, App. II.

[4] Informers working under patents in other offenses are often found. Two examples are mentioned herein, see above, Chap. I, n. 52, and below, n. 7 (probably a patent). Another apprenticeship informer working sometimes for a patentee was Thomas Veale, London haberdasher, who besides informing on various statutes in the two Westminster courts, also took a number of processes out of the Exchequer in 1575 "at the request of" three deputies under the Mackwilliams and Colshill patent (mostly for usury). (For his apprenticeship cases, Q.B.C.R., Hil. 18 Eliz., m. 63, Pasch. 19 Eliz., m. 36, 37. Reference to his other activities, from MS. Notes of Edwin F. Gay, citing Exch. Q.R., Barons' Depositions, No. 242.)

Parker of Barnstaple, who calls himself in some inclosure prosecutions a deputy of John Martin under the latter's patent.[5] However, two other deputies elsewhere were also identified in the record of their inclosure cases as prosecuting under this patent, while no reference of the sort has been found for Otterey and Holmer.[6]

Parker himself seems to have been not only a deputy under Martin's patent but also a licensed municipal informer at Barnstaple, where in 1561 he was disallowed as an informer by the town authorities but reinstated at the order of the Exchequer. He had a long career, like Otterey, from at least as early as 1564 in the Exchequer when he informed against offenses under the Cloth Acts until his appearance there as Martin's deputy in 1589. In the meantime he informed in the Exchequer in apprenticeship cases in 1575, in the Queen's Bench in these and other suits from 1577 into the 1580's. He is described indifferently as clothier and as yeoman, and may be the Parker mentioned as resident in Barnstaple in 1583 and 1587.[7]

Barnstaple life provides a possible glimpse of that rarity, an informer in apparently good repute. Thomas Lugg, who has already been met when informing for the shoemakers there, was perhaps the same Thomas Lugg who in 1610 was a trustee of one of the town's charities and in 1614 was informing against an unapprenticed cooper.[8]

The most discernible imprint made on his times by any local apprenticeship informer was that of Nicholas Wright of Knapton, Norfolk. Since he is consistently described in his informations as "grocer" and always of Knapton, he can probably be safely identified

[5] John Martin of Minehead was seen as informer in two cases of unapprenticed weaving (Act of 1555), Exch. Q.R.M.R., Hil. 6 Eliz., m. 164, 164d. The reference to Parker as deputy, from MS. Notes of Edwin F. Gay, citing *ibid.*, Mich. 31 Eliz., m. 315, 317, 320–321.

[6] The two other deputies were a William Hutton of Whittlesbury, Northamptonshire, not named as deputy but a privy seal grant of 2 Eliz. authorized composition; and an Adam Sheperd of London, merchant-tailor, described as Martin's deputy under the 1560 patent. (References from MS. Notes of E. F. Gay, to Exch. Q.R.M.R., Mich. 18 Eliz., m. 82, Mich. 31 Eliz., m. 415.)

[7] The disallowance of 1561, B.M. Lansdowne MS. 171, f. 436 (for violating the sumptuary laws, his prosecutor being "the informer upon the statute of apparel"). As a resident of Barnstaple, see J. R. Chanter and T. Wainwright, *Barnstaple Records*, I, 43; *Acts P.C.*, Eliz., XV, 197. Some of his cases: Exch. Q.R.M.R., Pasch. 6 Eliz., m. 85, Pasch. 17 Eliz., m. 76, 77; Q.B.C.R., Hil. 21 Eliz., m. 55, 68, Mich. 28/9 Eliz., m. 106.

[8] Chanter and Wainwright, *Barnstaple Records,* II, 230; Exch. K.R.M.R., Trin. 12 Jas. I, m. 146.

with the Nicholas Wright of Knapton listed in the county muster roll of 1577 as of sufficient means to join with three residents in supplying a moderate quota of armor. His apprenticeship cases were only in Norfolk and Suffolk, but he was informing in the Queen's Bench for other offenses in these two counties during some fourteen years. Almost his first known appearance was inauspicious, since he was one of nine informers committed to the Fleet prison in December 1574 for taking unlicensed compositions, and it was not long before he was under examination again about prosecutions he had begun but dropped. He was evidently well-known in his own county, for Francis Wyndham (barrister, justice of the peace, soon to be serjeant-at-law and within four years justice of the Common Pleas) told his brother-in-law Nathaniel Bacon, in December 1575, that "one Nicholas Wright the promoter" had been among those complaining of Wyndham to the Lord Chancellor for various matters. Wright may have done his spying through such men as the convicted vagrant whom he saved from hanging by an offer of employment, thus presumably acquiring a willing tool. He was busy also in Norwich, where in 1583 he called down on his head the wrath of the city fathers. He had unwisely chosen for attack some of the leading Dutch craftsmen by serving process on them "out of the Queen's Bench" on various charges. The Norwich authorities asked the Privy Council to intervene in favor of the defendants. What happened to Wright is unknown, except that he was still informing at Westminster three years later.[9]

Perhaps somewhat higher in the social scale was John Leake, London mercer, appointed in 1560 as one of five assistants to the alnager of the City of London. He exemplifies Unwin's phrase, "half

[9] *The Musters Returns for Divers Hundreds in the County of Norfolk . . .*, ed. H. L. Bradfer-Lawrence, Norfolk Record Society, VI, 71; MS. Notes of E. F. Gay, from Exchequer Proceedings, Bundle 70, and from Barons' Depositions, No. 284; *The Official Papers of Sir Nathaniel Bacon of Stiffkey, Norfolk*, ed. H. W. Saunders, Camden Society, 3rd Series, XXVI, 188; Norwich City MS. Quarter Sessions Books of Proceedings, IV, f. 163d., 30 July, 18 Eliz.; Norfolk MS. Sessions Books of Proceedings, III, f. 121, September Sessions at East Dereham, 27 Eliz.; W. J. C. Moens, *The Walloons and Their Church at Norwich*, Huguenot Society I, Pt. I, 41, 45, 263. Wright's nine apprenticeship informations in Norfolk were in the Queen's Bench between 1573 and 1583; other observed references to his other informations are *Acts P.C.*, Eliz., XIII, 72 (June 1581), and Q.B.C.R., Hil. 24 Eliz. to Hil. 28 Eliz. In the last known entry he appears as informing jointly with another local professional, William Rochester of Norwich, described as a joiner.

informer, half amateur inspector,"[10] better than most of the known informers. From 1576 to 1579 he was informing in the Exchequer, probably in his official capacity, on various clauses of the Cloth Acts. The cases may represent the conflict between London searchers and country clothiers that is expressed in Leake's writings of the same period on abuses in the manufacture of broadcloth. But besides his official cases, he appeared from 1575 through 1591 in prosecutions unrelated to his duties as deputy alnager. Though he was not informing in apprenticeship cases from the selected counties, his name occurs in suits against inclosers and illegal importers. His record and his position were sufficiently reputable for him to escape the Exchequer investigation of the 1570's which caught Wright and several others for malpractices. He seems to have emerged unscathed also from a complaint made in 1576 by the Earl of Leicester, on behalf of a defendant whom Leake had continued to prosecute after dismissal of a previous charge. Leicester asked Lord Treasurer Burghley that "this promoter" be made "an example to the rest." But in 1589–90 Leake was still deputy alnager, when he is found as defendant in suits brought by west-country clothiers who were protesting London search of their cloth and as representative of the alnagers of 1591 in hearings of this dispute before the Privy Council. By 1595 he had become keeper of Leadenhall; the last glimpse of him is in the familiar role of informer when in 1602 he was prosecuting a merchant for exporting unfinished cloth.[11]

More checkered careers were perhaps those of John Chambers, fishmonger, alternatively described as of London, Norwich, or Suffolk,

[10] The informer thus described by Unwin, Peter Blackborowe of Frome in Somerset, clothier, seems in fact not to have been either a professional informer or an "inspector." At the time he appeared as an informer, he was seeking a grant of the alnage, but there is no evidence that he obtained it. A truer local example of the informer-inspector was one Edward Hedd who, in the late sixteenth century, was both an appointed searcher for the tile-making industry of Essex (under a statute of 1477) and a professional informer before the quarter sessions (Cal. Q.S., XVII, 36, S.R. 138/47, Trin. S. 39 Eliz.; XVII, 25, S.R. 137/73; XVI, 220, S.R. 131/88.

[11] G. D. Ramsay, *The Wiltshire Woollen Industry,* 55–58n.; Exch. Q.R.M.R., various terms 19–31 Eliz.; Exch. Decrees & Orders, various terms 20–22 Eliz., and for the suits by the clothiers, *ibid.*, Hil. 30 Eliz., Mich. 31 Eliz., Mich. 32 Eliz.; *Acts P.C.*, Eliz., XXI, 97; his description of the cloth industry, *Tudor Economic Documents*, III, 210ff; Leicester's complaint, B.M. Lansdowne MS. 22, f. 85. Leake's "Treatise" of 1577 was in reality a petition for a dispensing patent as "Supervisor over the Alnager, searchers and sealers."

and Benjamin Clere, yeoman of Boxted, Essex. The former was observed as prosecutor in the two Westminster courts in the 1580's for apprenticeship and other offenses in counties as widely separated as Norfolk and Worcestershire.[12] But he had been an informer for some years previously, long enough to have confessed during the Exchequer inquiry of 1574–75 to unlicensed compositions.[13] He seems to have been also, in 1573 at least, a bona fide dealer in fish.[14] Is he the same as the John Chambers of Dunwich, Suffolk, who was indicted twenty-four years later at Essex quarter sessions as a "common barrator and disturber of the peace"? [15] His companion in trouble then was Clere, of the same name and place as an informer of 1586 against an Ipswich merchant for exporting broadcloth illegally.[16] In 1607, a Benjamin Clere — now termed a clothier — was again before the Essex magistrates, this time for resisting the searchers of woolen cloth, who claimed they had found him stretching a length of the light-weight broadcloth known as azure.[17] This variety had long been manufactured in the Boxted area, and was usually destined for export from Ipswich, or for the domestic market. If the various Cleres can be assumed to be one, and the common denominators of Ipswich and broadcloth make it seem likely, then Clere illustrates the manner in which a legitimate business might be linked with informing.

In late Elizabethan Staffordshire, a small group of informers had

[12] His apprenticeship cases, Exch. Q.R.M.R., Trin. 24 Eliz., m. 100, Mich. 28 Eliz., m. 233, 233d.; Q.B.C.R., Trin. 26 Eliz., m. 64, Hil. 28 Eliz., m. 202, Pasch. 28 Eliz., m. 66, Mich. 28/9 Eliz., m. 153, Hil. 29 Eliz., m. 124. He was prosecuting Suffolk offenders also, in 1582 and 1584, and was observed as informer in usury cases.

[13] MS. Notes of Edwin F. Gay, citing Exch. Q.R. Procs., Bdle. 70.

[14] *Acts P.C.*, Eliz., VIII, 171, petition from Chambers for license to export sprat, referred to Suffolk Commissioners for Restraint of Export of Victuals.

[15] Cal. Q.S., XVII, 36, S.R. 138/45, 20 June, 39 Eliz.

[16] Q.B.C.R., Hil. 28 Eliz., membrane number not noted.

[17] Cal. Q.S., XVIII, 167, S.R. 177/112, Epiph. 4 Jas. I. The practice of stretching cloth on tenters was the chief "abuse" against which John Leake inveighed in 1577, and Suffolk the county he named as worst in this respect. As a London deputy alnager, he was biased against the areas making the colored cloth which was finished before export, since these escaped most often from London's effort to maintain a monopoly of cloth-finishing and exporting. For the Suffolk manufacture of colored cloth, see Unwin, *Studies*, 268ff; A. Friis, *Alderman Cockayne's Project and the Cloth Trade*, passim. For the Essex industry, see *Victoria History of Essex*, II, 382ff; the Cloth Acts of 1552, 1557, 1559, 1585 (which exempted Boxted among other Essex villages from the prohibition on country clothmaking), and 1606; Friis, *passim*.

close connections with the metal-working industries developing in the southern part of the county. Two of the most active were made known in 1596 to the then clerk of the peace, Mr. Linacres A Leonard Milton, who described himself as "serving Lord Dudley," wrote Linacres to ask him to prosecute three men "on behalf of" Milton's "kinsman" Edward Ashmore of Bromwich, treating the informations as if Milton were present in person. He mentions the bearer of the letter, a John Norris, as his own partner, "both enrolled within the Exchequer." [18] Ashmore and Norris were already active before the county quarter sessions and continued to appear there as informers through 1608, in apprenticeship prosecutions and others. A competitor or colleague, Thomas Lynton, cooper of Walsall, was an informer both in the Exchequer and at quarter sessions.[19] Of Ashmore and Norris, something more is known than the mere entries of their informations, in which they are always termed nailers. Ashmore comes on the stage first in 1590 as a witness in an indictment of assault and battery, typical of the restless life he seems to have led in a turbulent community. Next he is seen as sheriff's bailiff to Robert Stamford, Esquire (justice of the peace, sheriff 1589/90); Ashmore's first known information was this same year. By 1597 he was a servant to Thomas Parkes, ironmaker, and was called a "laborer" in a series of charges and counter-charges for breaking and entering, assault and battery, between Parkes and three other gentlemen operating iron mills and furnaces, with their respective servants. Another of Ashmore's avocations may have been that of professional bailsman, a capacity in which he, Norris, and another informer figure in recognizances between 1599 and 1604. Meanwhile Norris was evading service of a series of writs, at least one being to answer a charge of theft brought in the same term of 1596 in which Norris had

[18] *The Staffordshire Quarter Sessions Rolls*, ed. S. A. H. Burne, III, 205–206. There is no record that Linacres assented to this request. Milton explained that he was unable to come himself owing to the arrival at Dudley Castle of his "lady" with friends; this suggests that he was employed in the household. The three offenders mentioned by Milton had been prosecuted by Ashmore two years earlier for unapprenticed nailmaking.

[19] In 1595 in the Exchequer, Lynton was prosecuting two nailmakers as unapprenticed (Exch. Q.R.M.R., Mich. 37 Eliz., m. 198); and before quarter sessions from 1595 into 1601, men in several occupations for the same offense. See Staffordshire MS. Sessions Rolls, various sessions Trin. 33 Eliz. to Pasch. 43 Eliz. and later, for informations by Ashmore, Norris and Lynton among others; also the printed series, Vols. II–VI, *passim*.

himself laid two informations for apprenticeship. Appropriately, in the accusation against him he is called "an informer"; but when last seen in 1609, he had become a victualler.[20]

Neither the occupational status of the Elizabethan informers nor the scanty knowledge available of their outward behavior does much to explain the ill repute which seems generally to have attached to them. Few were apparently as low in the Elizabethan social scale, or as disorderly, as the Staffordshire group. Some were even styled "gentleman," though this was no guarantee of respectability. But contempt has been the lot of the informer in other worlds than Elizabethan England, rooted in impulses deeper than particular social codes.[21] For the sixteenth- and seventeenth-century "promoter," his frequent resort to illegal methods did nothing to diminish the antipathy his very name incurred, even though the illegalities were in part forced upon him by a whittling down of his lawful gains.

As revealed in the apprenticeship cases, the trade of informing was carried on by each informer sporadically in respect to any one class of offenses, and usually without specialization either in the occupations of apprenticeship offenders or in apprenticeship alone. The impression of discontinuity gained from such a record, for example, as that of William Nelson, yeoman of Westminster, whose name was seen in apprenticeship cases in 1565 but not again until 1587,[22] may be caused partly by lack of a complete dossier for individual informers. Thus Nelson's occasional partner, William Rysam, a Southwark haberdasher, was by chance noticed as a frequent informer for apprenticeship between 1565 and 1568 against offenders outside the selected group of counties although he appeared little in cases within the group.[23]

[20] *Staffordshire Q.S. Rolls*, II, 32, 98–99; III, 199, 297, 340; IV, 83, 100, 123; V, 34, 206–207, 209, 267, 316; [VI], ed. D. H. G. Salt, 10, 43, 85, 94. For Robert Stamford as justice of the peace from about 1577 to about 1604, see Libri Pacis as noted in Bibliography; as sheriff, see P.R.O. *Lists and Indexes*, IX, 128.

[21] For example, Aristophanes' *The Acharnians*, trans. J. H. Frere, *passim*, or in Murray's version "a lot of wicked little pinchbeck creatures, degraded, falsely stamped and falsely born," G. Murray, *Essays and Addresses*, 42.

[22] Exch. Q.R.M.R., Mich. 7 Eliz., m. 236, etc., Mich. 29 Eliz., m. 214d., Hil. 30 Eliz., m. 103, etc. His observed prosecutions were from five counties, an example of the lack of geographical specialization by London informers mentioned in the text.

[23] No exact references can be given for these cases.

Specialization did exist, consisting in selection of certain statutes as the chief targets.[24] But Otterey and Holmer alone exemplify any tendency toward this in apprenticeship informing, and random sampling indicates that it was not typical for other offenses. The following frequency table suggests the lack of it in apprenticeship prosecutions among the numerous informers frequenting Westminster whose names are recorded in such cases:

Exchequer and Queen's Bench
1563–1603

No. of Appr. Cases per Informer	*Number of Informers*
Under 1 to 1½	46 to 49
2 to 5	48 to 49
6 to 10	9
11 to 15	1
16 to 20	3
21 to 25	3
Over 25	2
	112 to 116

The dispersion of individual informers' apprenticeship cases in place was much less than in occupations of offenders or than the general scatter of their activities. The majority of the professionals appear in cases from one county only, and for over half of these it is the county of their own stated residence. But the London informers, 62 out of the total 112, tended to have a wider geographical range, several figuring in cases from three of the selected counties, four covering more than this number, and several also being noticed in apprenticeship suits in counties other than the selected. Of the locally resident informers, only two prosecute in as many as three counties apiece, another in six (while a few others were seen also in cases from outside counties). To determine an average range, knowledge of all the prosecutions of a fair sample of individual informers would be essential. For the Londoners it would undoubtedly be extensive, while

[24] Informers working under patentees represent this kind of specialization; see examples already given. It is illustrated somewhat differently by "one of the informers for defective measures" at Middlesex Sessions (*Middlesex Sessions Records*, ed. W. Le Hardy, I, 447). By definition, as already stated, the professional was unspecialized in the sense that his motive for informing was not that of a particular trade interest.

for local men it was probably considerable within any one county and sometimes within a whole region. In the seventeenth century, when informations on apprenticeship were increasingly restricted to the local courts, a few London informers prosecuting before quarter sessions still kept in touch with more than one locality. Thus Geoffrey Brooman, yeoman, entered informations against apprenticeship offenders in both Essex and Somerset; John Richards, yeoman, prosecuted in Somerset.[25] Informers operating far outside their own habitat must have drawn on many sources. Occasionally London and local professionals worked together.[26] Some London informers may also have had local business connections; a possible example is Edward Jennings, fishmonger, who prosecuted apprenticeship offenders primarily from the southwest in 1601–1603, if he can be identified with the London grocer of the same name and time who dealt in Somerset calamine.[27] But there is ample evidence that both London and country informers had local agents. Their "factors" were mentioned in 1571, and a generation later the Exchequer informers were said to rely "very often . . . upon letters or intelligence out of the country from persons known to them" who bring the proofs of the alleged offenses when they come up to London.[28] Most districts no

[25] Brooman may have transferred his attention from Essex to Somerset, since his known Essex cases, the first in 1612, end in 1627, while his Somerset cases are from 1630 on. (Essex Cal. Q.S., XIX, 93, S.R. 200/105; 102, S.R. 201/93; 113, S.R. 202/106; some informations by Brooman for other offenses, 191, S.R. 208/114–115; Exch. K.R.M.R., Trin. 14 Jas. I, m. 30d.; Assizes Records, Southeastern Circuit, Indictments, Bdle. 69, March Assizes, 3 Chas. I; Somerset MS. Sessions Minute Books of Recognizances and Orders, IV, Mich. 6 Chas. I and seq.). For Richards, Exch. K.R.M.R., Hil. 11 Jas. I, m. 89d., Mich. 16 Jas. I, m. 97d.–98d.; Somerset MS. Sessions Indictment Rolls, No. 31, Items 44, 45, 47, 48, various sessions 13 and 15 Jas. I; No. 33, Items 79–80, Mich. 14 Jas. I. Brooman was among the informers who certified compositions to "Dr. Chambers' office," for the years 16 Jas. I to 13 Chas. I; his were for engrossing (reference from MS. Notes of Edwin F. Gay, to Exchequer K.R., Proceedings, Bdle. 84).

[26] William Rysam joined a merchant of Devonshire in prosecuting weavers (under the Act of 1555), Exch. Q.R.M.R., Hil. 12 Eliz., m. 356–357; Edward Jennings shared with a Coventry yeoman an information against Warwickshire country bakers, Pasch. 43 Eliz., m. 188. A few other instances were noted in apprenticeship informing.

[27] Jennings' apprenticeship cases in the Exchequer were from Devon, Somerset, Wiltshire, Worcestershire, Warwickshire, in various occupations. For Jennings the grocer, see *Victoria History of Somersetshire*, II, 389.

[28] *Cal. S.P.D.*, Eliz., Addenda 1566–1579, 346, draft of an act to control informers, read in Commons 23 April 1571; B.M. Lansdowne MS. 167, f. 144, a memorandum of about 1609 by the King's Remembrancer.

doubt had the equivalent of the system of communications reported from Wiltshire in 1619–20, when the justices of the peace were rounding up informers "grievous to the country," local operators who were "the evil under-agents of other more notable informers who have their residence in and about London." [29] Local informers also had their "men." [30] But whether any of the known apprenticeship informers were "under-agents" in their apprenticeship cases has not been discovered.

Another open question, but one with a bearing on the adequacy of the informer's profits, is the amount of time the average "promoter" devoted to his spying. Was it for many of them only a by-occupation, or did they often, like one of their number, "by the space of [a] twelvemonth . . . labor to note in writing" the offenses of their victims, putting their names in a "paper book"? [31] The apparently discontinuous nature of their activities, if in fact generally characteristic, favors the hypothesis that informing was a sideline for most of them. A number kept it up over many years. Some must have taken to it in preference to other business, like John Emery, held to have become "a very lewd and idle person . . . leaving that honest trade whereunto he was first bound . . . and liveth by promoting." [32] For those who made their living by this occupation alone, were its legitimate returns sufficient or were the bona fide operations a cover for private payments from the accused? If the latter, is it possible to judge the proportion of illegal to legal gains? This question is pertinent to the task of estimating the degree of correspondence between the recorded apprenticeship cases and the actual extent of violations.

The informer's legitimate receipts could be of two kinds: his share of the statutory forfeiture due on conviction; or a composition which by customary procedure the court might license him to make with the defendant before verdict. The first kind of reward he rarely received. Among the Elizabethan apprenticeship informations in the two Westminster courts only one instance was found of trial followed

[29] S.P.D. Jas. I, CXII, No. 14.

[30] In the North Riding, Robert Bainbrigg, styled "informer of the Exchequer," had his man Christopher Rockley (*Quarter Sessions Records*, ed. J. C. Atkinson, North Riding Record Society, II, 86, January Sessions 1615).

[31] Leadam, *Select Cases*, II, 220, information in 1540.

[32] MS. Notes of Edwin F. Gay, from Exch. Q.R., Procs., Bdle. 70. Emery was an informer in the Exchequer for apprenticeship between 1574 and 1594 against offenders from Devon, Essex, Norfolk, Cheshire (Exch. Q.R.M.R., *passim*).

by recorded conviction; only two in the Stuart period to 1643.[33] Observation indicates that this condition was typical in other offenses.[34] Quarter sessions records of the selected counties appear to contain only one entry of the statutory penalty in apprenticeship informations, and none of convictions in the later years.[35] In the occasional convictions in various offenses and in any court, however, the full penalty claimed by the informer in his accusation was generally greatly reduced by the jury's practice of bringing in a verdict of guilty for only a fraction of the alleged offense — with apprenticeship, for example, for one or two months out of an alleged eight to twelve months' illegal exercise of an occupation.[36]

From the Crown's viewpoint, the procedure corresponding to the licensed composition, and probably normally associated with it, though the record is seldom clear, was the mitigated forfeiture allowed the defendant when "to save expenses" he asked admission to a "reasonable fine." [37] Though only about five per cent of the Elizabethan professional informations for apprenticeship at Westminster, from the selected counties, carry a record of admission to fine, this

[33] Exch. Q.R.M.R., Pasch. 43 Eliz., m. 205 (professional); Exch. K.R.M.R., Mich. 11 Jas. I, m. 447 (professional), Pasch. 13 Jas. I, m. 174 (professional). No forfeitures were recorded. Two apprenticeship informations in counties outside the selected group recorded the full penalty (Q.B.C.R., Hil. 10 Eliz., m. 66).

[34] At least for the reign of Elizabeth, for which no convictions were seen in cases under three provisions of the Cloth Acts (seven-year apprenticeship, country clothmaking, keeping too many looms); apparently only two convictions were recorded in the Elizabethan prosecutions in the Exchequer for inclosures (MS. Notes of Edwin F. Gay).

[35] Essex Cal. Q.S., XVII, 133, S.R. 147/76, Mich. 41 Eliz. (nonprofessional). Judgment was given against the defendant when he failed to appear, for the full penalty claimed, £24. Nearly two years later he was arrested for nonpayment of the fine (Cal. Q.S., XVII, 183, S.R. 152/99; 218, S.R. 155/18).

[36] In the Elizabethan instance of a Westminster conviction (n. 33 above), an eleven months' exercise of the trade had been alleged but the jury verdict was for two. Examples occur in the seventeenth-century apprenticeship indictments before quarter sessions. A similar whittling down of the extent of offense was observed in a conviction for illegally made cloth: the allegation was sixty cloths, the jury found the accused guilty for only ten (Q.B.C.R., Trin. 7 Eliz., m. 54). In each of the two inclosure convictions (n. 34), the jury held the defendant guilty of conversion of less acreage over a shorter period than the informer had charged.

[37] For descriptions of Exchequer practice, B.M. Lansdowne MS. 171, f. 407 seq. (dated 1572); MS. 167, f. 10, 140; 168.2, f. 40 (dated 1609). The formula of the license to compound employs the same phrase, "to save expenses," and this was retained in the late seventeenth century. William Brown, *The Practice of His Majesty's Court of Exchequer*, 2nd ed. (London, 1699), 528.

compares favorably with the virtual lack of records of convictions. The amounts set by the court range from 6/8 to 20/–; the most frequent were 10/– and 13/4. The alleged duration of the offense in these cases was generally eleven months with a minimum of six, the full statutory penalty being 40/–per month.[38] There were no admissions to fine observed for the Stuart period in the Westminster apprenticeship cases. In quarter sessions records, only three entries of admission to fine and two of mitigation after conviction were found for all the apprenticeship informations of eighty years, in amounts from 1/– up to £11.[39] William Lambard condemned the practice from his own experience in Kent quarter sessions as a "mockery of the law," regarding the usual justification from the revenue standpoint as ill-advised: "though it may seem good husbandry" to take a fine before conviction instead of risking all profit to the crown on the chance of acquittal, "yet who seeth not that the other way is much more serviceable." [40] But the practice continued. In the apprenticeship informations it may be assumed to have been at least the intended accompaniment to the entries of licenses to compound, which in the sessions records, though not in the Westminster courts, are more numerous than admissions. Actual record of the two together was found in only one sessions and twelve Westminster apprentice-

[38] The number in professional informations was 25 or 26: Exch. Q.R.M.R., Fines, Pasch. 8 Eliz. (?), Pasch. 9 Eliz., Mich. 10 Eliz., Pasch. 18 Eliz. on information of Mich. 13 Eliz.; Q.B.C.R., Fines, Hil. 8 Eliz., Pasch. 11 Eliz., Mich. 13/14 Eliz., Hil. 17 Eliz. (3), Hil. 21 Eliz., Mich. 21/22 Eliz., Hil. 22 Eliz. (2), Pasch. 22 Eliz., Trin. 22 Eliz. (2), Hil. 23 Eliz., Hil. 24 Eliz. (2), Mich. 25/26 Eliz., Pasch. 26 Eliz., Mich. 27/28 Eliz. (3), Trin. 30 Eliz. One entry also was found in a nonprofessional information (Hil. 8 Eliz.). Of the professional informations on the three clauses of the Cloth Acts in the Westminster courts, about a tenth were admitted to fine, with 13/4 the most usual amount. This was a great reduction from the statutory penalties of £20 for a single offense of unapprenticed weaving (by the Act of 1555), and £5 for each illegal country cloth. The gap was even greater in the few instances of admission to fine in inclosure informations, where the statutory and actual penalties were £900 and £5, £230 and £2, £400 and £2, even £4000 and £6–13–8, etc. (MS. Notes of Edwin F. Gay).

[39] Wiltshire MS. Sessions Minute Books, I, Mich. 40 Eliz., case of Alexander Pearse, 10/– (not a professional information); Somerset MS. Sessions Minute Books of Recognizances and Orders, IV, Trin. 6 Chas. I, two fines of £11 and 40/–, "for mediation of the penalty," each one-half of total due on conviction; Nottinghamshire MS. Sessions Minute Books, VIII and IX, fine of 12d. entered Trin. 6 Chas. I on information of Epiph. 4 Chas. I; *ibid.*, fine of 5/– and license to compound Easter 7 Chas. I on information of Easter 6 Chas. I.

[40] *Eirenarcha* (1582), 464; (1588), 582.

ship informations.[41] According to contemporary Exchequer practice the grant of license to compound and the informer's certificate of the amount of the composition should precede the court's imposition of the mitigated fine.[42] No informers' certificates have survived from the twenty-one licenses known to have been granted during Elizabeth's reign in all apprenticeship informations in the two Westminster courts.[43] But the amounts recorded for mitigated forfeitures, since these were the equivalent of the informer's reported compositions, help to supply the lack. The total return to one informer, John Otterey, from four of his apprenticeship cases between 1578 and 1580 must have been, on this basis, £3–6–4; at the same period he was getting about £5 from six informations under the Cloth Acts. Andrew Holmer meanwhile would have received £1–13–4 from three apprenticeship compositions, some years later £1–10–0 from three more and later still another 10/– composition. A London informer in 1582 got 13/– from an Essex offender.[44] Similarly modest sums were

[41] The one sessions example in apprenticeship informations is that from Nottinghamshire cited in n. 39 above. Occasionally others were noticed in other offenses, such as a fine of 13/4 with composition of the same amount for an offense against leather regulations, and a fine of 10/– with composition of unrecorded amount for retailing illegally, both in Nottinghamshire. The Westminster cases were among those in the Queen's Bench listed in n. 38 above. In prosecutions at Westminster on the three clauses of the Cloth Acts, eleven such entries were found.

[42] See n. 37 above for descriptions of Exchequer procedures. Exchequer grants of licenses may include a proviso "that the said informer do procure the said defendant to make his fine" or "so as the Court be made privy to the said composition." An early seventeenth-century form specified that the license must be entered in the Exchequer Book of Orders and the amount of composition sworn to on oath. (Exch. Q.R., Decrees and Orders, Series I, VI, 280d., 21 Eliz., and VIII, 31, 23 Eliz.; B.M. Lansdowne MS. 168.3, f. 44, copy of original license of 1606 to Robert Bedoe who was an apprenticeship informer some years later; for Bedoe as applicant for a patent, see above, Chap. I, n. 45.)

[43] Entries of a few certificates of compositions on other offenses show rates correspondingly low in comparison to the informer's potential share from the full statutory penalties: 20/– in a case of forestalling (a high penalty by statute), £16 in one under the Tillage Act of 1563, 40/– in cash and 10/– worth of leather in another case, etc. (Exch. Q.R., Decrees and Orders, Series I, V, 320, 339d.). One of those certifying was James Langrake, an active apprenticeship informer; for his imprisonment two years before, for unlicensed compositions, see below, Chap. III, n. 16.

[44] The apprenticeship fines, from which Otterey's total is assumed, Q.B.C.R., Pasch. 21 Eliz., m. 68–69, Fines, Trin. 22 Eliz.; Mich. 21/22 Eliz., m. 103, Fines same term; Pasch. 22 Eliz., m. 89, Fines, Trin. 22 Eliz. The Cloth Act cases, in Exch. Q.R.M.R., Fines, Hil., Pasch., and Trin., 21 Eliz. Holmer's assumed receipts, Q.B.C.R., Fines, Hil. 23 Eliz., Hil. 24 Eliz., Pasch. 26 Eliz., Mich.

reported as the informers' compositions in the few apprenticeship informations at quarter sessions for which this record exists — about eleven entries in the eighty years. Their amounts, from 5/–, 5/10, up to 30/–, can probably be attributed also to the remaining instances, in which the amount of composition was not reported, out of the total thirty-one licenses recorded as granted during this entire period.[45] The varying sums agreed upon in compounding were probably, like the mitigated forfeiture when independently set by the courts, adjusted to the defendant's ability to pay.[46]

The sum of numerous such payments through a year constituted the informer's gross operating income from legitimate business in court, unless he supplemented it as no doubt many did by the fees of a professional bailsman or by retainers from special business groups for defensive informing.[47] But for his own legitimate prosecutions he

27/28 Eliz., Trin. 30 Eliz. The London informer, Q.B.C.R., Fines, Hil. 24 Eliz.

[45] The lowest sum, 5/–, is assumed from the mitigated fine in the same case, in Nottinghamshire; see n. 39 above. The highest is based on interpreting the Norfolk procedure in composition: the sum reported by the informer was £3, but an identically reported composition forty years later has a further entry that 30/0 was paid "to the use of the king" (Norfolk MS. Sessions Rolls, 20 Jas. I, Swaffham June Sessions; 14 Chas. II, Swaffham August Sessions). The other compositions in: Somerset MS. Sessions Indictment Rolls, No. 27, Pt. 1, Items 26, 27, 29, 31, 33 (all in 1613); *Quarter Sessions Records of the County of Somerset*, ed. E. H. B. Harbin, Somerset Record Society, XXIV, 35, Easter or Trin., 3 Chas. I; Staffordshire MS. Sessions Rolls, Mich. 12 Chas. I.

[46] Adjustment of the forfeiture to suit the defendant's purse is recognized in some quarter sessions' entries, for example, Essex Cal. Q.S., V, 30, S.R. 45/67, Midsummer, 1573; XIX, 7, S.R. 193/46, Epiph. 8 Jas. I. A Staffordshire informer of the Restoration explained the amount of his compositions, in one, "20/–, and no more, he [the defendant] being very poor" (MS. Sessions Rolls, Epiph. 14 Chas. II). In a patent scheme of the early seventeenth century, the proposed "Surveyor of the King's Casual Issues" was to rate forfeitures on penal statutes according to the value of the defendant and the nature of the offense (B.M. Lansdowne MS. 167, f. 144, article No. 8).

[47] Numerous instances of informers as bailsmen have been noticed in the record of the Westminster courts and quarter sessions. An example of retainers to informers to protect the interests of trade groups was the fee paid by the London Clothworkers in 1630 for informing against violators of the restriction on the number of apprentices (Dunlop and Denman, *English Apprenticeship*, 85n.). Presumably a fee was paid to the two feltmakers who were campaigning against unapprenticed feltmaking in 1578–79 and who claimed to have been "put in trust by a number of the feltmakers for all suits that concern the said science" (Exch. Q.R.M.R., Pasch. 20 Eliz., m. 69–73, 91–94, 138–139, etc.; Unwin, *Industrial Organization*, 133). The one probable illustration of the practice detected among apprenticeship cases in the selected counties was that of Thomas Pilkington, busy in Lancashire in Charles I's reign; his activities are described in Chap. X. The present writer has elsewhere suggested a possible

had to meet the costs; occasionally he had to be prepared for the rare event of a full-dress trial and even for paying costs and damages to a defendant on acquittal. He did not apparently recover costs from a defendant who did not appear or who was convicted.[48] He must also have had to pay for his "intelligences," and for his witnesses, who might have to be brought to London or to the local assizes. Such operating expenses cannot be discovered. But some of the legal costs can be itemized, although the total for a single prosecution is impossible fully to determine.

Fees charged in the Exchequer about 1610 (excluding some minor sums clearly payable by the defendant alone) came to a minimum of over £2–0–0 for a single information during any one term. Since prosecutions tended to carry through several terms, additional recurring fees would be payable to the attorney at 3/4 a term, 4/– for every continuance, and the like.[49] Lists of fees officially charged, moreover, do not tell the whole story. Bailiffs, justices' clerks, even occasionally a clerk of the peace, were accused by suitors in one court or another of demanding more than the established rates. Clerks in the Westminster courts were said to be in collusion not only with informers to inflate the information in number of words but with defendants to make willful errors in pleading, the latter to increase the informer's costs.[50] No sixteenth-century awards of costs against

employment by London interests of the informers responsible for much of the southwest apprenticeship prosecution of the sixteenth century (M. R. Gay, "Aspects of Elizabethan Apprenticeship," *Facts and Factors in Economic History*, 134–163); but this remains unproved.

[48] A demonstration of the informer's responsibility for his own costs is recorded in the Essex information in which judgment was given against the defendant, for nonappearance, and one-half the forfeiture awarded to the informer with no mention of costs. (See above, n. 35.) In a proposal for a collecting patent, the informer was to be allowed his expenses on all cases in which his share of penalties would be under £15 in any one trial (B.M. Lansdowne MS. 152.8, f. 132, endorsed 1609). His liability for an acquitted defendant's costs and damages was made mandatory by the Act of 1576 (18 Eliz., c. 5, perpetuated by 27 Eliz., c. 10).

[49] B.M. Lansdowne MS. 168, f. 94–95, ostensibly pertaining to the Lord Treasurer's Remembrancer's department, but the fees are what might be expected from contemporary descriptions to concern the business of the King's Remembrancer. See App. III for the fees in detail.

[50] A Somerset defendant alleged that the clerk of the peace had refused to take less than 20/– to discharge his bond, the proper fee being 3/4 (Exch. K.R., Decrees and Orders, Series II, II, 225d., Pasch. 5 Jas. I). For the Westminster accusation, see B.M. Lansdowne MS. 167, f. 18. Mention of the problem of controlling fees recurs through sessions records.

the informer in favor of a defendant were observed for apprenticeship cases in the Westminster courts; in three for other offenses they ranged from 20/– to 50/–. In two apprenticeship informations of the seventeenth century the awards were £3–6–8 and even £6–0–0.[51] The Staffordshire justices of the peace assessed a bill of £1–9–10 against one professional informer, while in Essex the energetic Geoffrey Brooman was faced in 1613 with an itemized accounting from the victorious defendant in an apprenticeship information.[52] This is the most detailed bill of costs and damages discovered for sessions work; it ran as follows:

Costs	Clerk of Peace for copy of information	4/4	
	Appearance in court at last January Sessions	2/–	
	Clerk at Easter Sessions	2/–	
	To Clerk for *venire facias*	2/–	
	To Sheriff for warrants thereupon	2/–	
	To Bailiff for warning the jury	8/6	
	To the jury at trial	7/–	
	To Bailiff for attending the jury	12/–	
	To Counsel at trial	£1–0–6	
	To Counsel for advice to plead	10/–	
	To Clerk of Peace for indictment, suit, and *capias ad satisfaciend.* for the cost	6/–	
	Sum	£4–5–4	[£3–16–4]
Damages	Defendant's attendance in London and Clerk of Peace for writ of *ven. fac.*, also his attendance, and to Sheriff for warrants thereupon	10/–	
	His "travale" to the Bailiff to call the jury	5/–	
	His attendance at the last three quarter sessions	15/–	
	His witnesses at the trial	13/4	
	The loss of his work during these travels	. . . .	
	Sum	£2–3–4	

[51] Q.B.C.R., Hil. 23 Eliz., m. 76, Hil. 24 Eliz., m. 91, Pasch. 23 Eliz., m. 54; K.B.C.R., Hil. 2 Chas. I, m. 21; Exch. K.R.M.R., Hil. 13 Chas. I, m. 53.

[52] *Staffordshire Q.S. Rolls* [VI], 85. The Essex bill, Cal. Q.S. XIX, 123, S.R. 203/129, Midsummer, 11 Jas. I. Brooman's information was against a husbandman for unapprenticed bricklaying (Cal. Q.S., XIX, 93, S.R. 200/105, Mich. 10 Jas. I). The informer was nonsuited, presumably for failure to prosecute. In two of the earlier cases the awards were made after the attorney general discontinued prosecution.

But the justices in fact "taxed" the informer only a total of £4.[53] The defendant, who did not himself know how to charge for the important item, the loss of his time, might have ruefully wished he had paid the informer privately.

Two other itemizations of defendants' costs in apprenticeship informations of the same period and county reveal that, though individual fees might be standardized (an attorney's fee at 3/4 as in the Exchequer, entering the plea of not guilty at 2/4), the items included in the bill of costs, the total costs, and the justices' award of costs might all vary widely from one trial to another even when the offense charged was identical. In these cases, the totals were £1–13–10 and £3–10–10, the first sum being recorded as "allowed by the court," while the second defendant's costs were assessed at only 20/–.[54]

Thus at one blow an informer might lose as much as the gross legitimate receipts of several informations. In apprenticeship informations at quarter sessions which went through to a trial, the odds seem to have been in the defendant's favor.[55] Even so, the informer's net yearly income may have compared favorably with average incomes of the lower middle class,[56] and if his informing was only part-

[53] Marginal notation in the bill.

[54] Essex Cal. Q.S., XVIII, 243, S.R. 184/29, Midsummer, 6 Jas. I, judgment for the defendant in an information for unapprenticed trading as mercer or grocer; XIX, 92, S.R. 200/100, Mich. 10 Jas. I, judgment for the defendant in an information for unapprenticed weaving; both brought probably by nonprofessional informers.

[55] The observed numbers in sessions records of acquittals and convictions on professional informations are, respectively, by periods: in 1563–1603, 0 or 1, and 0 or 1; in 1603–1625, 8 to 12, and 0; in 1625–1642, 3 and 0. The acquittal of the first period and one of the second may be in nonprofessional cases; and in three others of the second, the entry may refer to a plea of not guilty rather than to the verdict. There was also, in a professional information of 1617, a so-called acquittal on the informer's failure to prosecute, which is in fact a dismissal and therefore not included here. The nonprofessional acquittals totaled 6 to 8 for the entire span of years, convictions 1 or 2.

[56] By the 1630's, an income of about £40 a year seems to have been typical of the lower levels of the yeoman class — to which so many informers belonged, according to their case entries — while the more substantial were getting £100 and upwards (Campbell, *The English Yeoman*, 162, 216–218). For tradesmen, income data are nonexistent. Some bakers in Essex in 1597 were reported as having each sold some sixty dozen loaves in two months at 2d; if this rate of sale could have been maintained, each would have realized £36 a year, but since these were all loaves below the standard weight the bakers may have had a trade also in "honest" bread. (Cal. Q.S., XVII, 33, S.R. 138/32). For skilled labor, rough guesses can be made from daily wage-scales. At the highest rates paid in the building trades in Elizabethan Norwich, with adjustment for a lower

time work his position must have been considerably improved by the additional sums. Nevertheless, the gap between the statutory and the actual shares in penalties, the prolonged expenses of taking prosecutions through to trial, and the risk of costly upset thereafter, must have strongly tempted informers to make illegal use of the first entry of an information and the writ issued thereupon. Thus they could cut their expenses to a minimum and perhaps hope to squeeze more from the accused.[57]

Settlement out of court must often have been preferred by the accused themselves to avoid the court fees [58] and much loss of time and earnings. The practice of composition was widespread by the sixteenth century in many public duties, even though recognized as an abuse,[59] and the ordinary man probably saw little difference between a licensed and an unlicensed composition except that the latter might forestall his going to court at all. The defendant's very real interest in meeting the unlawful informer halfway was no doubt a substantial cause of the apparent infrequency of prosecution for informers' "abuses." [60] It may also help to explain why dispensing patents flourished as long as they did.

The informer's illegal receipts could take several forms: compositions under license but for more than the reported sum; unlicensed compositions on actual informations; compositions extorted by forged or pretended process on pretended informations; fees from defendants for false informations to prevent the entering of valid prosecutions, or for collusion of other kinds with defendants. The first two, since they

---

winter scale and for days off, annual earnings might have been about £18 or £19 (MS. Books of Chamberlain's Accounts, vols. 1553–1567, etc.). In Wiltshire, the half-year's pay of a smith in 1589 from one employer (full-time?) was £8–3–6 (H. Hall, *Society in the Elizabethan Age*, 3rd ed., 23, 204).

[57] The discouraging effect on informers of high costs of prosecution was succinctly stated in 1650: "if it cost the prosecutor more for his intelligence than a quarter part, no man, after he has once burnt his fingers, will put himself to certain expense for uncertain reward." (Suggestions for controlling the export of bullion, *Cal. S.P.D.*, Commonwealth, vol. 1650, 201.)

[58] The writer quoted in n. 57 above argued that licensing compositions with offenders was essential because few of them would "stand to a trial, as the charges of the suit will go a good part of their fine."

[59] Men compounded to escape jury or constable service, or military service in the county levies. Sir Stephen Proctor in urging his patent claimed that clerks of the market compounded for illegal weights and measures, clerks of the peace for unlicensed alehouses (B.M. Lansdowne MS. 167, f. 18).

[60] See below, Chap. III, n. 21.

were based on proceedings actually begun in a court, involve no concealment of the defendants' offenses. For apprenticeship, they are probably the most frequent illegalities.

The first of these has left no discovered trace before 1642.[61] The prevalence of unlicensed composition is suggested by the number of schemes for patents designed to tap the flow of payments to informers. It is demonstrated by the predominance of inconclusive prosecutions both in the Westminster and the local courts. This category constituted about four-fifths of the professional informations at Westminster in Elizabeth's reign, all those in the Exchequer in the next reign except for two convictions, and four-fifths or more of those in quarter sessions for the whole period 1563–1642.[62] Such bad prospects for definitive results — and these proportions can hardly be characteristic of apprenticeship prosecutions alone — would assuredly have caused an early decline of professional informing unless offset in other ways.[63] That the informers were finding compensation outside the courts is suggested most clearly by the occasional entries of admissions to fine, "the informer not present," and of "cease process, the informer not appearing." The chief gain, however, from these private settlements may have been in cutting expenses. Recorded amounts taken by Exchequer informers without license, on various unspecified offenses, though tending to average higher than the known licensed amounts, were still moderate — from 5/– up to £5 — and sometimes partly payments in kind — "24 dozen knives," "a gammon of bacon," a "sugar loaf," a "chalder of coals."[64] In the quarter

[61] Unless the confessions of Exchequer informers included unreported as well as unlicensed compositions (see n. 64 below). The only case involving this abuse by informers which was noticed in sessions records occurred in 1654 when a professional informer was accused of taking 11/6 from three men (their offenses not stated) while certifying only 1/6 for each. (Nottinghamshire MS. Sessions, Minute Books, XIII, July 1654, warrant of good behavior for A. Pepper.)

[62] See below, Chap. VI, for the proportion in prosecutions by other private interests, and for differences from one reign to another both in professional and other private prosecutions. See App. II, Tables II and III, for the absence of figures from the King's Bench (and Exchequer after 1624). The category of "inconclusive" here comprises cases with (a) no record of process, (b) initial process or process up to the stage of trial.

[63] Elton finds numerous cases among those brought by one informer in the reign of Henry VIII which were "non-suited" in the Exchequer, that is, of which the court took no notice; but he does not mention the practice of composition (see his "Informing for Profit," *passim*).

[64] A list of confessed compositions taken without licenses by nine informers

sessions records the occasional entries of accusations against informers rarely carry a statement of the sums involved, and the observed instances in the selected counties in which amounts of their takings are reported appear to be cases of extortion on pretended informations rather than of unlicensed compositions on actual prosecutions.[65]

The extortion was also on a modest scale. In the sole known entry of specific levies on apprenticeship offenders, the blackmail was no more than 5/– and 10/–.[66] Other offenses paid off at similar rates or even lower, 4d. and 6d. being recorded, though heights of 40/– or so can be seen, and of one London informer it was asserted that "butchers and victualers . . . he taketh at his own price and pleasure."[67] But the informer's total, from these threats of prosecution based on forged or faked process, was limited only by his enterprise and by the susceptibility of his prey. A "pretended informer" in Wiltshire was said to have extracted over £200 from several tradesmen, whose alleged offenses the report unfortunately does not mention.[68] A professional informer, who brought actual prosecutions for apprenticeship and for many other offenses in the Westminster courts, for a time successfully collected annuities in Norfolk at the rate of 20/– for each promise not to inform. Another elsewhere had been more demanding, £3 down with an installment of 13/4 and the obligation to pay a life annuity of 20/–.[69] There is no evidence whether these two rackets, or others, included apprenticeship offenders. That they had only a minor place among extortioners' victims is suggested

questioned in the Exchequer investigation of 1574–75 (MS. Notes of Edwin F. Gay, citing Exch. Q.R., Procs., Bdle. 70). Other confessions by informers, Exch. Q.R., Barons' Depositions, Nos. 241, 242, Hil. 17 Eliz.

[65] The accusation does not always state whether actual or faked process was used as the basis for pressure. In Middlesex a few unlicensed compositions are recorded as 12/–, 25/–, 22/–, and one sum of 17/– "on the statute of Laborers," *County Records*, II, *passim* (*temp.* Jas. I). In Essex an "illegal composition" of 10/– on an information for engrossing was the subject of an indictment against a London professional informer, Cal. Q.S., XIX, 105, S.R. 202/33 (1613).

[66] Norfolk MS. Sessions Rolls, Bdle. 6 Chas. I, indictment of Robert Reve, blacksmith of Helgay. Reve was a busy professional, informing at quarter sessions for some ten years and often in apprenticeship cases.

[67] MS. Notes of Edwin F. Gay, citing Exch. Q.R., Procs., Bdle. 70.

[68] Privy Council Register, Chas. I, XLVIII, 69 (1637).

[69] The first was Edward Body, London clothworker, active in apprenticeship informations in the last twenty years of Elizabeth's reign. For these illicit dealings he counterfeited the green wax seals on Exchequer subpoenas (Exch. Q.R., Barons' Depositions, Oct. 36 Eliz.). For the other, also a London professional, Exch. Q.R., Decrees and Orders, Series I, III, 65d., Nov., 7 Eliz.

by the virtual absence of apprenticeship informers from the number of men accused of extortion by false process or bribery not to inform.[70] For illegal extortion by informers, as for the authorized extortion by holders of dispensing patents, the profitable openings would be on laws more generally broken than those for apprenticeship, such as the regulations governing taverns and inns, commodity wholesaling, exporting and importing, and money lending. The extent of the abuse for all offenses may have been exaggerated by contemporary complaint. The informers' continued resort (on a large scale for a number of statutes) to genuine informations in the courts is the best possible witness to difficulties encountered in simple blackmail with no shadow of authentic legal ground.

Collusion with defendants, the fourth source of the informer's illegal gains, is even less likely to have been useful in apprenticeship offenses. In either of its forms — fictitious suits prearranged between informer and defendant to bar other prosecution, or the omission of certain names from informations against a group of offenders — collusion seems to have been a cause of complaint primarily where organized dealers wanted impunity for repeated violations heavily penalized.[71] Apprenticeship did not lend itself to group prosecution. In Tudor and Stuart England neither towns nor country villages offered sufficient opportunities in any one occupation over short periods to lure unapprenticed intruders en masse. Moreover, an apprenticeship charge had to specify for each offender not only the occupation and place in which, but also the length of time during which, the offense was committed.

The foregoing review of the informer's methods and rewards leads to certain conclusions. The total number of informers, London and local, operating at Westminster in Elizabeth's reign was so large and their sources apparently so diverse that they can probably be credited

[70] Two exceptions were in the North Riding and Wiltshire (N.R.R.S., III, 125, 118; MS. Sessions Minute Books, IV, April, 17 Jas. I). The informer involved, accused here of extortion on pretended informations in the Exchequer, was William Hackett of Frome, Somerset. He was at this time (1619) the center of an inquiry into the organization of Wiltshire informers. A decade later he was still informing in Somerset, on apprenticeship and other offenses.

[71] For example, among the London wooldealers and importers; and the London Company of Dyers was accused of collusion to enable them to use logwood in dyeing (prohibited by statute). See S.P.D., Eliz., XL, No. 38 (c. 1572); *Acts P.C.*, Eliz., XXI, 66 (1591); *Cal. S.P.D.*, Addenda 1580–1625, 510–511 (c. 1608); B.M. Lansdowne MS. 167, f. 18. For suppression of names, B.M. Lansdowne MS. 167, f. 144.

with adequate discovery of most offenses. A change in this respect for apprenticeship offenses after 1589 will be considered in the next chapter. But both before and after 1589, informers probably followed up their detection of apprenticeship offenders by beginning genuine prosecutions: concealment of violations by collusion is unlikely to have played any important part in the informer's operations in this field, and therefore unlikely to have caused appreciable distortion of a correspondence between actual and reported violations. How effectively the proceedings once initiated were pursued is another matter. The informers' potential gains as represented by the statutory penalties tended to be drastically reduced by the customary allowance of mitigated forfeiture and composition. They might secure somewhat higher returns by private agreements with defendants, which had the advantage for both parties of reducing expenses. Unreported and unlicensed compositions, probably the most widespread abuse in the system of professional informing, thus gave the informer a yield in an unknowable proportion of the discontinued and dismissed prosecutions from which the crown got no return and the accused suffered no recorded penalty. The efforts at restraint which the various malpractices made necessary, and the further impairment of the informer's reputation to which they led, will next be discussed.

III

REGULATION OF INFORMERS

Efforts to control the excesses of informers during the Elizabethan and Stuart periods took four principal forms. The first, short-lived, was to supplant the system of informing altogether. A second was to regulate it by proclamation and legislation: the early essays were designed to reduce irresponsible and penalize illegal informations; the later also to close the Westminster courts to the private information as a mode of proceeding on statutes of minor financial benefit to the Crown and of disproportionate annoyance to the subject. A third was to correct particular situations by special investigations and the strict punishment of individual informers. The fourth was to regulate the informer locally, by exacting some responsibility from him toward the local authorities.

Several themes can be followed through the history of these various methods. Setting the key for them all was the tendency to prejudge individual informers as "lewd," "for the most part of the meaner and worst kind of people." [1] Only exceptionally did the idea occur that they might be otherwise under different conditions. One theme was the continuing and unquestioning acceptance, apparently interrupted only twice, of informers as indispensable agents of enforcement. The general opinion then was that they were "necessary in every well-governed state"; this was expressed by a Restoration comment that the common informer was "more necessary than credit-

[1] The adjective was one often used about an informer; Andrew Holmer was thus characterized by the Exeter authorities in 1592 (*Acts P.C.*, Eliz., XXII, 404). The generalization is quoted from the Star Chamber's censure of Sir John Stafford for turning informer. J. Hawarde, *Les Reportes del Cases in Camera Stellata, 1593–1609*, ed. W. P. Baildon, 331–332 (1607).

able . . . ; yet such as govern themselves well are to be encouraged as furtherers of the public good."[2] A second element was the pervasive fiscalism of the era, which stimulated but also limited the attempted reforms. A third was the recurrent popular unrest caused by the manifestations of the system of informing; to soothe this became a principal motive of the ameliorative steps taken or accepted by the government. Their result was the gradual achievement of a degree of restraint on the informer, but in effecting this, of the serious limitation of his usefulness, at first for a few and then for the majority of mercantilist regulations.

The development of controls over informing began early in Elizabeth's reign with a plan to replace it for certain statutes by a more efficient community presentment of offenses, under the supervision of selected justices of the peace in every county. The object was stated as that of relief from the extortion of common promoters, "to repress their unlawful and undue practises and vexations," yet to secure execution of the statutes. The justices of assize were asked to consider whether such a commission composed of justices of the peace would not be "more grateful to the people and profitable to the realm" than enforcement of the statutes by informers; to what number in each county the informers should be restricted; whether the informers should not also be prohibited from informing on certain additional statutes "as the execution thereof may be more grievous to the people than profitable to the commonwealth." The commissioners were to receive presentments from any two residents of a locality, who were to be paid expenses and attendance out of the forfeitures.[3] One other proposal to supplant the informer in Elizabeth's reign would have entrusted all discovery of offenders under penal statutes, so that these "may be with more speed put in execution," to two justices of the peace in every county.[4]

[2] Hawarde, *Les Reportes*, 331–332; M. Dalton, *The Country Justice* (1682), 525, with additions, of which the quotation in the text is one, by an anonymous writer. The editions published during Dalton's lifetime contain no comment on the informer.

[3] *Cal. S.P.D.*, Eliz., Addenda 1566–1579, 20, dated 1566, possibly in November, and identified as in William Cecil's hand. Some of the statutes are identical with those on which William Tyldesley was reporting to Cecil in 1561 (*Tudor Economic Documents*, I, 330). They do not include the Statute of Artificers. Another form of the same scheme set the pay for expenses and attendance at 1/– a day (B.M. Harleian MS. 589, f. 310–315).

[4] MS. Notes of Edwin F. Gay, from Exch. Q.R., Procs., Bdle. 75; undated.

The first project, which implied great faith in the system of local community presentment, was accompanied by the draft of a bill for Parliament, limiting the informers in each county to a maximum of four, who would be authorized only by the lord chancellor, lord keeper, or lord treasurer and must give bond to pay the defendant costs for groundless vexation or delay.[5] Both the project and the bill may have been inspired by the same circumstances as a proclamation of November 10, 1566, "against such as abuse informers or promoters." In this, riots against informers were described, "especially in and about Westminster Hall and the palace of Westminster"; "great routs and companies . . . being assembled" had "not only beaten and very evil intreated divers of the same informers: but also have made great outcries against the same persons." [6]

Some concern with the problem is again apparent in Parliament in 1571 when another draft bill got as far as a second reading, and when in debate on the subsidy one member linked difficulty in levying it to the drain on people's purses attributable to licensees' and informers' abuses.[7] But no measure was enacted until 1576. This provided for registration and payment of costs by the informer, and imposed severe penalties for unlicensed composition (the pillory, a fine of £10, and disablement from informing).[8] Further reform was under consideration, probably about 1580–81, with intent "to cut off all the lewd and beggarly informers" by requiring all to give bond of £200, and to encourage the worthy by additional rewards from the exchequer.[9]

The proposals of 1566 and 1580/81 have in common a realization that existing rewards were insufficient to attract competent men to

[5] *Cal. S.P.D.*, possibly the "bill concerning informers" discussed October 1566 (*C.J.*, I, 73–74). A bill had been drafted for one of Mary's Parliaments (*Cal. S.P.D.*, 1547–1580, 114).

[6] *A Booke Containing All Such Proclamations . . . during the Reign of . . . Elizabeth*, collected by H. Dyson, 98.

[7] *C.J.*, I, 85, 87–88, 91; J. E. Neale, *Elizabeth I and Her Parliaments, 1559–1581*, 218–219.

[8] *Statutes of the Realm*, IV, 18 Eliz., c. 5, perpetuated by 27 Eliz., c. 10.

[9] Exchequer Miscellanea, Parliamentary and Council Proceedings, No. 25. This is bound in with the draft of a bill to reform "the negligences" of under-sheriffs and bailiffs, and of informers; and on January 30, 1581, a bill was read in the Commons dealing with the abuses of undersheriffs and bailiffs (*C.J.*, I, 120). No. 27 in the same collection is another draft bill about informers which provides harsher penalties than those of 1576, resembling the draft bill of Mary's reign mentioned in n. 5 above.

the work of detection and prosecution and to keep them honest. The earlier proposal is indeed unusual in recognizing the problem of expenses.

The statute regulation of informers which was crucial in the enforcement of the Statute of Artificers was that of 1589, already mentioned. For apprenticeship informations the vital clause of the act was Section 6, that all suits "for using any art or mystery in the which the party hath not been brought up . . . shall be sued in the general quarter sessions of the peace or assizes of the county where the offense was committed . . . or in the leet in which it happens and not in any wise out of the same county." Suits on all penal statutes in which forfeitures were payable to an informer were to be brought within a year of the commission of the offense.[10] The background of this legislation is unknown. Had there been renewed clamor against informers, troubling signs of unrest at a time when the meaning for England's security of the Armada's fate could not be realized? One of the annoyances associated with the common information was the expense and waste of time for jurymen summoned to Westminster, where the venue was often laid.[11] But the Act of 1589 revives the suggestion of 1566 that for some offenses informing was more trouble to the government than it was worth. Its provision that for all statutes in which the penalties were under £20 the venue must be that of the county where the offense was committed points to an intent to clear the Westminster calendars for lawsuits that were the better suppliers of Crown revenues.[12]

Whatever the chief purpose of the act may have been, its results for the professional informer in prosecuting apprenticeship offenses are not in doubt. It decreased the number of apprenticeship informations in the Exchequer and probably in the King's Bench,[13] although

[10] 31 Eliz., c. 5, §5. This restriction seems to have been generally complied with in apprenticeship informations before it was made mandatory by this law. Two other statutes were mentioned in Sect. 6 with the apprenticeship clause as specifically limited to the local courts, one prohibiting unlawful games, the other requiring the possession and use of archery equipment.

[11] The Act of 1576 had provided that trial juries should not be compellable to appear at Westminster in cases in which the offense was committed more than thirty miles away without reasonable cause shown by the attorney general (18 Eliz., c. 5, §3). In 1575 James Langrake had been summoned to answer for delaying trial in a case in which Leicestershire freeholders were on the jury (Exch. Q.R., Decrees and Orders, Series I, VI, 80, 5 May, 17 Eliz.).

[12] 31 Eliz., c. 5, §§2, 4.

[13] Lack of search of the Queen's Bench Coram Rege Rolls from 1589 to 1603,

conflicting interpretations left room for a few informations still to be brought by common informers in their own names. In the King's Bench, informers could make use of the ex officio information.[14] Business conditions contributed to the decline in informations on apprenticeship, but cannot alone have been responsible for a permanently lower level of informing activity at Westminster for this offense. The bearing of the Act of 1589 on the professional informer's effectiveness in enforcing the apprenticeship requirement will be considered in a later chapter.

While controls by legislation were being developed, reform by special orders or in particular situations by *ad hoc* inquiries had been tried. The Privy Council wrote in 1565 to the justices of assize, evidently directing them to take steps against extortionate informers.[15] Little trace is apparent of anything accomplished, unless an investigation begun in the Exchequer late in 1573 was based on orders framed eight years before. But more probably it was a campaign initiated within the Exchequer to collect from informers some of the unreported compositions of preceding years. Proceedings against informers found guilty may have temporarily improved the certifying of compositions to the court.[16] An obstacle, however, to a consistent program

and inadequate sampling thereafter, prevent a definite statement as to decrease in this court.

[14] There was a tendency in the reported cases in which the point was argued to hold that the Westminster courts could entertain apprenticeship informations. In one of 1605 the court agreed to advise on the question as one (they said) which concerned many informations. Not until 1620 does there seem to have been a clear-cut decision that according to the statute an information for apprenticeship must be brought originally in the county of the offense before quarter sessions or assizes. *The Second Part of the Reports of Sir George Croke in the King's Bench and Common Pleas*, 4th ed., II, 85: *Kenn v. Drake. The Reports of Sir H. Hobart . . .* , 5th ed., 327: *Nevill v. Yarwood.* The ex officio information was entered in the name of the king's attorney "at the relation" of a private informer (Holdsworth, *English Law*, IX, 237), a device that was not available in the Exchequer court. By the Restoration this and the action of debt had become the usual procedures for common informers in apprenticeship cases in the King's Bench.

[15] *Acts P.C.*, Eliz., VII, 199, a memorandum that letters were to be sent "concerning informers," without indication of their contents. But punishment of Edward Body, the Exchequer informer, a few months later was based on orders issued by the justices of assize: for extortion contrary to these orders he was imprisoned until he repaid what he had taken and 20/– costs. On his release he was ordered to give bond in £200 not to inform within three years unless specially licensed by the Exchequer court; this license was granted him three months later (Exch. Q.R., Decrees and Orders, Series I, III, 65d., Nov., 7 Eliz.).

[16] Examinations of informers and penalties imposed, Exch. Q.R., Decrees and

of regulation within the central courts lay in their competition for fee-paying business. To a later complaint that there were more informations in the King's Bench and Common Pleas than in the Exchequer was joined a proposal that all three should undertake similar reforms: if the Exchequer should act alone, it was claimed, the informers would be driven out, yet fees from them were "one of the chiefest heads left" of the clerks' "maintenance." [17]

The paralysis created by this situation in the central courts was not broken by any renewed energy displayed by the central executive branches of government. Whence the initiative came for the shaping and enacting of statutory control it is impossible to say. The piecemeal resemblances between the plan of 1566 in which William Cecil had been interested and the series of draft bills and completed acts suggest that his interest continued. But the directions of 1565 to the justices of assize were not repeated and no other effort was made to stimulate local authorities. The normal method employed for exhorting these to enforce the measures regarded by the government as especially important was through the address delivered by some one of the high officers of the Crown at the beginning of each term to the judges of assize and repeated to the grand jury at the opening of the assizes in every circuit. This "charge" might be accompanied by "articles of presentment," a list of the offenses particularly to be dealt with. This was transmitted by the justices of the peace at quarter sessions to the presenting juries and local officers of the peace. Sir Edward Coke in his first year as chief justice charged a grand jury to repress the abuses of informers.[18] But neither the articles of presentment attributed to him as issued at an earlier assizes,[19] nor the other such lists which have come to notice, include informers' of-

Orders, Series I, VI, 64, 18 Nov., 16 Eliz.; 69, 2 Dec., 17 Eliz.; 74d., 10 Feb., 17 Eliz. Penalties consisted of imprisonment (terms unknown); fines (usually fractions of the confessed compositions, from one-tenth to one-sixth, but in one case twice as much as the compositions); and a one-year disallowance from informing in any court. One offender had to undergo the pillory. Several apprenticeship informers, including Wright and Langrake, were among those imprisoned and disallowed.

[17] B.M. Lansdowne MS. 167, f. 45 (undated, but the arrangement of subjects corresponds with that in f. 40 endorsed 1610). The yearly salary received from the queen by one official of the House of Commons has been estimated at one-eighth or one-tenth of his total earnings, the balance being from fees and gratuities. Neale, *House of Commons,* 348.

[18] *The Lord Coke His Speech and Charge* (London, 1607), H.

[19] S.P.D., Eliz., CCLXXVI, No. 72.

fenses. Presentments by local juries seem equally blank, with rare exception.[20] At the level where local knowledge of rapacious informers would have been most immediate and accurate, there appears to have been no request for or acceptance of responsibility for the periodical reporting which the presentment system achieved for some offenses.

Direct attack on abuses was thus left to those aggrieved by them. The self-interest involved in escaping lawsuits by private arrangements with the informer has already been mentioned as a reason for inaction on their part; another might have been the natural reluctance to prosecute on the part of men themselves offenders against regulations. For whatever causes, known proceedings against erring informers are very few in proportion to the numbers and importance of these agents of the law.[21]

Partial control was intended and perhaps achieved by a licensing system which has left slight but unmistakable traces. In the sixteenth and early seventeenth centuries it may have operated through authorizations by the Westminster courts and the prerogative jurisdictions; later it may have been taken over in some counties by the justices of the peace.[22] Informers at Westminster appear to have had a recognized status, whatever its basis.[23] Another means of control,

[20] Two exceptions were in Essex: one presentment by the grand jury, one by a hundred jury, at quarter sessions (Cal. Q.S., IX, 61 [1580]; XIX, 331–332 [1619]).

[21] From 1563 to 1642, about a dozen were seen in the Exchequer (from all counties); about seventy-five from selected sessions records. Since no thorough search could be made for this type of offense, more such cases undoubtedly existed, but not large numbers. In the Essex Assizes Rolls only two indictments for unlicensed composition were observed (Assizes, S. E. Circuit, Indictments, Bdle. No. 51, 1609). Out of all the prosecutions, only one was identifiable as involving an apprenticeship offense: the informer was convicted of unlicensed composition with a baker he had informed against as unapprenticed, and was sentenced according to the Act of 1576 to two hours in the pillory, a fine of £10, and disallowance from informing (Wiltshire MS. Sessions Minute Books, VIII, Jan., 16 Chas. I).

[22] At a North Riding quarter sessions in 1606, two men were ordered to be punished for acting as informers "without the authority or license from his Majesty's Attorney in the North" (N.R.R.S., I, 44). By the later seventeenth century the North Riding justices of the peace were licensing informers (V, 73 [1651], VI, 222 [1674]; mention in 1650 of an "Informer General" for the Riding, V, 46). In Wiltshire a sessions order in 1670 referred to recognizances taken from men licensed to be alehouse-keepers, badgers, and informers (MS. Sessions Order Books, III, Easter 22 Chas. II). The power of disallowance itself implied the authority to allow.

[23] Occasional phrases imply this, for example a North Riding informer mentioned as "informer for the Court of Exchequer" (N.R.R.S., II, 86); one in

occasionally employed by the justices of the peace, was the requirement of a bond from the informer to pay costs if adjudged.[24] The attempt of the Wiltshire justices to supervise informations for apprenticeship offenses seems to have been unique, and has left no record of its application.

The willingness of the justices of the peace to restrain the informer probably varied with circumstances. When their own authority was evaded, Norfolk justices appealed to the lord treasurer to suppress an extortioner, fearing that otherwise his operations would "move a murmuring among the queens majesty's liege people." The local perturbation he caused seems out of all proportion to his success, for the final charge against him — after testimony that he had "molested a great number of honest dealing people" with threats of legal proceedings at Westminster — listed only eleven persons from whom he had taken sums ranging from 5/– to 40/–.[25] The apparent intensity of protest and the sensitiveness of the justices to it show how readily extortion could become self-defeating. The incident may illustrate another facet in the many-sided problem of regulating the informer: a tendency of local authority to turn for help outside its own sphere rather than to devise controls based on the available organs and methods of local government such as the system of presentment. Besides the resort to high officialdom, as individuals or in its collective form of the Privy Council, there was Parliament and the panacea of old or new legislation. In 1585, a Northamptonshire justice urged upon Burghley the renewal of the Act of 1576 before the end of the current session of Parliament.[26] His view was probably shared by many. After all, in that Parliament of which one session did renew,

---

Essex accused of taking money on a pretended court process "under color of his office of informer on penal statutes in the courts at Westminster" (Cal. Q.S., XIX, 508–509, 519). This was an informer active in Charles I's reign in prosecuting apprenticeship and engrossing cases at quarter sessions.

[24] Only a few scattered instances were encountered: Essex, 1646 (Cal. Q.S., XXI, 199, S.R. 330/67); Warwickshire, 1671, 1673 (*Orders Made at Quarter Sessions, 1665–1674*, ed. S. C. Ratcliff and H. C. Johnson, Warwick Record Society, V, 169, 198); Northamptonshire 1683, 1719 (MS. Sessions Minute Books, II, Epiph. 1683, MS. Sessions Rolls, Epiph. 1718/19). As with licensing, no statutory basis is known for the apparently local and spontaneous adoption of this method of control.

[25] MS. Notes of Edwin F. Gay, from Exch. Q.R., Procs., Bdle. 70, papers dated October and November 1575, one endorsed by Burghley with a note to make out a commission to the justices of the peace for an inquiry.

[26] *Cal. S.P.D.*, Eliz., 1581–1590, 227, letter from Roger Cave.

and in perpetuity, the "act against common informers," the House of Commons consisted mostly of present or future justices of the peace.[27] This undoubtedly was true of the next Parliament which in the session of 1589 passed the second statute of the reign affecting informers. A considerable percentage of the enlarged Jacobean commissions of the peace must have sat in the Commons which framed and discussed a series of bills "for the reformation of the abuses of informers" between 1604 and the enactment in 1624 of a companion to the famous Statute of Monopolies.[28] The complementary grievance of dispensing patents was canvassed at several of the same sessions, and the committees of the lower house to which bills on both subjects were referred contained a majority of members experienced as justices of the peace.[29]

The effort of the Commons in 1621 to push through legislation on the intermingled grievances was the most determined and most nearly successful until that time. There was much to explain this. In 1619 and 1620 in several districts the important commodity trades had been disorganized, if the strong tone of the complaints can be credited, by informers' prosecutions under statutes controlling middlemen. In October 1619, the Wiltshire justices of the peace appealed to the Privy Council for help in dealing with the informers who were interfering with the county's necessary importation of "commodities" from neighboring shires by compelling even licensed dealers to compound, so that the trade was "almost quite overthrown."[30] The justices complained that the informers had eluded their jurisdiction by certioraris removing prosecutions against them to the upper courts. Others later fled the county to escape arrest, but the justices reported to the Council three who had been taken and would be punished. Meanwhile the Council summoned at once before it the most notorious of the Wiltshire informers, William Hackett, and appointed a committee to inquire into the situation in the county. But Hackett was imprisoned in November only until the following term, and by February was

[27] Neale, *House of Commons*, 308.

[28] *C.J.*, I, 225, 229, 256–257, 396, 401, 442, 443; *Parliamentary Debates, 1610*, ed. S. R. Gardiner, Camden Society, 16.

[29] This statement is based on study of a number of the commissions of the peace, the composition of the committees being given in some instances in the Commons Journals.

[30] *Acts P.C.*, Jas. I, V, 42. The entry does not explain whether the "commodities" were foodstuffs or raw wool.

among the informers again complained of as molesting Wiltshire while residing "in and about London"; though the committee was directed by the Council to summon these men and examine them in the presence of such Wiltshire justices of the peace as might be in London, no further steps toward reform are recorded.[31] An equally mild remedy was adopted in the case of an informer who had been troubling Halifax wool buyers under the regulations for wool dealing: he was committed to the Marshalsea until he should withdraw the informations.[32] In the grain-producing counties, the autumn and winter of 1619–20 brought low prices after good harvests, accompanied by a similar recognition of the middleman's utility. The Kent justices forwarded to the Council a petition from farmers for relief, claiming that merchants at the port towns would not buy grain from them for shipment elsewhere in England because they were so harassed by informers; the Council replied that grain on account of its cheapness might be sent anywhere in the kingdom, and that further disturbance from informers was to be stopped by reporting their names to the Council.[33] In May 1620, the Council sent on to the justices of Huntingdonshire a complaint received against an individual informer who in the meantime was imprisoned. In June the Council ordered the withdrawal of a "multiplicity of informations preferred into the Exchequer" on the Act of 1551 for wool dealing, of which Cornwall had complained.[34]

Members of Parliament and of the Privy Council, therefore, had ample opportunity to know that the country was seriously disturbed over the ubiquitous informer, at the same time that complaint of the dispensing patents was rife. An example of the latter comes from Lincolnshire late in the winter of 1620, when the justices of the peace reported to one of the judges of assize that informers were abounding in the county, evidently because of the "new commission" to compound for the recognizances of victualers, butchers, and innkeepers.[35] To some the available measures of restraint applied by the Privy Council on request may have seemed inadequate.

[31] *Acts P.C.*, Jas. I, V, 46, 63, 85, 128–129; S.P.D., Jas. I, CXII, No. 14.

[32] *Acts P.C.*, Jas. I, V, 65, 17 November 1619.

[33] *Cal. S.P.D.*, Jas. I, 1619–1623, 112, January 1620; Privy Council Register, 1619–20, 114, January 28, 1620.

[34] *Acts P.C.*, Jas. I, V, 196, 227. These examples of informers' activities admirably illustrate their immediate response to situations of profit, especially those in which quantity of offenses would permit a quick raid.

[35] *Cal. S.P.D.*, Jas. I, 1619–1623, 130–131, March 1620.

Within a few days of the opening of Parliament in January 1621, one or more drafts of bills "against certain troublesome persons, commonly called relators, informers, and promoters" had been introduced. Sir Edward Coke favored one of the bills under debate and described the "articles" which the king had been ready to apply to the Westminster courts in default of Parliamentary remedies: one would have prohibited trial of all informations outside the county of the offense. Sir Hamond L'Estrange, a Norfolk justice of the peace, urged that the bill's passage be hastened. The king's speech in March supported it. But it was twice returned from the Lords with objections and amendments, and lost from sight. In February, consideration had also been given to reducing the number of penal statutes, and there had been some discussion of dispensing patents.[36]

The bill which at length became law was first read in the lower house of the new Parliament on February 24, 1624; it passed the Commons within two weeks, and the Lords on March 16. Its preamble emphasizes the burden on the king's subjects imposed by the necessity of appearing in the Westminster courts to answer informations or compounding to escape such appearance; this was one of the causes of vexation which had been mentioned in earlier debates. The object of the new act was similar to that of the king's proposed order in 1621, to confine all informations on penal statutes to the lower courts, even those brought by the attorney general, and to restrict the venue for trial to the county of the offense.[37]

In the same session, Parliament outlawed dispensing patents by the Statute of Monopolies and repealed sixty penal statutes. But the common information, though restricted, was not abolished.[38] A sig-

[36] *C.J.*, I, 510–511, 514, 538, 542–543, 562, 582; *Cal. S.P.D.*, Jas. I, 1619–1623, 238; *Commons Debates*, II, 31, 43, 115, 244, 300, 307, 324, 443, 460, and VI, 257–258. The abortive act of 1621 would also have limited trial to the county involved. Another of the king's "articles" would have required a signed warrant for every entry of an information in the name of the king's attorney; this method of evasion of the law of 1589 has been noted as employed in apprenticeship cases.

[37] *C.J.*, I, 672, 678; *Journals of the House of Lords*, III, 249, 252, 263; *Statutes of the Realm*, IV, 21 Jas. I, c. 4. Certain statutes important for Crown revenue were excepted from the act, so that informations on them could be laid in any county: the recusancy laws, regulations for export and import, etc.

[38] There seems to have been some contemporary doubt whether the Statute of Monopolies in prohibiting dispensing patents extended also to compositions by informers on penal laws. But the practice of composition continued; and the dispensing patent in fact revived.

nificant difference in status between the information and the dispensing patent had been demonstrated by the decisions of the judges in 1604 in the Case of Penal Statutes. Although their first report had unequivocally condemned grants of the authority to take forfeitures without legal proceedings or to dispense with penalties, three weeks later their second report, on penal statutes which merited and required better execution, accepted the common informer by implication. Its recommendations included better enforcement of the Acts of 1576 and 1589 against specific abuses, particularly in the practice of composition in which licensing should be made effective.[39] Continuing reliance on the system of information was displayed in the course of debate in 1621: Sir Edward Coke argued that "informers must not be quite taken away but regulated"; another member had already suggested that informers should be encouraged in order better to enforce the recusancy laws.[40] Only rarely was a different view expressed. A member of Parliament in the 1610 session had urged that all informers "be taken away and to proceed by indictment," but this proposal apparently found no sponsors.[41]

One objection to abolishing procedure by common information was fiscal. Some of the opposition to the bills of 1621 originated with "officers of the courts to whom all the profit came by these informers" [42] — the same vested interests that had prevented a housecleaning within the central courts before. Informers' operations when duly controlled might be seen as bringing a larger yield to the crown. Archbishop Sandys, reporting in 1587 to the lord treasurer the punishment of one informer at York for unlicensed composition, appeared to credit the informer's claim "that he had brought in one sitting to the council at York £80 odd money. If thus much by one promoter, how much by all the rest? And if thus much at one sitting, how much at all the sittings?" [43] The possibility cannot altogether be dismissed

[39] *Cal S.P.D.*, Jas. I, 1603–1610, 165; B.M. Lansdowne MS. 168, f. 344.

[40] *Commons Debates*, VI, 257–258; *C.J.*, I, 519. Use of informers seemed the natural resort in plans for law enforcement, for example in the measures requested by the New Company of Merchant Adventurers (*Acts P.C.*, Jas. I, III, 16, 18–19).

[41] *C.J.*, I, 401; *Parl. Debates, 1610*, 16. In one version of the debate, this suggestion is attributed to Sir Edwin Sandys, who had just called informers "ever odious, commonly varlets"; in another to the Earl of Salisbury during debate in the Lords.

[42] *Commons Debates*, II, 307.

[43] J. Strype, *Annals of the Reformation . . .* , III, Pt. 2, App., Book II, 464.

that local jurisdictions looked with envy at the hoped-for profits from informers' operations elsewhere and that a wish to increase the fees of local clerks was a factor in the enactment of 1624. But there is no evidence that county justices of the peace thought in such terms. The long-lasting and massive advance in prices, however, put under heavy and continuous pressure all holders of offices or employments from which the returns tended to be fixed: legal fees, pensions, or the shares in statutory forfeitures, mitigated fines, and licensed compositions. A basic cause of the evil of extortion in its various forms was thus also a cause of the difficulties in restraining it.

The general toleration of procedure by the common information throws into sharp relief the strength of contemporary hostility to the marauding informer, which against the weight of this toleration was able to push through, by the Act of 1624, a severe reduction of original informations in the Westminster courts. This at least can be assumed to have happened with many of the statutes to which the act applied. In apprenticeship prosecutions, the exclusion intended by the statute of 1589 was now made virtually complete.[44]

The triumph of the informer's enemies, celebrated by Coke in the declaration that "the vexatious swarm of informers, who are best trusted where they are least known, are vanished and turned again to their former occupations,"[45] owed much to the mounting wave of resentment against dispensing patents with their attendant "knaves" whose exactions were lumped together in the popular discontent with those of the individual informer. Paradoxically, the same class of men who in Elizabeth's reign had been applicants for or holders of such patents, country gentry who were justices of the peace or of the same social level, now in their capacity as legislators turned against them. A number of Jacobean patentees sat on commissions of the peace, but membership of these had been diluted by that time by "new" men. Was opposition to dispensing patents aroused by something more specific than the generalized dislike of their multiplication in the hands of king's favorites and financiers which has long been recognized as a factor? Was it nourished by specific jealousies on the part of the older class of country magistrates who saw taken from them opportunities for investment that they had once

[44] See note for Table III, App. II below, for the few entries of ex officio informations which probably disguised the professional informers' cases.

[45] E. Coke, *Institutes of the Laws of England*, 3rd ed., Part IV, 76.

cultivated, for bestowal on men who had pushed their way into the narrow circle of county government and influence?[46] The complex of motives which (temporarily) ended the dispensing patent, and crippled the informer, put an ironic twist into the history of English mercantilism: the justices of the peace, to whom was entrusted by statute most of the responsibility for enforcing its policies, had a major part in weakening the position and impairing the usefulness of the chief agent by whom in fact these policies had been activated — the professional informer.

[46] The present writer is not equipped to test the question raised in the text. Sir Francis Mitchell and Sir Giles Mompesson were the two most notorious patentees of James I's reign; both were justices of the peace and attached to the Buckingham circle. Some justices of the peace of established Elizabethan families held Stuart patents more reputable than the dispensing grants, such as that for discovery of recusants' lands held by Sir Edward Greville of Warwickshire and his brother-in-law Sir Henry Bromley of Worcestershire (though this later in the hands of Sir Henry Spiller was not favorably known); or the patent to print law reports granted to Sir William Woodhouse of Norfolk.

IV

THE DISTRIBUTION OF PRIVATE PROSECUTIONS AMONG AREAS AND OCCUPATIONS

In the present chapter, attention must again center on professional informations for two reasons: their preponderance over the whole period; still more their importance in the one segment of the whole for which comparability among areas is possible, the years 1563–1589. Then, unhindered access to the Westminster courts from every county provided a record unaffected by intercounty differences in quarter sessions activity, in the presence or absence of informers, and in survival of archives.

After 1589, only three of the selected counties have sufficient sessions rolls or books in the last thirteen years of Elizabeth's reign to permit appraisal of the nature of sessions business; for four others, sampling is possible. For the next reign, the records of six counties have adequate continuity, though from the sessions rolls of one, Wiltshire, crucial years are missing in the second decade; in four others, serious gaps impair their value for the present purpose. By the 1630's, ten counties can be included as adequate.[1] But even were all records equally perfect, the occurrence of the professional appren-

[1] See Bibliography for descriptions of the sessions records of each county. In the first period (1590–1603): Cheshire, Essex, Staffordshire; Norfolk, Somerset, Wiltshire (almost in the first three), Worcestershire. The second (1603–1625): Cheshire, Essex, Nottinghamshire, Somerset, Wiltshire, North Riding; Devon, Lancashire, Norfolk, Worcestershire. The four additional in the 1630's: Devon, Lancashire, Staffordshire, Warwickshire. Staffordshire sessions archives between 1610 and 1632 were not utilized for the present study. The West Riding records exist only for the last four years of Elizabeth's reign, and from 1637, except for Order Books between 1611 and 1642.

ticeship prosecutions and thus comparisons among counties would be subject to distortion because districts attracted professionals unequally. This must have affected to some degree the occurrence of cases before 1589 in the Westminster courts, but then rather to exclude the remoter country villages and hamlets (where for most occupations few unapprenticed intruders would be found in any event) than to deprive any large areas of the informers' attentions. But when the professionals had to appear at county quarter sessions instead of Westminster to prosecute apprenticeship offenses, they may have tended to neglect them except in areas abounding in middlemen's potential marketing offenses, or in customs violations. In such counties, more apprenticeship cases might be brought because they were conveniently incidental to other prosecutions. Unevenness in the distribution of apprenticeship informations from this cause might become still more likely when after 1624 the professional had to transfer his operations to the quarter sessions for the majority of the penal statutes. Within certain counties, however, the pattern of distribution of apprenticeship prosecutions in place and occupation has some meaning.

Mere aggregates of cases have none, when the varying sessions records alone must be relied upon. Their significance in the sixteenth century for the two Westminster courts is restricted by the possibility that some were brought in the third court of the group, Common Pleas, omitted from the present study. At first sight, the total of less than 700 for the Elizabethan period, when until 1589 the efficiency and ubiquity of the informer in apprenticeship prosecution should have been at their peak, seems unacceptable as even approximately representing actual violations. Should not informations be numbered in the thousands, like those on other regulations central to the mercantilist policy and the economic life of the era? But this yardstick cannot be applied. Ample evidence of a wide acceptance of apprenticeship and, to a somewhat less extent, of the seven-year term, can be seen throughout contemporary records, whereas equal evidence exists that others of the chief attempts at economic control did not fit economic needs. No surprise should be occasioned by the contrast in the rolls of the Westminster courts between the parchments crowded with the names of offending middlemen, exporters, usurers, and those containing scattered entries of the unapprenticed.[2]

[2] See Introduction for comment on the prevalence of apprenticeship. The

If satisfactory explanations can be given for apparent agreement between contemporary business conditions and the most striking concentrations or absences of apprenticeship cases, they will have a double interest: in testing effective enforcement, and the value of patterns of distribution of the apprenticeship cases as "tracers" for economic changes. Analysis of the relationships will deal principally with these problems: the wide discrepancies in number of recorded apprenticeship prosecutions among the counties of the selected group; their unequal distribution among occupations; and the marked differences in the number of cases within certain industries or occupations among the various regions.

In some respects the professional informations of the Elizabethan period clearly fail to correspond to actual violations.[3] The first and most obvious is the existence of prosecutions by private agencies other than the professional informers, their recorded number amounting, before 1603, to something less than a third of those by professionals. Most of the offenders in these additional cases were not attacked by the professionals. Some perhaps were not discovered, others may have been known as already prosecuted. In other instances, the professionals' lack of interest may be attributable to the timing of the offense in a business depression.[4] A second gap between offense and prosecution on the Act of 1563 during Elizabeth's reign is revealed in the professional informations on the Acts of 1552, 1555, and 1557 for lack of apprenticeship in textile crafts, numbering more than did the professional cases in textile crafts on the Statute of Artificers, and duplicating them only rarely.[5] Size of the penalty and therefore a greater pressure to compound may have influenced the informers' choice of the older statutes, but their preferences in any period look from this distance merely indiscriminate. A third gap is visible in the occasional prosecutions against violators of the apprenticeship regulations laid down by the statutes applicable to feltmaking and the

---

largely unused material in the Westminster prosecutions of middlemen and usurers should be a valuable means of extending knowledge of the flow of commodities and credit in Tudor and Stuart England.

[3] The likelihood of such failure after 1589 has already been emphasized.

[4] See next chapter. A negligible number of additional cases were the work of public agencies, see App. II, Table I.

[5] Apprenticeship cases on the Cloth Acts in the selected counties total about 200, of which one-half were in Devon and nearly one-third in Somerset. (See next chapter.)

manufacture of leather goods. Within the selected counties, however, these were few, and in feltmaking rarely by professionals.[6]

Considerably over one-half of the Elizabethan professional apprenticeship informations in the Exchequer and Queen's Bench came from Norfolk, Devon, and Essex; the three counties with the next largest share had only one-fifth, Somerset, Wiltshire, and Worcestershire, for the last of which Warwickshire and Staffordshire are alternates; six others had somewhat over one-tenth together.[7] Among the counties with the small numbers, four belonged in whole or part within special jurisdictions whose courts could have entertained prosecutions on the Statute of Artificers as on other penal statutes: the West Riding, Cheshire, Lancashire, and Worcestershire.[8] But it seems unlikely that many apprenticeship cases would have been brought before them. Lancashire, the West Riding, and Cheshire were basically similar in their relative isolation from the main currents of Tudor and Stuart traffic, except for their few larger centers of which Chester was the busiest, and for the districts of woolen cloth production in the West Riding and in southeast Lancashire. Remoteness from Westminster did not deter informers from prosecuting in the Exchequer many Yorkshire dealers in wool and hides, clothiers using tenters to stretch

[6] For prosecutions in feltmaking, see above, Chap. II, n. 47.

[7] See App. II, Table I, for the aggregates. The higher percentages are: Norfolk, 24 per cent, Devon 20 per cent, Essex 15 per cent; Worcestershire, Warwickshire, and Staffordshire about 5 per cent each. If all the apprenticeship informations at Westminster be considered professional, the first two groups would not alter, but Warwickshire, Lancashire, and Staffordshire would compete for the third place, together making over one-seventh of the total.

[8] These jurisdictions were: the West Riding, under the Council of the North; Cheshire, under the Palatinate of Chester; Lancashire, under the Palatinate of Lancaster; Worcestershire, under the Council of the Marches of Wales. For evidence of informations before the first, though not of particular statutes, *West Riding Sessions Rolls, 1598–1602*, ed. J. Lister, Yorkshire Archaeological Association Record Series, III, 101–102. For one estimate of the Council's competence and effectiveness in enforcing penal statutes, see Reid, *The King's Council*, 288–289, 293ff. On the exemption of Cheshire in 1569 from the jurisdiction of the Council of the Marches, see C. A. J. Skeel, *The Council in the Marches of Wales*, 131, and on the competence of the Council to execute penal statutes, 89. For the present study, no search of the few and scattered surviving records of these courts was possible. (On judicial records of the Palatinates, see S. R. Scargill-Bird, *A Guide . . . to the Documents . . . in the Public Record Office*, 2nd ed., 185–187 and 192–193.) The omission of West Riding cases from this study's examination of Exchequer apprenticeship prosecutions can hardly have affected the total shown as recorded for Elizabeth's reign, since only ten from all Yorkshire are listed in the Agenda Books.

cloth, or Lancashire recusants, while both London and Yorkshire informers were responsible for the few apprenticeship cases recorded in the Queen's Bench from the West Riding.

Worcestershire, Warwickshire, and Staffordshire, different as they were in their industrial specialization, are alike in the lack of dispersion of the apprenticeship informations. These are grouped in each around a few centers far more developed than the rest of the county. The interpenetration of industry and agriculture characteristic of the age was constituted in these shires as a whole much more by production for nearby local markets than was true in certain limited areas within them or in the principal "clothing counties" dependent on a national and export market. An apparent connection between the occupational distribution of the apprenticeship cases and the character of the market will be noticed again in later pages.

Economic life moved at an even more sluggish pace in the three counties claiming (except for Cheshire) the fewest apprenticeship prosecutions: Northamptonshire, Leicestershire, and Nottinghamshire. The first two possessed a handful of towns whose traffic may have already felt the stimulation induced by the rise of the large-scale grazier. But in general, a contemporary comment on Northamptonshire is applicable to all three, at least through the second quarter of the seventeenth century and, for much of the region, for far longer: "there is no special trade in the county to set the people on work . . . though it contain many parishes, yet they are very small ones."[9]

Discussion of the two regions where the bulk of the Elizabethan cases are concentrated — the southwest and East Anglia — will require a separate chapter, which will also offer an explanation why numbers differ between Devon and its neighbors Somerset and Wiltshire.

Comparison of the intercounty distribution of professional cases from one reign to the next is not feasible for the reasons outlined at the beginning of this chapter.[10] The chance of arbitrary changes in the pattern from the uneven availability of quarter sessions records can be illustrated by the shift in the Elizabethan proportions when

[9] Sir Edward Montagu (one of the county's most noted landowners and magistrates), writing in 1614, *The Montagu Musters Book*, ed. Joan Wake, Northamptonshire Record Society, VII, xiv–xv, 235.

[10] Except in respect to the differing proportions of Westminster informations from Devon and from East Anglia in the two periods 1563–1603 and 1603–1625, see next chapter.

account is taken of the professional informations for apprenticeship in surviving sessions files added to those of Westminster. Staffordshire then ranks fourth in number of cases. Does this suggest that the ranking of Somerset and Wiltshire as given by the Westminster cases alone is misleading and likely to be altered radically were their sessions records whole? The answer is probably in the negative for Wiltshire, since its records are not markedly inferior in completeness to Staffordshire's. For Somerset, the true number of cases may have been considerably larger.[11]

The geographical distribution of cases, however, depends on the occupations involved. Summaries of the occupational distribution for professional informations and for other private prosecutions are presented here.[12] The defects in sessions records again impair the analysis of both sets and in all periods to which they apply. In Table 1, for example, in the years 1609–1632, metal-working crafts cannot be properly represented because of the gaps in the Worcestershire sessions files and in the use of those of Staffordshire. In the sixteenth century the converse is true, that the accident of survival of Staffordshire records in greater fullness than those of counties of important but unlike industrial specialization, such as Devon, has skewed the figures toward too high a proportion of metal-working cases. A further defect of the sessions records in the third period is the large number of entries for which the illegal occupation is unknown — about a fifth of the total.[13] Table 2 must be used even more cautiously because individual cases, of undue weight among the low totals, may have little or no connection with economic conditions if they resulted from private quarrels or represent the effort of a master to retain an apprentice. In Wiltshire a glover who in 1606 had brought two others into court on charges of unapprenticed use of their craft was himself sued the next year. In Somerset another twice prosecuted his deserting apprentice who had set up independently. Four blacksmiths in the Mendips were at loggerheads in 1621–22. In 1638 a

[11] The cases in Staffordshire quarter sessions are discussed in the next chapter.

[12] See also the tables in App. II which show that useful intercounty comparisons of the distribution of "other private prosecutions" cannot be made, since they total less than 100, widely scattered, in the Elizabethan courts. In the seventeenth century they suffer like the professional cases from inequalities in sessions records.

[13] Chiefly in Somerset in years when the original informations or indictments were missing from the Sessions Rolls and the corresponding entries in the Minute Books were incomplete.

TABLE 1

AGGREGATE OF PROFESSIONAL INFORMATIONS FOR APPRENTICESHIP, BY OCCUPATION

1563–1642

Selected Counties

Seven-Year Term, Act of 1563

Occupation	Exchequer and Queen's Bench [a]		Quarter Sessions		
	1563–1603	1603–1625	1563–1603	1603–1625	1625–1642
Textile industry	166 to 172	15 or 17	1	52 or 53	16 to 18
Textile processing [b]	20	3 or 4	2	3	5 to 6
Dealing and retailing	102 to 107	10	2 or 3	28 to 34	99 to 107
Food processing	91 to 93	16	4 to 7	127 to 147	283 to 295
Leather processing	43 to 44	7 or 9	0 or 1	17 to 22	18 to 19
Metal processing	18	2	20	0 [d]	6 to 8
Wood processing and building trades	9	2	2	13 to 15	17
Miscellaneous [c]	8	0	0	3	6
Unknown	0	0	0 or 1	6 to 8 [d]	74 to 115
	457 to 471	55 to 60	31 to 37	249 to 285	524 to 591 [e]

[a] In Elizabeth's reign, the Exchequer 1563–1603, the Queen's Bench 1563–1588 inclusive. In James I's reign, the Exchequer 1603–1625, the King's Bench Easter 1603 to Hilary 1607, Easter 1616 to Hilary 1617 incl.

[b] Includes tailors, feltmakers, hatmakers, hatters, upholsterers.

[c] Includes surgeons, barbers, potters, limeburners, ashburners, ropemakers, soapmakers.

[d] Four of the "unknown" cases occurred in Staffordshire; some or all were probably against metalworkers.

[e] To this should be added 28 to 30 cases in Essex Assizes: 27 to 29 food processing; 1 retailing.

Lancashire plumber and a glazier sued one another.[14] Accidental factors may qualify the professional informations also, perhaps the inspiration of personal animus or chance gossip, but presumably less than other private prosecutions.

Nevertheless, some features of these tables deserve comment and invite speculation. The first question is what influenced the numbers of apprenticeship cases in various occupational groups.

The most general was obviously the character of a region in its industrial or agricultural specialization or its trading activity. Effects on the geographical distribution of cases have been briefly noticed. For the occupational distribution, in its broad outline, a rough com-

[14] Wiltshire MS. Sessions Rolls, No. 4, Easter, 4 Jas. I, No. 5, July, 5 Jas. I; Somerset MS. Sessions Indictment Rolls, No. 11, Pt. I, Item 79 and No. 13, Pt. II, Item 155; *ibid.*, No. 42, Pt. I, Items 76, 111, and 113; Lancashire MS. Sessions Indictments, Bdle. No. 15, 14 Chas. I.

TABLE 2

AGGREGATE OF NONPROFESSIONAL PRIVATE PROSECUTIONS FOR APPRENTICESHIP IN COUNTIES OF CHIEF OCCURRENCE, BY OCCUPATION

1563–1642

Selected Counties

Seven-Year Term, Act of 1563

Quarter Sessions

Occupation	1563–1603 [a]	1603–1625 [c]	1625–1642 [e]
Textile industry	19 to 29 [b]	64 or 65	39 to 43
Textile processing	1	7	4
Dealing and retailing	9 or 10	24 to 29	21 to 23
Food processing	5 to 9	68 to 71	79 to 87
Leather processing	0	10 to 11	32 or 33
Metal processing	0	10 to 15 [d]	16 [f]
Wood processing and building trades	7	13	9
Miscellaneous	1	25	5
Unknown	2 to 12 [b]	1 to 5	9 to 14

[a] Two counties only, Wiltshire and Essex.
[b] Ten of the "Unknown" are textile prosecutions but may not be for violation of the seven-year term.
[c] Four counties: Somerset, Wiltshire, Essex, Norfolk.
[d] May include five cardmakers, i.e. makers of cards for wool-combing.
[e] Five counties: Somerset, Wiltshire, Essex, Norfolk, Lancashire.
[f] Includes eleven cardmakers.

parison of proportions in the selected counties with those for all counties may illustrate the same point, using the Elizabethan cases in the Westminster courts for all informations (a) in the selected counties, and (b) in all counties.[15] Percentages in the three largest occupational groups for (a) and (b) respectively are: in the textile industry, 38 per cent and 21 per cent; dealing and retailing, 20 per cent and 19 per cent; food processing, 19 per cent, 23 per cent; other occupations, under 10 per cent in both (a) and (b). The difference in the first arises from an exceptionally large number of textile prosecutions in Devon, a situation requiring special consideration later.

[15] For counties outside the selected group, cases in the Exchequer were tabulated from the Agenda Books only, in which the names of prosecutors are not entered. This record is defective also in frequent abbreviation of the entry to "ex. art," so that the classification by occupation has to include a large number of "Unknown" — about one-eighth of the total. Furthermore, there is a wider margin of error in the total, since the count was not kept with the same effort at accuracy as for the selected counties.

The difference between (a) and (b) so far as any may in fact have existed, in the third group, is consistent with their composition. Certain counties in (b) had a considerable business in food processing. Two of these were Kent and Sussex, known for their numerous mills and conspicuous in the record of apprenticeship cases for the prosecutions of millers, 29 in Kent, 19 in Sussex. In Kent — a well-traveled granary and hop-growing center — prosecutions of bakers and brewers were also relatively numerous, 18 and 15. In Suffolk, Gloucestershire, Surrey, and Berkshire, prosecutions of bakers were above the average in number (19, 13, 12, and 8), which may be associated with relatively densely settled districts of textile workers at the level of cottager and laborer, virtually landless and barely housed. The spread of commercial baking is likely also to have accompanied everywhere the increase of accommodation at inns and alehouses. What, however, made the difference between these three "clothing counties" and the broadcloth districts of Wiltshire and east Somerset in which almost no prosecutions of bakers were brought to Westminster? Perhaps a difference in the local availability of grain supplies or in the general prosperity and activity of the areas making colored cloth and those of the white broadcloth? [16] Another type of activity may help to account for the similarity between the percentages for (a) and (b) in both food-processing and in dealing and retailing. In Essex and Norfolk, prosecutions of brewers were higher than in most counties, 9 and 16 compared to 15 in Kent and to only one or two in most of the fifteen counties registering any such cases; [17] those of millers and bakers were more than the average in Norfolk (6 and 9) if not as high as in Kent, Sussex, or Suffolk. In dealing and retailing, Kent and Sussex also outrank others,[18] with 39 each, while from Essex there were 27 and from Norfolk 19; elsewhere the numbers usually

[16] Or, obviously, the difference may be due to defective records or to an accidental presence or absence of informers. The county of Surrey claims twelve cases of bakers in the two Westminster courts during the years under review, not as many as might be expected from the bustling streets of Southwark alone, but other prosecutions may have been lost with the sessions records or have been brought in the borough court. For business conditions in the southwest textile areas, see next chapter.

[17] All these figures belong to the two Elizabethan Westminster courts, 1563–1603 for the Exchequer, 1563–1588 inclusive for the Queen's Bench.

[18] Surrey was next with 26. The larger aggregates in several of the counties in (b) as compared with (a) are offset for (b) in the percentages by a greater number of prosecutions in miscellaneous crafts and trades.

were under 10.[19] All four counties included areas of active traffic. Essex and Norfolk both contained large textile districts, and through parts of each ran a busy overland trade with London, while along their coasts and from their ports went a considerable share of England's coastwise commerce. Norfolk like Kent was a producer of hops and barley, and one of England's chief malt-making regions.

Differences among and within occupational groups in the incidence of prosecutors' activity arose from conditions in the groups themselves, as well as from the general economic character of whole regions. Such conditions were: how much an occupation was dispersed through an area; whether an occupation was in a period of expansion, perhaps with the accompaniment of increasing dispersion; what type of market it served; to what extent it offered part-time or seasonal employment; how far the workers in it were physically isolated. The influence of each will be considered for some illustrative occupations and areas. Some attention will be given to the reasonableness of the total numbers of apprenticeship cases in relation to the probable size of various occupations. The fundamental condition to which the apprenticeship cases are only an imperfect clue was, in all occupations, the extent to which the apprenticeship requirement was accepted as the norm. Two factors important here were the degree of skill and experience necessary and the social prestige of the occupation; a third factor allied with these was the utility of established connections; a fourth the need of capital.

The first occupational group to which some of these considerations will be applied is that of woodworking and building. Most, though not all, of its component crafts were to be found in every large district; yet apprenticeship prosecutions against the craftsmen are everywhere few.

From all counties, the Elizabethan Westminster prosecutions of the unapprenticed in building and woodworking crafts totaled 39 and 52 respectively. Among the building trades, only one case involving a mason was observed, and occasional prosecutions of tilers and tilemakers were the most frequent. In the woodworking crafts, those of carpenters and joiners were most numerous. From the selected counties only, the Westminster cases of Elizabeth's reign numbered 4 in the building trades, and 6 in woodworking; during the period 1603–

[19] Some further comment is made later in this chapter on the acceptability of the small size of these totals.

1642, the total seen was 3 building, 5 woodworking.[20] In the available quarter sessions records from 1563 to 1642, only 34 apprenticeship prosecutions by private agencies were found in building trades, and 51 in woodworking crafts.[21] In the woodworking cases, chiefly from Essex, Norfolk, and Nottinghamshire, carpenters were in the majority with 19, wheelwrights were 7.

Part of the difference in number of prosecutions between woodworking and building may have been caused by the wider dispersion of the former through the countryside and by a more general demand for this occupation. In Jacobean Gloucestershire, the relatively small proportion of the county's manpower reported as in the building trades (2 per cent for the whole county) has been attributed to extensive part-time employment of agricultural servants and laborers, and to self-help in the erection of country cottages.[22] Neither activity would invite prosecution as an unapprenticed use of the trade, and both would characterize much local construction. The demand for masons tended to be localized by the availability of building stone and was lessened further wherever was practiced the use of portable wooden frames, illustrated by an incident in Essex. A resident of Rayne who had secured a "piece of ground . . . half a mile from the market" of Braintree, where he hoped to set up "the frame of a house" he had prepared, petitioned the justices of the peace for a license to proceed without the statutory four acres to each new cottage.[23] These frames, presumably similar to or identical with the "crucks" characteristic of the simpler Elizabethan village houses,[24]

[20] All totals above represent all private prosecutions. Building: 2 tilers, 1 glazier, 1 house-carpenter, 1 mason, 2 bricklayers. Woodworking: 1 carpenter, 3 joiners, 5 wheelwrights, 2 coopers. Plumbers have been classified in these occupational groups in metal processing, except for two offenders, each accused of using the crafts of carpenter and plumber together.

[21] Nearly half of the building trades offenders were in the North Riding (12 masons, 3 slaters); one-third of the woodworking cases were in Essex. One presentment of a tilemaker was the sole prosecution by public agencies of offenders in this occupational group.

[22] A. J. Tawney and R. H. Tawney, "An Occupational Census of the Seventeenth Century," *The Economic History Review*, V, No. 1, 36, 38–39, 39n. This is a study of the muster returns of 1608 which are unusual in giving occupations of the men reported.

[23] Cal. Q.S., XV, 118, S.R. 109/54. He is probably the tailor of the same name, described as of Braintree, who in 1591 was a professional informer in a small way at the quarter sessions. (*Ibid.* XVI, 65, S.R. 117/65–67; for some of his other cases, *ibid.*, S.R. 117 & 118, *passim.*)

[24] Hoskins, *Essays*, 55 and *passim*.

may not have required a carpenter, as apparently Portway's did not. But the need of the ordinary village for farm implements, for the cruder household furnishings when these were not joiner's work, and even still for wooden utensils in spite of the spread of pewter and other metal dishes and spoons, called for the carpenter's skill where more specialized craftsmen were lacking.[25] Either the local carpenter or wheelwright probably constructed and repaired looms and spinning wheels for textile workers.[26] But not every small community enjoyed the presence of either craftsman. The Gloucestershire survey reported 410 carpenters and joiners, 22 wheelers and wheelwrights, a difference which corresponds to a considerably larger number of apprenticeship prosecutions of carpenters and joiners than of wheelwrights.[27]

The apparent lack of illegal entrants into the building trades agrees with the leisurely pace of operations, except in such a dizzy world as Elizabethan and Stuart London. Even at the end of the seventeenth century, a tiler of Milverton, Somerset, had worked for twenty years on the "new" mansion house of the Francis family; in an earlier time, a plasterer had been employed from 1614 to 1629 on the overmantels and other decorative work of George Luttrell's residences.[28] At this rate, local demand could be satisfied by a very few craftsmen. The number needed in Essex tilemaking is supplied by contemporary statement. Two appointed searchers for this industry, who claimed to have surveyed all the tile kilns in Essex about 1595, reported forty-six.[29] On such a scale of magnitude, three apprenticeship prosecutions in the reigns of Elizabeth and James I seem not unwarrantably few.

The tradition of apprenticeship was probably stronger in the build-

[25] The craft of a turner was perhaps a more specialized one than would be available in most villages.

[26] One prosecution of an allegedly unapprenticed sleymaker was found, the offender residing in the heart of one of Wiltshire's chief broadcloth districts (MS. Sessions Minute Books, IV, Mich. 17 Jas. I, Mich. 18 Jas. 1).

[27] Tawneys, "An Occupational Census," 60. The Gloucestershire figure gives a different picture for this county from the wheelwright-to-every-village distribution described for the midlands (W. G. Hoskins, *Midland England*, 71–72). The Lancashire justices of the peace in 1592 licensed a cottage without four acres in order to bring a carpenter to the village of Haslingden, *Lancashire Quarter Sessions Records*, ed. J. Tait, Chetham Society, New Series, LXXVII, 56.

[28] V. A. Batchelor, "The Manor of Combe Florey," *Somerset Archaeological and Natural History Society Proceedings*, LXXXIII, 121; L. Weaver, "The Court House," *ibid.*, XCII, 38.

[29] Cal. Q.S., XVII, 25, S.R. 137/73. Some of their output may have been sold outside the county.

ing and woodworking occupations than in textiles or retailing, and perhaps is reflected in the rarity of prosecutions of glaziers, although this was a rising industry from the late sixteenth century. The increase in numbers engaged, however, was probably gradual: Gloucestershire in 1608 had only a few; in the town of Leicester by the early 1590's there were four or five; the city of Norwich could keep more at work, seventeen being admitted to the freedom during Elizabeth's reign. But there must have been some localization of the craft, for example, not a single apprentice to it was enrolled in Elizabethan or Stuart Northampton.[30]

Greater conformity in apprenticeship in the building trades than in woodworking, or fewer inducements to "intruders," or perhaps only the smaller size of the first group of crafts, is suggested by a difference in the shares of professional and nonprofessional prosecutors. Cases involving woodworkers, as recorded in quarter sessions from 1563 to 1642, were brought in equal proportions by the two classes of private prosecutors. But of those in the building trades, almost three-quarters were the work of nonprofessionals.[31]

The degree of dispersion, even though it may have influenced the difference in amount of apprenticeship prosecution between woodworkers and building craftsmen, has no simple correspondence with the number of apprenticeship cases. The Gloucestershire returns already mentioned afford the only available quantitative study of occupational dispersion in Tudor and Stuart England, though the findings for this county may not be representative. For some occupations they agree with observation elsewhere. For example, the frequency of presentments in Elizabethan Essex from a variety of places against tailors "working at their own hands" points to a wide distribution of this craft; in Gloucestershire its dispersion is greatest. At the other extreme, evidence in Worcestershire that numerous parishes in the 1630's lacked a baker[32] is consistent with the finding in

[30] Hoskins, *Essays*, 111–112; Tawneys, "An Occupational Census," 60 (ten were reported from the county); *The Register of the Freemen of Norwich, 1548–1713*, ed. P. Millican, 65–66. The statement about Northampton is based on notes of the enrolments of apprentices' indentures, for the use of which the present writer is indebted to the kindness of Miss Helen M. Cam.

[31] The proportions between the two craft groups in the number (given above) of Westminster informations, which are mostly by professionals, agree with the suggestion in the text.

[32] *Calendar of the Quarter Sessions Papers*, ed. J. W. Willis Bund, Worcestershire County Records, 483–657.

Gloucestershire that bakers were present in only 12 per cent of the manors reporting manpower. A lack of correspondence between dispersion as measured in Gloucestershire and apprenticeship prosecution is shown in Table 3.

TABLE 3

DISPERSION OF OCCUPATIONS IN GLOUCESTERSHIRE AND APPRENTICESHIP PROSECUTION IN SELECTED COUNTIES

Occupations	Per cent of Gloucs. manors with one or more of the listed occupations [a]	Number of apprenticeship cases in Elizabethan Westminster courts	
		Selected counties	All counties
Tailors	62	22	73
Woodworkers [b]	57	7	52
Metalworkers [c]	48.5	18	54
Builders	36.5	3	39
Millers	26	12	87
Butchers	25	23	52
Leatherworkers [d]	15	33	76
Bakers	12	37	150
Brewers	3	33	92–93

[a] The table is arranged from the analysis of manorial returns (Tawneys, "An Occupational Census," 41) with omission of some occupational classifications.

[b] Chiefly carpenters and joiners, with occasional wheelwrights; in the apprenticeship prosecutions, the numbers of the latter are 3 and 5.

[c] Chiefly smiths; also includes plumbers.

[d] Chiefly tanners and curriers, also includes saddlers, etc., but not shoemakers.

The most striking divergences at one end of the scale between dispersion and apprenticeship prosecution are in the occupations of baking and brewing and to a less extent in those of milling and leatherworking and, at the other end, in those of tailoring and woodworking.[33]

The common denominator here appears to be the type of market. The craftsman belonging to any of the first four groups, those most dispersed, worked primarily to order for a customer, selling his services rather than his product, and his market was therefore circumscribed. Butchers at most inland places must also have had only a

[33] The disparity for textile crafts, not shown in the table, would be of a somewhat different kind: they would rank third in degree of dispersion but the number of prosecutions would be disproportionately greater than for the tailors and the woodworkers.

local market. Bakers, brewers, millers, tanners, curriers, like the textile workers, might feel the forces of a wide selling area, and those in some districts, even of an export market. But inducements to new enterprises were rare outside the occupations which met a more than local demand.

Variations in prosecution may have reflected not merely the different impact of local or distant market but the range of demand within the local market: for bread, from the middle class down into the lower levels, the demand must have been greater than for butcher's meat, in an age when dairy produce commonly had the name of "white meats" since it provided the meat substitute for the poor.[34] The association of retailing bread with keeping an alehouse or inn also evidenced this range of demand. Instances of this union of enterprises occurred in Essex, to mention no others.[35]

Affecting the quantity of apprenticeship prosecutions was the physical isolation of many occupations when carried on in small rural communities, which protected them from the inquiries of the professional informer and the trade jealousy of competitors. Indispensability might also shield them. The sole village representative of a particular craft, so long as he was a competent workman, was likely to be accepted by his neighbors regardless of how he had learned his trade.[36] The most widely dispersed occupations therefore may have been those in which prosecution fails most often to match apprenticeship offenses. An outstanding exception is the craft of weaver, in which wide distribution and frequent prosecution went together in some regions, such as Devon. This suggests that what conferred immunity was not so much the isolation of the craftsman as the restriction of his product to the village bounds. When this was delivered or sold outside, to a middleman or a nearby weekly market, he was exposed to attack.

In the foregoing survey, for one occupational group, of variations in the activity of apprenticeship prosecutors, the dispersion of the craft or trade has been treated as static. Possible relations between the occurrence of prosecution and changes both in the size of an occupation and in the extent of its scattering through an area can be

[34] *Acts P.C.*, Eliz., XXV, 25, 55.

[35] Cal. Q.S., XVI, 11, S.R. 112/62 (1590); XIX, 172, S.R. 208/51 (1614) and 219/131 (1617).

[36] Note that the sleymaker mentioned above, n. 26, was acquitted.

illustrated from the two groups, dealing and retailing trades, and food processing.

Over the whole span 1563–1642, the majority of the apprenticeship prosecutions in Essex and Norfolk were of retailers and food processors.[37] In the Elizabethan Westminster cases the two counties, especially Essex, contrast sharply in this respect with Devon, and to a less degree with Somerset. The divergence in the aggregates between the two eastern and three southwestern counties is shown in Table 4.

TABLE 4

AGGREGATES OF PRIVATE PROSECUTIONS OF RETAILERS AND FOOD PROCESSORS

County	Westminster Courts				Quarter Sessions					
	1563–1603		1603–1625		1563–1603		1603–1625		1625–1642	
	Re-tailing	Foods	Re-tailing	Foods	Re-tailing	Foods	Re-tailing	Foods	Re-tailing	Foods
Essex	27	18	3	5	10	10	17	36	11	24
Norfolk	19	33	1	8	0[a]	0[a]	9	114	60	220
Devon	8	12	1	0	. .	. .	0[a]	1[a]	0[a]	3[a]
Somerset	10	6	2	2	0[a]	0[a]	14	43	24	61[b]
Wiltshire	6	12	2	2	1	2[b]	9	16	6	38

[a] Indicates sessions records too defective for use here.
[b] Indicates unknown occupations probably belonging to this category.

The sessions records of the four counties exclusive of Devon are, for the present purpose, roughly comparable in continuity from 1604 on, though the totals for Essex are likely to be the most accurate, and those for Norfolk are probably minima. To judge from the Essex assizes records, resort to this court was increasing a little for prosecutors on apprenticeship offenses. The Essex cases of James I's reign, however, were only 13, all prosecutions of bakers by a trade competitor; those of the next reign numbered 29 in food processing, 1 in retailing, all, or nearly all, being professional. Since the amount of apprenticeship prosecution lost with the assizes records of the

[37] Retailers prosecuted were: mercers, grocers, chandlers and tallow-chandlers, drapers (woolen- and linen-), haberdashers. In Norfolk two stationers also were included, in Essex two cheesemongers. Food processors were: bakers, millers, brewers, butchers. One poulterer was included in Essex with the food trades.

other counties is unknown, the real activity of unapprenticed intruders and of their discoverers cannot be gauged.

In the sixteenth century, when comparisons among counties are permissible, at least a part of the larger amount of retailing and food-trades' cases in East Anglia has already been explained by the general economic life of the region. Elizabethan Essex, with its close relationship to the London market and its thriving export and import trade flowing through the seventy-five or more lading places it boasted for coastal vessels,[38] can be supposed to have had more lively currents of traffic through its towns and villages than the southwest counties. Devon's ports of Exeter, Plymouth, and Barnstaple were larger and more important for overseas trade than anything Essex had, but this localized bustle can have been transmitted to the countryside only indirectly and weakly. In Somerset and Wiltshire, also, the impulse of trade ran along fewer arteries than in Essex even though it ran strongly. In Norfolk, commercial activity centered in the two ports of Yarmouth and King's Lynn; the coast in between was fringed with small ports and lading places; the principal market towns were in the east. The county lacked the numerous industrial villages of northern Essex, and among its more self-contained districts trade was probably less generally diffused. Norfolk's lead in food-processing cases was due to those against brewers, reflecting the position of Norfolk in the late sixteenth century as a principal producer and exporter of malt and beer.[39]

The differences among these counties in their number of cases of unapprenticed retailers and food processors might be attributed to the presence of more informers in the two near London, were it not for the record of prosecution in all five by both London and local professionals on a variety of statutes. But the differences may have been partly created by differing dispersion of the crafts and trades in the two occupational groups. The normal function of small towns in the sixteenth and seventeenth centuries was to act as distributive

[38] E. P. Dickin, "Notes on the Coast, Shipping, and Sea-borne Trade of Essex, from 1565 to 1577," *Essex Archaeological Society Transactions*, New Series, XVII, 153–164. Chief imports via the Essex coast were groceries, household utensils and ironmongery, from London, and overseas merchandise including mercery wares.

[39] T. S. Willan, *The English Coasting Trade 1600–1750*, passim; B. Cozens-Hardy, "The Maritime Trade of the Port of Blakeney, Norfolk, 1587–90," *Norfolk Record Society*, VIII, 19. Like Essex, Norfolk's imports included mercery wares from the Netherlands, groceries and ironmongery from London.

centers for the adjacent countryside.[40] Local courts in many of them — not only in the cities of Norwich, Exeter, and Salisbury, but in boroughs such as Colchester, Yarmouth, Taunton, Chard, or Barnstaple — would hear suits brought by informers and trade competitors for apprenticeship offenses within their jurisdiction. In the regions of least dispersion of retailing and food processing there is thus the greater probability that apprenticeship violations would not be fully reflected in cases in the Westminster courts or quarter sessions.[41] Besides this negative factor, tending to decrease cases recorded in the central courts, the positive influences of growth in the occupations may be present in some areas and periods, possibly also an increased dispersion in country places.

In the following discussion of the distribution between town and country [42] of prosecutions in some of the retail trades, their numbers will appear absurdly low, as do in fact the totals, unless a scale of size for the occupations can be estimated. The Gloucestershire survey again provides assistance. Here, in one of the important textile-making counties, the proportion of men engaged in dealing and retailing was 3 per cent and with food processing was still under 5 per cent for the whole county exclusive of the three largest towns; about 6 per cent with the towns included. For the three towns alone, it was 26 per cent. But though this illustrates the place of the town in distribution, and though in the city of Gloucester retailers were about 10 per cent of the male population returned for musters, the number of master tradesmen in the city was not large: 34 mercers, 16 drapers, 5 haberdashers. Only twelve haberdashers and one grocer were reported for the whole county.[43] Evidence of size elsewhere tends to confirm the impression that even in the towns only a few retailers were

[40] Tawneys, "An Occupational Census," 38; Wadsworth and Mann, *The Cotton Trade*, 55.

[41] This hypothesis would apply to apprenticeship prosecutions in any occupation, but the tendency of the merchandising groups to constitute or dominate the organized companies in corporate towns makes it more applicable to retail trades than to other occupations.

[42] By "town" in this analysis will be meant a place having the right to a market, the term including the larger boroughs, corporate towns, and cities. The most nearly contemporary descriptions have been utilized where possible for the classification, but complete accuracy cannot have been achieved.

[43] Tawneys, "An Occupational Census," 38, 61–62. The return of only one grocer suggests that the numbers reported in the Gloucestershire survey must not be taken too literally, but they remain a useful indication of relative size of occupations.

required to supply local needs. At Stratford-on-Avon, only two retailers were recorded between 1562 and 1588 as having paid for admission to the freedom of the borough, a payment which "foreign" tradesmen would have been unlikely to evade easily at that period.[44] A century later in Derby — in Camden's time already a malt-making center as well as the assize town — the general trading association contained four grocers, sixteen mercers, and only single representatives of other trades.[45] In late seventeenth-century Nottingham, the few enrolled burgesses of 1693–94 included no mercer, chandler, or grocer, although some retailers may have been tolerated in the town who were not members of the restricted group of burgesses.[46]

There were various competitors with settled and specialized or semi-specialized retailers for the limited demand of the country village or town. A strong contender was the weekly market, in which the resident shopkeeper might himself retail, and another the series of fairs specializing in one commodity or another, which were a feature of nearly every part of England. The petty chapmen, the peddlers, the hawkers, were a recurrent source of annoyance to the established tradesmen and carried their wares far afield.[47] Raw materials for food, drink, and industry were distributed in the countryside by middlemen such as the badgers, kidders, and carriers who might be licensed by the justices of the peace to sell grain, fish, and dairy produce to private individuals for household use; by the wool-brokers, the flaxmen, the drivers with iron and nails, and the rest.[48]

Still other competitors were the craftsmen who retailed goods from

[44] *Minutes and Accounts*, I–IV, *passim*; the two entries mentioned, III, 76–77, 95.

[45] S. Kramer, *The English Craft Gilds*, 43n.; and for discussion of the small number of retailers normal to Tudor and Stuart towns, 43ff. Derby had an unusually high proportion of ironmongers, 12 in the trading company, and they may have operated as retailers of other wares.

[46] *Records of the Borough of Nottingham*, ed. W. H. Stevenson, and others, V, 97.

[47] E. Lipson, *The Economic History of England*, II, 90–93. These could not be attacked through the apprenticeship law, unless they attempted to retail as residents. Identifiable offenses of this type are very rare among the apprenticeship cases.

[48] N. S. B. Gras, *The Evolution of the English Corn Market*, 152; Unwin, *Studies*, passim; E. Lipson, *The History of the Woollen and Worsted Industries*, passim; Wadsworth and Mann, *The Cotton Trade*, 47, 59; W. H. B. Court, *The Rise of the Midland Industries, 1600–1838*, passim.

their houses, and they must have been numerous. But almost nothing is known of the extent to which differentiation between the craftsman and the retailer did in fact prevail in the smaller places. Retailing by the craftsman might take at least three forms, selling the product he made, selling an allied product such as his raw materials, or selling a quite unrelated product. The first form would not have violated the apprenticeship laws, while the usefulness of the apprenticeship prosecutions in tracing competition of the second and third kinds is severely limited by the frequent lack of mention of the defendant's occupation. Less than a hundred such cases have been identified in all courts for the whole period 1563–1642, and from both towns and villages. In approximately a third of the prosecutions, tailors were the retailers, primarily as woolendrapers and drapers; in less than a sixth of the total, weavers tended to retail as mercers or drapers; about the same number of shoemakers were operating as chandlers, mercers, and grocers; while the remainder was made up of smiths, building craftsmen, butchers, and a scattering of other crafts in various retail trades.[49]

In favorable coastal areas another kind of competition must have retarded the development of retail dealing in the smaller port towns and lading places. This was akin to the plantation trade of later colonial settlement and can be seen operating along the Essex coast, where individual country-dwellers in the sixteenth century were shipping outward cargoes and receiving inward orders direct from London. A gentleman of Little Bentley with access to numerous lading points on the northeast coast sent cheese, butter, and logs to London; one at St. Osyth in the same area, a little port with vessels of 15 to 35 tons belonging to it, also was sending local produce, and men like this ordered grocery and chandlery wares from metropolitan suppliers.[50]

A further justification of the usual scantiness of apprenticeship cases in retailing is the likelihood of a fairly general acceptance of apprenticeship as a normal means of entry into trade. Scattered ref-

[49] Unspecialized retailing was hard to prevent even in corporations. At Colchester in 1622, an alien was retailing at home linen cloth and haberdashers' wares though he was a loom-maker, while the wife of a bay-maker sold lace, thread, and other goods imported from Holland. The loom-maker reportedly pursued his retailing in spite of being "troubled by informers" and having promised to deal only in his own trade. (S.P.D., Jas. I, CXXIX, No. 70.)

[50] Dickin, "Notes on Essex," 161ff.

erences make it reasonably certain that the practice prevailed before the Civil War, and probably long after, even in small country towns. A writer of the Restoration takes this for granted.[51] During the same period, a mercer's apprentice in a little Lancashire town who kept a diligent diary was unique only in his articulateness.[52] In this occupation, some of the advantages of apprenticeship might count for much: experience, established connections, the need of a little capital if the trade were to furnish the whole living of the tradesman, and not the least important, a social prestige which raised some branches of shopkeeping a little above the ruck.[53]

Exactly the opposite conditions could also have tended to reduce prosecutions for apprenticeship, not so much in towns as in villages and their environs. Despite the undoubted advantages of apprenticeship for the full-time settled shopkeeper, selling was an occupation easily taken up on a part-time basis and only a tiny stock in hand was necessary for the country dealer.[54] Equally the part-time nature of much agricultural work lent itself both to in-and-out trading and to seasonal or part-time employment in building and other crafts.[55] The status terms so often used in entries of apprenticeship offenses to identify the defendant, "yeoman," and "husbandman," undoubtedly described in an unknown number of cases the basic occupation. Essex inventories of the seventeenth century disclose a little of the situation of a few apprenticeship offenders of the period, both those who had nothing but their craft or trade and those who ranked occupationally and socially as husbandmen or yeomen. John Draper

[51] Dunlop and Denman, *English Apprenticeship*, 201, citing *Trade of England Revived* (1681), 30.

[52] *The Diary of Roger Lowe, 1663–1674*, ed. W. L. Sachse.

[53] A higher social status of the wholesale merchant and of certain branches of retailing is reflected in the property qualifications set by the Statute of Artificers, though to maintain the exclusiveness of merchandising for reasons of social distinction was not its aim. The superior prestige of the merchant's occupation to manual crafts however skilled is a familiar phenomenon of sixteenth- and seventeenth-century life. But that much if any social difference obtained between the craftsman and the small retailer of a country town seems doubtful.

[54] For example, a dealer in flax near Preston who kept a little cloth and some grocery wares (Wadsworth and Mann, *The Cotton Trade*, 59); and some of the Essex inventories mentioned in the text above (*Farm and Cottage Inventories of Mid-Essex, 1635–1749*, ed. F. W. Steer, Nos. 127, 169, etc.).

[55] The builder might also have an alternative craft: an Essex offender was accused of being a tilemaker in summer and a tailor in winter (Cal. Q.S., IV, 228, S.R. No. 44/40, 1573).

of Writtle exemplifies the second sort: when he was prosecuted in 1661 for unapprenticed baking, he was called a tailor; but when he died in 1672 he was described as a yeoman, though he had been keeping a baker's shop. The inventory of his goods gives no idea what land he held, but among his movables, besides his bakery tools, were twenty-one sheep.[56] Temporary and part-time business enterprises of this sort favored the evasion of apprenticeship and may also have discouraged the prosecution of the offenders, since without serious loss the illegal occupation could be laid aside until a safer opportunity. But how far prosecution was actually repressed by this it is impossible to tell. Professional informations rarely accuse the defendant of much less than the maximum possible term of illegal exercise of an occupation, one year, but it is vain to speculate on whether this was mere form to maximize the claim for reward or whether the professional informer attacked only those who offended on a full-time basis.[57]

A centrifugal tendency in the retail trades, perhaps felt before the reign of Elizabeth, may have given rise to an effort at statutory repression in one branch, the act of 1554/55 which prohibited the retailing of mercery, drapery, and haberdashery wares in corporate towns by nonresidents.[58] Occasional informations were brought on this statute in the Westminster courts and at quarter sessions.[59] Their apparent infrequency is consistent with the view that in the sixteenth century and early seventeenth century retail occupations normally centered in the larger towns. The evidence of apprenticeship prosecu-

[56] *Inventories*, No. 75. Several examples of village craftsmen who were also farmers are mentioned in Hoskins' *Midland England*, 72–73; and yeomen in trade, in Campbell's *The English Yeoman*, 156–159.

[57] In one of the largest concentrations of retailing cases, in Norfolk in the 1630's, the charge was almost always for eleven months' illegal use of the trade. These were all professional informations except one. In this, against a yeoman, the charge was two months.

[58] 1 & 2 P. & M., c. 7.

[59] The importance, in relation to apprenticeship cases in retailing, of tracing prosecutions on this act was not realized by the present writer when opportunities were available to search the archives. No count was kept, and it is possible that they were more numerous than is thought. Some were seen in sessions records, but only occasionally noted. In Essex in 1607, a trade competitor, a village mercer, prosecuting several mercers in nearby villages for lack of apprenticeship, accused one also of retailing drapery wares at Chelmsford though living outside a borough, corporate, or market town (Cal. Q.S., XVIII, 193–194, S.R. 180/11, 12); in Nottinghamshire in 1633 a professional informed on the same statute against two village traders near Nottingham (MS. Sessions Minute Books, IX, July and Mich. 9 Chas. I).

tions, however, opens up a glimpse of a possible trend here and there toward greater dispersion. The Elizabethan cases give only a vague hint of this: in the five counties named above, only those from Essex include offenders in country villages, making about a quarter of the total; but among the Essex prosecutions of town retailers were eight residents of villages accused of unapprenticed retailing at the market town of Chelmsford and at the village of Brentwood a few miles away on the London road.[60] In Northamptonshire, three cases at country villages out of ten Westminster prosecutions of retailers during Elizabeth's reign represent the only other such sign of country retailing in the selected counties in this period.

But in the next period, 1603–1625, the distribution of the cases suggests some increase. In Somerset, though six-sevenths of the still modest total[61] were in towns, about a fourth of these places earned the name only by the accident of a medieval grant of market rights and in size were probably indistinguishable from the larger villages. All of the few Jacobean prosecutions of unapprenticed retailers in Wiltshire were of village traders; in Essex these made three-fifths of the county's larger total, and in Norfolk over one-half. The trend, if it was one, appears in the following period also, to some extent: one-third of the increased Somerset total was country cases, while these made up four of Wiltshire's six, four-fifths of Essex's reduced number. In Norfolk, however, town cases were again in the majority, though there is a hint of a greater dispersion than in the sixteenth century in a larger proportion involving offenders in the small market towns instead of in the chief ports.

The significance is not clear of a difference in the shares of professional and other private prosecutors. In Somerset, the prosecutions of both town and country offenders were brought mostly by professionals, in Norfolk entirely so (with one exception). In Wiltshire all the sessions cases of the seventeenth century were nonprofessional, in Essex the majority of all periods were, while in both counties several of the prosecutors are clearly identifiable as local competitors. This difference between the two pairs of counties parallels the further contrasts, that in Somerset and Norfolk there are not only the greater proportion of town cases but in the third period, 1625–1642, the

[60] Westminster and sessions cases, if any, are considered together in the discussion of the town-vs.-country distribution of cases. The Essex reference is to Cal. Q.S., IV, 48, S.R. 39/25.

[61] For the totals in each of these counties, see Table 4 above.

greater total number of retailing prosecutions. The dissimilarities might suggest that the professional informers were not as efficient in searching out the country offenders. But in the same period the distribution of prosecutions in food processing in these counties, resembling the retailing cases in being more the work of professionals in Somerset and Norfolk, reveals the professionals as very active in both country and town cases. The differing shares of professional informers cannot be attributed to their neglect of Essex or Wiltshire, for in both counties some were informing on other statutes and others indulged in a bit of unlicensed composition or extortion.

Both the total numbers and the activity of professionals agree with the hypothesis that a movement of expansion was occurring after 1625 in the distributive trades in certain counties, but chiefly as a growth in the principal centers, though in Norfolk with some spread into the little market towns of the busier districts. There are symptoms in the apprenticeship cases of a slight expansion in Nottinghamshire and Lancashire also.[62] But the existence and location of such a movement require investigation. For the Tudor and Stuart periods, knowledge of the distributive trades is still very slight.[63] Observation of sessions records indicates a decided upturn in the activity of professional informers on the statutes regulating middlemen in Nottinghamshire, Somersetshire, Norfolk, probably to a lesser amount in Essex, an upturn which began in the late 1620's. Apprenticeship prosecutions by professionals increased also in the first three of these counties, and especially in food processing and retail trades. The smaller number in Essex, if it is not merely the result of losses of informations from the sessions files, may indicate a condition in Essex of less growth in this later period. This county because of its proximity to London may have seen an earlier spread of small-town and country shopkeeping.[64]

[62] Out of Nottinghamshire's total 59 apprenticeship cases, 1625–1642, at least a sixth and probably more were of retailers. (The illegal occupation is unknown in some 13 cases.) Professional informers were very industrious in this county from about 1629.

[63] This is least true of the food trades, thanks to the valuable work of Professor N. S. B. Gras on the corn market (already cited) and Mr. F. J. Fisher's brief study of the development of the London food market (*The Economic History Review,* V, No. 2, 46–64). There is useful information also in Willan's study (cited above).

[64] Compared to Gloucestershire, which has supplied a sample of occupational distribution, Essex's apprenticeship cases in retail trades bulk large: only two from Gloucestershire were observed in the Elizabethan Westminster courts.

It would be easy to exaggerate the extent of settled shopkeeping by country residents and to misunderstand the nature of dispersion as applied to retail trades. Competition by country retailers with the town need not have taken the form of new shops opening in the villages. The Essex instance already quoted, of villagers retailing in the nearest market town, shows that country competition might be felt in the stalls of the market-place. This type of retailing was the primary object of the pre-Elizabethan statute.[65] A double pressure was felt in Northamptonshire among other areas, where early in James I's reign fifty-five tradesmen of the towns petitioned the members of Parliament for the county to improve the enforcement of the Statute of Artificers, complaining of those who made and sold wares in country villages and came weekly to the markets.[66] The appearance in county sessions records of occasional prosecutions of the unapprenticed for retailing in cities such as Exeter and Salisbury is probably owing to the same sort of offense, the competition of nonresidents with town freemen.

The different force and timing of demand in individual retail trades would have produced growth of varying extent and period. In the trades of mercer and draper, for example, the county of Kent resembles Essex and Norfolk in having a relatively larger number of apprenticeship cases concentrated between 1581 and 1589.[67] The aggregates were low, as with all the retail prosecutions, yet above the average. They suggest an accelerated growth of the distributive trades in areas near London in the later sixteenth century, and in these three counties an obvious stimulus to the mercer's business was the past and continuing immigration of the Dutch and Flemish settlers among whose specialties was the making of various mercery wares. This may have increased also the direct import of such goods, traded in earlier generations chiefly through London. Native manufacture of many of them — pins, needles, and thread, for example —

[65] Defendants in the observed prosecutions on this statute are invariably described as of places which are identifiable as villages; sometimes the charge specifies that they are not resident in a borough, corporate, or market town.

[66] Hist. MSS. Comm., XLV, *MSS. of Duke of Buccleuch*, III, 138.

[67] Prosecutions of mercers and drapers in the two Westminster courts for these three counties were, for the whole reign and for the decade 1581–1590: Kent, 23, 18; Essex, 15, 14; Norfolk, 12, 8. There were none in this decade in Essex quarter sessions. Only the evidences already cited of the small numbers actually engaged in these trades in the sixteenth- and seventeenth-century town permits the use of so few prosecutions as a basis for speculation.

was only beginning to compete with imports. Basically the stimulus was the rising middle-class standard of living with its greater demand for accessories of dress.[68] However, the three counties mentioned had no monopoly of cases against mercers and drapers. Equal or larger numbers were brought in Sussex, Suffolk, and Surrey, and concentrated in earlier years. Were special causes at work, iron and glassmaking in the Weald, for example, or only random factors in all six? [69]

Whatever may be the causes of the greater numbers of prosecutions in retailing merceries and drapers' goods, they will account for about two-thirds of all the Elizabethan retail cases in Essex. Nearly another quarter was made up by offenders in chandlery. Two of the county's specialties were cheeses and hops, both dealt in by chandlers.[70] Together these trades, closely related to Essex's products and sources of supply, were responsible for most of the county's lead in the retail prosecutions in this period.

The Norfolk retail cases in Charles I's reign are partly attributable to local rather than general conditions. The majority were bunched in 1631 and early 1632 and probably reflect a sudden and temporary increase of illegal entrants, not long-term growth. Most were in the southeast region of Norfolk, later well known for its linen-making and already a specialized district therein.[71] Many of these men, to

[68] The classification of "mercery wares" is a shifting one, as in the term "mercer." For fifteenth-century definitions of these, which may have changed little by the beginning of Elizabeth's reign, see S. Thrupp, "The Grocers of London," in *Studies in English Trade in the Fifteenth Century*, ed. E. Power and M. M. Postan, 268. An Elizabethan description of trade lists "cords, pins, points, bolts of black thread" as among small wares imported from Brittany and Normandy for mercers ("A Speciall Direction for Divers Trades," ascribed to 1575–1585, in *Tudor Economic Documents*, III, 201). In one of the informations on the act of 1554–55, the defendant was charged with selling mercery wares listed as "cambric, holland, lockram, and canvas" (Q.B.C.R., Mich. 27/28 Eliz., m. 204).

[69] Sussex had a total of 32 mostly in the 1560's and 1576–1580; Suffolk, over 14, mostly in 1566–1570; Surrey, 12, mostly in the 1560's. No other county than the six named had more than 8 cases in these trades and several none, from 1563 to 1603.

[70] By the later sixteenth century, London chandlers sold hops, oil, soap, and vinegar (Kramer, *English Craft Gilds*, 114n.). Dealers in butter and cheese for the London market in James I's reign included tallow chandlers; see the Act of 1623 (21 Jas. I, c. 22).

[71] See next chapter for discussion of apprenticeship prosecutions of linen-weavers which pinpoint this area. Diss and East Harling, two of the market towns where several of the retail prosecutions were located, were famous by the

judge from the charges against them, were general shopkeepers, each prosecuted in four separate informations for exercising the trades of linen-draper, mercer, tallow-chandler, and grocer.

General dealing of this type, and the overlapping of one trade with another so frequently evidenced in the Tudor and Stuart periods,[72] might have been expected to cause demarcation disputes and consequent apprenticeship prosecutions. But few instances are visible. From 1563 to 1642 less than fifty prosecutions, for the unapprenticed exercise of two or more retail trades together, were traced in the Westminster courts and in quarter sessions, and many of these came from Norfolk alone in the 1630's. Still fewer were those in which the defendants shifted from one retail trade into another; unapprenticed retailing by tailors appears at least as often.[73]

In food-processing occupations, instances of shifting from one into the other appear to be very infrequent, while virtually the only cases of exercising two such occupations together occurred in Norfolk.[74] In this occupational group too, a potential cause for apprenticeship prosecution thus seems not to have operated.

The large place taken by the food trades in the aggregate of all

---

late seventeenth century as linen markets (F. Blomefield and C. Parkin, *An Essay towards a Topographical History of Norfolk*, 2nd ed., I, 38, 333). See the next note for a grocer's interest in linen.

[72] Differentiation among retail trades has been described for fifteenth-century London as consisting merely in the greater proportion and regularity with which one class of wares might be traded in by an individual dealer (Thrupp, "The Grocers of London," 280ff). The inventory of a Northampton grocer in 1556 listed various fabrics of worsted, linen, and linen with cotton (Northampton MS. Assembly Books, I, 252). An Elizabethan grocer at Colchester received a shipment from London which included ironmongery and pots, just as London grocers in the preceding century had imported pots and pans from the Continent (Dickin, "Notes on Essex," 163; Thrupp, "The Grocers of London," 279). A later Essex tailor was presented for unapprenticed trading as a grocer and for engrossing cheese (Cal. Q.S., XX, 363, 286/13, Mich. 10 Chas. I, Grand Jury presentment).

[73] Occupational shifts cannot be traced in any completeness from the apprenticeship cases, owing to the frequent description of the defendant as yeoman or husbandman (occasionally laborer), which is likely to be an occupational term as well as one of status but may disguise a part-time craft or trade. Often also neither status nor occupation is given; or the occupation is identical with that of which the defendant is accused.

[74] The combination seen usually was that of baker and brewer. Less overlapping in the food-processing occupations is to be expected than in retailing, since their needs differed more widely in amount of capital, location, supplies, and market.

apprenticeship prosecutions is deceptive in respect to their importance among the apprenticeship prosecutions of most counties studied. The five counties whose retailing cases have been compared supply also the bulk of those in food processing in the Elizabethan Westminster courts from the selected counties, all others of this group having only about twenty together. The seventeenth-century total from available sessions records is composed largely of the Norfolk cases, which make up almost two-thirds of those from the five counties, and approximately half of those from all. However, the prosecutions before the Essex assizes in the Stuart period, almost wholly of bakers and brewers, are a reminder how incomplete may be the aggregate of cases preserved in sessions records.[75]

The low aggregates in most of the counties probably correspond to normally small numbers engaged in food processing. Like retailing, this did not fill a quantitatively important place in the economy except in a few centers. To refer again to Gloucestershire, there all the occupations making food and drink absorbed less than 2 per cent of the reported manpower exclusive of the three largest towns. But in these, nearly 7 per cent was in the business of milling, baking, malting, brewing, or cooking.[76] The numbers and dispersion of the individual crafts must everywhere have varied from one district to another and differed from each other. The apprenticeship prosecutions in four principal branches — baking, brewing, butchering, and milling — are too unlike in amount and distribution to discuss as a group.

Prosecutions of bakers in most counties outnumber those in the other food-processing crafts. In Elizabeth's reign, however, the highest total in the Westminster courts for any county was under 20. The county of Gloucester recorded 13. Rural Gloucestershire in 1608 reported few bakers.[77] In the late sixteenth century in so busy a city as Chester, whence troops were transported to Ireland and ships provisioned, master bakers numbered only 26 to 33.[78] Though Essex and Norfolk each registered only nine apprenticeship prosecutions of bakers in Elizabeth's reign, the next reigns show a relatively con-

[75] All 13 of James I's reign were in 1609, trade prosecutions of Colchester bakers. What produced this attack is not known. Between 1625 and 1642, the 31 cases recorded involved 15 bakers and 14 brewers, the latter in the smaller market towns, the former mostly in the country. All the prosecutions were brought by professionals.

[76] Tawneys, "An Occupational Census," 36.

[77] "An Occupational Census," 41, and Table 3 above.

[78] R. H. Morris, *Chester in the Plantagenet and Tudor Reigns*, 422.

siderable increase in the number of cases in both counties and in Somerset. The cases in each county are distributed throughout the period with minor variations, and may perhaps trace a growth of commercial baking associated with expansion in other business activities.[79] An interesting correspondence exists in Devonshire, after the Restoration, between the known era of growth in the Exeter and Devon serge manufacture and trade, and a series in the county quarter sessions of numerous and dispersed apprenticeship prosecutions in food processing. The distribution of the apprenticeship cases in the early Stuart period follows a pattern suggesting some slight spread of country bakers in Somerset and Norfolk; in Essex, country cases outnumbered those in towns throughout.[80]

No single cause explains why, in all periods and most counties, considerably fewer millers and butchers were prosecuted than bakers. According to the Gloucestershire testimony, both crafts were found in a high proportion of rural districts. Appropriately, the few cases in Essex and Norfolk were mostly in country places.[81] But entrance to

[79] The numbers were, from Westminster courts and sessions in 1603–1625, Essex 27, Norfolk 30, Somerset 20 (compared to 3 in 1563–1603); from sessions only (no such cases found in the Westminster courts) in 1625–1642, Essex 22, Norfolk 9, Somerset 51 or more. Essex had in addition the assizes prosecutions of bakers; see above, n. 75. The variations are probably related to local or general business fluctuations, of which little is known with any accuracy in the Stuart period. The Somerset cases are mostly in the years 1614–1615, 1627–1628, and from 1631 on. Those of Essex are more evenly distributed, except for the Colchester group in 1609, another small group in the country in 1618, and eleven cases, mostly country, in 1640–1641.

[80] The reference to Devonshire is based on analysis by the writer of apprenticeship prosecutions recorded in the MS. Sessions Rolls, in which such cases begin to appear in some quantity only from the 1650's. For the growth of Exeter and the serge industry, W. G. Hoskins, *Industry, Trade and People at Exeter, 1688–1800.*

[81] In Essex the number of offending millers was only three in Elizabeth's reign, of whom one was the object of prosecution by separate informers in Westminster and in quarter sessions. He was milling at Wethersfield, in what John Norden described as the best grain-growing region of the county (*Speculi Britanniae Pars . . .* , by H. Ellis, Camden Society, IX, 8). At nearby Finchingfield, where a mill still stands in the village street, a miller was a busy informer twenty years later against unapprenticed competitors in that district and near Chelmsford (Exch. Q.R.M.R., Mich. 44 Eliz., m. 199; Cal. Q.S., XVII, 272, S.R. 159/101, 286, S.R. 160/39; XIX, 396, S.R. 220/61, 496–497, S.R. 239/113–114). Norfolk's three butchers were, suitably, in the rich marshland pasture district between the coast and the town of North Walsham which in the eighteenth century if not before was known as a cattle market. (N. Riches, *The Agricultural Revolution in Norfolk*, 38).

milling was restricted by the need of capital and suitable location. In butchering, the narrowness of the local market perhaps best explains the rarity of prosecutions of intruders.[82]

The importance of brewing in the Norfolk economy has already been commented on. The prosecutions in this county in the Elizabethan courts came almost wholly from the two large ports of Yarmouth and King's Lynn and the smaller one of Cromer. For this there was good reason, in their large inward traffic in hops and Newcastle coal for the brewhouses, and in the outward trade in malt and beer, as well as their business of provisioning ships. Brewing everywhere tended to be a town occupation. In Gloucestershire it had the least scatter of any of the nonagricultural occupations reported from country places.[83] Port towns may have especially attracted the brewing business in the developing Age of Coal. Though Gloucester reported in 1608 only nine brewers, Barnstaple twenty years earlier had at least twenty-nine, probably more.[84]

The concentration in towns, where municipal and craft oversight was at least available if not always effective, and the requirements of location, fuel, and capital, would have helped to protect the brewer's craft against the unapprenticed intruder during normal times. The number of apprenticeship prosecutions in most counties is slight, and the majority are of offenders in smaller towns.[85] In Norfolk alone was any clear increase observed in the seventeenth century. Here the numbers rose to 71 in 1603–1625 and to about 200 in 1625–1642,

[82] Somerset and Wiltshire had more than the average number of cases in this occupation, though still few: Somerset in the three periods, 2, 13, 9; Wiltshire 7, 6, 1. Wiltshire's were mostly in the southwest corner of the county, just north of the eastern limits of Dorset's Vale of Blackmoor, where cattle were fattened for the London market (*Victoria History of Dorset*, II, 275). The absence of such cases from sixteenth-century Leicestershire (only one in the Westminster courts), where at Leicester and at Rugby the trade of butcher was growing in numbers and influence in the Elizabethan age (Hoskins, *Essays*, 108–122) is not surprising. Outside the centers of control in the towns, and except in its grazing, the economic life of the county was not active compared with the shires treated in the text.

[83] See above, Table 3.

[84] Tawneys, "An Occupational Census," 38; Chanter and Wainwright, *Barnstaple Records*, I, 47. On the increasing use of coal by brewers, see J. U. Nef, *The Rise of the British Coal Industry*, I, 157, 186.

[85] Gloucestershire had only five prosecutions of unapprenticed brewers in the Westminster courts. In Essex, two of the eleven Elizabethan prosecutions were at the port of Maldon; six were at Saffron Walden, on the edge of a hop-growing district (Norden, *Speculi Britanniae Pars* . . . , 8; Essex Cal. Q.S., XVI, 180, S.R. 128/81, 82; Exch. Q.R.M.R., Hil. 31 Eliz., m. 110–113d.).

with a trend toward occurrence in the inland market towns and a few villages instead of only in the ports. But they are concentrated in certain years: in 1613–1615, when professional informers were attacking other occupations also, especially food processing and retailing, in Somerset as well as Norfolk; in 1622; and markedly in 1631–32. Like the professional informations of these last years in retailing, the sharp increase appears to correspond less to any permanent expansion than to a widespread multiplication of probably temporary enterprises. Their possible connection with business fluctuations will be commented on in the next chapter.

The shares of professional and other private prosecutors in the seventeenth-century food-processing cases differ among the four counties of east and southwest in much the same way as those in retailing. Throughout, professionals predominate in Norfolk, nonprofessionals in Wiltshire. In Essex the shares are about equal in the first period, as they were in this county in the sixteenth-century cases, but from 1625–1642, professionals brought none (or one) of the prosecutions in the food trades in quarter sessions, though they were responsible for those in the assizes. In Somerset the respective amounts are reversed between the first and second periods, professionals bringing about one-third from 1603 to 1625, two-thirds thereafter. The vigor of the professional informer seems to be associated with times of apparent expansion and activity, rather than with the location of offenders in country or town.

V

BUSINESS FLUCTUATIONS AND APPRENTICESHIP PROSECUTIONS

Since private agencies mainly enforced the seven-year term of apprenticeship, private interest and not public policy supplied the motive power. Among the forces affecting the intensity and direction of private interest few can have been stronger, yet harder to isolate and trace, than fluctuations in business activity. Of necessity, appraisal of their relationship to apprenticeship prosecution must be limited to the very few areas and occupations for which some pattern of "good times" and "bad times" can be pieced together. So far, this has been possible over an extended period for only one region and its principal industry, the textile manufacture of the southwest.

The central subject of business fluctuations is as yet little explored, except in the indispensable pioneer inquiries of W. R. Scott and the fruitful short study of F. J. Fisher.[1] The first attempts an outline of alternations of "good and bad trade" for England as a whole; the second deals with long-range results of the severe depression of the early 1550's. The apprenticeship prosecutions of Elizabeth's reign have a unique value, in the absence of quantitative data, as indicators of varying conditions in individual industries and occupations, which

[1] W. R. Scott, *The Constitution and Finance of English . . . Joint-Stock Companies to 1720*, I, both text and the "Table of Years of Good and Bad Trade" (pp. 465ff); F. J. Fisher, "Commercial Trends . . . ," 95–117. The statement in the text excludes general works or special studies in which there is material bearing on the subjects in question.

may not coincide with ascriptions of prosperity or decline to the economy as a whole.[2]

Increasing demand for products and services probably exerted more pressure on the system of apprenticeship than a shrinking market did. Resort to a secondary occupation without qualification by apprenticeship undoubtedly was apt to occur when the primary craft or trade of an individual was in a slump.[3] But a more general assault on the walls between occupations might begin when there was need for a quickly enlarged supply of a commodity. In the absence of technological improvements this required more workers. If short-run calls on the labor supply were prolonged by their coincidence with one of the major upward movements in business activity, and still more if both were buoyed up by one of the great long-term rises in the general price level, barriers imposed by statute on occupational mobility would be weak indeed. Such conditions would offer a rich harvest to the professional informer, and they appear to have done so in the narrow-cloth woolen industry of Devon and west Somerset during much of the first half of Elizabeth's reign.

Special studies for this or the Stuart period of the various branches and regions of England's then principal industry, the making of cloth, are almost nonexistent. For the southwest the only published work is that by G. D. Ramsay on Wiltshire.[4] The present argument has had to develop its own supports, to explain the wide difference in number of the Elizabethan apprenticeship prosecutions between Devon, with west Somerset, and the adjoining districts of east Somerset and Wiltshire. The chief cause is believed to be a growth in the market for narrow cloth at a faster rate than, or at the expense of, the traditional broadcloth of the southwest.[5] Part of the larger demand undoubtedly came from greater domestic use of the lighter fabrics.

[2] The large numbers of informations in the Westminster courts on the middlemen and usury regulations should be useful in the same way.

[3] In the nature of things, with incomplete descriptions of defendants' occupations in the apprenticeship cases and lack of knowledge of conditions in particular crafts, the possible reasons for illegal entrances into occupations cannot be discovered.

[4] *The Wiltshire Woollen Industry in the Sixteenth and Seventeenth Centuries.*

[5] This theme has been presented briefly elsewhere by the present writer (M. R. Gay, "Aspects of Elizabethan Apprenticeship"). The number of cases there tabulated has been increased by additions from the Queen's Bench Coram Rege Rolls gathered after the article's publication.

There were other elements which must have made for less observance of the apprenticeship requirement in the woolen industry of Devon and west Somerset than in Wiltshire or east Somerset. One was the organization of the industry, which seems to have been more widely scattered in the first two areas. Evasion of rules would have been easier in their lonely hamlets and cottages than in the clothing villages of the Wiltshire-Somerset border. Perhaps another was the kind and quality of the fabrics made in the former region, chiefly narrow cloth of half the weight or less of the standard fine broadcloth which was the principal product of east Somerset and Wiltshire in the sixteenth century. Much of the narrow cloth was of coarse quality, more readily made by the inexperienced. There may have been an older tradition in the broadcloth branch of standards of skilled workmanship, although compulsory apprenticeship by national enactment was recent even in this.[6] Granted, however, that there was less force normally in the apprenticeship law in the making of narrow cloth, the outburst of activity in Elizabeth's reign by the pair of professional informers Otterey and Holmer is not accounted for, or the fluctuations in their recorded cases.

The chief varieties of cloth made in Devon were kerseys, a related cloth called a "dozen," and straits. These could all be woven by one operator, whereas broadcloth required two men at the loom.[7] Straits were lighter and coarser than kerseys, and a specialty of the Totnes area in the south, while the making of kerseys was widespread, especially through the valley of the Exe and through the northwest from Exeter to Barnstaple and beyond, though found also in the Totnes and Tavistock districts.[8] At and about Crediton a fine kersey

[6] 5 & 6 Ed. VI, c. 8, a seven-year apprenticeship required for clothmakers and putters-out; modified by 1 Ma. sess. 3, c. 7 to exempt cities and towns; restored by 2 & 3 P. & M., c. 11, § 7, to apply to broadcloth weavers; broadened by 4 & 5 P. & M., c. 5, § 22, to cover all weaving and clothmaking in broadcloth and narrow cloth including kerseys.

[7] There was a slight difference in quality and price between the dozen and the kersey, but both were narrower and lighter than the "dozen" of Yorkshire, which was a short broadcloth. H. Heaton, *The Yorkshire Woollen and Worsted Industries*, 108–109. The statutes regulating dimensions and weights are informative on the accepted differences among types of cloth at least in theory (Acts of 1552, 1557, 1606). On the Devon dozen, see the Act of 1593 also (35 Eliz., c. 10). On the kersey, see R. Ehrenberg, *Hamburg und England im Zeitalter der Königin Elisabeth*, 269ff; *Acts P.C.*, Eliz., XXX, 492.

[8] Mapped largely from the occurrence of prosecutions for clothmaking under the Act of 1557, in which varieties of cloth are specified. Reference in statutes

was made. In Somerset, the cloth industry of the west differed greatly from that of the east. Along the Wiltshire border, with its center at Frome, was the western boundary of the heavy broadcloth manufacture. But from Bridgewater south to Chard the leading variety of cloth, though a broadcloth which in type resembled the northern dozen, was coarser and lighter than true broadcloth, and normally a colored cloth, unlike fine broadcloth or the Devon kersey both of which were usually sent out from their respective counties without dyeing and finishing.[9] The subvarieties made within this area, and in the Dunster region, covered a broad range of qualities and prices. Kersey making was scattered through the county, from Taunton, Ilminster, and Chard west to a district more or less continuous with that of north Devon; the kerseys were of both the Devon type and the Reading, the latter a larger and finer kind. There were local specialties in the light cheap cloths. Some serge manufacture was to come later.[10]

The cheaper fabrics entered markets so different from those for fine broadcloth that their manufacture was subjected to different external stresses. Whereas the standard "whites" of Wiltshire from the late 1550's were exported primarily to the Netherlands and to German markets, to which access was controlled by the Merchant Adventurers and the Hanseatic League, the principal market for kerseys from the southwest was across the channel, in Normandy and Brittany, and down the French coast to Spain and Portugal. A chief market for straits also was in Brittany.[11] To these lay the natural trade routes of the western and southwestern ports, and a sign perhaps of expanding trade rather than contraction was the in-

is almost the only other available evidence of the location of the industry in Devon.

[9] The sketch is again based on statute specifications, clothmaking prosecutions, and casual mention. See Ramsay on the predominance of white broadcloth in Wiltshire. The intention here is to aid the discussion of prosecutions in relation to business activity.

[10] Taunton serges may be the "stuffs" mentioned by Thomas Gerard in 1633 as made at Taunton (*The Particular Description of the County of Somerset*, Somerset Record Society, XV, 55); they were well known before being listed by Thomas Fuller (cited in *An Historical Geography of England*, ed. H. C. Darby, 410).

[11] "A Speciall Direction . . . ," 201–202: fine white Devon kerseys to Rouen, Morlaix, St. Malo; for Andalusia, "fine white kerseys" (Reading and Hants. kerseys named but not Devon). The Act of 1553 (7 Ed. VI, c. 9) stated that the straits of Devon and Cornwall were exported to Brittany.

corporation of the Exeter Company of Merchant Adventurers in June 1560, "trafficking the realm of France and the dominions of the French king." [12] The ability of three western ports — Exeter, Bristol, and Chester — to maintain local courts of merchant adventurers is in notable contrast to the failure of the Eastland Company to develop western branches. The growth of an active export trade from the outports depended not only on the market but on a local supply. In turn, one cause of the prevailing structure of the Devon industry, with its numerous independent weavers and small clothiers and a putting-out system only partially developed, was probably a ready access to nearby merchants.[13]

Other destinations for Devon cloth at the opening of Elizabeth's reign were Italy and northern Europe: kerseys were part of the transit trade handled by Italian merchants in Antwerp and Brabant, and Venetian ships were lading in the later sixties at Devon ports with cargoes of kerseys, cloth, and tin, while small amounts of Devonshire cloth went to Hamburg, at least through the seventies.[14] In the late sixties, too, if not earlier, southwestern merchants were engaging in the Baltic trades.[15] What part, if any, Devon cloth had in the development of more distant markets is not known. The description of exports already quoted lists other kerseys than the Devon type for the Levant market and insists that for this and for Barbary the cloth must be of the finest.[16] Kerseys of some variety went to the

[12] C. Gross, *The Gild Merchant*, II, 371–373. The organization had been first sought in 1558. Despite Mr. Fisher's persuasive argument in the article already cited, it seems unnecessary to attribute all the restrictive organization of the period to the effects of a slump.

[13] See Ramsay's suggestion for the opposite situation in Wiltshire, in *The Wiltshire Woollen Industry*, 20.

[14] *Cal. S.P.D.*, 1547–1580, 188, No. 15, 198, No. 57; *Cal. S.P.*, *Venetian*, VII, 455, No. 480; 442, No. 468; Ehrenberg, *Hamburg und England*, 269ff.

[15] The charter of the Eastland Company in 1579 offered special entrance terms for merchants from various outports (including several in Devon, and Bridgewater in Somerset) who had exported through the Sound since 1567 (*The Acts and Ordinances of the Eastland Company*, by Maud Sellers, Camden Society, 3rd Series, XI, lxi, 147). Among English ships seized by Denmark after 1565 was at least one from Plymouth (N. R. Deardorff, "English Trade in the Baltic during the Reign of Elizabeth," *Studies in the History of English Commerce in the Tudor Period*, 238ff).

[16] "A Speciall Direction . . . ," 201–202. Another market analysis a few years earlier agrees in stating France and Spain as chief destinations for west country kerseys and coarse cloths, but includes both Barbary and the Baltic for the latter (*Historical Geography*, 379, citing Roger Bodenham's memorandum of 1571 to Cecil).

Persian market, and during the 1580's the Levant Company's newly opened and growing trade with Turkey could maintain the connection with Persia begun by the Muscovy Company's overland trade through Russia.[17]

Somersetshire's narrow cloths were shipped to much the same areas as those of Devon, and the coarse cloths of the broadcloth type made in the Taunton-Bridgewater area were exported rather more widely, it would seem, to districts in Spain and the Azores, the finer cloth to Portugal.[18] Consultations of the Exeter Merchant Adventurers with merchants of Taunton and Chard show their common interest in the French market, though these two towns were grouped with the smaller Devon towns in assessments for common expenses, paying much less than Exeter or Totnes.[19]

At home a market may have been growing even before Elizabeth's reign for the lighter and cheaper varieties of cloth. Complaint of "slight and subtle making" and detailed standardization in the 1550's may have reflected not merely poorer quality resulting from unfavorable cost-price differentials, but a real change in demand.[20] The modifications of standards in 1557, inspired by clothiers' complaints, were all in the direction of lighter weights.[21] A growth of the narrow-cloth industry is revealed in the extension to it of the restrictions on country clothmaking already in force for broadcloth.[22] Fragmentary indications of the domestic uses of kerseys show a middle- and lower-class market: some variety of kersey was in de-

[17] Scott, *Joint-Stock Companies*, I, 68; M. Epstein, *The Early History of the Levant Company*, 245ff. In the latter citation, a reprint of Sir Francis Walsingham's paper of 1580 on trade with Turkey, the statement is made that the kersey export handled by Italians and Ragusans had been going chiefly to Turkey.

[18] "A Speciall Direction . . . ," 201–203. In 1588, a group of Taunton merchants adventured a ship to Guinea (*Acts P.C.*, Eliz., XVI, 294).

[19] W. Cotton, *An Elizabethan Guild of the City of Exeter*, passim.

[20] 3 & 4 Ed. VI, c. 2; 5 & 6 Ed. VI, c. 6; Fisher, "Commercial Trends," 112, suggests the squeeze of high wool prices and falling cloth prices in 1550–51. However, in July 1551, the London drapers reported price increases in kerseys and dozens of 75 per cent to nearly 100 per cent within four years (*Tudor Economic Documents*, II, 192–193). At least as early as 1538, a professional informer prosecuted a number of Devon clothiers for kerseys not conforming to the dimensions of the statute 27 Hen. VIII, c. 12 (Elton, "Informing for Profit," 152).

[21] 4 & 5 P. & M., c. 5. The specifications for Devon straits had already been modified in 1553 (7 Ed. VI, c. 9).

[22] 4 & 5 P. & M., c. 5, § 21.

mand for the long hose of the early Elizabethan period which the sumptuary laws tried so vainly to control; in the Stuart period Devon kerseys were used for breeches and petticoats for the poor, and for decorating the waists of ships.[23] The market, illustrated by the phrase "russet yeas and honest kersey noes," [24] was one destined to grow in size and variety, and its strength is suggested by the rapidly increasing demand for the very similar and partly competing fabrics of worsted, the "new draperies."

But like the market for broadcloth, it fluctuated in volume. Some of the external causes of variation for the broadcloth manufacture are easily traceable and well-known. Analysis of their effects, however, has necessarily been limited either to a particular area of production such as Wiltshire, or to general treatment. Prosecutions of offenses under the several Cloth Acts and under the apprenticeship clause of the Act of 1563 are not only new sources of knowledge of the distribution of the textile industry within Devon and Somerset. They prove also a rough indicator to hitherto uncharted fluctuations in industrial activity there, which do not always coincide with those otherwise identified.

Prosecutors utilized the apprenticeship clauses of the Acts of 1555 and 1557 for some years before making use of the Act of 1563. Table 5 shows the totals of apprenticeship cases in the Westminster courts under the Cloth Acts and the Act of 1563 combined, for three southwest clothing counties, by the same triads of years selected by Mr. Fisher for his averages of cloth exports.[25] Mr. Fisher's figures are quoted for comparison.[26]

[23] *Cal. S.P.D.*, 1547–1580, 200; *Victoria History of Essex*, II, 325; *Prices and Wages in England*, ed. W. Beveridge, I, 637.

[24] Cited from *Love's Labour's Lost*, Act. V, Sc. II, in *Minutes and Accounts of . . . Stratford . . .*, III, 15, in connection with the purchase of kersey for the beadle's hose, 1577.

[25] No apprenticeship prosecutions in textile crafts have survived in the quarter sessions records of the three counties for the period covered by the table.

[26] Fisher, "Commercial Trends," 96; informations are from Exchequer Queen's Remembrancer Memoranda Rolls and Queen's Bench Coram Rege Rolls, except for 1559–1562 when they were taken, for the Exchequer, merely from the Agenda Rolls. Both professional and other private prosecutions are included, since the latter fell within the same years as the former, except in east Somerset and Wiltshire (to be commented on shortly). In several cases they are not definitely identifiable in the Devon and Somerset series. The probable non-professional prosecutions in the above table total 15 for Devon, with 2 more unknown (under 1/10 of Devon's total); 11 for west Somerset (about 1/10); 4 for east Somerset (½); and 8 in Wiltshire (⅓).

TABLE 5

APPRENTICESHIP INFORMATIONS IN TEXTILE TRADES
1559–1588

(Exchequer and Queen's Bench)

Years	Devon-shire	West Somerset	East Somerset	Wilt-shire	Average exports of shortcloth from London (in 1000's)
1559–61	18	2	0	2	94
1562–64	58	28	1	1	61
1565–67	34	28	1	1	95
1568–70	45	19	1	3	94
1571–73	0	0	0	7	73
1574–76	0	0	0	4	100
1577–79	32	10	5	6	98
1580–82	20	4	0	0	98
1583–85	5	0	0	0	101
1586–88	5	4	0	0	95

The same sharp contrast in amount of prosecution, between Devon with west Somerset and Wiltshire with east Somerset, is to be seen in the informations of the same period, shown in Table 6, for the offenses of country clothmaking and keeping too many looms.[27]

TABLE 6

INFORMATIONS FOR COUNTRY CLOTHMAKING (A) AND KEEPING LOOMS (B)
1559–1588

(Exchequer and Queen's Bench)

Years	Devon		W. Somerset		E. Somerset		Wiltshire	
	A	B	A	B	A	B	A	B
1559–61	0	27	0	2	0	0	2	2
1562–64	6	23	3	11	0	1	0	9
1565–67	57	6	32	1	0	0	0	2
1568–70	53	9	17	3	3	0	2	0
1571–73	0	0	0	0	0	0	1	1
1574–76	0	0	0	0	5	1[a]	7	0
1577–79	27	5	4	0	0	0	3	1
1580–82	15	5	0	0	0	0	0	0
1583–85	2	0	0	0	0	0	0	0
1586–88	0	0	0	0	0	0	0	0

[a] Repeats information of 1564 against same offender.

[27] Under the Acts of 1557 and 1555 (4 & 5 P. & M., c. 5, § 21; 2 & 3 P. & M., c. 11, §§ 1–4).

This contrast is no accident. The significance of the Devonshire cases cannot be appreciated unless it is realized that in no other county is the amount of such textile prosecutions nearly so large. The disparity between the two different districts of the southwest woolen industry, with their distinct products, cannot be accounted for solely by a possible directing influence hostile to the narrow-cloth manufacture, by a weaker tradition of apprenticeship, or by random factors. The explanation must lie in a greater activity of enterprise in the narrow cloths and in the kersey branch particularly, during the late 1550's [28] and 1560's, renewed in the late seventies and early eighties. It is more than a coincidence that the prosperous career of Devon's outstanding clothier, Peter Blundell of Tiverton, maker of kerseys, spanned much of Elizabeth's reign, while those of his peers in stature, John Winchcombe of Berkshire and William Stumpe of Wiltshire, belonged to the reign of Henry VIII.[29] The London deputy alnager, John Leake, attributed the beginning of the Devon dozens' manufacture to about 1530, a dating which at least suggests that its growth was known to be recent; yet he described it, in 1577, as "a marvelous great commodity." [30] The development of the west central textile district of Somerset must have begun soon after Leland's travels there (between 1535 and 1543), for he does not mention clothmaking at Taunton, and as to Bridgewater refers only to the recent "decay" of "above 200 houses." [31]

The appearance of prosecutions for illegal looms earlier than for other offenses corresponds not unreasonably to the probable first response in expanding production: the addition of an extra loom or so by workers already established; then a later entry of newcomers. All the small total of illegal looms in west Somerset and most of

[28] Until 1557 prosecutions on the Act of 1555 were rare; yet in that year 12 informations were brought against Devon and Somerset weavers keeping too many looms. Restrictions on rural industry had been suggested for Devon three years earlier, in a Commons bill requiring craftsmen to live in towns (Cunningham, *Growth of English Industry*, II, 26–27, n. 5).

[29] Lipson, *Woollen and Worsted Industries*, 45–48.

[30] *Tudor Economic Documents*, III, 211.

[31] *The Itinerary of John Leland*, ed. L. T. Smith, Parts 1–3, 161, 163. Possibly another indication is the location of the market where the offending Devon clothiers in 1538 (see n. 20 above) were offering their kerseys for sale — at Norton St. Philip in the east Somerset broadcloth district. By 1555 the spread of the industry, in the colored light broadcloth and/or narrow cloth characteristic of West Somerset, was sufficient to inspire another act (2 & 3 P. & M., c. 12) on behalf of control by the towns of Taunton, Bridgewater, and Chard.

those in Devon occurred in kersey-making areas. Almost half of the west Somerset cases of unapprenticed weaving, which were the next to appear in any quantity, were in the kersey district around Wiveliscombe, while those in Devon can be assumed to be chiefly against kersey-weavers.[32]

In treating the whole group of informations as indicating an expanding industry, it must not be assumed that all those for lack of apprenticeship and country clothmaking were against newcomers. In the apprenticeship cases, there are only a few repetitions,[33] in two of which the second prosecution was ten years or so later than the first. From these it can be inferred that other defendants had been in the business longer than the information makes evident. Some cases of country clothmaking show, by an earlier information under some other regulation, that the defendant had been established in the location specified as clothier or weaver, or both, over a period of years, thirteen in one instance, nine in another.[34]

The meaning of uncertainty as to the number of actual newcomers is obvious, in considering the relation of the prosecutions to business activity. At best, there is only a general correspondence in the increase of the two, nothing that can be dignified with the term "correlation." A technical reason preventing immediate response of prosecution to offense was the necessity for the informer to wait for the penalty to cumulate.[35] This lag, therefore, has to be allowed for in the survey which follows of fluctuations in business conditions and in prosecutions.

The winter which saw the enactment of the Statute of Artificers was set in the middle of three years of recurring disturbances to the chief export trade, that of broadcloth. In 1562 the Antwerp staple was closed for a time to the Merchant Adventurers and again in November 1563, in retaliation for restrictions on Flemish merchants

[32] The variation in number of the informations for the different offenses listed in the tables above may have been caused in part by changing anticipations of rewards; in part by exhaustion of the informers' knowledge under any one head; in part perhaps by temporary reform.

[33] Devon 5, Somerset 2, Wiltshire 1.

[34] Devon about 8, Somerset 6, Wiltshire 1.

[35] Unapprenticed weaving, under the Act of 1555, was the sole offense of those discussed in the text in which there was a flat penalty (£20); with the others, the penalty was set by the week, month, or piece of cloth. A possible explanation for these prosecutions of apparently long-established craftsmen is the in-and-out nature of work in many occupations. Such offenders may have reëntered the industry after an interval.

in England but on the excuse of the epidemic of plague which had broken out in London in August and was severe through most of 1564; in England all exports of cloth were prohibited for a time in the winter months 1563–64, though the ban was lifted in late March except to the Low Countries. The average exports from London for the period 1562–1564 probably reflect the inability of the temporary staple at Emden to take up the amounts formerly sent to Antwerp, and the effects of the plague. The impact of the grain scarcities in the autumn of 1563 on general trade is uncertain. Meanwhile, in the southwest, though Wiltshire cloth output had declined, no complaints of depression in Devon and west Somerset are recorded. Trade to France had been made difficult by the outbreak of the wars of religion in the summer of 1562, and in August Exeter merchants were complaining to the Privy Council of bad treatment at Morlaix; then Rouen was shut off when the Huguenots lost it in October. But the northern French markets were presumably available once more in time for spring and summer sailings in 1563, with uneasy peace established by the edict of Amboise, despite the struggle still going on at Havre to oust the English force there. The incidence of plague in the southwest is not clear. However, by the spring of 1564, a kersey trade was being carried on again by the Italians. A memorandum by William Cecil, undated but ascribed to this year, argued against restoring intercourse with Antwerp that "this . . . will breed no stay of clothing to such as make any colored cloths, or to them which make kerseys, or to them of the north that make coarse cloths, for that the vent of them remaineth as good as before, both into Spain, France, and the East countries. And the kerseys that were wont to be sent into Italy by experience may pass thither from Emden." [36]

The schedule of prosecutions in Devon and west Somerset is consistent with this comment on the narrow-cloth trade. In 1560, in one of three years which have been supposed "good" years in general, there was the first increase in cases under the Cloth Acts against

[36] The difficulties with the Netherlands, based on Ehrenberg, *Hamburg und England*, 64ff; Unwin, *Studies*, 176, 208–209; Scott, *Joint-Stock Companies*, I, 32; Fisher, "Commercial Trends," 106. The prohibition and renewal of exports, *Cal. S.P.D.*, 1547–1580, 231, 235, 236; complaint from Exeter, *ibid.*, 205; Italian traffic in kerseys, *ibid.*, 239. Grain scarcity, Scott, *loc. cit.*; decline in Wiltshire, Ramsay, *The Wiltshire Woollen Industry*, 66. The memo. by Cecil, in *Tudor Economic Documents*, II, 45.

Devon offenders since 1557, the majority for keeping too many looms, the others for unapprenticed weaving. In 1562 there was a slight increase again in the latter class of cases, but the first considerable jump, relatively speaking, came in 1564. It is difficult to make a guess at the necessary lag for these narrow cloths between new orders, or promising prospects of good sales, and the output: according to a "trade" estimate, a week was required for one weaver to produce eleven kerseys of the northern type, a somewhat longer cloth than the Devon.[37] However, the prosecutions for country clothmaking against Devon offenders, in which it would be to the informer's advantage to maximize the alleged output, claim a good deal less than a year's volume calculated on this basis.[38] Orders from clothiers or prospects of sales thus might result in the setting up of additional looms half a year to a year ahead of the expected shipping season; the increase in prosecutions of 1564 might be reflecting signs of improvement in trade in the spring or early summer of 1563.

The few Somerset prosecutions in these years, which can be identified certainly or with probability as against kersey-makers or weavers, follow much the same course as those of Devon. Their number, however, is so small that it looks as though informers were devoting most attention to the Devon scene where expansion may have been greater.[39]

Little is known in detail of the years 1565–1569. Short-cloth exports recovered to slightly better than the average before the troubles of 1563–64, with the reopening of Antwerp and trade up the German rivers. In the summer of 1566, the Exeter Company of Merchant Adventurers was able to charter five ships for Malaga, Portugal, and Gibraltar; but there is no indication other than this, and than the prosecutions for country clothmaking, of the level of business activity. The Exeter Company's prohibition in the same summer of shipments in the Spanish and Portuguese trade by nonfreemen, or by freemen

[37] Heaton, *Yorkshire Industries*, 109: cited from a document of 1588.

[38] Nearly two-thirds of the Devon offenders were charged with having made 20 cloths (kerseys and "plains") within nine months or a year; only a few with 60 to 80 cloths. In prosecutions for unapprenticed clothmaking, a half of the defendants were alleged to have made 60 cloths or less within the year, but two-fifths of them as much as 100 to 200 cloths.

[39] The informer John Otterey was chiefly responsible for prosecutions in the kersey area of west Somerset; but analysis of the distribution of his Devon and Somerset cases by districts shows that his area of operation was not governed by his own ascribed residence at South Molton in the Devon kersey area.

of the company with any nonfreeman, might have been either a response to intruders brought in by good business or to a contraction in 1566.[40] For domestic demand, there is probably relevance in the issue in February 1566 of another proclamation on apparel, regulating the amount of kersey in hose; the proclamation complained, like its predecessor in 1562, of the excess in dress.[41] The making of bays, the worsted fabric so similar to kersey in many of its uses, flourished in the years immediately following alien settlement at Norwich in 1566: in the summer of 1567 immigrants were urging their relatives and friends to join them, trade was so good.[42]

The informations under the Cloth Acts and the Statute of Artificers suggest industrial activity in Devon and west Somerset in the second half of the sixties, and perhaps especially in 1566–1568.[43] In this period, however, prosecutions for country and unapprenticed clothmaking outnumbered those for unapprenticed weaving four to one. Some of the offenders, as was pointed out on a preceding page, had already been prosecuted some years before as unapprenticed weavers or for excess looms. It is certainly possible that the new clothmaking prosecutions, against such as these and others, reveal a development of the putting-out system in the Devon kersey industry. An interesting parallel is to be seen in west Somerset, where there was also an increase in cases of clothmaking in country places or without apprenticeship. But in Somerset the district chiefly involved is that of the coarse broadcloths, the Tauntons and Bridgewaters rather than the kersey areas (so far as these are distinct). Even, however, in the latter, the proportion of apprenticeship cases for clothmaking as compared to those for weaving is higher than in Devon.

For both counties, the onset of the widespread depression usually held to have been initiated by the Spanish-English embargoes of 1568–69 put a stop to informers' activity in textile offenses. Seizures

[40] The chartering and the ruling mentioned in Cotton, *An Elizabethan Guild*, 31–32, 177. The ships were of 40 to 60 tons, apparently a fair average at the time for merchant ships from most outports. (The report of the Surveyor of the Port of London for the year Mich. 1571 to Mich. 1572 shows that of Exeter's total 124 ships "trading in merchandise," only 8 were over 60 tons, and 76 per cent were under 40 tons (*Cal. S.P.D.*, Eliz., Addenda, 1566–1579, 441).

[41] F. E. Baldwin, *Sumptuary Legislation and Personal Regulation in England*, 223.

[42] *Tudor Economic Documents*, I, 299–300.

[43] Most of the prosecutions in the period 1566–1570 were in 1568–69.

of English goods in Spain, and at Rouen in 1569 as a result of the renewal of the French wars of religion and English partisanship therein, must have hit the southwest narrow-cloth industry as severe a blow as the stop on the Flanders trade did the broadcloth — perhaps even harder for lack of alternative outlets such as the Merchant Adventurers had acquired at Hamburg in 1567. Plague and the northern rebellion disturbed domestic markets.

The importance of the French trade to Devon is illustrated in 1572 by the invitation to western merchants, among whom those of Exeter and Totnes were named first, to send representatives to London for the discussions preliminary to negotiations over the commercial clauses of the Treaty of Blois.[44] But the actual resumption of trade was delayed by war in the Netherlands and France, and in May 1573 inability to meet the expense of trained men for the musters was reported from the county of Devon, as due to decline in their trade.[45] There is no evidence to show when recovery began in the southwest. Possibly the organization of the Spanish Company in late 1576 and 1577 is proof that this trade had again increased to a point where the Merchant Adventurers wished to secure an immediate control of expansion.[46] The French markets had been reopened, and in 1578 it was said that the western merchants' greatest traffic was to St. Malo. Kerseys, Devon dozens, and Somerset cloth were being shipped by Hansards and interlopers to Hamburg.[47] West Somerset's cloth went to Spain, Russia, and the Baltic.[48] In 1577–1579 there was a reappearance of prosecutions against both Devon and west Somerset offenders, for lack of apprenticeship and for

[44] Cotton, *An Elizabethan Guild*, 62–65.

[45] *Cal. S.P.D.*, 1547–1580, 460. See Scott, *Joint-Stock Companies*, I, 51–56. Yet for the Shrewsbury drapers, dealing in Welsh "cottons" for which a chief export market was Rouen, the years 1572–1575 were prosperous, as measured by the enrolment of new freemen in the company (Mendenhall, *The Shrewsbury Drapers*, 86).

[46] A similar suggestion has been made by Mr. Lawrence Stone, in "State Control in Sixteenth-Century England," *The Economic History Review*, XVII, No. 2, 117.

[47] *Cal. S.P., Foreign*, Eliz., 1577–1578, 507; Ehrenberg, *Hamburg und England*, 330-331.

[48] Or so it would appear from the appointments to a committee to hear the answer of Taunton clothiers to John Leake's charge of false clothmaking. Two London aldermen were on the committee, who had long been associated with trade to these regions — Thomas Pullison and George Barnes (*Acts P.C.*, Eliz., XI, 160, 168).

country clothmaking, which continue in Devon into 1588, though never as numerous as in the earlier years and dwindling to a mere handful after 1582; in west Somerset they are, as in the 1560's, fewer than in Devon.

The beginning of the next recession is generally assigned to the years 1586–1587, and the export figures from London are consistent with this.[49] But there are some suggestions that in Devon the recession may have begun earlier. The merchants at Totnes had complained in 1581 to the Exeter Company of country intruders, but it seems not to have been until November 1584 that the company felt pressure enough to take steps toward control, which came to nothing.[50] A contrary indication of improved markets for one of the cheaper narrow cloths, the white straits, appears to be given by the statute early in 1585 which repealed the standard specifications and permitted both country clothmaking and the use of three instead of two looms in the manufacture of this variety of fabric.[51] Yet it is conceivable that such a relaxation of restrictions was either a delayed legislative response to better sales in the earlier 1580's, or that in 1584–85 the cheaper and lighter cloth could compete in a market that had become less favorable for the kerseys and dozens.

Merchants were having difficulties with new customs duties in Brittany in 1583 and 1584; in 1584 negotiations over impositions were still in progress with the French government.[52] By October 1585, the Exeter Company was considering how to safeguard its shipping from raiders off the French coast, and decided to petition for a corporation of western merchants to shift trade from Brittany to the Channel Islands, a proposal which they had rejected two years before.[53] Spanish raids on shipping were hindering access to Spanish markets also in 1585. The year 1586 brought the seizure of English ships in Spanish ports, the fall of Antwerp, and in France confiscation of English goods at Morlaix.

[49] Scott, *Joint-Stock Companies*, I, 88; Unwin, *Studies*, 201ff; Ramsay, *The Wiltshire Woollen Industry*, 67; Fisher, "Commercial Trends," 96.

[50] Cotton, *An Elizabethan Guild*, 129, 159. The company then agreed to instruct Exeter's members of Parliament to petition for a law excluding from export trade all country merchants, and all those not engaged in export trade for eighteen years before or apprenticed seven years to an "ancient merchant."

[51] 27 Eliz., c. 18.

[52] Cotton, 66–72, 73–75; *Cal. S.P.D.*, Eliz., 1581–1590, 221.

[53] Cotton, 67, 133, 136–137.

The sharp decrease in apprenticeship prosecutions and of cases under the Cloth Acts after 1582 suggests that the expansion in Devon and west Somerset had spent its force, and that the volume of output either did not increase as much proportionately in narrow cloths as the export averages indicate for the broadcloth production, or that it could be handled without calling into the industry enough "new" entrants to attract informers. By the early months of 1586, the recession had begun sufficiently for the effect of decreased orders to be felt by the industry. Kersey weavers petitioned the Privy Council, who referred their complaint to the local authorities, with directions to enforce the apprenticeship laws against "certain farmers and others in the counties of Exeter, Devon, and Cornwall . . . not being apprentices to the art of making kersey [who] set up looms in their houses and buy wool in the markets to regrate the same, to the hindrance of those that have been apprentices. . . ."[54] This illustrates a tendency of trade interests during recessions to attempt protection by means of the apprenticeship law.

There may have been another reason for the virtual disappearance of informations. At some date previous to October 1585, a dispensing patent for "the reformation of kerseys" had been granted to Sir Edward Stafford, long ambassador to France, whose deputies were assured in that month by the Exeter Company of assistance in executing it.[55] His monopoly may have made it unprofitable for professional informers to bring further suits at Westminster.

Prosecutions at Westminster for apprenticeship and under the Cloth Acts against Devon and Somerset offenders do not reappear in the 1590's.[56] The Act of 1589, in diverting apprenticeship informations on the Statute of Artificers from the Westminster courts, may also have discouraged informations under the Cloth Acts.[57] But conditions in the narrow-cloth industry of the southwest after 1586 were perhaps the chief obstacle to informing. The entire interval from 1586 into 1603 has been summarized as one of depression.[58] Other occupations than the cloth trade provide evidence to contradict this, and in fact, broadcloth export appears to have recovered quickly in

[54] *Acts P.C.*, Eliz., XIV, 21, 27.

[55] Cotton, *An Elizabethan Guild*, 129, 131–132.

[56] At least in the Exchequer. When none were brought in this court, prosecutions in the Queen's Bench are very unlikely.

[57] Since it applied to all penal statutes where the penalty was £20 or less.

[58] Scott, *Joint-Stock Companies*, I, 465.

1589–1594.[59] But the western merchants had recurrent difficulty up to the mid-1590's: their usual markets in Normandy and Brittany were closed by the embargo on trade into areas controlled by the Catholic League, except by special license for which various merchant groups seem to have petitioned in vain. Even after the power of the league had been broken, English traders in northern France suffered from a variety of new restrictions and impositions.[60] It is not known, however, whether the narrow-cloth industry in general shared in the brief trade revival apparently occurring in the broadcloth industry at the end of the century.[61] A local situation of decline in kersey-making may be traceable at Crediton. Some manufacture of the new draperies had developed in Devonshire by the middle of the 1580's,[62] though probably on a minute scale. By 1600, residents of Crediton were complaining to the justices of the peace about unapprenticed weavers of bays and other cloth; [63] and in the preceding year, a Crediton weaver had brought informations for unapprenticed weaving against men of the town and its neighborhood.[64] A generation later, a writer was looking back to past glories of the Crediton kersey industry, "before the perpetuanoes were wrought." [65]

In the broadcloth industry of east Somerset and Wiltshire, the

[59] Fisher, "Commercial Trends," 96.

[60] Cotton, *An Elizabethan Guild*, 132, 134–136, 160–161; B. Reynolds, "Elizabethan Traders in Normandy," *The Journal of Modern History*, IX, 294–297.

[61] Fisher, 96; Ramsay, *The Wiltshire Woollen Industry*, 61.

[62] The informer John Otterey prosecuted two Barnstaple merchants in 1586 for unapprenticed clothmaking of bays (Q.B.C.R., Hil. 28 Eliz., m. 92, 104).

[63] Devonshire MS. Sessions Minute Books, I, Easter 42 Eliz. The only record of the response of the justices of the peace is an order referring the petition to three justices of the Crediton area.

[64] Exch. Q.R.M.R., Pasch. 41 Eliz., m. 123, 123d., 124, 124d.

[65] T. Westcote, *A View of Devonshire in 1630*, ed. G. Oliver and P. Jones, 120. A recent study of muster returns shows, so far as the return can be trusted, a sharp drop between 1569 and 1577 in the number of able men at Crediton, a similar one at Hartland, and a lesser decrease at Tiverton. (Rich, "The Population of Elizabethan England," 256–257.) At all three, informations before 1569 had been plentiful, but were few after the resumption of informing in 1576. It looks as though particular Devonshire centers, perhaps of the finer kerseys, never recovered from the depression of the early seventies. Apprenticeship and Cloth Acts prosecutions in the later years of Elizabeth's reign tended to group around Exeter and Totnes, the latter being the center of a manufacturing area of cheaper cloth. In the Crediton situation in 1599–1600 there may be the beginnings of the growth which was to make the county's output of new draperies sufficient by 1616 for its inclusion in an inquiry into the use of wool in these fabrics (*Acts P.C.*, Jas. I, II, 644).

slight amount of prosecution on the various regulations, shown in the tables above, seems consistent with the condition of the industry in Elizabeth's reign. Its great expansion had come in the first half of the sixteenth century, and though it was still dominant in the economic life of the country, there was no thrust of new growth during the second half.[66] The lack of informing activity for apprenticeship offenses is probably associated with this situation rather than with the structure of the industry. In a comparatively narrow district from the eastern edge of the Mendips and Cotswolds to the western edge of the Wiltshire downlands, it was carried on in a series of small towns and villages linked by interspersed hamlets. Its closely knit organization, "under clothiers" as was said in 1597 of the parish of Kingswood, and the existence of a system of apprenticeship backed by tradition and local ordinance from a time preceding national regulation, undoubtedly had some force in restraining the entry of newcomers.[67] Local organizations of weavers, in market as well as corporate towns and with a jurisdiction apparently over neighboring villages, are known by the end of Elizabeth's reign and may have been of long standing. The widely scattered industry of Devon and west Somerset could hardly have come under such close supervision. But everywhere the impress of a traditional practice of apprenticeship, so generally found in the medieval towns, appears to have penetrated the countryside. Its strength is well illustrated in connection with the spread of the new draperies. These seem to have been generally regarded as outside the scope of existing legislation, and only occasional prosecutions were attempted against individual offenders.[68] Yet a complaint in 1622 of their freedom from apprenticeship restrictions alleges that "two-thirds" of the whole — not the whole — of the Suffolk makers of new draperies were unapprenticed.[69]

[66] Fisher, and Ramsay, *passim*.

[67] For the location and organization of the industry, Ramsay, *passim*; for the description of Kingswood, *Acts P.C.*, Eliz., XXVII, 221. Ramsay on apprenticeship in Wiltshire, 60–61.

[68] Early in the seventeenth century it was claimed that the new draperies were not covered by the Cloth Acts, and it was the view of the deputy alnager and writer John May that the Act of 1563 did not apply (S.P.D., Jas. I, XVIII, No. 85, about 1606; J. May, *A Declaration of the State of Clothing*, 1613, cited by Unwin, *Studies*, 292). Doubt as to the law's application was expressed by an Essex justice of the peace in 1602.

[69] S.P.D., Jas. I, CXXIX, No. 59. Some exaggeration of the extent of unapprenticed manufacture can probably be allowed for. But there is no reliable

In the broadcloth area itself, the repeated insistence in the enactments of the 1550's on the seven-year term of apprenticeship betrays a breakdown of the customary restrictions in the boom years of the preceding decade. In the reign of Elizabeth, the local weavers' organizations were unable to maintain control over apprenticeship during the apparent upturn after 1597, already mentioned. By 1602 recession and unemployment had set in and the weavers enlisted the support of public opinion and the justices of the peace. The measures then taken are discussed later in this chapter.

Special situations, random causes, or personal animosities may be reflected in the small groups of prosecutions recorded from Wiltshire and east Somerset from 1559 to 1589. Too much emphasis should not be put upon the third of these elements in accounting for apprenticeship prosecution in any period or place, for even the first entry of an information at Westminster or quarter sessions was an expensive pleasure for the average small man of the time to indulge in, and cannot often have been the sole motive. The most interesting of these groups of cases lies in the years 1577–1579. Ten of the sixteen prosecutions were brought by two weavers of Bradford and Westbury against unapprenticed weavers and clothmakers in their neighborhood. Their residence and partnership resemble those of the two cloth searchers twenty-five years later whose prosecutions formed a part of the campaign already referred to against the unapprenticed, but in 1577–1579 they did not prosecute for the offenses of particular concern to the working weaver and small clothier — excess apprentices, unqualified journeymen — as the later informers did, and there is no mention of them as searchers. Their cases, however, coincide in time with a few brought by the Peter Blackborowe who made a brief but puzzling appearance on the Wiltshire scene in the 1570's and had ambitions for an alnage patent. John Leake, the London deputy alnager, was also informing in these years in several textile districts, including the broadcloth area in the southwest, and in 1577 had prepared his diatribe against "abuses" in clothmaking. That same year, representations of "decay" from east Somerset, possibly inspired or made by Blackborowe, had induced the Privy Council to order an inquiry into "abuses" there and in Wiltshire.[70]

---

indication of the prevalence of apprenticeship among English workers in these fabrics.

[70] The two informing weavers, Richard Howse and Thomas Hawkins, may

The Council had also been moved by reports from the colored cloth industry of Suffolk and Essex on the high price of wool to grant the clothiers leave to stretch the cloth exported to eastern markets.[71]

This stir in two widely separated areas of broadcloth manufacture suggests the possibility that there had been a mild recession following the revival of 1574–1576. In this event, the informations by the Wiltshire weavers illustrate the difference which tends to occur in the timing of professional and nonprofessional prosecutions, the former lessening or disappearing during trade depressions, the latter sometimes coinciding with them.

In two other great textile regions of England, the rarity of prosecutions on the Cloth Acts and the Act of 1563 calls for brief comment.[72] The county of Essex made a variety of textiles. Broadcloth manufacture had long been established at such towns and industrial villages as Coggeshall, Bocking, and Braintree. Most of the cloth was like that of Suffolk, exported principally to the Baltic and southwestern Europe in the 1570's, but then and in the following century also to Germany and the Low Countries, France, Barbary, and the Levant. The making of worsteds had long antedated the settlement of the

have been instigated by Blackborowe (Ramsay, 139) or have been partners (M. R. Gay, "Aspects of Elizabethan Apprenticeship," 149, n. 2) or they may have been acting independently, perhaps sponsored by the weavers' organization. Their cases were for lack of apprenticeship, country clothmaking, and excess looms, involving eight offenders (Exch. Q.R.M.R., Mich. 19 Eliz., m. 82; Hil. 20 Eliz., m. 63; Pasch. 20 Eliz., m. 76, 76d., 87d., 105d.; Mich. 20 Eliz., m. 105; Hil. 20 Eliz., m. 64; Pasch. 20 Eliz., m. 74; Q.B.C.R., Pasch. 21 Eliz., m. 56; Mr. Ramsay refers to another, Exch. Q.R.M.R., Mich. 18 Eliz., m. 74). In 1579, Hawkins was the informer in a suit against a Westbury weaver for usury (Exch. Q.R., Decrees and Orders, Series I, VII, Mich. 21 Eliz.), but this does not by itself put him into the professional class. For Blackborowe, see Ramsay, 59, 139; the Council inquiry into clothmaking, *Acts P.C.*, Eliz., X, 28, 157. All the cases in Wiltshire and east Somerset from 1575 to 1579 may be associated with internal politics in the alnage, perhaps the recurrent struggle between London and local alnagers for the right to search west-country cloth. One informer of 1578 against Taunton clothiers for evading search, William Harte, merchant of Taunton, was a local deputy of the alnager for Somerset and Dorset, and was himself prosecuted by John Leake for the same thing (Exch. Q.R.M.R., Pasch. 20 Eliz., m. 75; Hil. 21 Eliz., m. 76ff).

[71] *Acts P.C.*, Eliz., IX, 385.

[72] In Essex from 1559 to 1603, a total of 33 under the clauses of the Cloth Acts enumerated in Tables 5 and 6 above, and under the Act of 1563 (seven-year term). In Norfolk, 42, all under the Act of 1563. The absence of cases under the Cloth Acts in Norfolk is natural in a county where broadcloth manufacture always had been of minor importance.

Dutch at Colchester in 1568, but so little is heard of it that it may never have been extensive in Essex. Manufacture of the "new draperies" by English workers seems to have developed only slowly; the chief signs of growth of a native industry in the "new draperies" belong to the early seventeenth century. An old specialty of the Coggeshall area, a white cloth, seems to have had sufficient resemblance to the new "bays" to have acquired their name, a testimony to the saleability of the newer worsteds.[73] The demand for these developed in part with the rising standards in house-furnishings of the middle class, especially in hangings and coverings, since cushions, coverlets, and carpets were typical worsted end-products.[74] There was also some kersey-making in the county.[75]

No special study has yet been published of conditions in these branches of the Essex textile industry during Elizabeth's reign or later.[76] There is no positive evidence now available of growth in the broadcloth or kersey industries other than the additional exemption in 1585 of two villages, Boxted and Langham, from the prohibition on rural clothmaking.[77] Signs of stress in 1577 have been mentioned, and again in 1590 clothiers of Suffolk, Essex, and Norfolk petitioned

[73] Yet "Coggeshall bays" were listed among new draperies in the alnage grant for these in 1578 (N. J. Williams, "Two Documents concerning the New Draperies," *The Economic History Review*, Second Series, IV, No. 3, 354); and see n. 75 below.

[74] Heaton, *Yorkshire Industries*, 264–265; Hoskins, *Essays*, 59–65, 117–118.

[75] This sketch is based on *Victoria History of Essex*, II, 382ff; Unwin, *Studies*, Chapter VII; the statutes of 1552, 1557, 1559 (exempting three Essex villages from the country clothmaking restrictions), 1585 (exempting two more); references in the state papers, and the evidence of Westminster informations. For the mention of markets, Unwin, *Studies*, VII; Friis, *Alderman Cockayne's Project*, passim; *Tudor Economic Documents*, III, 173–199 ("Project for a Staple at Ipswich"); *Cal. S.P.D.*, Eliz., Addenda, 1566–1579, 356. The basic difference between the old East Anglian worsteds and the "new draperies" was in the weft, which in the former was of combed wool like the warp, in the latter of carded wool or of silk or cotton (Friis, 2; Heaton, 268). The Coggeshall "whites" were called "handywarps," which suggests that their warp was of thread spun by hand on the rock and distaff instead of the tighter thread of the wheel; after weaving they were treated to look like bays. On English in the new draperies, see the statute of 1609 (7 Jas. I, c. 7); T. Cromwell, *History and Description of . . . Colchester*, II, 286–287; *Victoria History of Essex*, II, 390. For kersey-making, the only source is the prosecutions for clothmaking, Exch. Q.R.M.R., Trin. 5 Eliz., m. 129–130d.; Hil. 7 Eliz., m. 88d., etc.

[76] The discussion of the Suffolk "old" and "new" draperies in Unwin, *Studies*, 262–301, contains mention of Essex, but the essays do not deal with the problem of trends of growth or decline.

[77] 27 Eliz., c. 23.

to have the standard dimensions of "Suffolk" cloth modified.[78] It can be assumed that the Essex prosecutions on the Cloth Acts and the Act of 1563 were in the broadcloth and kersey branches, not the new draperies, with the exception of two cases involving baymakers.[79] The timing of the Essex cases contrasts in one respect with those of Devon, one-half of the former having been in the years 1577–1585 whereas the majority of the Devon cases antedated 1571; but, as in the southwest, textile prosecutions in Essex virtually disappear after 1585. They are too few to analyze from the standpoint of short-run business fluctuations.[80]

There is no more reason for Essex than for the broadcloth districts of the southwest to assume so effective a self-enforcement of apprenticeship that it could have withstood much pressure to increase quickly the supply of textile labor. Essex did not lack active professional informers, two of whom brought also prosecutions in the southwest. If the apparent lack of professional interest in offenders from the textile crafts in this county corresponds to a condition of no marked advance in the older branches of the industry,[81] the absence of recorded prosecution by textile workers themselves suggests, as in Wiltshire, no marked depression either. An occasional prosecution of an unapprenticed weaver by one of the craft occurs in the sessions rolls, but not till 1614 is there evidence of attempted control of conditions of employment by a local "company" of weavers, one at Coggeshall.[82] This year affords the first glimpse of craft

[78] *Tudor and Stuart Proclamations*, Nos. 823, 824.

[79] Only the prosecutions for unapprenticed and country clothmaking under the Act of 1557 state the type of cloth made by the defendants. In fourteen of the Essex cases of this sort, eight were for kersey-making, four for broadcloth, two for bays. One of the baymakers, in 1579, was a Henry Freeman of Maldon (Exch. Q.R.M.R., Trin. 21 Eliz., m. 80); in 1577 a Mr. Henry Freeman, stapler, was the subject of complaint by the Coggeshall clothiers as a dealer in wool, making bays at Maldon "to the hindrance of all clothiers" (S.P.D. Eliz., CXIV, No. 47). An informal complaint against a fustian-maker was apparently entered at quarter sessions in Essex in 1602. See below, Chap. IX, n. 70.

[80] The three-year intervals in which occurred the largest numbers of the Essex prosecutions were: 1565–1567, six cases; 1583–1585, eight. All were professional. Both sets of years were prosperous, as gauged by broadcloth exports from London.

[81] Most of the textile prosecutions in Essex in Elizabeth's reign were by professionals, with the exception of two at Colchester in 1583 for unapprenticed weaving and perhaps four at and near Chelmsford in 1563 for unapprenticed kersey-making. There are no prosecutions of textile crafts in quarter sessions until the seventeenth century, the few thereafter being chiefly nonprofessional.

[82] Cal. Q.S., XIX, 156, S.R. 206/105, Easter 12 Jas. I, recognizance of Daniel

organizations in the industrial market towns and villages similar to those in Wiltshire and sufficiently formal in structure to act through "wardens." [83] The notorious depression of the early 1620's was felt in the effort of the company of weavers in the village of Bocking to prevent unemployment for journeymen; and in 1627–28, at a time of local recession in the Essex manufacture of new draperies and apparently also in that of woolen cloth, the Bocking company renewed its efforts at control.[84] Proof of the kind of conditions associated with such attempts of craftsmen to enforce apprenticeship restrictions comes from the same district in the following year. The weavers of Bocking and Braintree petitioned the justices at the Easter sessions of 1629 for relief, alleging a want of work for the past six years, and this complaint was supported by a second petition from Bocking residents about the "lamentable condition" of the town and the decline of trade.[85]

Industrial life in Norfolk centered chiefly in the worsted manufacture, in which Norwich was dominant. How widely distributed through the county either worsted making or the new draperies were at this period is not known. Some broadcloth of the Suffolk type was manufactured.[86]

The apprenticeship prosecutions in textile crafts in Norfolk can be

---

Sutton to answer for discharging three journeymen before their year's term ended.

[83] The view that guilds seldom existed in "non-autonomous market towns" may require modification (Heckscher, *Mercantilism*, I, 243).

[84] Cal. Q.S., XIX, 492, S.R. 239/49, Epiph. 20 Jas. I, recognizances of nine weavers of Bocking and adjacent villages to answer for keeping an illegal proportion of apprentices to journeymen, and like offenses, including three rare examples of the application of the property qualification of the Act of 1563 for apprenticeship to country weaving. For the 1627–28 cases, *ibid.*, XX, 137, S.R. 259/40 and 41, 219, S.R. 265/73; *Cal. S.P.D.*, Chas. I, 1627–28, 156, complaint in April 1627 of decay in trade of new draperies at Colchester.

[85] Cal. Q.S., XX, 233, S.R. 266/120, 121.

[86] On the worsted industry, *The Records of the City of Norwich*, ed. W. Hudson and J. C. Tingey, II, *passim*; Moens, *The Walloons and Their Church . . .*, passim. Both Yarmouth and Lynn shared in its development. Apprenticeship indentures enrolled at Norwich in Elizabeth's reign suggest that the town of North Walsham was the center of a worsted-weaving district (*Register*, 226, 231). The city officials claimed in 1578 that a variety of figured worsteds introduced by the aliens was being made everywhere "in all parts of the country . . . as other the strangers' commodities be" (Moens, 77). The location of the broadcloth industry in the county is also unknown. The absence of prosecutions under the Cloth Acts (see above, n. 72) leaves no available source of this kind by which to map the distribution of woolen manufactures.

divided, with minor exceptions, into two distinct groups. About one-half of the total forty-two refer to textiles of undeterminable kind.[87] The other group may provide a clue to an otherwise unidentified expansion in the 1580's. These cases concerned weavers in villages of the southeast, along or near the Suffolk border, the district in which a fairly definite localization of linen-making is known to have existed by the latter seventeenth century.[88] Only five of the offenders are specified as linenweavers, but the region and the identity of the informers in the various prosecutions (five local professionals of whom three were from the northeast Suffolk linen district) make it a safe assumption that the others were also in linen-making.[89] Confirmation of the sixteenth-century location of the industry here is to be found in a series of informations twenty years later in the Norfolk quarter sessions against men in this area described as linenweavers, some of whom bear the same family name as offenders prosecuted at Westminster in the 1580's.[90]

All but three of the twenty informations against the linenweavers in the southeast were brought in the years 1581–1585, the remainder and three repetitions in 1586. Like the prosecutions in the woolen industry observed elsewhere, they appear to belong to a period of growth which had slackened by the second half of the decade. There is little in apprenticeship prosecutions in other counties to suggest a more general development in this branch of the textile industries.[91]

[87] Of this group, however, 12 prosecutions, brought by one professional in 1568 at country villages near Norwich, Aylsham, and East Dereham may reflect some effort by the Norwich russell-weavers to restrain growth outside the city (Exch. Q.R.M.R., Mich. 10 Eliz., m. 303–303d., 309–310d., 317–318d., 320–320d.).

[88] The medieval linen industry in Norfolk had flourished in the northeast, in Aylsham and other towns. One information was brought in 1581, probably by a nonprofessional, against a linenweaver near Aylsham (Q.B.C.R., Hil. 24 Eliz., m. 91).

[89] Two of the five informers have already been introduced, John Chambers and Nicholas Wright. For the cases: Exch. Q.R.M.R., Hil. 28 Eliz., m. 152–153d., Pasch. 28 Eliz., m. 116d.; Q.B.C.R., Hil. 25 Eliz., m. 106, Pasch. 25 Eliz., m. 72, 77, Hil. 26 Eliz., m. 92, 149, Pasch. 26 Eliz., m. 103, 105, Trin. 26 Eliz., m. 59, Hil. 27 Eliz., m. 55, Mich. 27/28 Eliz., m. 165, Hil. 28 Eliz., m. 59, 113, 148, Trin. 28 Eliz., m. 40, 145, 164, Mich. 28/29 Eliz., m. 107–108.

[90] MS. Sess. Rolls, 2 Jas. I, Mich. Sess. at Norwich; 3 Jas. I, Easter Sess. at Norwich, Epiph. Sess. at Norwich.

[91] In Suffolk there is one known prosecution of a linenweaver in 1586 and seven of weavers in 1581–1585 who cannot be identified without knowledge of the district in which the offenders were living. Two cases in Kent and one in Lancashire, between 1586 and 1589, make up the total observed in the West-

The preceding review of textile prosecutions shows them, in all the principal clothmaking regions surveyed, to agree in their decrease after 1585 with the external evidence for a recession in the woolen industry beginning in 1586, with a local recession indicated earlier in Devon and related districts. But the timing of apprenticeship prosecutions in three other occupations provides cause to question how far the decline in the various branches of the textile industry coincided with a downturn in other business activity. The three are food processing, retailing, and nailmaking. At least in part, the pressure of employment of which the apprenticeship cases in these crafts and trades are a symptom was the result of war-time demand and can be confirmed by independent observation. Unfortunately the exclusion of apprenticeship informations from Westminster after 1589 precludes tracing their correspondence with business conditions beyond this year, except in one area and occupation. The closing decade of the century requires a careful study of its uneven texture of boom and slump, prosperity and near-famine, which is beyond the scope of the present work.

The volume of trade was not at once affected by the disturbances in the Continental markets. It may, on the contrary, have been expanded by the war threats and preparations of these years. Sir Francis Walsingham's receipts from his farm of the customs at various outports appear to have reached their peak in the fiscal year beginning Michaelmas 1587, though they declined in the following year to somewhat less than in 1585/86 and 1586/87.[92] Not until the spring of 1589 did Walsingham petition the Queen for release from accumulated arrears of rent, on the ground that revenues were seriously reduced by restraints of trade, troubles in France, and fear of war with Spain.[93] From 1585 to 1590 the shipping employed by the Turkish and Venetian trades increased, and in spite of the times a considerable intercourse was maintained with the eastern Medi-

---

minster courts. These informations were in the Coram Rege Rolls and, since in counties not among the selected group, were not noted in detail.

[92] C. Read, *Mr. Secretary Walsingham*, III, 388. Professor Read mentions the "enormous increase in the net return" between 1584 and 1590 as "no doubt largely due to a very considerable expansion of trade in spite of wars and rumors of wars" (391). The general impression of an overall increase is no doubt sufficiently reliable, despite the tricks played on customers' entries in outports such as King's Lynn (N. J. Williams, "Francis Shaxton and the Elizabethan Port Books," *The English Historical Review*, LXVI, No. 260, 387–395).

[93] Read, III, 386.

terranean in 1589–1591.[94] Even to embargoed areas on the Continent, licenses to trade could be obtained.[95]

Meanwhile the domestic market for foodstuffs was increased by the mustering of troops in areas near the coasts and the victualling of the Navy, and local dealers must have felt the stimulus. Those of London had to be ordered to divert supplies.[96] There was also the spur of a prolonged period of scarcity and high prices, felt from the late winter of 1586 into 1587. To judge from mention in the state papers, the smuggling of commodities outward to the Continent was on the increase.[97]

In counties within London's metropolitan area, prosecutions in the Westminster courts of unapprenticed processors of foods exceeded in the four years 1586–1589 any ten-year period earlier.[98] In Essex, cases involving the food crafts and trades were as numerous in 1586–1589 as in the whole reign theretofore; in Norfolk they were more than in any previous five-year interval.[99] In both counties prosecutions of brewers accounted for most of the concentration in the late 1580's. The location of the six in Essex at this time, close to a supply of hops, has already been mentioned.[100] An interesting sidelight on the demand for hops is given by a group of prosecutions for haircloth-weaving at the village of Wethersfield in the hop-growing district of Essex. Here the six intruders constituted a massive increase without doubt in the numbers engaged in this obscure occupation

[94] Cheyney, *History of England*, I, 389, 394.

[95] See *Cal. S.P.D.*, Addenda, 1580–1625, 156, licenses granted by Walsingham's deputies for trade with St. Malo. Exeter merchants were permitted in January 1590 to resume trade with France via the Channel Islands (*Acts P.C.*, Eliz., XVIII, 311). Control apparently became tighter in succeeding years; see above in this chapter.

[96] *Acts P.C.*, Eliz., XVI, 204, order that the "beerbrewers and others occupying the trade of conveying of beer to and fro" should supply the troops in Essex and Kent, 30 July 1588.

[97] For example, *Cal. S.P.D.*, Addenda, 1580–1625, 176–177 (illegal shipments from London and Essex to Dunkirk, 1585); 232 (Bristol merchants supplying Spain with munitions and provisions, 1587); 251–252 (smuggling by the Hythe town officials, one of whom was a butcher, of horses, tallow, oats, "ready killed beef and pork in barrels," 1588).

[98] The cases are tabulated from the Exch. Q.R. Agenda Books and Q.B.C.R. Rolls. The total in 1586–1589 was 82; the next highest had been 53 in the five years 1581–1585.

[99] A total of 8 in Essex in 1586–1589, and 10 in Norfolk. There were no food-processing cases in Essex quarter sessions before 1590.

[100] See above, Chap. IV, n. 85. All six were in 1589.

whose product was utilized in drying malt and hops.[101] Meanwhile in the hops- and food-handling retail trade of chandler, five offenders had been proceeded against between 1587 and 1589, four of them in the London area at Barking and Epping. In Norfolk, the occurrence in 1586–1588 of two-thirds of the county's retailing cases (in mercery and drapery) during the decade may have been associated with dealing in foods, but more probably with the increased flow of trade through the Norfolk ports.

The evident activity in the brewing industry was reflected by apprenticeship prosecution less strongly in Norfolk, the county where it might most have been expected.[102] This was perhaps owing to the apparently marked localization of the industry during the sixteenth century in Norfolk's three largest centers with their autonomous jurisdictions. But in prosecutions of bakers also, the effects of the scarcity years of 1587–1588 show more clearly in apprenticeship prosecutions in other counties than in either Norfolk or Essex. For all other shires in these two years, such prosecutions were about two-fifths of their aggregate in the Elizabethan period, the response to scarcity prices not so much for the actual exercise of the craft of baking as for the chance to secure a license for grain-dealing on a small scale.[103]

Only a faint echo of the continued stimulus to the provision trades in the 1590's provided by the needs of the armed forces is found in the Essex sessions records, in prosecutions in 1594–97 of brewers at Maldon and of bakers and millers at and near Barking and Epping.[104]

[101] Cal. Q.S., XV, 177, S.R. 111/2, Epiph. 32 Eliz., a list of offenders in bail. The hair-weavers were two yeomen, two tailors, a smith and a shoemaker. The prosecutor is not named. Despite the importance of maltmaking and brewing in Norfolk, only three "hair-makers" or "hair-weavers" were admitted to the freedom of the city of Norwich in the course of more than a century (*Register*, 84). One professional information against a hair-weaver accompanied a number of prosecutions of brewers in Norfolk quarter sessions in 1615.

[102] Only five prosecutions of brewers in 1586–1589; but this was a third of the Norfolk total of Elizabethan Westminster prosecutions of brewers, the same proportion as in all other counties combined.

[103] The pattern of London development, with city and county retailers competing as middlemen with the wholesale traders — the mealmen, maltsters, and millers — was no doubt repeated in miniature in and around provincial towns. Favorable conditions must have drawn temporarily into food processing a number of little men, just as small traders moved in and out of the coastwise grain trade according to the situation of the moment. (Gras, *English Corn Market*, 195–196, 198n; Fisher, "London Food Market," *passim*.)

[104] Cal. Q.S., XVI, 180, S.R. 128/81, Midsummer, 36 Eliz.; XVII, 36, S.R.

But there is possible confirmation from this county that the decade was not one of unrelieved decline in the rarity of presentments by local juries in Essex quarter sessions, between 1592 and 1600, of "single-men working at their own hands." Such men competed with those in settled employment and with married householders, and efforts to suppress them appear to accompany disturbed conditions and unemployment.

Apprenticeship prosecutions in one county only have survived from the last decade of the sixteenth century in sufficient numbers to trace a pattern of industrial activity confirming the existence of rising demand and employment in individual industries. In the metalworking district of south Staffordshire a series of professional informations against unapprenticed metalworkers, the majority nailmakers, is too prolonged to attribute merely to accidental factors.[105] From 1583 through 1601, a total of 28 or 29 cases were recorded in the sessions records and the Westminster courts, most of them after 1590.[106] The relative dimensions of this campaign can be realized by comparison with the total of 44 Elizabethan apprenticeship cases in metalworking crafts from all counties.[107]

138/47. The second set were laid before quarter sessions in the early summer of 1597, among years of extremest scarcity and high prices. They were informations by the professional Edward Hedd whose name had occasionally appeared in the files since the mid-nineties in informations for engrossing. There might be a larger number of apprenticeship cases to record were it not for the loss of some whole sessions in this decade. A statute of 1593, requiring the return of beer barrels or an equivalent amount of clapboard from overseas, testifies to a continued export of beer in quantity; so does the complaint in 1595 from the London Coopers' Company of apprentices who set up for themselves outside the company's jurisdiction before completing their terms (35 Eliz., c. 11; *Acts P.C.*, Eliz., XXV, 60). Casks were among the "sea victuals" reported as having risen in price 100 per cent and more between 1584 and 1595 (*Cal. S.P.D.*, Eliz., 1595–1597, 101).

[105] The local professionals who brought most of the series were introduced in Chap. II above.

[106] The metal crafts represented by the offenders were: 18 or 19 nailers, 5 smiths, 3 bucklemakers, 1 bitmaker, 1 pewterer. Almost two-thirds of the cases after 1590 occurred in the years 1594–1596, a tendency to bunching found among the few apprenticeship informations still brought in the Exchequer after 1589. From all counties and occupations, these are the most frequent in 1594–1596 and 1598–1602. Examination of the Coram Rege Rolls during this decade would probably add to the total and might agree with the Exchequer distribution by years.

[107] In nearly half of the total from all counties, the offenders were blacksmiths, and about one-quarter were cutlers.

Most of the Staffordshire offenders lived in the district between Wolverhampton and Birmingham, which overlapped the area where exploitation of the coal mines had been accelerating.[108] Access to larger supplies of fuel helped metalworkers of the region to fill an increasing demand. Nailmaking must have become part of the "war industry" requirements of these years — for the pioneer contingents, for shipbuilding (so far as the increase in shipping came from home-built ships),[109] for new construction at the ports.[110] Meanwhile there was an enlarging market in the equipment of coal mines and salt pans, and in the continued new building in London itself as well as the increase in the "cottages without four acres of land." [111] How far the impact of these nonlocal demands was transmitted to the midland metalworking areas is another question. It has been thought that until the seventeenth century the London market for ironmongery was supplied from London sources.[112] Apprenticeship cases witness to some increase in smithing and cutlery-making in the London area, but a greater localization of nailmaking is implied by the absence of Exchequer prosecutions of nailers from any area except south Staffordshire. Nails may have been marketed more widely than other ironmongery such as the farm implements, harness, and house equipment, which were turned out by local smiths all over the country. A more than local market had developed, however, for the ironmongery of Staffordshire.[113] By the beginning of James I's reign, Walsall dealers took their wares to London, in spite of the bad roads thither. This town, lying a little to the northwest of what seems to have been the chief nailmaking district, was not only a center of production of saddlers' ironmongery but apparently both of the wholesale handicraft system and the putting-out system which existed side by side in nailmaking and the manufacture of other

[108] Nef, *British Coal Industry*, I, 65–66.

[109] Nef, I, 173, 173n.

[110] See for example a memorandum of 1594 that the victualing of 8000 men for three months requires that advance orders be given to prepare storehouses, breweries, and bakehouses at Portsmouth and Dover (*Cal. S.P.D.*, Eliz., 1591–1594, 420).

[111] Nails were a frequent purchase by the corporation of Stratford-on-Avon for repairs and new construction (*Minutes and Accounts*, passim).

[112] Court, *Midland Industries*, 134.

[113] Even in the fifteenth century, London grocers had among their debtors some nailers of Lancashire and Staffordshire (Thrupp, "The Grocers of London," 276). By 1590 bar iron came to Walsall from as far away as Nottingham (Nef, *British Coal Industry*, I, 171n).

small iron wares, as in so much of the woolen industry. A petition of 1603, which serves to illuminate the organization of the metalworking crafts, complains (as of a recent development) of a shift of former craftsmen from Walsall into trading in iron and in the finished goods. There is strong evidence of recent expansion too in one of the regulations sought by the craftsmen, that no nailer was to employ more workers at once "than shall dwell in his own (house or shop)."[114]

The pressures of recent growth in the nailmaking industry are probably already to be seen in a bill of 1585 which never became law. This was aimed at applying the seven-year term of apprenticeship specifically to nailmaking as "a trade of itself," as well as to limiting the apprentices to two for every journeyman hired; apprentices were to be prohibited from setting up for themselves until they were thirty years old or married (another application of provisions of the Statute of Artificers).[115] The type of regulation sought here, however, is defensive, reminiscent of the Wiltshire weavers in 1603 and similar to legislation proposed for nailmaking in 1621, a year of undoubted decline in business activity.[116] The combined evidence of proposals for regulation, of apprenticeship prosecutions, and of market conditions sketches a rough pattern of fluctuations in the nailing industry: "good years" in the early 1580's; a setback about 1585; renewed and vigorous expansion from the late 1580's with the best years perhaps over by 1595; recession in the early 1600's.

Nailmaking was not confined to south Staffordshire. The bill of 1585 was to apply to Staffordshire, Worcestershire, and Shropshire; the petitioners of 1603 described themselves as of the counties of Stafford, Warwickshire, Worcestershire, and Shropshire, and these are the four counties enumerated in the bill of 1621.[117] The lack of

[114] *Staffordshire Quarter Sessions Rolls*, V, 19. Trin. Sess. 1 Jas. I. In the interest of the small handicraftsmen, chapmen and "drivers" of ironmongery were also to be prohibited from putting out iron. The reply of the Walsall chapmen refers to carrying wares "to London and elsewhere" and claims that without them the poorer sort of craftsmen, lacking ready money, would be unable to supply themselves with iron.

[115] *Victoria History of Worcestershire*, II, 272; *Staffordshire Rolls*, I, 288.

[116] Court, *Midland Industries*, 61; *Commons Debates*, VII, 141, App. A. The bill was phrased as for "the handicraftsmen in iron and steel" but was endorsed as "Bill concerning the nailers."

[117] There were minor localizations of nailmaking elsewhere, as in the Forest of Dean (Tawneys, "An Occupational Census," 44, quoting the 1608 return of

comparable series of apprenticeship prosecutions for the three counties other than Staffordshire is attributable partly to differing survival of sessions records, partly to a competing jurisdiction, partly perhaps to differing rates of growth. Even for Staffordshire the cases in the Exchequer are too few to suggest a definite pattern, so that the lack of sessions records for Warwickshire may hide a movement similar to that of Staffordshire. Shropshire was omitted from the present study, but like Worcestershire came within the special jurisdiction of the Court of the Marches of Wales.[118]

For the seventeenth century, lack of knowledge and space prevents even so tentative a sketch of business fluctuations in particular industries and trades as has been ventured for Elizabeth's reign. Evidence both of the sequence of apprenticeship prosecutions and of business conditions is even less adequate than earlier. But the occurrence of apprenticeship cases in the best surviving series of sessions records tends to confirm impressions derived from the Elizabethan distribution. The course of apprenticeship prosecution throughout emphasizes such distinct economic characteristics and patterns of change differentiating the various regions that analysis of times of "good" and "bad" trade applied to the national economy as a unit would appear likely to be unrewarding, except for the major depressions. That beginning in 1621 or 1622, for example, is traceable in apprenticeship prosecution by a general decrease, affecting principally 1623–1625; in Norfolk it was evident after the April quarter sessions of 1622. As "tracers" for conditions of stress or of activity in individual industries, the apprenticeship cases suggest furthermore the presence of such varying short-term fluctuations that discussion of general alternations will require wide and detailed "business annals" so far as these can be pieced together.[119] As an illustration, the inci-

---

54 nailmakers for the county); and in the West Riding near Wakefield and Bradford (*Sessions Rolls 1598–1602*, I, 203).

[118] The Council of the Marches certainly intervened in cases within the jurisdiction of the city of Worcester: in 1575, it ordered a stay of process in a suit pending before the city bailiffs against a blacksmith for lack of apprenticeship, until the charge should have been heard before the Court of the Marches (Worcester MS. Liber Recordum, entry of year 1575–1576, the order dated from Shropshire).

[119] In an unpublished paper delivered before a Huntington Library seminar in 1941, the late Edwin Francis Gay suggested that "detailed study of the cause and character of earlier fluctuations should show that the 'random perturbations' do not, after all, play a much more decisive part in them than in

dence of apprenticeship cases in Wiltshire, Somerset, and Norfolk, may be examined for the reign of James I.

The period begins for Wiltshire before James's accession, after a probable interval of increased production. Symptoms of declining employment and, it would seem, of pressure to reduce costs, are visible in the numerous presentments brought in 1602 and 1603 by Westbury weavers, two of whom were entitled cloth-searchers, against unapprenticed competitors — those who took apprentices and journeymen contrary to the provisions of the Act of 1563, and those operating too many looms. Local and central authorities intervened, with approval in quarter sessions of orders for the weavers' companies and with the enactment of compulsory minimum wage-fixing for textile workers.[120] But in 1605 there was another though smaller effort to suppress the same sort of offenses.[121] Petitions in 1647 by weavers of Westbury and Devizes for better enforcement of the 1603 regulations tend to confirm the reading of the earlier situation as one of local distress, for 1647 was a year of unemployment in the broadcloth industry, at least in the northern part of the county.[122] Meanwhile in Norfolk the outburst of professional prosecution of linen-weavers in 1605–06 suggests a condition of expansion in contrast to the apparent Wiltshire slump.

those of the nineteenth century." Within obvious limits, the study of apprenticeship cases as reflecting variations in employment tends to bear this out.

[120] Wiltshire MS. Minute Books from July, 44 Eliz. to Oct., 1 Jas. I. On the opening years of the seventeenth century in the Wiltshire woolen industry, see Ramsay, pp. 61–62, 71, who treats them as comparatively prosperous. Cheap apprentice labor in place of journeymen, the hiring of unqualified journeymen or their employment for less than the legal term of a year, and the obvious pressure on wages might all have accompanied a quick upturn in production, but are more likely to have been the subject of court action by craftsmen when employment had slackened. See the similar response by Essex weavers in 1623, n. 82 and n. 84 above. Exchequer prosecutions in the textile industries under the Cloth Acts, as well as the Act of 1563, continued to be scanty during the reign of James I, either as the result of the Act of 1589 or because conditions in the textile industries did not attract professional informers. The Act of 1603 for minimum wage assessment, 1 Jas. I., c. 6.

[121] MS. Sessions Rolls and Minute Books April and Oct., 3 Jas. I. At the July Sessions a long list of clothiers were presented for not paying wages according to the statute; it includes two of the prosecutors of 1602–03.

[122] Hist. MSS. Comm., *Various*, I, 114; MS. Sessions Rolls, Easter 23 Chas. I. In July some of the petitioners appear as prosecutors of unapprenticed broadcloth weavers, and at the same sessions broadweavers from the region around Calne and Chippenham complain of a "great want of work" (MS. Sessions Rolls, Trin. 23 Chas. I).

In Somerset, signs of possible strain in the west Somerset industry were visible in 1608–1610 and again in 1612 in apprenticeship prosecutions of weavers near Taunton and in and near Wellington, by craftsmen who appear in more indictments than they could probably afford from their own purses.[123] Public presentments at quarter sessions in 1608, a year of grain scarcity, by juries for Taunton borough and for the hundred, of unapprenticed textile workers in Taunton and nearby may be associated with the complaint by the parish of Taunton St. James that it could not relieve half its poor who "do so fast increase." [124] In the following year, merchants of Chard were protesting that they had never recovered their losses in the 1590's.[125] Nevertheless, there were no prosecutions at this period of offenses under the other provisions of the Act of 1563, and attempts by the working weavers to restrict entry into the industry might have accompanied an increase in production and employment instead of a decrease. Conditions of these years, therefore, in the west Somerset textile industry must remain uncertain.

In years usually considered to be those of active trade, from 1613 into 1616, conditions in Somerset about which little is known evoked both professional and other private prosecutions of unapprenticed brewers, bakers and butchers.[126] There was no parallel activity in Wiltshire, although professional informers were operating in that county, and though the spring of 1614 was marked by riots in the clothing districts because of a severe grain shortage.[127] But in Norfolk there was a similar though larger wave of wholly professional inform-

[123] Somerset MS. Indictment Rolls, Trin. 6 Jas. I to 10 Jas. I.

[124] *Ibid.*, Trin. 6 Jas. I; *Quarter Sessions Records for the County of Somerset*, XXIII, 29.

[125] E. Green, "On the History of Chard," *Somerset Arch. and Nat. Hist. Soc. Procs.*, XXVIII, Pt. 2, 55. The merchants may have been exaggerating their poverty since they were refusing — like other southwest towns — to join a proposed corporation for trade with France (*Cal. S.P.D.*, Jas. I, 1603–1610, 516–517, 534–535).

[126] Scott, *Joint-Stock Companies*, I, 141, 465, classifies these among his "good" years until the disturbance to the woolens market caused by the Cockayne experiment began to be felt in the broadcloth districts. The prosecutions in Somerset were geographically distinct: those against brewers concentrated at Taunton; of bakers mostly in the busy industrial and trading area of Dunster and its vicinity; of butchers, at Axbridge on the edge of the mining district of the Mendips, and between Axbridge and the coast, at places such as Mark and Weare where in the late eighteenth century were lands described as rich and with many small dairy and grazing farms (Collinson, *Somerset*, I, 182, 184).

[127] Ramsay, *The Wiltshire Woollen Industry*, 71–72; *Acts P.C.*, Jas. I, I, 457.

ing against brewers and bakers. In this county, a common denominator in the situations of the food-processing trades in 1613–1616, 1621, and 1631–32 may have been the inducement already mentioned to temporary newcomers to enter small-scale wholesaling, especially in a county producing and exporting grain in such quantity as Norfolk. This was the opportunity to get licenses from quarter sessions, under guise of baker, brewer, and the like, for the purchase of grain ostensibly to process. During the reign of Charles I, Somerset like Norfolk had relatively numerous professional informations against food processors, though in a more continuous series from 1627 through 1631.[128] Their activity seems to have been little affected by the recession in the textile industry which began in or before 1629,[129] unlike Wiltshire, Essex, and Norfolk where no apprenticeship cases or very few are recorded for the years 1629–1630. Continuing food shortages and the plague marked the year 1630. The plague's varying severity in the towns during 1630–31 may in part account for subsequent apprenticeship prosecutions here and there against country intruders. At Preston in Lancashire, the local drapers proceeded in 1634 against country retailers within a radius of some nine miles who had set up without qualification during "that woefull tyme" when Preston had been decimated by plague for a twelvemonth.[130] A commentary on the relation between the number of prosecutions and of offenses is found here: eleven or twelve retailers were actually named in the Preston company's complaint, but their petition to the Privy Council for assistance claimed that "where there was almost no trading in the country, not above three or four men, in the same compass there is fifty or sixty. . . ." Allowing for normal exaggeration, the discrepancy illustrates a probably frequent selection of a few offenders to prosecute as a warning to the remainder.

The Preston campaign was paralleled during 1633–1637 in Lancashire and near Chester by the efforts of several organized or semi-organized crafts in the towns to assert themselves against the compe-

[128] The large number of cases entered only as "contrary to 5 Eliz." has already been noted, and the actual range of occupations prosecuted may have been wider than appears.

[129] The onset of recession is variously assigned to 1628, early 1629, and late 1629 (Scott, *Joint-Stock Companies*, I, 193–194, 466; Leonard, *English Poor Relief*, 152–153). Evidence of localized recession in Essex as early as the beginning of 1628 or possibly some months before is mentioned above, n. 84.

[130] Wadsworth and Mann, *The Cotton Trade*, 58.

tition of countrymen said never to have been apprenticed. This defensive movement by trade interests seems to have occurred during a period of "good trade" (unless local difficulties existed), and demonstrates, if so, that nonprofessional prosecution might be undertaken during business activity as well as in business decline.[131] Not enough is known of conditions in 1637–38 to tell whether an increase at that time in both Somerset and Wiltshire of apparently nonprofessional prosecutions in foods, chiefly of bakers, corresponds to local "good trade" or to the reverse; but from 1636 possibly into 1638 there was decline in the woolen industry.[132] In the disturbed period from 1639, apprenticeship prosecution appears generally to have dropped.[133]

[131] *The Cotton Trade*, 60–61; see below, Chap. X, for references to the attitude of the Privy Council. On business conditions, see Scott's classification, I, 466. Improvement in food supply and local order may be gauged by the decrease in monthly reports from justices of the peace after their first year following the council order of January 1631. Nearly a hundred of these certificates are known before 1632, but thereafter each year appears to record fewer until 1635. (Tabulated by the writer from Leonard, *English Poor Relief*, passim, and from originals in S.P.D. Chas. I.) Their distribution in every year but 1631 is concentrated in certain divisions of only a few counties. See Leonard, 159, on negligence in making the returns.

[132] Scott, I, 217, 466; Leonard, 160, 163. Monthly certificates of the justices of the peace increased in number in 1636–37.

[133] Except in Nottinghamshire, where because of some special situation in saddlery-making, there was a renewal in 1639–40 of professional informations first brought in 1633–34 against offenders in this occupation. In Essex also there was a bunching of prosecutions of bakers, partly in quarter sessions by nonprofessionals, partly in assizes by a London professional.

VI

EFFECTIVENESS OF PRIVATE INTERESTS

An effort to appraise the effectiveness of private agencies, professional and other, as enforcers of the apprenticeship requirement naturally begins with the record of results achieved in prosecutions. For analysis of results, the cases have been classified as "effective," "ineffective," and "inconclusive." The first class includes instances of (a) conviction, with or without entry of fines imposed; (b) admission to fine and (c) license to compound on informations. The second includes (a) acquittals; (b) dismissals, discontinuances, and pardons; (c) removals to a higher court, unless the final outcome in the upper court is known to be "effective" [1]; and (d) rejections of bills of indictment by the grand jury, or "ignoramuses." The third is made up of cases with no record of proceedings or an incomplete one.

In the Elizabethan Westminster courts, the proportion of effective results was virtually the same for both classes of prosecutors, the professional and all others,[2] about one-fifteenth of the total; ineffective, about one-eighth for the professional, from one-eleventh to one-sixth for the others. For each class, about four-fifths of the total were "inconclusive." Of the Westminster cases in the reign of James I, nearly all the professional and all the others are inconclusive; two

[1] Removals by certiorari have been included in the "ineffective" rather than the "inconclusive" class on the assumption that if the defendant had the funds and a sufficiently strong case to appeal, the deterrent effect of prosecution was unlikely to be appreciable whatever the final verdict. In the period 1563–1642, certioraris in apprenticeship cases appear to have been under one per cent of the total in the selected counties. Only two cases were found from the selected counties among those removed to the King's Bench by certiorari, in which a result was recorded: one was acquitted, the other dismissed.

[2] It will be remembered that the demarcation of the second class in the Westminster cases is very imprecise and the possible total small.

convictions were recorded among the professional informations. From 1625 to 1642, with only six original informations,[3] four were ineffective, two inconclusive.

In the one extant series of assizes prosecutions, one-sixth were effective, all these being nonprofessional; the remainder were inconclusive.[4] Results in quarter sessions cases differ from one period to the next. In Elizabeth's reign, the proportions both of effective and ineffective prosecutions by professionals were slightly higher than in other private prosecutions.[5] In the next reign, there were fewer effective professional cases though about the same proportion of the others. But a considerably larger share of the nonprofessional than of the professional prosecutions were recorded as ineffective.[6] From 1625 to 1642, the share of effective prosecutions by professionals slightly exceeded the nonprofessional, while again the latter had the greater proportion of recorded "ineffectives." [7] Over the whole eighty years, more than four-fifths of the professional prosecutions were inconclusive, over nine-tenths of the nonprofessional informations, but less than one-half of the indictments.[8]

The method of noting the history of a prosecution differed widely among the county sessions records. Norfolk has had to be omitted

[3] Five of the six were ex officio informations probably disguising professional informers; the sixth may be nonprofessional. The results in the few removals by certiorari traced in King's Bench are counted in the quarter sessions cases. It seems probable that the proportions in the results would not be very different even if the K.B. Coram Rege Rolls had been searched throughout the period 1603–1642.

[4] Or, seven cases out of a total of only forty-four in Essex Assizes, 1563–1642: they were in 1609 against Colchester bakers. A measure of their "effectiveness" is the size of the penalty, 3/4 apiece on the submission of the seven, the charge having been for a full year in each case. (Assizes, S. E. Circuit, Indictments, Bdle. 51, Lent 7 Jas. I.) For this circuit, the minute books, which probably contained notes on the results of prosecutions, have not survived.

[5] Professional cases: a little under one-tenth recorded as effective; perhaps nearly one-fifth as ineffective. Nonprofessional: less than one-twentieth effective; perhaps nearly one-seventh ineffective.

[6] Professional cases: from about one-eighth to less than one-tenth ineffective. Nonprofessional: about one-third ineffective.

[7] Professional cases: one-tenth or a little more, effective; under one-twentieth ineffective. Nonprofessional: less than one-tenth effective; one-third ineffective.

[8] All indictments have been classified as nonprofessional except for 9 (10 counting a repeat by a different informer) brought in Nottinghamshire in 1628–29 by professionals who had been prosecuting by information before then. A similar change from information to indictment occurred after 1636 in Somerset, but here the names of the prosecutors are not recorded in most of the entries.

from the foregoing analysis because of a complete lack of entries of process and results in the numerous apprenticeship cases there.[9] But it is clear enough that the direct effects of court prosecution were felt by a small minority of the defendants everywhere and in every period. From 1603 to 1625, the increased proportion of nonprofessional prosecutions definitely recorded as ineffective is due not only to better preservation of entry books of sessions proceedings but to the greater share of procedure by indictment with the consequent notation of those which were "ignoramus."[10] With these rejected bills, almost a sixth of the total indictments, and with acquittals forming over one-fifth, the proportion of recorded ineffective indictments in James I's reign rose to over one-half. From 1625 to 1642 it is not quite one-half, with discharges and rejected bills making up over two-thirds of all the "ineffectives" and about one-third of all the nonprofessional indictments of the period. Among the professional informations, however, in Somerset and Nottinghamshire the number of licensed compositions increased slightly and in Somerset several unlicensed compositions were detected and recorded.[11]

The terms "effective" and "inconclusive" need scrutiny. With both professional and other private informations, a recorded "effective" result meant licensed composition with or without admission to fine, fine and composition together making a penalty always well below the statutory level.[12] The actual penalty in an indictment, except in the rare instance of conviction followed by full fine,[13]

[9] The series of Books of Proceedings, containing a record of the issue of process and abstracts of the outcome in individual cases, is broken in the Norfolk files by a long gap for the period when all the apprenticeship cases before 1643 occurred in this county, i.e., from 1587 to 1639. In some counties, notations were made on the parchment bills of indictment filed in the roll for each sessions, but apparently not in Norfolk.

[10] As suggested in the preceding note, record of proceedings and results is found most often in the abstract of sessions proceedings kept in the minute books where these survive. But they do not contain usually any record of ignoramus bills, which are generally to be found in the sessions rolls.

[11] Some eight defendants in apprenticeship informations were fined for having compounded with the professional informers (MS. Sess. Min. Bk. of Recogniz. and Orders, Vol. 1620–1627, duplicate in rough draft, and *ibid.*, IV, 1627–1638, Regular Series). To penalize the defendants rather than the informers appears to be a unique innovation in Somerset, and one for which no statutory basis is known.

[12] See above, Chap. II, especially nn. 38, 39, 41, 43, 45–46.

[13] Some eight cases of the full fine for the number of months originally charged, in the whole period 1603–1642.

usually corresponded on the defendant's submission to the mitigated fine imposed with an information and might range from 6d. and 2/6 up to the full fine for the number of months charged in the indictment.[14] A tendency for the term of the original charge to be reduced by the jury in a verdict of guilty has been mentioned. In some twelve indictments before quarter sessions, in which this reduction was made, it ran from convicting for one month out of an original two months to a verdict for only one out of twelve months. Two practices persisting in at least one city court of quarter sessions have not been observed in any county, but unless some protest brought them to light they could not be known: mitigating a fine privately outside the sessions court, and remitting a part of a fine on payment.[15] The extent to which the so-called "effective" prosecutions, thus moderated, could actually oust defendants from their crafts and trades is commented on later in this chapter.

To what extent the large "inconclusive" group of prosecutions may be thought to contribute, if full details were available, to the "effectives" or their opposite depends chiefly on its composition. Where it is made up mostly of indictments, it must probably be assumed to belong to the "ineffectives." To judge from the Westminster courts, the lack of full entries is only in part the result of loss or of contemporary carelessness,[16] and to have a substantial proportion of incompleted cases was normal for a Tudor or Stuart law court. These apparently were simply dropped by the prosecutor or non-suited by the court. But the proportion of completed cases to all types of prosecutions is higher for quarter sessions, where procedure by indictment was so frequent, than for the Westminster courts in which the professional informer reigned. Moreover, within the quarter sessions record, the proportion of inconclusive cases is higher for informations in all three periods than for indictments. This similarity between the fate of informations in central and in local courts confirms the view previously stated that the informer did not push his cases to a con-

[14] About eight to ten cases of submission and six to eight of mitigated fine. So far as can be ascertained the defendant in an indictment, when he had submitted, did not pay the equivalent of a composition to the prosecutor.

[15] *Minutes of the Norwich Court of Mayoralty 1630–1631 . . .*, ed. W. L. Sachse, Norfolk Record Society, XV, 17, 218, 224.

[16] An entry on the wrapper of one sessions roll notes that "no process was filed to this sessions because the sheriff made no return or sent a writ." (Essex Cal. Q.S., XIX, 396, S.R. 229/62, Midsummer, 18 Jas. I.)

clusion in court if he could arrange a private settlement. In an undeterminable number of the inconclusive informations, a "penalty" on the offender may have been imposed through an unlicensed composition. To the extent that this tended to be higher than the amounts set by the courts, the professional's illegal methods were more "effective" than the correct procedures; and this may apply equally well to the comparatively few nonprofessionals using the information, since among these cases the proportion of incomplete entries is even higher than with the professional informer. So far as money penalties were any deterrent to setting up in a craft or trade without apprenticeship, the prosecutors who exacted a composition outside the court were relatively more effective agents of enforcement than those who kept within the law in prosecuting, or than public agencies whose cases seem as frequently to have been dismissed or dropped as any others.[17]

The relation between the level of monetary penalty and its preventive efficacy is problematical in all times and societies, but particularly in those so affected by inflationary trends as the Elizabethan and early Stuart periods. The impact of the lesser forfeitures is especially difficult to gauge for the incomes of the lower middle class, relatively rigid as many of these incomes tended to be. For the scores of little men among the informers' victims — textile workers, bakers, brewers, shopkeepers, many of them in tiny hamlets — payment to an informer must have been more than merely a nuisance tax on a going business. Yet men like John Otterey apparently found it worth their while to prosecute the scattered Devonshire weavers even though the craft had no reputation for prosperity — "the common speech is rife . . . to be a weaver's wife is to live poore." [18]

From scattered times and places come instances of intervention by authority to protect the unapprenticed worker from prosecution. Some of these will be discussed later as illustrations of the attitude of central and local government toward enforcing apprenticeship.[19] But that there should be occasion for such protective efforts proves that lawsuits could be a very real burden on defendants. During the

[17] See below, Chaps. VIII and IX, for prosecutions by public agencies. It is possible, but there is no way of testing how possible, that prosecutors by indictment even when nonprofessionals arranged out-of-court payments.

[18] *The Pepys Ballads,* ed. H. E. Rollins, II, 1625–1640, No. 73, "A Wench for a Weaver," c. 1630.

[19] See below, Chaps. IX–X.

attack on country competitors launched by various town groups in Lancashire and Cheshire in the 1630's, friends of a shoemaker of Frodsham, petitioning authority on his behalf, testified that prosecution for alleged lack of apprenticeship had forced him to leave his trade and sell all he had to defend himself. Intervention secured promises from the Chester Company of Shoemakers that neither this defendant nor a second also accused should be further prosecuted.[20] Escape from the same sort of pressure was sought in 1628 by a former tenant of Viscount Conway in Warwickshire who was charged before the assizes with using some trades without an apprenticeship. Lord Conway wrote to the judges of assize, suggesting that the suits were "only for vexation, of which there is some appearance by their [the prosecutors] putting in frequent indictments, and informations, and avoiding trials."[21] A generation earlier an impoverished gentleman of Sandwich was helped by the Privy Council to gain immunity from prosecution for adopting the trade of a baker in the town though he was never actually apprenticed to it.[22]

Occasionally local custom might be adapted to protect the unapprenticed. In corporate towns, marriage to a qualified person was generally recognized as one of the three modes of qualifying under the Act of 1563 in lieu of apprenticeship.[23] So in the North Riding in 1607, when two unapprenticed bakers of Thirsk were informed against, evidently as whipping boys for other offenders, the justices

[20] B.M. Harleian MS. 2104, f. 464, 469, 471. Authority in this instance was Thomas Lord Savage, chancellor to the queen consort; the petition itself is undated but his letter to the Recorder of Chester was 22 September 1633. His son, Sir John Savage, who like his father was a justice of the peace of Cheshire, also intervened.

[21] S.P.D., Chas. I, CIX, No. 45, letter from Secretary Conway to the judges of assize, July 7, 1628. John Wolmer, Conway's tenant, was probably identical with the John Wilmore of Stratford who was prosecuted by professional informers before quarter sessions in 1626 and 1635, on the second occasion (when he was termed "gentleman") for engrossing, on the first for an unknown charge. He may also be identical with the John Wilmore who was an "enterprising young ironmonger" of Stratford about 1585. (*Quarter Sessions Order Books*, I, 30, 229; *Minutes and Accounts . . . of Stratford . . .*, III, lix.) All this suggests that he was a prosperous merchant extending his business operations into several fields, whose case may offer another example of trade interests prosecuting on an apprenticeship charge during times of "good trade."

[22] *Acts P.C.*, Eliz., XXIV, 352, Privy Council's letter to the town authorities. This is an example of entry into an occupation as second best.

[23] The other two were by patrimony and by redemption.

of the peace appointed eight of the unapprenticed whose wives were qualified bakers to continue in the trade. The six among them who had thus been saved from prosecution were ordered to contribute one-half of the "charges and fines already spent and paid in defense of that trade upon the said informations" by the two previously accused.[24]

The hardships of prosecution or of informers' demands evoked appeals to the Privy Council from numerous other groups offending against various regulations. Repeated orders were issued to preserve the immunity of aliens in their principal communities from prosecutions for lack of apprenticeship, to stop informations for stretching cloth, and for dealing in wool, butter and cheese, or grain.[25] For the poorer defendants, the burden of any prosecution was not alone the fees or even the possible money penalty, but the loss of days of work while attending in court.[26] A tilemaker in Essex, indicted by a competitor in 1615 for not having served an apprenticeship, got neighbors to testify for him at a subsequent quarter sessions, asking relief from being bound to appear and petitioning for the use of his trade ["with-

[24] N.R.R.S., I, 81. The informations were brought originally before the Council of the North, another illustration of the existence of more prosecutions than can now be discovered.

[25] Orders were sent out on behalf of the aliens in 1591, 1611, 1615 and 1616, 1617, 1622, 1626, and 1635. *Acts P.C.*, Eliz., XXI, 275, July 11, 1591; XXII, 506, June 2, 1592; Moens, *Walloons Church at Norwich*, 64, 248, 65, 69; *Acts P.C.*, Jas. I, II, 301–302, and 482, October 11, 1615, and April 9, 1616; *Cal. S.P.D.*, Jas. I, 1611–1618, 377–378, June 1616 (the June order was rescinded in October, at least for London, *Acts P.C.*, Jas. I, III, 31); *ibid.*, 223; S.P.D., Jas. I, CXXXI, No. 12, June 5, 1622; *Cal. S.P.D.*, Chas. I, 1625–1626, 474, November 1626; *ibid.*, 1635, 85–86, May 1635; *ibid.*, 150; *ibid.*, 371, September 1635. Most of these years were in scarcity periods, several coinciding with outbursts of prosecution in food processing and distribution which have already been noted in Chapter V above: thus the orders of 1615 and 1616 concerned the aliens in Norwich and in London, and the Norwich city records show a number of professional prosecutions of bakers in these years. Cloth-stretching, Unwin, *Studies*, 273; *Acts P.C.*, Eliz., IX, 385; *Cal. S.P.D.*, Chas. I, 1631–1633, 55, 58. Wool dealers protesting prosecution, *Acts P.C.*, Jas. I, V, 207, 288. Dealers in butter and cheese, *ibid.*, II, 524, and see below, Chap. X, for the Council's reply as significant of the attitude toward enforcing economic regulations. See above, Chap. III, for the Council's intervention on complaints of the interference of informers with the grain and wool trades.

[26] The court fees were not negligible, whether from their size or unpopularity: an Essex justice of the peace, Sir Francis Barrington, declared in a Commons debate on a recent proclamation increasing the fees of clerks of the peace, etc., that he "had much ado to appease the people, for they would rather go to the gaol than pay fees" (*Commons Debates*, II, 120).

out hindrance"] as his only support.[27] Two Norfolk collarmakers begged the justices of the peace for a prompt hearing of a common informer's charge against them for lack of apprenticeship; they had been summoned for three successive sessions at which they had given their "diligent attendance" though without other means of maintenance than their craft.[28] Every now and then a casual reference will light up strongly the continual struggle of Elizabethan and Stuart craftsmen and laborers on the edge of destitution, for example, the need of spinners and weavers of flax near Preston for local retailers to supply their raw material since they could not take time from their work to buy it at the Preston market.[29]

Time and expense together made prosecution in a Westminster court a greater hazard than a lawsuit brought locally. The compulsion to come to Westminster for trial, described by Sir Henry Poole in 1621 as the core of the grievance against informers, was a valid threat.[30] In the majority of the known cases of extortion by pretended informations, the informer claims to have a Westminster suit pending.[31] In Jacobean Somerset, four men of Merriott deposed before a justice of the peace to the extortion of various sums of money from them. They had been "sent for to an alehouse" by two men who there told them "that they had process . . . to call them into the Exchequer to answer their fustian weaving" and that if they did not agree with these two for some money "it would cost them twenty nobles apiece to answer the same"; whereas if they agreed to pay up, "they would never be called in question again." Upon this, one of the four paid 4/–, a second 2/–, a third 4/6, while the fourth cannily "spent in their company 8d. but gave them nothing."[32] The incident has interest not only for its authentic picture of these minor blackmailers at work but as an illustration of the resistance they encountered — a skeptical craftsman and resort to local justice. This sort of reception

27 Cal. Q.S., XIX, 211, S.R. 211/95; 215, S.R. 211/112; 236, S.R. 213/91. The neighbors testified that the accused had served his apprenticeship with his father and "makes better stuff" than the prosecutor.

28 MS. Sessions Rolls, May Sess. at Swaffham, 19 Jas. I, April Sess. at Lynn, 20 Jas. I.

29 Wadsworth and Mann, *The Cotton Trade,* 59.

30 *Commons Debates*, VI, 257.

31 This was also the manner in which the Spence patent was alleged to have been effective.

32 MS. Sessions Indictment Rolls, No. 2, 5 Jas. I, Item 15, examination before Sir Edward Hext, September 7, 1607.

must have made the possession of actual writs from an initiated Westminster prosecution seem to the professional informer worth their cost in fees.

It is difficult to judge by how much, if at all, the threat of the expense of Westminster prosecutions was exaggerated. The total of court costs, travel, lodgings and board in London, lost work, to say nothing of witnesses brought up, might run very close to the £6–12–9 forecast by the extortioners. Here and there occur accounts of expenses for journeys to London. In 1590, a trip to London from Stratford-on-Avon, on legal business for the corporation, which required two days' travel each way, with a stay of a little under a fortnight in the metropolis, cost two aldermen £1–7–3½ apiece. Since this was a journey that went on the expense account, it was probably not the cheapest. Closer to what an artisan might have to pay merely to get to London, and from nearly the same part of the country as the Somerset quartet, is the allowance of 2/6 made at the same period, presumably to a servant or an agent, by William Darrell of Littlecote.[33] But even at the lowest reckoning, these are vast outlays measured on the scale of a skilled craftsman's daily wage of perhaps 1/0 to 1/4 in the late sixteenth century.[34]

A summons to appear in a Westminster court was a weapon possessed until 1589 chiefly by the professional informer. Before that year, few nonprofessionals utilized the Westminster courts in apprenticeship prosecutions, and after it, few of either class. But for the prosecutor there may have been an added advantage in bringing suit outside the defendant's county, besides the greater menace to the accused: to take him out of the zone of any local influence he may have had. Counsel for one professional informer in a suit against

[33] *Minutes and Accounts of . . . Stratford . . .* , IV, 86–87; Hall, *Elizabethan Society*, 202. The lowest figure in Darrell's accounts, among several of varying sums for travel by one person to and from the city, was 1/4.

[34] Wage entries in the Norwich MS. Chamberlain's Accounts. Wages assessed for master craftsmen tended to run somewhat lower elsewhere: as in Devon (A. H. A. Hamilton, *Quarter Sessions from Queen Elizabeth to Queen Anne*, 12); at Chester in 1597 the yearly rate for a smith was £5–10–0, a master carpenter £6–6–8, a woolen-weaver £4–0–0 (Morris, *Chester* . . . , 367), and these had just been raised. In early seventeenth-century Somerset, the daily wage assessed for master masons and carpenters was 1/– (MS. Wage Assessments, 2 Jas. I, in bundle at Taunton Shire Hall). The foregoing are the rates without meat and drink. The daily rate at Canterbury, however, was comparable to the Norwich wage payments (Civis, "Minutes Collected from the Ancient Records and Accounts . . . in . . . Canterbury," *The Kentish Gazette*, 1800–01, No. 13).

a Staffordshire usurer urged the Exchequer court to permit the venue to be at Westminster, because the defendant was "greatly allied in the county and . . . the plaintiff is like to have no indifferent trial." [35] While this possibility cannot often have affected an apprenticeship information, occasionally its subject was a man of substance: John Wolmer was helped by local influence. Another ironmonger, described also as a merchant, Bartholomew Wormell of King's Lynn in Norfolk, twice evaded penalty, even in a Westminster court, on a charge of unapprenticed ropemaking; while prosecutions for unapprenticed brewing at Yarmouth of two merchants, one of whom was a shipowner and later a bailiff of the borough, were discontinued by the attorney general.[36]

With how much effective thoroughness was a prosecutor able to press home his attack against defendants who were not greatly allied and who feared the waste of time and money? In the majority of the inconclusive cases and even of those where a penalty of some sort was recorded, it seems improbable that the offender was driven from his allegedly illegal occupation. This assumption can be tested, however, only in a small minority of cases, either by accidental knowledge of a defendant's later occupation or by repetition of the charge against him, even occasionally by both means. A John Smith of Stratford-on-Avon was prosecuted three times by three professional informers for unapprenticed baking; yet there was a John Smith, baker, still living in Stratford several years later.[37] Richard Barber of Berrowe in Somerset, a tailor, was informed against two or three times in 1615 for carrying on the trade of a butcher, but nine years later was described as a butcher there.[38] Six men of Norwich were prosecuted by a professional for setting up as tailors without apprenticeship; at least two were still tailors in Norwich at a much later

[35] Exch. Q.R., Decrees and Orders, Series I, XXII, 237d., Mich. 37 Eliz. The request was allowed by the court.

[36] For Wormell, Q.B.C.R., Mich. 10/11 Eliz., m. 64; Exch. Q.R.M.R., Pasch. 11 Eliz., m. 126d. He appears as a shipowner in 1580 (*Stiffkey Papers*, 5). For the two merchants at Yarmouth, Henry Stanton and Nicholas Williams, Exch. Q.R.M.R., Mich. 8 Eliz., m. 98, 98d.; *Stiffkey Papers*, 7; C. J. Palmer, *The History of Great Yarmouth*, 68, 303.

[37] Q.B.C.R., Pasch. 26 Eliz., m. 101, Mich. 27/28 Eliz., m. 101, Trin. 28 Eliz., m. 141; *Minutes and Accounts . . . of Stratford . . .*, IV, 144.

[38] Somerset MS. Indictment Rolls, No. 30, Pt. 2, Items 162 and 232, indictments, probably Mich. 13 Jas. I; No. 31, Item 19, indictment, probably Easter 13 Jas. I; Som. Rec. Soc., XXIII, 348.

date.[39] In Somerset, two of the defendants in apprenticeship prosecutions of the 1620's may be identical with tradesmen issuing tokens in the 1650's or sixties.[40]

Instances of repeated prosecution of one offender are not frequent. Among the Elizabethan cases at Westminster, there were fourteen repetitions from the southwest counties involving apprenticeship offenses on the Cloth Acts and the Act of 1563; in each of four other counties there was one repetition (on the Act of 1563). In quarter sessions cases, the chief occurrence of "repeats" was in the two series of professional informations in Somerset and Norfolk in Charles I's reign. In two prosecutions in the former county at this time, the defendants continued in their illegal occupation of baker even though they had not only paid the first informer an unlicensed composition but had been fined for doing so. Other repetitions of various periods in this county and elsewhere demonstrate the continuing use of the supposedly illegal occupation over periods of six, eight, or ten years, but there were only about a dozen instances in all.[41] No difference is observable between professional and other prosecutions in frequency of repetition.

A difference of real importance, however, appears to have existed between the professional informer and other private prosecutors in the timing of their activities. This has been pointed out in several connections in the preceding chapters. The professional seems to have been attracted to apprenticeship offenses in periods when expansion and the presumable entry of newcomers, or the resumption of work by part-time or occasional "intruders," made it worth his while; just as he responded quickly, for prosecutions on the statutes

[39] Exch. Q.R.M.R., Pasch. 30 Eliz., m. 109–112d.; *Register*, 127–128, 131.

[40] John Gardner of Cheddar, chandler (MS. Indictment Rolls, No. 42, Pt. 1, Item 64, ignoramus bill at Epiph. 18 Jas. I; W. Boyne, *Tokens Issued in the Seventeenth Century*, 393); Robert Horewood of Ilminster, tallow-chandler (MS. Indictment Rolls, No. 45, Item 10, information at Epiph. 22 Jas. I; Boyne, 396).

[41] As illustration: in Somerset, MS. Indictment Rolls, No. 13, Pt. 2, Item 101, indictment probably at Mich. 5 Jas. I of Hercules Dun als. Ley for unapprenticed shoemaking at Taunton, same informed against by a professional at Trin. 15 Jas. I (*ibid.*, No. 31, Item 49). In Essex, Cal. Q.S., XVI, 65, S.R. 117/65, Midsummer, 33 Eliz., professional information against John Allison of Coggeshall, termed "draper," for setting up as a linen- and woolen-draper; the same man had been prosecuted in the Queen's Bench in 1584 (Q.B.C.R., Hil. 26 Eliz., m. 96) when he was described as a tailor. John Draper of Writtle, mentioned in Chap. IV above, is another case in point.

for middlemen, to the conditions which caused an increase in the number of middlemen operating in commodity distribution. His loss of interest during "bad" times may have meant a widened gap in such years between actual offenses and their prosecution, although the number of offenses undoubtedly dwindled during recessions. In Elizabeth's reign especially, the gap was seldom filled by the trade competitor's efforts to restrict entry into his field of business. For reasons at present unknown, before the late sixteenth century ordinary folk seem to have resorted little to quarter sessions courts to enforce the law against their neighbors in economic matters.[42] Ignorance may often have been a cause. The retailers of Chelmsford and Brentwood who petitioned the justices of the peace for remedy against unlawful competitors during the depression of the early 1570's, when professional apprenticeship cases almost vanished from the Westminster courts, evidently did not know how to proceed in due form. Although the court ordered the issue of process against the eight accused retailers as the petitioners had requested, counsel's plea has survived for three of the trials to show what use could be made by the defense of technical errors in procedure. He pointed out that the "indictment" was merely a petition not found by the grand jury.[43] By the seventeenth century, both individuals and groups knew better how to use quarter sessions to put down unwanted competition, and in other periods when professional informations were few, lawsuits by trade interests still occur: the Wiltshire weavers in 1602–03, the Essex weavers in 1623, a group of Essex potters the year before. Yet the potters employed the same method of a complaint first to the justices of the peace.[44]

Another gap in enforcement was opened by the interval which the

[42] See above, Chap. I.

[43] Essex Cal. Q.S., IV, 48, S.R. 39/25, Easter 14 Eliz.; 244, S.R. 44/58, 59, 60, Easter 15 Eliz. One of the defendants, here described as a laborer, had already been informed against in 1571 for setting up as a mercer (Exch. Q.R.M.R., Mich. 13 Eliz., m. 193); now he was accused of exercising the trades of "mercer, haberdasher, and grocer"; in 1589 he was mentioned as a draper (Cal. Q.S., XVII, 149, S.R. 148/160).

[44] For the Wiltshire and Essex weavers, see above, Chap. V. Only one prosecution is recorded by what may have been another semi-organized craft group, "the potters of Stock and Buttsbury" (Essex Cal. Q.S., XIX, 465, S.R. 236/14, indictment of a husbandman as an unapprenticed "earthen potmaker" during eleven months, Easter 20 Jas. I; *ibid.*, 473, Item 84, his recognizance dated in January 1622 to answer the earlier complaint).

professional informer permitted to elapse before bringing suit, in order to maximize his claim for reward, a practice not regularly adopted by other private prosecutors. For many small offenders, working on the in-and-out basis, the "free" time thus allowed them may have been all or most of what they needed, and subsequent prosecution must in such cases have lost a good deal of its force.

On the whole, however, the professional informer who carried the larger share of the work of enforcement seems also to have been more effective than the other private prosecutors. In results, so far as these are measurable by success in securing a money penalty, he achieved more than others. Over the entire period professional prosecutions fared better than other private prosecutions, and the unsuccessful were relatively fewer. As for the inconclusive cases, since professionals continued to prosecute apprenticeship offenses, a considerable number of private settlements can safely be presumed. Their greater effectiveness was aided, at least during the quarter century after 1563, by easy access to the Westminster courts.

In thoroughness of prosecution, the tendency of the professional to keep the golden goose alive may have been paralleled by the probable infrequency of the cases in which trade competitors had the funds for a protracted campaign of suppression.

In adequate coverage of offenses, apart from his neglect of them in slack periods, the professional had a distinct advantage over all other prosecutors. For apprenticeship enforcement until 1589 and in some individual instances thereafter, the system of professional informing secured for the state a network of police superior in scope and cheapness to any other then practicable. Even when the Act of 1624 had completed the effect of the earlier statute in turning the professional informer into a provincial rather than a national agent of police, he remained the only agent other than the justice of the peace within any one county whose operations were not inherently parochial.[45]

Because the professional informer did not specialize on particular types of offenses, his sources of gossip were wider and more varied. If there was an accompanying risk for the statutes carrying the lesser penalties that they would be ignored in favor of those more profitable, the risk was reduced by the apparent tendency of mitigated fines and of compositions to yield a fairly uniform rate of return which con-

[45] Using the term in a broad sense for the high constables and juries of the hundred, and in its strict sense for the petty constables of the parish.

trolled to some extent what the informer could demand out of court. The extralegal payments secured by the professional gave him the same advantage in effectiveness over public agencies of enforcement which he possessed over other private prosecutors.

At its worst, the system of informing did more merely to keep the mass of regulations alive in the public mind than any other agency available to Tudor and Stuart governments. This was perhaps all that was desired by the age. As Sir Edwin Sandys remarked, if penal statutes were enforced "to the utmost, it would be unsufferable."[46] For observance of the apprenticeship requirement, the known presence of informers familiar with small and large communities must have been an inducement to qualify for an occupation and to keep at hand the duly registered indentures to prove the seven-years' training.

But the social cost of reliance on the professional informer was higher in the long run than mercantilist regulation could pay. It was not only that the informer's bad name and general reputation for dishonesty suggested to potential offenders that he could be bribed to protect their illegalities, the practice of unlicensed composition thus feeding on itself. The informer was not a good advertisement for his wares; contempt for the individual was transferred to the function. From the beginning, the "character of an informer" was drawn in harsh lines, and informers were admittedly "not well favored in the counties where they dwelt."[47] The Somerset justices of the peace had unusual difficulty in 1627 in arranging the settlement of one Thomas Warre, probably the active informer of the same name and time. The parish not only "most wilfully and obstinately" refused to accept his family, but "combined together to prevent him getting a house" so that the family had to "lie abroad in barns and stalls and outhouses."[48] In upper and lower classes, to act like an informer was a reproach. The case of Sir John Stafford, who as a "relator" brought suit in the Star Chamber, well illustrates the attitude of the first: he "was greatly blamed by the Court [of Star

[46] *C.J.*, I, 396, February 17, 1610.

[47] See above, Chapters II and III, for characterizations of the informer. The quotation is from a memorandum on Sir Stephen Proctor's project for registering informations, one objection being that informers could not obtain local endorsements for the proposed certificates of residence (B.M., Lansdowne MS. 167, f. 144).

[48] Som. Rec. Soc., XXIV, 46. Warre appears as an informer in apprenticeship and other offenses before the quarter sessions during the 1620's.

Chamber] that being so worthy a gentleman, . . . he would stoop to so base an office as to be an informer."[49] The effect of this contempt on the whole structure of the system of community presentment of offenses is foreshadowed in the objection of two tradesmen in Jacobean London to jury service. Each was indicted before quarter sessions for disregarding a summons to serve on a presentment jury because he would not be an informer.[50]

By the close of the seventeenth century, the stand taken by the London Bakers' Company toward procedure by information is probably symptomatic. The company was refusing to take action against violations of its standards on the evidence of informers;[51] and it is in the last fifteen years of the century that informations for apprenticeship in the quarter sessions courts markedly decline without later increase, persisting thereafter only in the assizes. A fundamental change may have occurred in the general estimation of the informer's office and function.

This apparent decline of the office of the informer in public acceptance, after long contempt for individual informers and for the abstract character of informer had been undermining its status, was accompanied in the late seventeenth and earlier eighteenth centuries by a search for expedient substitutes,[52] although procedure by information continued to be recognized in statutory regulation of economic life. But it is not too much to say that the professional informer made his important contribution not only to the history of mercantilism but to that of the growth of *laisser faire*, as distaste for a principal method of enforcement came to taint the whole concept of regulation by the state.

[49] Hawarde, 331–332.

[50] *Middlesex Sessions Records*, I, 368, Sessions Register, 1613–14. Was this considered sufficient ground for refusing service? Both indictments were discharged.

[51] S. Thrupp, *The Worshipful Company of Bakers of London*, 52–53.

[52] The practice of paying a public informer may perhaps have developed because of increased resistance to the private informer. It was not until after the middle of the eighteenth century that proposals were made to assume the costs of prosecution at public expense as a remedy for the situation of having to choose between prosecution by informers or no prosecution.

Part II

ENFORCEMENT BY PUBLIC AGENCIES

INTRODUCTION

A paradox of Elizabethan and Stuart government was the co-existence of contradictory attitudes toward the maintenance of law. On the one hand, there was consigned to private hands, to private profit, and to the service of the crown's financial needs, as much of the apparatus of law enforcement as it suited private persons to take. With this there went an accepted dilution of the law's force and legalized evasion of its intent. On the other hand, throughout England every local community was served voluntarily by unpaid holders of public office who assumed with little outward compulsion onerous duties involving personal discomfort or even danger, sacrifice of time, and financial risk. The two types of behavior interpenetrated one another to some extent. A justice of the peace bought or was granted a dispensing patent; a searcher of cloth or of tiles, whose office paid for itself by the sale of immunities, belonged to the same social class as the unpaid "conservators of peace," the petty constables or members of a presentment jury. The two attitudes must have been more closely assimilated than the records usually reveal or than an idealized view of local government wishes to perceive. If collusion to evade the law was not open and unblushing in this sphere as it was with the informer and the patentee, there often might be a willingness to overlook, or indifference and indolence; and if the local authorities had no frequent and certainly no admitted financial reward for closed eyes and silence, their personal interest might be advanced in less tangible ways, by peaceable relations with a neighbor, by avoiding annoyance to the more powerful or their dependents, or by their own unscathed sharing in illegal activities. But the deeply rooted and ancient organisms of local government seem to have resisted in the main the infection of fiscalism, potent as this was in an inflationary economy. Some who knew them well urged their continued strength as the only alternative to the manifestations of private profit in government. Lambard, that experienced justice, must have believed in the honesty if not the energy of the juries of presentment when he wished that jurors would take good care in their service, "which is the chief and almost the only ground, whereupon the justices are to work: considering that rarely any other than common promoters (that hunt for private gain and are not led by zeal of justice) will be entreated to inform against offenders." [1]

The majority of the legislation which embodied English mercantilist policy had no other public means of enforcement than local authorities who operated through institutions and practices of venerable age. The centralization of the Tudor monarchy stopped short of creating an administrative officialdom; and execution of policy had to wait upon the readiness or reluctance of local individuals and bodies to enlarge their traditional circle of duties and responsibilities. The cohesive strength of customary obligation, so essential to the functioning of voluntary local government, operated also to retard its adoption of novelties. The fate of the apprenticeship regulations at the hands of local authorities suggests that the enforcement of new statute law was effectively taken up into the mass of pre-existing obligatory duties only when it met an urgent need of the local community or was in harmony with strong public sentiment.[2]

Four classes of local authorities and several levels of county society were involved in the enforcement of the Statute of Artificers, individually or collectively: the justices of the peace, the high constables of the hundreds,[3] the petty constables of the parish, and the juries of presentment. Specific duties were committed to the first three authorities by the Statute, which will be described in connection with each class. Apart from those of an administrative and police character, the responsibilities of local government for the Act

[1] Lambard, *Eirenarcha*, 4th ed. (1599), enlarged by himself, 387. This passage does not appear in earlier editions. Does its presence reflect a decade's increase in the number of informers operating before quarter sessions?

[2] Illustrating the former is the relatively quick absorption into the list of offenses regularly presented of two created by statute late in Elizabeth's reign, the building of cottages without a minimum four acres of ground and the taking of "inmates" or lodgers (31 Eliz., c. 7). Control of "inmates" being exercised earlier, by presentment at petty sessions in S.E. Essex, was probably under the pre-Elizabethan statute applying to London and its environs. Illustrating the latter might be the local variation in presentment of those who absented themselves from church.

[3] "Hundred" was the term used in some counties for an ancient administrative unit; other names were "wapentake," "lathe," etc.

of 1563 as for all statute law committed to its care were discharged through the medieval system of presentment. This was the only means of setting the law in motion against offenders,[4] other than by the presentments of appointed searchers in certain industries,[5] or by the informations or indictments originating with private persons. Such presentments were by definition capable of initiating legal process against the individuals or upon the matters of which they took notice.[6] Together with executive orders issued by the justices of the peace in or out of quarter sessions, they are the external record of the local authorities' enforcement of a given law. The contribution of local government to the implementing of mercantilist policy cannot be measured in statistical terms by the number of lawsuits or orders. The pressure exerted by the whole local system of inquiry toward maintaining due observance of the laws escapes any simple estimate. Nevertheless, the recorded interest shown in enforcing the different economic and social regulations throws light on their varying importance in the local community and the varying degrees of local support they received. The central government expected or hoped that its own rating of relative urgencies would be accepted locally, and to that end issued periodical directions for inquiry, and specific orders for execution. A comparison of these with the local measures actually taken on any given statute helps to indicate agreement or conflict between the aims of central and local government.

Presentments of violations of the apprenticeship requirements by local agencies, used as an index of local concern to enforce them, suggest a minimal place in public policy. In the reign of Elizabeth, official presentments on the provision for the seven-year term constituted less than a sixth of all the apprenticeship prosecutions on this section of the Act brought before quarter sessions. They were about a fiftieth part of all such prosecutions in all the courts examined. From 1603 to 1625, they made up about one-fourteenth of the quarter sessions cases, a twentieth of those in all courts. In the third period, they amounted to a hundredth or less.[7] These figures are

[4] Except for minor offenses that could be dealt with summarily by one or two justices.

[5] Such prosecutions are exceedingly rare in quarter sessions records.

[6] Holdsworth, *English Law*, I, 76–81, 266–279. But their validity in this respect was not so clear in practice; see Chap. XI.

[7] See App. II below. Since presentments were also made to the assizes in

astonishingly low, considering what vitality the system of presentment possessed. But they can be tested for the Elizabethan period from the sessions records of Essex, a county with a more continuous series of public presentments than any other of this time.[8] Here they composed nearly one-fifth of the apprenticeship cases in the sessions files and about a twentieth of the prosecutions against Essex apprenticeship offenders in all courts. The higher share in the one county than in the group may be largely accounted for by probable differences in the number of documents lost. The papers of presentments, miscellaneous in size, were apparently filed in the sessions rolls with even less regularity than informers' documents; in many instances they may never have come into the hands of the clerk of the peace, if the high constables who were responsible for collecting the presentments of the petty constables, or the foremen of the presentment juries, neglected to leave them with the court. The factor of loss may lead to understating the attention given to prosecution of apprenticeship offenses by the local authorities. There is compensation, however, in the fact that presentments of individual kinds of wrongdoing were not made singly. Each return from constable or jury dealt with a list of matters, so that how often each type of offense was included in the lists is also indicative of the importance assigned to its enforcement. This question is discussed more fully elsewhere, but the absence of apprenticeship from the articles for presentment confirms the evidence of the offenses presented.

To try to account for the apparent indifference of local authorities to evasions of the apprenticeship law will be the task of the succeeding pages. Even within the Act of 1563, sharp contrasts in local enforcement are observable between the apprenticeship provisions which set up totally new regulations for rural crafts (except for a

---

each circuit, the loss of all but the Essex indictments series may have destroyed evidence of greater effort to enforce apprenticeship. But surviving articles of inquiry do not indicate this (see Chaps. VIII and X below).

[8] The present writer does not know the Kent sessions records, which form as old a series as those of Essex. Within the selected group, Essex alone has material before the last decade of the century for the study of the Elizabethan presentment system; the apparently long Norfolk series lacks most of the essential documents, the surviving Cheshire and Somerset rolls are incomplete, and for Wiltshire only brief entries in sessions minute books are available before the seventeenth century. The abundance of extant presentments by constables and juries in Elizabethan Essex is almost duplicated in Restoration Northamptonshire.

ten-year old precedent in the woolen industry), and those provisions which had a long history — the service clauses and (to some extent) the wages regulation. Presentments for service offenses occur often; those for wages less seldom, it is thought,[9] than for apprenticeship. Presentments for breaches of the elaborate property requirements imposed on rural and town apprenticing are nonexistent.[10] Does the explanation of these divergences lie chiefly in a different reception of old and new regulations, in a greater or less bearing on local needs and problems, in more or less trouble in detection; or did general causes create a distinction in enforcement between regulations applicable primarily to crafts and trades and those which clearly affected the orderly life of the community as ratepayers and consumers? A short survey of the nature of local government in personnel and problems is a necessary first step in finding an answer.[11]

[9] This is little but a general impression.

[10] Except for a few in the special conditions for 1602–03 in Wiltshire; see below, Chap. VIII.

[11] For a general outline of local government, the reader is referred to the basic work of the Webbs (S. and B. Webb, *English Local Government: The Parish and the County*); Holdsworth, *English Law*, I and IV; to Heckscher, *Mercantilism*, I, 246–253, for a brief summary of generally accepted views on the effectiveness of enforcement of mercantilist legislation by the justices of the peace; to Cheyney, *History of England*, II, 313–341, for a compact review of their appointment and duties. For the constables, *ibid.*, 389–408; H. B. Simpson, "The Office of Constable," *The English Historical Review*, X, 625–641.

VII

CONSTABLES AND JUSTICES

At all levels of county government a common basis and interest were the land and the relationships of land tenure. Within their degrees all holders of office were subject to some pressures of personal and group dependency on greater men,[1] which might influence their treatment of an offender. Most breakers of the apprenticeship regulations were, like Francis Bacon's constables, men of so "inferior condition" that personal influence except on behalf of manorial tenants or former servants might seldom be exercised by those above. How local authorities regarded apprenticeship enforcement was affected more vitally by their primary concern for whatever touched the land — disturbed the security with which men held and worked it, diverted into burdensome rates the income from it, or upset the ordered community life which was arranged and valued in terms of land.

In the Act of 1563, the petty constable is named only in connection with the duties of making out the certificate of discharge required for servants leaving an employer, and of securing compulsory service in harvest time. In other legislation affecting economic and social life, his apparent role was equally inconspicuous. Nevertheless his undistinguished shoulders carried the base of the pyramid of local government: the "stacks of statutes" rested thereon. In his own sphere he was, quite as truly as the justice of the peace in his, the man-of-all-work for the community and the central government, and the union of policing and administration involved in his two

[1] For clientage in the upper ranks of Elizabethan society, see Neale, *House of Commons*, 24.

functions under the Act of 1563 is typical. He was the agent of the justices of the peace, in the execution of their warrants and in the collection of public funds; executioner of petty justice on vagrants, pilferers, runaway servants and apprentices, scolds and users of abusive language, temporary gaoler; the township's sole official detector and "relator" for criminal offenses, public nuisances, personal habits and vices offensive to the community, social conduct subversive of public order, and breaches of some of the more important economic legislation (the dealings of middlemen, for example) for which no special official had been designated. He had, in short, a wide and undefined responsibility for the preservation of order and the detection, presentment, and punishment of crime.

A continuing problem of the constableship was expressed by Michael Dalton, the author of one of the most popular of the seventeenth-century manuals for justices of the peace, when he recommended the selection of substantial men for the office: "constables chosen out of the meaner sort," he wrote, "are either ignorant what to do; or dare not do that they should; and are not able to spare the time to execute this office." [2] In theory the constable was the appointee of the court leet, where this was kept.[3] The selection was not always the best that could be made. The township of Goldhanger in Essex was presented at the quarter sessions in 1624 by the jury for the hundred for choosing as constable a "poor man . . . having no estate to live by, but only his day labor." [4] If, on the other hand, a gentleman was chosen, he might refuse to serve, as one did in 1614 after selection by the "whole jury and inquest in the king's court and leet" for the township of Gray's Thurrock in the same county.[5] Or for some reason — the failure of the court leet to sit, or,

[2] Dalton, *The Country Justice*, 5th ed. (1635), 47. As a justice of the peace for Cambridgeshire, Dalton had first-hand knowledge of the difficulties of local government. This passage does not appear in the earlier editions; had the level of county office holders been declining? In 1630 he described them as usually husbandmen in his county (4th ed., 4).

[3] Either by actual election or by the steward of the leet.

[4] Cal. Q.S., XIX, 532, S.R. 243/34, Epiph. 21 Jas. I.

[5] Cal. Q.S., XIX, 142, S.R. 205/82, Epiph. 11 Jas. I. Another Essex case of a gentleman's refusal after his nomination by the court leet, *ibid.*, XVIII, 249, S.R. 184/81, Midsummer, 6 Jas. I. Occasionally gentlemen are found serving as petty constables, but they appear to have got excused more often than any other class; witness various instances throughout sessions records, and see Campbell, *The English Yeoman*, 319.

if it did, to choose a constable — a place might be left without a constable "or any other officer to serve the queen." [6] In some counties the practice of "houserow" or rotation among residents seems to have been a widely accepted method of filling local office, together with that which attached to certain tenements the duty of performing local services.[7]

The statutory requirement that constables take their oath of office before a justice of the peace was in keeping with the earlier development which had made the constable subordinate to the justices before the end of the fifteenth century.[8] By the seventeenth century the quarter sessions had become a court of appeal for those who felt aggrieved in regard to the constable's office by the action or inaction of the leet courts or by the incidence of tenure. In numerous instances the justices of the peace on such appeals designated a fit inhabitant, sometimes by the nomination of the outgoing constable.[9]

In the rural parishes of the Elizabethan and early Stuart periods, the office of constable tended to be filled from the class of middling yeomen, artisans, and shopkeepers. "Custom and current opinion had made it a public obligation of men of [the yeomen's] station, just as the office of justice devolved upon their neighbors of the gentry." [10] Occasionally in Essex the office might fall to a clothier, who in that county would generally belong to a group of employers separate from, and a peg above, the weavers, yet so similar in condition that they could be described on occasion themselves as

[6] Essex Cal. Q.S., IX, 65, S.R. 73/72, the township of Wennington presented by the "jury of the hundred" at the high constables' petty sessions, January 4, 1580. In 1574, three townships in one hundred had no constable (*ibid.*, V, 139, S.R. 48/51). The North Riding justices had to issue a general order in 1609 fining every township which did not have a sufficient constable. (N.R.R.S., I, 172; fines levied in accordance with a similar order, 91, 98, II, 48, IV, 110).

[7] Either one or the other way of filling office, according to tenure or residence, has been observed by the present writer as in use in the seventeenth century in Somerset, Wiltshire, Warwickshire, Nottinghamshire, the West Riding of Yorkshire, and Lancashire. In S. and B. Webb, *Parish and County*, p. 16, are cited similar instances.

[8] For the oath of office, 27 Eliz., c. 12, and for this and for the change in the position of the constable, Simpson, "The Office of Constable," 639.

[9] For examples, see Warwickshire, *Sessions Order Book*, I, 12 (case in 1625) and 196 (1634); II, 126–127 (1645). Also in Somerset, Som. Rec. Soc., XXIV, 147 (Jan. Sess., 1631); XXVIII, 160, 164 (Sept. Sess., 1651, Jan. Sess., 1652), 190–191 (Oct. Sess., 1652).

[10] Campbell, *The English Yeoman*, 319.

weavers.[11] In Norfolk, husbandmen, weavers, butchers, or an occasional tradesman, served as constables, but yeomen most frequently.[12] They were ordinary men going about what was to them a commonplace and burdensome business, and rarely known outside their own parishes or hundreds. The obscurity in which they performed their office is reflected in the query written on the margin of a Restoration presentment, "Who knows their names?" [13]

The high constable was the intermediary between the petty constable and those lofty luminaries of the county, the justices of the peace, or the distant comets, the judges of assize. In social rank he was also intermediate, though perhaps tending to approach more closely to the lower ranges of the heights above him than to the levels beneath.[13a] Francis Bacon's somewhat acid tone toward the holders of local office may color his assignment of the office of high constable to "the ablest freeholders, and substantiallest" of yeomen "next to the degree of gentlemen," [14] which gives the impression of an average a step lower than it seems to have been. Yeomen often did fill the office but perhaps not as often the country over as gentlemen.[15] In some counties the service may have been solely by the latter; in others, the share taken by gentlemen varied from one division of the county to another.[16] Occasionally high constables were drawn from

[11] Examples of clothiers as constables, Essex Cal. Q.S., XIX, 238, S.R. 214/22, July 1616; 278, S.R. 217/57, April 1617. The Essex cloth industry still lacks an historian; and the attempted definition of the clothier's status is merely that of the present writer on the basis of a good deal of familiarity with the sessions records. But see J. E. Pilgrim, "The Cloth Industry in Essex and Suffolk, 1558–1640," *Bulletin of the Institute of Historical Research*, XVII, No. 51, Abstract of M.A. thesis, 144.

[12] A glimpse of economic position is given by a statement from the constable of Griston in Norfolk that he is a "townsman" of the same, resident for twelve years past in a farm of £45 a year (MS. Sessions Rolls, 10 Jas. I).

[13] Assizes, S. E. Circuit, Indictments, Bdle. No. 112, roll for Essex Summer Assizes, 1671; at this period the petty constables' presentments made before the petty sessions of the justices of the peace, on much the same topics as the Elizabethan presentments (including cases of living out of service), were forwarded to the assizes. The presentment quoted was made by a high constable against some petty constables who had defaulted in making their returns.

[13a] The Webbs, (*Parish and County*, 491), assign him a social position somewhat lower than is indicated in the text here, but for a later period.

[14] Bacon, *Works*, VII, 751. Of the petty constables Bacon observed that "they be men, as it is now used, of inferior, yea of base condition."

[15] Campbell, *The English Yeoman*, 345–346, for examples of yeomen in the office.

[16] A sampling of the sessions rolls in Norfolk indicates variations from one

the upper levels of industry: a Suffolk clothier, employing in 1622 some two hundred workers, was mentioned as "long a high constable." [17] This, however, was an accidental association: undoubtedly his qualification for the office was landholding. A Cheshire justice of the peace criticized his colleagues' selection of a candidate on one occasion as unfit, because he was "a shopkeeper" with only an "exceeding small" freehold.[18]

As the seventeenth century wore on, the office may have been filled more often from the higher rank; unless the apparent change is in reality only a significant change in terminology — that men of the class who in Elizabeth's time were content to be called yeomen were later not satisfied with anything less than the appellation of a gentleman. Throughout, however, appointment to the office was usually by the justices of the peace.[19] The quarter sessions was the court of appeal when the choice of high constable was questioned, or when the officer wished release from his post. The justices appear to have had an unquestioned right to discharge for unfitness either high or petty constables.[20]

No fixed term of service seems to have been established. The variation in practice was greater than in the term of petty constables for whom service of more than a year was probably unusual. High constables seldom served less than three years, often for four to six, sometimes ten years and more, and very occasionally twenty to thirty.[21]

---

hundred to another. The varying social distribution of land tenures would be the chief cause of the differing prominence in office of gentlemen or yeomen.

[17] *Cal. S.P.D.*, Jas. I, 1619–1623, 395.

[18] *Quarter Sessions Records*, ed. J. H. E. Bennett and J. C. Dewhurst, The Record Society [of] Lancashire and Cheshire, XCIV, 74.

[19] A transfer of control from local hands to those of the justice of the peace seems to have occurred to a large extent before the reign of Elizabeth, though where the old hundred court had survived, often by coming into private hands, selection might still be at this court. On both high and petty constables two valuable introductions to printed sessions records are useful: *Minutes of Proceedings in Quarter Sessions . . . for the Parts of Kesteven in the County of Lincoln*, ed. S. A. Peyton, Lincoln Record Society, and *Quarter Sessions Records of the County of Northampton*, ed. J. Wake, Introduction by S. A. Peyton. In Somerset where in the reign of James I the chief constables seem usually to have been elected at the hundred court, appointment by the justices was the practice by the middle of the seventeenth century, and in one instance the reason is evident: "the leet incident to the hundred having for some time discontinued the election" (Som. Rec. Soc., XXVIII, 117).

[20] But the exercise of this right was restricted by practical considerations, mentioned later in this chapter.

[21] *Nottinghamshire County Records*, ed. H. H. Copnall, 16. The Essex high

Length of service provided continuity in what was an administrative as well as a police position. This, however, may have perpetuated variations in efficiency as much as it brought experience to county problems.[22] One cause of the longer terms was probably the scarcity of substantial residents able to assume the financial burdens of the office and willing to undertake it. Yet it may have carried sufficient local prestige to make it desirable. The reputation of being a "very honorable, wealthy, and substantial man" rested for one individual on his service as high constable.[23] Even the unpleasant and so often unwanted office of petty constable could confer a sense of importance relatively to social inferiors: a Norfolk holder of the post boasted to a cleric "you are but a parson and I am a constable."[24]

The view that a given social position entailed the customary obligation to serve in local offices, and its natural corollary that they became hallmarks of status, were most fully developed for the relative newcomer in prestige, the office of the justice of the peace. The second half of the sixteenth century saw a decisive growth in the social esteem and the actual local leadership and influence of this office. The appearance of epitaphs commemorating service in the commission of the peace is a sure sign of the importance attributed to it for family rank in the county.[25] Before the next century, it was a disgrace to be put out of the commission.[26] Though for the knights and squires

---

constable who asked discharge in 1572 after ten years was still serving in 1579, Cal. Q.S., IV, 77, S.R. 40/3 (cited in Campbell, *The English Yeoman*, 345) and IX, 63, S.R., 73/71. By Charles I's reign the term had been stabilized in the West Riding at three years, by custom and by order (*West Riding Sessions Records*, II, ed. J. Lister, Yorkshire Archaeological Association Record Series, LIV, 126, 131, 201, 394).

[22] A justice of the peace in Essex commented on the incumbent high constables of one hundred that they "have taken more pains in service this one year than their predecessors in many years before." (Cal. Q.S., XIII, 12, S.R. 94/15, letter of September 1585 from Arthur Harris, Esq., to his colleagues at Michaelmas quarter sessions.)

[23] W. B. Willcox, *Gloucestershire, A Study in Local Government, 1590–1640*, 49n. See also below, n. 81.

[24] Norfolk MS. Sessions Rolls, 11 Chas. I, article of complaint probably at July Sessions, undated. The constable is described as an alehouse-keeper.

[25] For example, the monument to three members of the Blount family in Worcestershire, of whom the father Walter and eldest son Francis were justices of the peace. Walter died in 1561; the monument appears to be contemporary with the death of his second son Robert in 1575 though possibly with the later (? undated) death of Francis. (T. Habington, *Survey of Worcestershire*, by John Amphlett, Worcestershire Historical Society, II, 15.)

who were its working majority,[27] no higher external qualification than the outmoded property requirement of the fifteenth century had ever been laid down,[28] the accretion of responsibilities heaped on the justices of the peace by Elizabethan statutes and by the central government had conferred on them an increasing primacy among county authorities.[29]

By far the greater number of those who attained to a place on the Elizabethan commissions of the peace derived their income chiefly from landholding. For the majority this had been the principal concern and source of income of at least their immediate forbears. The commission was rarely if ever to be reached in one generation from small beginnings, even in land, still less in trade or business. It took the Temples of Stowe, springing from "the younger son of the younger branch" of an old family and full of vigor and push, two generations to achieve it.[30] The exclusiveness of the gentry was growing as their network of family connections was interwoven with increasing complexity and strength throughout the country. The consolidation of their economic and social position with and after the

[26] A late sixteenth-century protest from Cornwall at being dropped from the commission, see Rowse, *The England of Elizabeth*, 342; a plea not to be dismissed, in 1610, see *Cal. S.P.D.*, Jas. I, 1603–1610, 624. Debating the bill in 1621 to prevent wrongful imprisonment, the solicitor-general argued against a penalty proposed for justices of the peace of a year's dismissal from the commission, on the ground that it was dangerous for the county services, since the disgrace would be such that the former justice would "not be willing to come in again." (*Commons Debates*, VI, 172).

[27] The high officers of state who were ex efficio members, the few lay (and ecclesiastical) peers, and the justices of assize for the circuit, seldom took much part in the active local duties of the commission.

[28] An estate of £20 in land had been required in 1439 (18 Hen. VI, c. 11).

[29] S. A. Peyton has contrasted the secondary part assigned the justice of the peace in the duty of caring for the county highways by the statute of 1555 with the power given him in 1562: by the earlier act, the courts leet were still the courts of first instance for presenting highway defaults, by the second, the justice was to present such offenses of his own knowledge. The same writer has also emphasized the importance of two poor law enactments in establishing the authority of the justice of the peace over other local officers: that of 1572 empowering the justices to assess the county for the relief of the poor and of prisoners, and that of 1597 giving them control over the appointment and supervision of the newly created office of overseer and over the levy and use of the necessary funds. (See Peyton's Introductions, especially that in Northamptonshire *Q. S. Records*, passim.)

[30] E. F. Gay, "The Rise of an English Country Family," *The Huntington Library Quarterly*, I, No. 4, 369.

distribution of monastic properties may have heightened the barriers within the upper middle class against associations with industry and trade, except where these involved exploitation of minerals, of new processes, or of new branches of wholesale and export commerce.[31] Entry into the "county" through success in the law was another matter. This bestowed distinction, when combined with the landed wealth which was its usual result in Tudor and Stuart England. Moreover, competent lawyers were indispensable for the work of the commission of the peace.

A general recognition nowadays that the predominant element in the county magistracy of the sixteenth and seventeenth centuries was land has not saved the justices of the peace from an accusation of bias in favor of industrial interests.[32] A short review of typical commissions of the peace shows how rare were their connections with any industrial interests of the types affected by the economic controls of the period. Connections with trade and finance existed, and justices of the peace were some of them "great corn-masters" no doubt; such interests might have predisposed them in individual cases to deal gently with middlemen, usurers, alehouse-keepers. Bias in these directions is plausible but irrelevant to the present study. A few illustrations of the origins and associations of justices in various counties provide a background for understanding their attitude toward industrial and craft regulations.

[31] The most detailed study of the acquisition of former monastic properties by the gentry in one county is that of A. L. Rowse, *Tudor Cornwall.* Much useful material is available in the later volumes of the Victoria History of the Counties of England for certain counties such as Worcestershire and Warwickshire. For a general discussion, R. H. Tawney, "The Rise of the Gentry, 1558–1640," *The Economic History Review*, XI (1941), 1–38, and "The Rise of the Gentry: A Postscript," *ibid.*, Second Series, VII, No. 1, 91–97, written in answer to Trevor-Roper, "The Gentry 1540–1640." Ramsay, *The Wiltshire Woollen Industry*, 45–46, believes there was a growth of social barriers between Wiltshire gentry and clothiers in Elizabeth's reign.

[32] Heckscher, *Mercantilism*, I, 249, referring to the "danger of making cloth manufacturers themselves justices of the peace" as "a real one." However, on preceding pages he described the "majority" of justices as having "not much of a personal concern" in industrial problems (246–247). The context in the statement first cited is the one in which bias is usually alleged, i.e. the enforcement of the anti-tentering act in Yorkshire at the close of the sixteenth century. But the danger of bias which was guarded against in the statute for assessment of wages in the textile industry was evidently that of clothier-justices of the peace within corporate jurisdictions, not in the county at large (1 Jas. I, c. 6, §6).

In Essex, if anywhere outside Middlesex and Surrey, an infiltration of trade into the ranks of the justices of the peace might be looked for, because citizens of means were already in the sixteenth century resorting thither for the summer. But of about 132 justices in the commission during Elizabeth's reign,[33] only two, both of London, are known to have been themselves in trade: James Altham, London merchant and member of the Clothworkers' Company, alderman until 1561, Essex justice of the peace by 1564, father of two knights of whom one became a baron of the Exchequer; [34] and Sir Thomas Lodge, adventurer in the Guinea trade, who was lord mayor of London in 1562.[35] Four more were sons or descendants of London mercantile wealth: Henry Capel of Rayne Hall, Sir William Fitzwilliams of Northamptonshire and Essex, Bernard Whetstone of Woodford, and Sir William Smith (son of a London draper and nephew of the secretary of state; rather a special case).[36] Only one justice of the peace appears to have had a connection with the cloth industry, and this only through an earlier generation: John Abel (justice for a few years in the 1570's) was said to have descended from a clothier of the late fifteenth or early sixteenth century. But nearly one-sixth of the knights and esquires who were on the commissions of the peace in this county from 1559 through 1596 were in the law: [37] at different periods this profession was represented here by men of the caliber of the revered William Bendlowes, old when Elizabeth was young; Sir Richard Weston, judge of Common Pleas, and his barrister son Jerome; James Morrice, recorder of Colchester; Sir John Tyndall, doctor of civil law and master in Chancery.[38] Less than one-tenth of the bench were office holders or cour-

[33] Here and in the following discussion, the number of justices of the peace refers to those on the commission from 1559 through 1596 (the latest commission examined for Elizabeth's reign except in one or two counties), exclusive of: officers of state, peers, bishops, judges of assize, and a somewhat arbitrary selection of the justices of the peace who are known to appear only on the commission of 1559.

[34] P. Morant, *History and Antiquities of the County of Essex*, II, 488; E. Foss, *Biographia Juridica*, 12–13; A. B. Beaven, *The Aldermen of the City of London*, passim.

[35] *Dictionary of National Biography*; Beaven, *passim.*

[36] Morant, *History of Essex*, I, 138, II, 401; I, 160; I, 38.

[37] Several of the hitherto unidentified justices of the peace may have been professional lawyers.

[38] Morant, *History of Essex*, passim; Foss, *Biographia Juridica*, passim. Sir Clement Higham, privy councillor to Mary and in 1558 chief baron of the

tiers, such as Thomas Fanshawe, remembrancer of the Exchequer, and Henry Mackwilliams, gentleman pensioner and patentee. On the whole, some two-thirds of the Essex bench were not "new men" in the Elizabethan generation, though the majority owed most of their position to the efforts of their sires in the preceding forty years. The influx of "new men" was noticeable in this county, however, under the Stuarts, with financiers of the stature of Sir Martin Lumley, Sir Stephen Soame, Sir Paul Bayning, and lesser merchants like Richard Hale, a grocer, coming in from London.

In Somerset and in Wiltshire, where entry into the "county" from the long-established textile industries might be expected, the story is much the same. In the former, two justice-of-the-peace families of the sixteenth and seventeenth centuries may have sprung from early sixteenth-century clothiers, the Babers and Bysses, but this connection, if any, is obscure.[39] Bristol trade provided access to the county bench for three sons of the city's mayors, Hugh and Matthew Smith, and George Sniggs, the last being aided also by his profession: recorder of the city and later a baron of the Exchequer. Sir John Young, a Bristol citizen who had inherited landed as well as mercantile wealth, held estates in three counties and was justice of the peace in both Somerset and Wilts.[40] Lawyers on the bench constituted probably one-tenth at least of all the knights and esquires on the known Somerset commissions of Elizabeth. But earlier generations of established families had been nourished by the law in this county, as in so many others. An example here is the family of Portman, for

---

Exchequer, was only on Elizabeth's first commission of the peace for Essex, but may have remained on the Suffolk bench until his death, since he signed in Suffolk the declaration for the Act of Uniformity in 1569 (S.P.D. Eliz., LX, No. 62). His son and grandson were both Essex justices of the peace.

[39] A possible cousinship between the Bysses who were justices of the peace and the Bisses or Bysses of Croscombe, "gentlemen," of whom one at least was a clothier in the early seventeenth century, seems unlikely to have given the former family an economic stake in the industry. On indications of ancestry, see *Somerset Enrolled Deeds*, ed. S. W. B. Harbin, Somerset Record Society, LI, 3, 21–22, 42, 44.

[40] For Somerset families in general, the *Visitation of Somerset in 1623*, ed. F. T. Colby, Publications of the Harleian Society, XI; Collinson, *History of Somerset*, passim. On the justices of the peace from Bristol, *ibid.*, II, 292–293; J. Latimer, *Sixteenth-Century Bristol*, 57, 119–120, and *The Annals of Bristol in the Seventeenth Century*, 15, 20, 22–23; G. Kidston, "Hazelbury Manor," *Somerset Archaeological and Natural History Society Proceedings*, LXXVIII, lv.

whom two generations of eminent legal talents had amply buttressed by the middle of the sixteenth century a position in the county founded by a fifteenth-century marriage to lands.

In Wiltshire, it appears that an industrial background was immediate for only one, hypothetical and remote for a second.[41] Sir James Stumpe, justice of the peace for the first four years after Elizabeth's accession until his early death, had succeeded in that office to his father, the famous clothier William Stumpe of Malmesbury, whose own case was rare in its direct step from industry to the commission. Alone of the Wiltshire justices, so far as is known, Sir James had a continuing connection with the cloth industry, since his younger brother maintained the family enterprise. But his connections by marriage with the Bayntons, and his vast properties, must have been far more influential in his aims and decisions. In the next generation his heiress's marriage into the powerful Knevett family was another step away from the loom-shops,[42] into the circle of those whose family origins were based primarily on inherited estates.[43] These made up almost two-thirds of the Elizabethan justices of Wiltshire whose origins are known.[44] Six of those who signed the orders in 1603 for the weavers of Westbury [45] provide a good cross-section, in family, profession, or length of service, of the type of men who were furnishing most of the active justices of the peace in this or other counties. In alphabetical order, they were: John Hungerford, justice

[41] The origins of about a quarter of the Wiltshire justices of Elizabeth's reign are still unknown to the present writer. The uncertain instance was Sir Jasper More of Heytesbury, a son of a Thomas originally of Bagborough in Somerset who had bought the priory of Taunton; the district suggests possible antecedents in the west Somerset cloth industry in the early sixteenth century. (A. B. Connor, "Monumental Brasses in Somerset," LXXVII, 96). Jasper was succeeded in 1610 by a half-brother Thomas, who was a justice of the peace in both Wiltshire and Somerset through 1625.

[42] Ramsay, *The Wiltshire Woollen Industry*, 31–37, 46–47. Several clothiers' descendants are mentioned as having become county families (pp. 42, 46) but none can be traced on the available commissions of the peace in Elizabeth's reign or thereafter. It would not be surprising to find them supplying high constables for the county or the lesser gentry who were so often called on to work alongside the justices of the peace in local inquiries.

[43] For other Wiltshire families, see J. Aubrey, *Collections for the Natural and Topographical History of Wiltshire*, ed. J. Britton, *passim*; R. C. Hoare, *The Modern History of Wiltshire*, I-V, *passim*. In this county again, at least a tenth of the justices were in the law; less than a tenth were office-holders or courtiers.

[44] To the present writer.

[45] See below, Chap. X. Seven signed, but one, Henry Martin, has not been identified.

from about 1600 to his death in 1636, probably belonging to the Cadnam branch of an old and widespread family in Wiltshire and Gloucestershire; Edmund Lambert, justice for fifteen to twenty years, son of a Londoner who had bought Wiltshire estates; James Ley, the later earl of Marlborough and chief justice of the King's Bench, son of a Wiltshire esquire; Sir James Mervin, justice for some thirty-seven to forty years, son of a knight and descendant of a family holding the manor of Fonthill since the early fifteenth century; Sir Henry Poole, knighted at the coronation, and on the bench in Wiltshire for perhaps forty-five years or more, justice in Gloucestershire and Oxfordshire also, where some of his estates lay; and last, Giles Tooker, counsel to the city of Salisbury from 1601 and its recorder from 1611 (probably related to the then prebend of Salisbury and later dean of Lichfield, William Tooker), justice for some twenty-two years and father-in-law of a Worcestershire justice.

In general, the Jacobean commissions of the peace were as little tainted with industrial connections as had been those of Elizabeth.[46] The exploitation of mining properties was not regarded as a debasing business in the scheme of Elizabethan or Stuart social values. Nor were capitalist enterprises in glassmaking (Sir Robert Mansell was a Norfolk justice of the peace), salt extraction, or ordnance, in the same category with the socially unacceptable "mean trades." [47] Association with a craft was contemned: when John Harington, later

[46] Professor John H. Gleason of Pomona College, who is engaged in an intensive study of Elizabethan and Stuart justices of the peace, corroborates this finding for the counties he has investigated. There were occasional exceptions. In Worcestershire, one wealthy clothier, his son, and the son of another were justices of the peace in the Stuart period (Roland Berkeley, Sir Robert Berkeley, and Richard Skinner, see Habington, *Survey of Worcestershire*, II, 281–282; *Victoria History of Worcestershire*, III, *passim*.).

[47] Interests in mining and saltmaking are found among justices of the peace particularly in the midlands and north, and in Somerset lead mining: among Staffordshire justices of the peace of the lesser sort there were Robert Stamford and William Whorewood, farmers of iron-mills (Staffordshire *Q.S. Rolls*., III, 297 and *passim*); in the West Riding, justices of the peace such as Sir Robert Anstruther and Sir William Slingsby had mining properties (Nef, *British Coal Industry*, I, *passim*); the Willoughbys and Strelleys among justices of the peace families in Nottinghamshire (*ibid*., *passim*). Robert Bowes, justice of the peace in several northern counties, was interested in saltmaking (*ibid*., I, 176); Worcestershire landed proprietors owned salt pans at Droitwich as probably did Cheshire families at Nantwich and Northwich. John Hippisley, an early Elizabethan justice of the peace in Somerset, was concerned in a Mendip lead mine. The list could be extended considerably.

knighted, better known as writer and courtier than as Somerset justice of the peace and printer, twice took a London apprentice away from his master, a "printer and graver," the Privy Council rebuked him for employing anyone "in that profession, being a matter contrary to your quality and calling." [48]

In the Stuart commissions of the peace, the proportions of entrants from trade and finance, and of "career men" other than those from the law, somewhat increased. An example from Devonshire is Sir James Bagg, son of a Plymouth merchant, magistrate and customs official; he succeeded his father in 1614 as comptroller of customs at Plymouth, was knighted in 1625, and was a justice of the peace by the 1630's.[49] In Somerset, a prosperous merchant Barnaby Lewis bought into the "county" in the reign of James I but felt himself to be cold-shouldered by his fellow-justices.[50]

Justices of the peace could and did engage in a number of lucrative occupations without loss of prestige. They held various kinds of patents: [51] many were keepers of royal parks; traffickers in appointments and reversions to office about the court and the government; investors in mortgages, and moneylenders,[52] avocations which they shared with many of their country neighbors.[53] In the southwest, maritime ventures and seizures of prizes were profitable to men like Sir Carew Raleigh, younger half-brother of Sir Walter and justice of the peace in Wiltshire and Dorset.[54]

[48] *Acts P.C.*, Eliz., XXII, 504, 31 May 1592. No reference has been seen elsewhere to this interest of Harington's.

[49] *Acts P.C.*, Eliz., *passim*; *Cal. S.P.D.*, Eliz. and Jas. I, *passim*; Devon *Libri Pacis*.

[50] Som. Rec. Soc., XXIII, xxvi.

[51] See above, Chap. I, nn. 34, 37, 45.

[52] References to keeperships are scattered through the state papers, as are mentions of land transactions (and in local histories); for dealings in offices, see *Trevelyan Papers*, Part III, ed. Sir W. C. Trevelyan and Sir C. E. Trevelyan, 52–53, 55–57, 63–64, 68; other mention in state papers, contemporary letters, etc. The largest creditor of the gambler-son of Sir Anthony Cooke, at the time he had to sell his inherited Warwickshire property to John Temple, was Sir William Waldegrave, colleague of both Cookes on the Essex bench, and the younger Cooke's father-in-law (E. F. Gay, "The Rise of an English Country Family," 387; and commissions of the peace for Essex). And see Tawney, Introduction to Wilson's *Discourse*, 53, for loans by Sir John Hollis, Nottinghamshire justice of the peace, to the Willoughbys and Strelleys.

[53] See collections of printed inventories, mention of compositions with creditors in state papers, etc.; Tawney, Introduction, *passim*.

[54] *Acts P.C.*, Eliz., XXII, 496, 28 May 1592; and XXIII, 165, 3 September 1592.

The bias which is mentioned by contemporaries most often was family and local influence.[55] In Essex, one of the most active of the lesser justices was accused of injurious dealing toward a cleric who had charged some of his servants with seditious talk. In Wiltshire, Sir Henry Knevett was rebuked by the Privy Council for having removed a former servant from Salisbury gaol without consultation with fellow justices. Fabian Phillips, member of the Council of the Marches of Wales and justice of the peace in Cheshire, Shropshire, Worcestershire, and some of the Welsh counties, was reported to the Privy Council as favoring one side in a case; the Privy Council excused him from further participation in it, but without rebuke. Numerous instances of this kind in the Council letters convey the impression that personal bias was accepted as a fact, not usually deserving reproof but merely calling for appropriate steps to avoid its consequences when possible.[56]

Local influence and authority were furthered by long and in most cases continuous service, usually ended only by death. A table of approximate frequencies of years of service in four counties shows variation, due in part to irregularities of compilation.[57]

The spread of family connections, by which the hold of those

Per Cent of Elizabethan Justices of the Peace by Years of Service 1559–1596

	Essex	Norfolk	Cheshire	Devon
1–10	39	45	26	38
11–20	33	24	36	28
21–30	16	13	26	18
31–40	11	13	11	15
41–50	1	5	1[a]	1
	100	100	100	100

[a] Two more justices served 51 and 52 years and one was on the commission 62 years.

[55] Sometimes to the point of criminal abuse of authority, see examples supplied in Willcox, *Gloucestershire*, 56–60 and notes.

[56] *Acts P.C.*, Eliz., XXII, 399; XXI, 387, 418; XX, 117. Commissions of the peace for the counties under the jurisdiction of the Council of Wales, and to some extent for neighboring counties independent of it like Cheshire, had during Elizabeth's reign a sizable common group of barristers and justices of assize for Wales — the most considerable amount of overlapping which occurs. Phillips was one of these.

[57] Officers of state, peers, bishops, and justices of assize have been omitted,

solidly established was strengthened, can be illustrated by a few examples. In Cheshire, Peter Warburton of Arley who himself served as a justice of the peace for over fifty years had four sons-in-law who were Cheshire justices of the peace also: Thomas Wilbraham of Woodhay, on the commission for twenty-six to thirty years, son-in-law through a first wife of another Cheshire justice of the peace, father of one Cheshire justice of the peace and father-in-law of three more; William Brereton of Ashley, justice for some twenty-five years under the first two Stuarts and father of a justice of the peace; Sir Peter Warburton the judge of Common Pleas, father-in-law of the justice of the peace Sir Thomas Stanley; Thomas Marbury, on Jacobean commissions of the peace.[58] Even in Essex, half-brothers, cousins, or brothers-in-law sat at the same quarter sessions and held alehouse sessions together.[59] At no one sessions in any county would it have been possible to array so overwhelming a list of family relationships as in a session of Parliament, but at the simultaneous quarter sessions of a number of different counties the same condition of family links which "almost defy description" could have been found.[60]

So customary was it, in those families rooted in the county, for son to succeed father on the commission of the peace that the absence of the next generation indicates failure of the line, disgrace — per-

---

and a number of justices of the peace who appear on only one commission. The table is calculated from the terms of service established by the various commissions examined (see Bibliography), dated as accurately as possible; plus interpolation of further information wherever available, as in sessions records and state papers. In most cases, it is believed the true term of service approximated the upper limit of each frequency group, since with very few exceptions all additional information has tended to lengthen the minimum. For the same reason, the percentage in the first group might be found too high, but there is the offsetting influence of a probably larger turnover in the lower brackets of the commissions among the justices of the peace barely qualifying for office.

[58] Peter Warburton of Arley was also father-in-law of Ralph Egerton of Ridley whose name has not been found on available commissions of the peace but who was father of the justice of the peace Sir Richard Egerton; father-in-law probably of a Lancashire justice of the peace; and posthumously of a West Riding justice of the peace.

[59] For example, Sir Thomas Golding and Henry Golding in 1565–66; Arthur and Vincent Harris in 1572; two sets of brothers-in-law at the Gaol Delivery of July 1574, Henry Medley and James Morrice, William Cardinal and Henry Appleton; cousins, John Sammes and Andrew Paschall, Lord Rich and Edward Rich (both assiduous justices). (Based on attendance at the sessions, Cal. Q.S., *passim;* and Morant, *History of Essex*, passim.)

[60] Neale, *House of Commons*, 312–313.

sonal or political — or failure of fortune. The last cause may explain, for instance, why a Cuttes serves only on the Cambridgeshire bench and not in Essex also, after the death in 1615 of the magnificent gentleman Sir John Cuttes, who lived with such princely ostentation that he was forced to sell up his Essex lands, including the manor and borough of Thaxted. This appears to be a good illustration of that essential basis of the office of the justice of the peace in local landholding, which prevented it from becoming a hereditary claim.[61] Local administration was confided "to persons who already possessed local authority, and who were confirmed in it, rather than given it, by the Crown." [62]

The question how many of these justices, so knit together in their landholding, so busy with their personal enterprises, had or took the time and attention necessary for their official duty is difficult to answer, probably impossible except for a rough approximation. Material is not yet available for a satisfactory study of attendance at sessions and much of it will never be; this applies still more to the work of the justices out of sessions. The mere numbers on the commission at different periods count for very little unless something can be known of the proportion resident in the county and their distribution. Only a few comments will be offered here.

In ten of the selected counties the average number of knights and esquires on the Elizabethan commissions of the peace ranged from 42 to 43 in Devon and Essex down to 24 and 26 in Warwickshire and Northamptonshire; the Jacobean commissions from 66 in Devon, 59 and 57 in Essex and Norfolk, to 26 in Warwickshire; those of the period 1625–1637, from 57 to 23.[63] A report in 1575 on justices of the peace resident in each county, compared with the average of the

[61] For Sir John Cuttes, Morant, *History of Essex*, II, 439; H. W. King, "The Descent of the Manor of Horham, and of the Family of Cutts," *Essex Archaeological Society Transactions*, IV, 30; various commissions of the peace. In Essex, in the Elizabethan group of justices of the peace whose family relationships have been identified (39 per cent have not), about 30 per cent were fathers of Essex justices of the peace, several being grandfathers also, 20 per cent were sons, 9 per cent were fathers-in-law of Essex justices, 8 per cent were sons-in-law.

[62] Tawney, *Agrarian Problem*, 384.

[63] The counties are, in addition to those mentioned in the text, Somerset, Wiltshire, Worcestershire, West Riding, Cheshire. The commissions of the peace included in the averages are for the following years: 1559, 1562, 1573, 1577, late 1579 or 1580, 1583 or 1584, 1584 or 1585, and about 1596; 1604, 1607 or 1608, 1621 or 1622; 1625, 1631 or 1632, 1636 or 1637.

two available commissions nearest in date, shows varying percentages: as high as 90 per cent in Devon and Somerset, as low as 58 per cent in Warwickshire.[64]

Location was one of the considerations in appointing to the commission, but recurring complaints of areas lacking nearby justices suggest that it was inadequately achieved. In a survey in 1587 of the commissions of the peace in each diocese, the bishops' recommendations were influenced by the number of existing justices in the area of residence of the candidate. The bishop of Bath and Wells suggested the reappointment to the Somerset commission of the peace of three men who had been removed, on the ground that their places of abode were "very convenient." The bishop of Peterborough lamented the poor distribution, with a great number in some parts, elsewhere few or none; he thought this created suspicion that the commission was used "as a countenance to the parties [rather than as] a benefit to the country." [65] An uneven distribution would tend to result from the location of "gentlemen's seats" in the more traveled and agreeable parts of a county; in the moors around Dulverton, Somerset, John Sydenham in 1564 was the only justice "nigh, saving Sir John Wyndham, who for age, sickness, and other causes is not now very meet to do service"; or in the "very rude" country between Axminster and the sea, there was only one justice "who for want of help is not able to answer every suitor." [66] The increase in the size of the commissions in James's reign did not necessarily affect such conditions, nor the reduction between 1622 and 1625. Again from Somerset a justice of the peace at the edge of the Mendip hills complains in 1626 that he is alone in his "division." [67] But usually the Privy Council, referring questions to the justices, were able to call upon three or four living near the place involved. This utilization of the nearest justices may well be responsible for somewhat exaggerated impressions that only a small number of justices were active.[68] In Essex, for example,

[64] See Bibliography for the commissions of the peace as given in various Libri Pacis; the report of 1575 in S.P.D. Eliz., CIV. In Essex the Elizabethan compiler in 1575 appears to have returned all the justices of the peace on the commission, a possible misunderstanding of his instructions.

[65] Strype, *Annals*, III, Pt. II, App. Bk. II, 450, 462–463.

[66] *A Collection of Original Letters from the Bishops to the Privy Council, 1564* . . . , ed. Mary Bateson, The Camden Miscellany, IX, 63–64.

[67] Som. Rec. Soc., XXIV, xx. Similar complaints were made in other counties.

[68] Some of these have undoubtedly been based on the Stiffkey Papers, which

which there is no reason to consider an atypical county, letters went from the council to at least thirty-one different justices through the years 1586–1596, or to about two-fifths of the total number of individuals on the two commissions of the peace of 1584 and 1596.[69] For the most important duties of state, the council relied on a few tried servants; thus the commissioners named for Essex on three special commissions during (probably) 1584–85 number twelve different knights and esquires, with Sir Thomas Mildmay appearing on all three, Sir Thomas Lucas and Sir John Petre on two.[70] The twelve were a quarter of the commission of the peace of 1584. Approximately the same fraction constituted the average attendance at Essex quarter sessions in 1587–1590, but included a number of justices of the peace not sufficiently senior or considerable to be put on special commissions.[71] However, often it was these smaller justices, to judge from scattered evidence in several counties and various periods, who were most important in not the least essential work of the magistrate — his daily accessibility for the settlement of neighborhood grievances and disturbances of the peace. Again illustrating from Essex, it appears that during the 1560's and 1570's, perhaps a half of the commission of the peace were available to sign warrants, license alehouses, commit offenders to gaol, deal with recalcitrant servants and apprentices.[72] In Worcestershire during James's reign, about 60 per cent of the bench seem to have performed their work out of sessions with fair conscientiousness.[73] Some allowance therefore must be made for the

---

tend to emphasize the activity of Nathaniel Bacon and the regional group of justices around Lynn and the northern coast. The statement above rests on classification of Privy Council letters in various years, from *Acts P.C.* In Somerset there was a group around Bristol, another near the Mendips, another near Crewkerne, etc.

[69] *Acts P.C.*, Eliz., XIV-XXVI, *passim*; B. M. Lansdowne MS. 737, f. 132–183, Liber Pacis about 1584, f. 136–138 for Essex; S.P.D., Eliz., Case F, No. 11. The net increase in number from 1584 to 1596 was five. Only knights and esquires again are included in these figures.

[70] B.M. Harleian MS. 474, f. 88, 93, 95; the undated commissions were for disarming recusants, the restraint of the transport of grain, and for examining passengers. In May 1585, lists of commissioners in certain counties for restraining the export of grain were compiled (*Cal. S.P.D.*, Eliz., 1581–1590, 243). Mildmay, Lucas, and Petre were all large landowners and leading justices of the peace.

[71] Based on lists of attendance at each quarter sessions, Cal. Q.S., *passim*.

[72] Based on signatures to documents in the sessions rolls, Cal. Q.S., *passim*.

[73] Based on signatures to documents in the sessions files, *Calendar*, passim.

justices' accomplishment in these outside services, as an offset to contemporary or later strictures on their lack of assiduity.[74]

Francis Bacon summarized the unavoidable contrast between local self-government and authoritarian bureaucracy when he pointed out the "great difference between that which is done by the distracted government of justices of peace, and that which may be done by a settled ordinance, subject to a regular visitation." [75] Other unfavorable opinions were expressed from time to time about the justices: they were indifferent to matters outside their own locality — "justices will not meddle out of their divisions"; they showed "much partiality, sometime malice"; [76] many get into the commission "more for particular authority than for public service," the Privy Council complained.[77] Yet they often displayed much initiative and public spirit. A considerable number devoted time and attention to duties out of sessions, even if sessions attendance was not high. A system of regional division of work and of private sittings of justices had evolved, with little direction from the central government which rarely proposed the administrative devices for executing its orders. Local action now lost to sight must have been taken without prompting from authority outside the county, like that of the Essex high constables who reported from a statute sessions of 1572 that they had apprenticed several poor children — this at a time when apprenticing by public authority had no statutory basis other than an act of 1535.[78] Traces have survived of the routine performance of many duties not usually recorded.[79]

As the editor's introduction points out, documents from several districts of the county have been lost; here as elsewhere, there can be little doubt that the surviving indications understate the actual work the justices of the peace did.

[74] Holdsworth, *English Law*, IV, 145, and Heckscher, *Mercantilism*, I, 247, cite Lambard's complaint of the scanty time that justices would give to quarter sessions.

[75] *Works*, XI, 252.

[76] *C.J.*, I, 1 Mar. 1620/21.

[77] Essex Cal. Q.S., IX, 26, S.R. 72/22, Mich. 21 Eliz., copy of Privy Council letter to the judges of assize, directing them to see that all justices of the peace took the proper oath before the judges before continuing to exercise the office.

[78] Leonard, *English Poor Relief*, 55, 76; Essex Cal. Q.S., IV, 151, S.R. 41/55, a statute sessions held after the justices of the peace had ordered in July 1572 that these sessions be kept regularly.

[79] Examples: the casual mention of the presence of searchers in cloth or tilemaking, in Essex (1607, 1597); in Wiltshire in the 1590's and early 1600's (cloth); in the West Riding in 1640–41 (order of quarter sessions to prosecute

The working relationship among the local officers of the county reviewed in the foregoing pages is difficult to define. In the early years of Elizabeth's reign, the justice of the peace was not yet the "ruler of the county." Apart from his supervision by a watchful and critical Privy Council seconded by the justices of assize, he was not yet in effective control of other local authorities. The rapid growth of his powers in this respect during the second half of the sixteenth century has been indicated above. By repetition and convenience, a direct administrative connection was established in an enlarging area of county government between justice of the peace and petty constable, in part new, in part replacing an old order in which the high constable had stood chiefly in immediate relation to the parish constables.[80] As for the high constable himself, the degree to which his status had declined by the middle of the seventeenth century beneath that of a justice of the peace can be gauged from the angry complaint of a Norfolk justice of that time. Protesting an accusation that he had aided royalist prisoners to escape, he wrote of his accuser: "whom I made not chief constable to repay me with malice and ingratitude for the many favors which he and his predecessors have received from me and mine."[81] But in enforcing their authority the justices of the peace were in effect limited to the sanctions of reprimand and fine, or so the apparent rarity of dismissals for negligence (or any cause) would suggest.[82] The justices in relation to the constables must have been in the same dilemma as the central government in relation to negligent magistrates — how to find replacements any more willing or able to do the work adequately. And the justices probably lacked, especially in regard to the petty constable, the

---

at county expense the use of a false search seal for cloth, *Sessions Records,* II, 240–241, and another mention of a searcher, II, 274).

[80] Much of this development came with the growth of poor law administration (see above, n. 29) but execution of the Statute of Artificers contributed to it through the operation of the wage-assessment and service clauses.

[81] H. L. Styleman, "L'Estrange Papers," *Norfolk Archaeology,* V, 128, a letter from Hamon L'Estrange, Esq., in October 1648. This family had supplied justices of the peace for several generations. The quoted remark has various interesting implications, among them that of the personal influence of one justice and that of the advantage of securing the office of high constable.

[82] Records of orders are scanty in the sixteenth century, even in Essex, and were not followed in detail by the present writer (except for apprenticeship) in either the sixteenth or seventeenth century. But the available printed Order Books of the seventeenth century appear to confirm the statement in the text.

sanction which the central government could and did employ, the mere threat of dismissal. This might have been useful against high constables, whose wish to hold office is suggested in several instances, but seems likely to have been usually ineffective for the uncomfortable post of the petty constable. Control by the justices of the peace had to take milder and more indirect forms, perhaps often sporadic, such as the order of the North Riding justices in 1612 that the high constables were to bring to the next sessions written lists of the names "of the several parishes and . . . constables" the lack of which the justices thought the cause of the neglect of "sundry services."[83] They could exert their influence better when a constable was to be appointed, as the Privy Council reminded them in 1609. They were to consider from time to time, the council directed, whether all constables of hundreds were sufficient men for their office. In regard to constables of townships, they were to "take the like care as far as it may any way concern you, as lords of leets or otherwise for fit and serviceable persons to be chosen."[84] This illustrates the vital part played by the manorial and parochial influence of the justice of the peace in his control of the other local authorities.

Much also depended for efficient administration on the justice's own vigor and leadership, as was observed in a later generation: the justices, it was complained, "are not fond of the severe and troublesome part . . . and if the justice shift it off from him, so will the constable as readily follow his worship's example . . ."[85] Equally important might be the justices' ability to protect the local officers in the discharge of their duties, but this had its limits. A Somerset justice complained in 1626 that three drunkards in his district had put to "expense and journeys" a constable who had got a conviction against them, by suing him at quarter sessions for libel; now, adds the justice, "the other constables will take heed how they meddle too much."[86]

The high constable, despite the gradual transference of his ancient dignities to the justices of the peace, continued to be technically re-

[83] N.R.R.S., I, 256.

[84] *Stiffkey Papers*, xxii, 26; a copy of the council letter is in the Cheshire MS. Sessions Bundles, 7 Jas. I.

[85] F. Brewster, *New Essays in Trade*, 47.

[86] Som. Rec. Soc., XXIV, xxi.

sponsible in many respects for the petty constables' performance of duty, especially in returning presentments to the justices' petty [87] and quarter sessions and in executing the justices' warrants. But these parish officers were probably not his subordinates in a legal sense.[88] His only way of coercing an unwilling or lazy constable was to exert whatever personal pressures he commanded through land or family,[89] or to present the offender to the sessions or assizes, at which the negligent officer might be fined or even committed to gaol.[90] Meanwhile the petty constable's station in life made adequate execution of his office even more difficult than his social superiors found it to accomplish theirs. Occasionally neglect of duty resulted from frivolous causes. Henry Bursey in the North Riding refused to make his presentments at a petty sessions "by reason he was to go to a horse-race." John Burke in Essex, constable of White Notley, was "a maintainer of unlawful games, and has not executed his office accordingly." [91] But more often the constable had to put first his own business of getting a living, whether at a craft or trade or as a husbandman who had to be "most part of the day in the fields." [92] The demands made upon his time and energy fully to carry out his multifarious duties under the many statutes were impossible to meet, as they were almost equally so on a voluntary basis for those above him.

[87] See below, Chap. IX.

[88] Contemporary writers differed in their views, see Peyton, *Proceedings in Quarter Sessions . . . for . . . Kesteven*, I, xlv.

[89] Sometimes the influence of a superior was used to prevent execution of duty: the Privy Council complained in 1617 that petty constables and other local officers failed to present to the commissioners for sea breaches in Norfolk and Suffolk the names of the owners of endangered lands who should pay assessments, and declared that "men of so mean condition durst not be so bold but that they receive encouragement from men of better estate" (*Acts P.C.*, Jas. I, III, 227).

[90] N.R.R.S., II, 96.

[91] N.R.R.S., I, 232, October Sessions, 1611; Essex, Cal. Q.S., VI, 105, S.R. 53/54, presentment by the grand jury at April Sessions, 1575.

[92] Dalton, *The Country Justice*, 4th ed., 4.

VIII

LOCAL PRESENTMENT

The responsibilities of local authorities for executing the Act of 1563, as for other statutes, were of two kinds — those specifically assigned by the statute and those belonging to their general duties. The former were few, for constables and justices of the peace alike. For the petty constables the Act's instructions concerned only the service provisions. For the high constables, the sole reference in the statute is the proviso that they shall continue to hold their petty sessions as accustomed.[1] The justices of the peace were required to validate the certificates of the estate of an apprentice's parents, to settle disputes between master and apprentice and discharge contracts of apprenticeship for cause; to compel apprenticeship on demand from householders needing apprentices; to enforce the service and wages provisions of the statute; and to supervise the Act's observance, by holding special sessions of inquiry twice a year.[2] The work of the justices will be discussed in a separate chapter. The subject of the high constables' petty sessions, in so far as these dealt with apprenticeship, is a part of the larger topic of the system of local presentment of offenses.

Many of the general duties of the high and petty constables were comprised within their function as agents for the presentment of offenses to one or another court, because this necessitated inquiry into or knowledge of local conditions or sometimes the original discovery of offenders, as well as the reporting of illegalities. On whom the responsibility then devolved for prosecution was another question, and failure to seek or find an answer to it resulted in one of the chief

[1] 5 Eliz., c. 4, §40; see App. I below.

[2] 5 Eliz., c. 4, apprenticeship, §§20, 22, 25, 28 (see App. I below); service and wages, §§3–4, 11–12, 15, 17, 31; special sessions of inquiry, §30 (see App. I below).

weaknesses of the system.[3] Besides the constables of both ranks, the primary sources of presentments to quarter sessions and to assizes were the grand jury "for the body of the county" and the juries for the hundreds or for equivalent divisions within the county. Though each agency of presentment made its own returns, those of the petty constable were the basic element, not only because they concerned the smallest unit area, the township, but also because they often supplied material for the others' returns.

The least of the courts to which it is certain that the petty constables made presentments of offenses against the Statute of Artificers [4] was that held, not universally but widely, by the high constables in their hundreds.[5] The only known sixteenth-century series of records for these petty sessions, outside of certain boroughs, is preserved in the Essex quarter sessions rolls, although presentments before them in sixteenth-century Norfolk left piecemeal traces.[6] The

[3] See below, Chap. XI.

[4] The possibility cannot be entirely dismissed, though it seems remote, that the older local courts, the remnants of royal or franchise jurisdictions, occasionally enforced apprenticeship regulations. The statute of 1589 named the court leet as one of the local courts to which certain suits including those under Section 24 of the Act of 1563 were to be restricted. Reference to the leet may have been only for the other regulations in question, but this cannot be certain in an age when the manorial courts were still sufficiently vigorous to receive new assignments of jurisdiction (see Peyton, Introduction, Northamptonshire *Quarter Sessions Records*, xliii). Manor courts did sometimes take notice of industrial offenses (an instance mentioned by Ramsay, *The Wiltshire Woollen Industry*, 61). The Essex records show that in Elizabeth's reign courts leet, courts baron, and the sheriff's tourn all paralleled the work of the high constables' petty sessions for some offenses and occasionally duplicated or alternated with them. In the seventeenth century, evidence of the continued vitality of manorial jurisdictions in Essex is less frequent, but even in 1631 a petty constable reported to quarter sessions that he was making presentments to a court leet (Cal. Q.S., XX, 284, S.R. 273/35).

[5] The growth and continued activity of these little courts of the hundred alongside the decaying hundred courts of more ancient lineage appears to be an unexplored subject; the Webbs drew attention to them (*Parish and County*, 492, n. 1). The prominence of their function as a labor exchange suggests an origin in the fourteenth-century statutes of laborers, though no mention is made in B. H. Putnam, *The Enforcement of the Statutes of Laborers*. Procedure and subject matter of presentments in part resemble those of the medieval sheriff's tourn (H. M. Cam, *The Hundred and the Hundred Rolls*, 120–121). The Act of 1563, Sect. 40, makes it clear that they did not then exist in all counties. They were active in some boroughs, for example in Thetford in Norfolk and in Great Grimsby in Lincolnshire; in the latter the oldest extant entry is in November 1539 (MS. Court Books).

[6] Evidence for the regular holding of the high constables' petty sessions with

Essex returns, however, provide the best sample of procedure and subject matter, beginning with the earliest extant in April 1562, until they disappear early in the seventeenth century.[7] Presentments were made by the petty constables of the townships within the hundred, together with one or more inhabitants. These made up presentment juries whose attendance appears to have been compulsory. The offenses on which it was their duty to report derived from ancient common and statute law and from recent legislation, and at least to some extent may have followed instructions delivered to the high constables from quarter sessions.[8] A memorandum of what was to be presented at a petty sessions of 1566 listed the main heads: the vagrants punished, how the watch and ward was kept, whether unlicensed alehouses had been suppressed, the activities of engrossers and forestallers, the playing of unlawful games; and "to inquire of servants, both men and women" with a marginal note, "for excessive wages." Three other subjects were the maintenance of butts for archery, "breakers of the peace" and "sowers of sedition." A jury presentment in 1572 was in response to nine "interrogatories delivered" to them which included the third and fourth subjects of the preceding memorandum as well as the assizes of bread and of beer.[9] The offenses presented at the Essex petty sessions, besides the time-honored matter of road and bridge repairs, included a wide gamut of local nuisances and personal habits. The importance of the sessions for enforcing contracts of service is demonstrated by the frequency with which presentments for violating these occur. But no present-

---

petty constables presenting to them antedates the Act of 1563 by some thirty years in Norfolk, but the quarter sessions files have preserved only a portion of their returns to the quarter sessions, made in accordance with the writs from the justices of the peace, which must be the direct descendants of those issued under the early statutes of laborers (Putnam, 66–67).

[7] Only two or three returns are known for the years between 1602 and 1642, and one in the late seventeenth century.

[8] No such instructions have been seen for the high constables' petty sessions, as distinct from those for their presentments to quarter sessions, unless the memorandum and the "interrogatories" described in the text were based on a "charge" delivered at quarter sessions.

[9] Cal. Q.S., II, 112–113, S.R. 18/61; IV, 39–41, S.R. 39/6. The jury presentment was from three parishes and was probably made early in 1572 although the record belongs to the Easter Sessions. It has the appearance of a return to petty sessions. The two documents immediately following it in the roll are reports from individual parishes of the supply of grain on hand, and all three items may reflect the special conditions of 1571/2 rather than normal procedure.

ments in four major classes of economic and social regulation are found in the Essex series: the whole array of apprenticeship requirements, regulations for particular industries (the Cloth Acts, the statutes controlling the processing of leather, and the like), inclosure, and usury.

Nevertheless the petty sessions made a contribution to the enforcement of apprenticeship which was not the less vital because indirect. In Essex as in other counties where the high constables' petty sessions were held, they had the important duty of providing both a labor exchange and a registry of service contracts.[10] Though there is no evidence at all that this function was expanded after 1563 to include for rural areas the systematic registration of apprentices' indentures, nevertheless, if Essex is representative, apprenticeship contracts were occasionally recorded: several petty sessions returns in this county list the wages and terms for apprentices as well as servants. For example, at the statute sessions for the hundred of Becontree in March 1574, seventeen apprenticeships were recorded to masters in seven different crafts. In the hundred of Lexden, one of the chief district of the Essex woolen industry, the hirings at the petty sessions of April 1575, though principally of servants to rural craftsmen, listed an apprentice to a fuller and one to a brickmaker, each for seven years. A similar record of service contracts which included some for apprentices is preserved from a petty sessions of 1610 held for Waltham half hundred in the same county. In the town of Waltham itself, a glover had three apprentices, a baker two, a butcher one, and in a neighboring village two tailors and a smith each had two apprentices; in every case the return affirms that the apprentice is "bound by indentures according to the law." [11] Few of the returns include a list of hirings at all; that any of them do is probably from the ignorance of some high constables of their precise function. Presumably, however, those better informed, who certified to quarter sessions only the offenses which required "hear-

[10] In some counties, this may have been their sole duty even in the sixteenth century; in later periods, generally so.

[11] Cal. Q.S., V, 175, S.R. 48/88; VI, 117–118, S.R. 53/50; XIX, 5–6, S.R. 193/40, petty sessions in December 1610 for Waltham half-hundred. It is quite possible that each of these returns comprehended the total of apprenticeships begun within the hundred during the quarter-year to which they applied; if so, the small number of such contracts, as well as the number of apprentices kept by each master, provide a further indication of the scale of economic activity.

ing and determining" there, kept a similar registry of their own. This is indicated by occasional mention elsewhere. In Jacobean Norfolk, for example, a maidservant claimed the entry in "the constables' books" as a proof of her contract of service.[12] Rare indictments for retaining apprentices without registering the indenture according to law within three months may imply the existence of recognized means of doing so.[13]

The petty constables' duty to keep themselves informed of conditions of employment may have contributed to enforcement of apprentices' terms. In the intervals between petty sessions, the constables made the rounds of the employers in the community, recording changes in hirings, new hirings, or the wages being paid. These inspections were the basis for their presentments at the statute sessions, and so far as they performed this duty, they may also have been in effect inspectors of apprenticeship. The system seems to have operated with a good deal of routine effectiveness where it existed,[14] and certain types of service offenses dealt with in petty constables' reports were connected with the observance of apprenticeship.

One was the reduction of the statutory term, either from a master's turning the apprentice away or from agreement between master and apprentice to end the contract. Each can be illustrated from petty sessions in Essex: one master was presented for attempting to "put away" his apprentice before the end of his term to avoid paying him the agreed wage; another for accepting 3/– from his apprentice to release him after six years had been served of his seven-year term.[15] Such breaches of contract, however, seem generally to have been brought directly before the justices of the peace.

[12] Norfolk MS. Sessions Rolls, 19 Jas. I, document recording examination of a servant complaining of ill treatment; she testifies she was hired at a petty sessions in September 1620.

[13] In Essex, one in 1614 of a fuller of Great Coggeshall (Cal. Q.S., XIX, 137, S.R. 205/38, Epiph. 11 Jas. I, under Sect. 25 of 5 Eliz., c. 4); another in 1628 of a Bocking weaver (MS. Sessions Rolls, No. 265, Bdle. of Ignoramus bills of miscellaneous dates). Alternatively these may have been merely nuisance prosecutions utilizing a disregarded provision of the statute.

[14] The sessions records of the North Riding alone contain adequate evidence for the early seventeenth century of the petty constables' activity in this function. (See N.R.R.S., I and II, *passim*). On the subject of hirings at statute sessions, though without reference to apprenticeship, see R. K. Kelsall, *Wage Regulation under the Statute of Artificers*, 56–60; his illustrations, however, are drawn mostly from the later seventeenth century and the eighteenth century.

[15] Cal. Q.S., V, 160, S.R. 48/61, Easter 16 Eliz.

The offense against Section 3 of the Statute of Artificers, refusal by single men under thirty to take service on demand, was frequently reported to the petty sessions by the parish constables. Such presentments must have had some effectiveness in detecting the unapprenticed worker. It is not clear from the context in a few of these cases whether the young men reported for "living at their own hands" had been apprenticed or not. At the petty sessions for Waltham half-hundred in March 1575, among "bachelors" out of service, two linen-drapers were presented for keeping shops in Waltham; the result of the accusation for one of them was an order that he leave town, but the other was allowed to stay since he had been apprenticed in Waltham.[16] In another instance the offender might have been, but was not, prosecuted as unapprenticed. At a petty sessions a bachelor was presented as out of service, a charge which took the following form in the presentment by the jury for the Duchy of Lancaster at the next quarter sessions, Easter 1573: "Roger Turner who was a husbandman now has forsaken his science and keeps the trade of buying and selling butchery ware without license."[17] The selection of offense by the two juries concerned suggests a greater interest on their part in preventing withdrawals from the supply of agricultural labor than in suppressing an untrained butcher. A mixture of motives appears in five presentments on the borderline between the two charges: single men working out of service and lack of the seven-year term of apprenticeship. The earliest of these, in 1574, was a petty sessions' presentment against a bachelor of Bocking for "occupying the science of shearman" though never apprenticed. The next cases were not until 1591, when the Chelmsford petty sessions presented three "singlemen," each for coming into a separate parish "without testimonial or certificate whence he came" and using there an art, "whereas to our knowledge he was never educated as an apprentice for seven years . . . contrary to the statute of the fifth year"; one set up as a weaver, the others as tailors. The fifth similar case is found in the petty sessions' presentment of 1610 for Waltham half-hundred, already mentioned, under the heading of "Masterless men and other

[16] Cal. Q.S., VI, 178, S.R. 55/9. The one ordered away may also have been apprenticed elsewhere. The strength of old statute law become custom is reflected in the permission given two tailors similarly offending to stay for forty days — the grace period provided in the act of 1388.

[17] Cal. Q.S., IV, 229, S.R. 44/42; 248, S.R. 44/61.

that work at their own hand contrary to the law": "John Knight, tailor, not having served seven years." [18]

These presentments appear only minor qualifications of the view that the enforcement of apprenticeship was not one of the normal objectives of the presentment system at the level of the township, the smallest unit of local government and the one closest to the rural offender. The motive for reporting the "singlemen" in these instances and in others like them was the community's interest in defending the earning power of its householders and heads of families. A later prosecution by the trade competitors of such an intruder shows the union of the two offenses: in 1622 William Mott, a single man, was required to give bond to answer at the next quarter sessions the complaint of "the potters of Stoke and Buttsbury" that he, as a bachelor, not only works at his own hand but also "setteth up the trade and occupation of a potter having never been bound apprentice thereunto, taking away the living of married persons who have wife and children." [19]

When such unmarried competitors were newcomers to the township, they came under the special notice of the constable for another reason, in connection with his duty to suppress vagrancy. The testimonial of discharge required from servants before they could legally leave a district, together with compulsory hiring for young unmarried men and women, attempted to regulate settlement for the more migratory class of workers for generations before the settlement law of the Restoration.[20] In such cases as have been cited, these labor regulations were used defensively to protect the resident craftsmen-householders. The same thing was happening in Wiltshire: at the July quarter sessions in 1623, the constables of the hundred of Mere presented a tailor who had been living in the town of Mere some six months, "having come a stranger"; he refused to leave, although warned, staying "to the hurt of the poor men of the same trade" who

[18] Cal. Q.S., V, 159–160, S.R. 48/61; XVI, 72–73, S.R. 118/38 and 38a; XIX, 5, S.R. 193/40. In the typescript Calendar, the 1610 entry appears as the presentment of the hundred jury at the January quarter sessions, but notes made from the original sessions roll suggest that it may at least have been taken over from the same petty sessions' return which had reported contracts of service (see n. 11 above).

[19] Cal. Q.S., XIX, 473–474, S.R. 236/84, Easter 20 Jas. I, recognizance dated January 14.

[20] The testimonial, or certificate of legal departure to seek work elsewhere, was necessary in order to leave even the parish (Sect. 7 of 5 Eliz., c. 4).

"suppose" that he is unapprenticed.[21] Such presentments raise a very important question about local enforcement of apprenticeship, from the township up through the quarter sessions: was the apparent slackness in executing the apprenticeship regulations due to the overriding need to minimize the problems of pauperism and vagrancy rather than to the stickiness of local custom controlling the acceptance of new responsibilities by the local officers? From this viewpoint, the established, or even the new, householder and family man might be permitted the use of an occupation, even though all the village knew he had never "served his time," so long as he did not tread on the toes of too many or too influential competitors. The unattached man, on the other hand, at once came under suspicion, and a rumor that he was unqualified for his trade provided an additional excuse for getting rid of him.

The integral connection, in the thought of the period, between regulation of the service contract and the perpetual fear of the menace of vagrancy is demonstrated in a petition to the Lancashire justices of the peace for better enforcement of compulsory service and for a house of correction because servants seek "liberty to work when they please," refusing to be hired by the year, and housekeepers, it is claimed, "cannot live in safety in the night," so great are the numbers of masterless people.[22]

Control of the "idle out of service" was sufficiently important at the end of Elizabeth's reign in Essex to be the subject of special orders at quarter sessions, possibly as part of a general campaign during the uneasy last months of the queen's life to tighten measures against potential rioters and "stirrers of sedition": petty constables were thereafter to certify monthly to the high constables not only the vagrants in their parish who had been punished and sent on with a pass and the number of alehouses and inns, but also those out of service. The high constables were to keep these reports in a "book" to present to the justices, and they were enjoined to hold their petty sessions twice a year.[23]

[21] MS. Sessions Rolls, Trin. 21 Jas. I, among the Presentments. Probably he was a bachelor "living at his own hands."

[22] MS. Sessions Recognizances, Bundle for 1625–26, petition dated May 1606, from the western district around Ormskirk. The petitioners ask that "a yearly meeting" be held for setting down servants' wages and their enrolment "as in the south parts."

[23] Cal. Q.S., XVIII, 278, S.R. 160/6, Epiph. 45 Eliz.

The watch kept by petty constables and their cojurors for the hundred on single men and newcomers in township or manor must have provided, for many village parents and children, a motive in itself to obtain the security of an apprenticeship, and its attestation in registered indentures. The safeguard which this could furnish even for the young unmarried man is illustrated by a case from Somerset: a nineteen-year old bachelor was presented at quarter sessions for using the art of a currier at Bruton to the hindrance of an established craftsman; two marginal notations tell the outcome — "and yet hath served his apprentice," "vacat." [24] To such indirect enforcement of apprenticeship the high constables also contributed by their responsibility for holding the petty sessions, wherever these registered apprenticeship contracts, and for the presentments brought in to them which helped to keep track of irregular conditions of service or use of independent occupations. With variations in the scope of subject matter, their petty or statute sessions appear to have functioned over most of England in the period 1563–1642, except possibly in the southwest.[25] In this region perhaps even in the sixteenth century presentments by petty and high constables direct to quarter sessions took their place. By the seventeenth century, there are indications that elsewhere the high constables' petty sessions were becoming or had become hiring sessions only, with their jurisdiction as a minor court

[24] MS. Indictment Rolls, No. 7, Epiphany Sessions at Wells, 45 Eliz. It is not clear why in this case the apprenticeship excused the young man from compulsory service until thirty unless he had sufficient personal or real estate to be exempt according to Sect. 3 of the Act of 1563, or unless no currier needed to hire him.

[25] William Harrison's *Description*, 103, does not provide additional evidence of their existence since it was probably drawn from Essex where he was a parson at Radwinter. The Norfolk sixteenth-century evidence has already been mentioned. In Staffordshire the Elizabethan petty sessions of the high constables may have been, as in Essex, a court of initial presentment for a number of offenses dealt with in quarter sessions (MS. Sessions Rolls, Nos. 7, 38, 42). The seventeenth-century vitality of the statute sessions in numerous shires suggests a long history earlier, but in few of any period is there evidence that they were more than hiring sessions. In Devonshire and Wiltshire the character of certain orders at quarter sessions indicates an absence of statute sessions. Devon, MS. Sessions Rolls, 1601, Calendar of Recognizances with memoranda of orders, cited in Hamilton, *Quarter Sessions*, 13: order at Easter 1601, accompanying a wage assessment, that constables must present to five regional subcommittees of justices the names of all masters and servants giving and taking wages over the assessed rates. Wiltshire, MS. Sessions Minute Books, III, Epiphany Sessions 13 Jas. I: order that parish overseers of the poor must keep registries of service contracts. In Somerset no mention has been seen of statute sessions.

transferred to the justices of the peace in private or in quarter sessions.[26] Their dwindling to mere labor exchanges suggests the possibility that whatever part of their earlier functions concerned the registration of apprenticeship contracts may also have shrunk as they dealt more exclusively with the hiring of farm and domestic servants.

To judge from the surviving Essex samples of petty constables' presentments of the Stuart period, most of which were probably returned to quarter sessions, they dealt with much the same list of offenses as in the Elizabethan, with statutory additions.[27] So also did those of the high constables, who were to add matters of their own knowledge to the presentments of their inferiors. Presentments to the assizes by both ranks of constables probably differed little if at all from those to quarter sessions.[28] There does not appear to have been any very systematic direction to either court. An Essex high constable in 1630, reporting to quarter sessions on the parish presentments for which he was responsible, explained their small number thus: four townships had sent in their returns to the assizes; one had reported "nothing worth presenting"; from four others he had not heard.[29] Existing examples of presentments to quarter sessions by both ranks of constables follow, with considerable local and individual variation, a roughly uniform pattern. Within this frame there was apparently little if any greater place for direct supervision of apprenticeship than in the work of the high constables' petty sessions;

[26] This apparent decline in the powers of the high constable can be inferred with most probability in Essex, from the disappearance there of the petty sessions' returns and scattered evidence that justices of the peace were holding private sessions at which presentments were made. More continuous illustration of the nature of such private sessions before two or a few justices is available in the North Riding.

[27] Only a few are extant in the Sessions Rolls 1603–1642: a group in 1609–10, more in the 1630's. The county archives include separate bundles of paper documents not examined by the present writer, which may or may not contain constables' presentments. Such bundles are mentioned in *The Guide to the Essex Quarter Sessions and Other Official Records*, ed. F. G. Emmison, 3. Presentments by high and petty constables in other counties confirm the generalization in the text above. New statute offenses were those added in the closing years of Elizabeth's reign: cottages without four acres, lodgers, and violations of the poor laws of 1597 and 1601. Recusancy was also a subject of constables' presentments to quarter sessions in the Stuart period.

[28] The Somerset sessions records contain occasional presentments made to the assizes by the high constables.

[29] Cal. Q.S., XX, 266, S.R. 271/29.

in the period 1563–1642, only two certain instances are known of direct presentment by either rank of officer for using an occupation without having served an apprenticeship, and four others which may be by high or petty constables.[30] The case cited above, of a bachelor currier in Somerset, is on the borderline between enforcement of apprenticeship and of service, like the five cases in Essex petty sessions in Elizabeth's reign. Such presentments of single men out of service, made to the quarter sessions, might be indirect means of overseeing apprenticeship no less than when made to the high constables' petty sessions.

The uniformity of pattern already noticed constitutes a long-term trend in the subject matter of high and petty constables' presentments toward an increasing attention to offenses involving vagrancy, poor relief, the overcrowding of areas by squatters and lodgers, and the whole class of nuisances, particularly as to roads and bridges. In several localities, service offenses appear frequently. Wider questions of economic regulation seldom or never are included. Did local officers select from a more comprehensive list the subjects most closely touching the community, or did they receive no instructions from above as to the subjects they ignored? Discussion of these points belongs to the topics of the responsibility of the justice of the peace for the presentment system and of the central government's relation to law-enforcement.[31]

Two agencies of presentment paid somewhat more attention to enforcing compulsory apprenticeship than did the constables, or the jurors at high constables' petty sessions. These were the juries for each hundred which presented at quarter or other sessions of the justices of the peace and at the assizes, and the grand jury for the county. Within the eighty years 1563–1642 in the selected counties, seven to nine presentments for exercising occupations without a seven-year apprenticeship were made by grand juries, and from forty-two to fifty-four by hundred juries.[32] The available evidence is in-

[30] The first two are in the North Riding, one in 1608 by a petty constable of an unapprenticed weaver, the second in 1611 by two high constables of an unapprenticed butcher (N.R.R.S., I, 122, 207). The doubtful four are also in the North Riding in 1608 (I, 106–108).

[31] In the next two chapters below.

[32] Two presentments in Essex may be by grand or hundred jury, and may be for service rather than apprenticeship. In the North Riding, either the original document or the form of abstract used by the editor of the printed sessions

sufficient to explain this difference in the number of such cases presented by juries to quarter sessions and assizes, and by constables to these courts or at the statute sessions. The general range of subject matter of hundred juries' presentments seems greater than that of constables,[33] suggesting either that the former were regarded as having a wider range of competence or that they were bolder because of their social position or the safety of numbers. But that there was any marked gap in social status is very doubtful. In Elizabethan Essex, the social level of the men summoned to each quarter sessions for possible service on the hundred juries of presentment was similar to that of the petty constables. Occasionally in this county the designation of "constable" is entered against all or many of the hundred jury, sometimes against only one or two, or none.[34] An identity of personnel with the jurors who presented to the high constables' petty sessions, or perhaps only with the constables presenting there, is several times suggested by references in the hundred juries' presentments: for example, at Easter Sessions in 1566 the jurors for Freshwell hundred, after reporting one highway needing repair, say that "as for all other things else we did present to the high constables at the petty sessions within six days . . . holden at Walden."[35] Northamptonshire at a later period is the only other county in which the practice has been observed of summoning petty constables for jury service, with a consequent narrowing of the sources of presentment. More widespread was a custom of summoning high constables

records makes uncertain the nature of nine cases, whether indictments or presentments. The remaining doubtful case may be a private individual's prosecution.

[33] In Essex, hundred juries presented reputed witches, offending purveyors, and offenses once presented in manorial courts such as overstocking pasture or pound breach, besides the standard subjects found in constables' presentments. Very occasionally a hundred jury presented an extortionate informer (Cal. Q.S., XIX, 331, S.R. 223/37).

[34] For example, at Epiphany Sessions, 1557, 13 out of 20 were constables on the jury for the hundred of Hinckford, only 1 out of 22 on that for Chafford hundred at the same Sessions, 6 out of 16 for the hundreds of Uttlesford and Freshwell (represented by one jury together), whereas the list for Chelmsford hundred is wholly constables, 22 in all, both at this Sessions and at Easter Sessions, 1562 (Cal. Q.S., I, 61–65, S.R. 3/35–41, 95, S.R. 5/29). In 1564 jurors for three hundreds were all described as constables (Cal. Q.S., I, 182a–183, 185–186, S.R. 11/13, 14, 17).

[35] Cal. Q.S., II, 113, S.R. 18/62. Other like instances in 1566, 1567, 1568, 1569, etc. (*Ibid.*, II, 111, S.R. 18/59, 151–152, S.R. 20/6; III, 14, S.R. 26/26, 53–54, S.R. 27/22).

to serve on the grand jury: Lambard testifies to it for Kent, Dalton in Cambridgeshire; in the North and West Ridings, individual high constables can sometimes be identified on the two grand juries which served in these Ridings at each sessions.[36] In Somerset, from the early seventeenth century some hundred presentments are described as by "the Constables and Jury" or "the Jury with Constables," but for other hundreds there continue to be separate presentments by the high constables.[37] In certain counties no overlapping of personnel is apparent: in Staffordshire, for example, at least in the sixteenth century, constables were not summoned as jurors, though occasionally in the seventeenth century high constables may have been called for the grand jury; and in Wiltshire juries and constables made separate and sometimes conflicting presentments.[38]

The anonymity of collective presentment hardly seems a necessary safeguard in prosecuting the small offender who was the usual object of local accusations for lack of apprenticeship, any more than for offenders of similar status in the subjects of presentment most frequently occurring. These for hundred juries included the problems of vagrancy, overcrowding of parishes, negligent officers, superfluous and disorderly inns or alehouses, and single men out of service. Hundred and grand juries alike tended to make the upkeep of roads and bridges a foremost concern. No doubt it touched the jurymen the

[36] In Northamptonshire in 1667, a hundred jury returns that everything has been presented by the petty constables, "several of us being constables ourselves"; and in 1657 a constable is identifiable with a member of a hundred jury (MS. Sessions Rolls, Easter Sess. 19 Chas. II, Warden hundred presentment; *Quarter Sessions Records*, 125 and 169). The Webbs cite the Jury of Constables in Coventry, *Parish and County*, 464–465. The use of constables' juries in the late seventeenth and in the eighteenth century had spread, as in Middlesex, Hertfordshire, and elsewhere. For grand jury service by high constables, Lambard, *Eirenarcha* (1581), 306–307; Dalton, *The Country Justice*, 7th ed., 514; N.R.R.S., I, 208, 210, 214, 228, 259, 261, II, 95, 97; *West Riding Sessions Records,* I, 8, 29, 105, 110. (Two cases involved in these references may both be petty constables of higher social rank than the average.)

[37] MS. Indictment Rolls, 1608, 1610, 1611, etc., through the series until 1625–26, when by a change in filing, presentments were no longer bound in with indictments. When presentments are found again, from 1640, and in the later seventeenth century, this styling continues; in 1652 there is one mention of the "juries of constables of hundreds"; but it seems possible that the assignment by some authorities to Somerset of the practice of "constables' juries" rests only on what was, in fact, joint presentment by high constables and jury.

[38] *Staffordshire Rolls,* IV, xxiii, V, 138, 153; Wiltshire MS. Sessions Rolls, Trin. 13 Jas. I, presentments by Heytesbury hundred jury and constables; Trin. 20 Jas. I, the same, and Warminster hundred jury and constables.

most nearly, and sometimes the most recently, as for those of four Essex hundreds in 1562 who united to report "a bridge which is very noisome . . . for it is now that we were afain to swim over with our horses as we came hither." [39]

When competition from the unapprenticed occurred under conditions that made it "noisome" to the community, it too was worthy of presentment. Over a half of the apprenticeship presentments by grand and hundred juries in the counties of Somerset, Wiltshire, Essex and Norfolk,[40] were made in anxious times, years of scarcity, increased vagrancy, or depressed trade. A high proportion, between a half and two-thirds, were against food processors, especially bakers. This is consistent with the attention given by the juries to presentments of the prices and quantities of bread and grain.[41] Local shortage may have caused two Essex presentments of unapprenticed bakers in April 1591 and October 1592, one of whom was also accused of starchmaking.[42] In Somerset and Norfolk, presentments by borough and hundred juries of offending bakers in April 1594 and January 1597 were in seasons of general scarcity: the Book of Orders was reissued in 1594 to enforce control of the grain trade, while 1596 was notorious for its dearth and disorder and in April 1597 rioting mobs in Norfolk seized grain on its way to the ports.[43] The depression years 1622–1623 were also a period of grain shortage, when in clothing counties such as Wiltshire the justices of the peace took measures to see that markets were supplied; and in Wiltshire at this time the

[39] Cal. Q.S., I, 132, S.R. 8/10.

[40] The only four counties with the exception of the North Riding in which jury presentments can be traced before 1642. Not enough is known by the present writer of economic conditions in the North Riding to include it in the above statement.

[41] In presenting violations of the assizes of bread and ale. Occasionally they reported directly on the quantity of grain available, as in Essex in 1572 (Cal. Q.S., IV, 41).

[42] Cal. Q.S., XVI, 53, S.R. 116/34, presentment for the hundreds of Dengey, Winstree, and Thurstable, of a basket-maker of Barking; *ibid.*, 110, S.R. 122/24, presentment for the hundred of Hinckford of a weaver of Halstead. In the latter case, the jury may have been protecting the use of grain despite local unemployment: about 1589, weavers there were complaining of insufficient work given them by English clothiers after the Dutch settlers had been driven away by jealousy (*Victoria History of Essex*, II, 390).

[43] Somerset MS. Sessions Indictment Books, II, Easter 36 Eliz., presentment by jury for Ilchester borough; Norfolk MS. Sessions Rolls, Epiphany 39 Eliz., presentment by Northgreenhoe hundred; Gras, *English Corn Market*, 236; Cheyney, *History of England*, II, 26; *Acts P.C.*, Eliz., XXVII, 88.

jury for the hundred of Westbury presented unapprenticed bakers near the chief textile village of the district.[44]

During the last two years of Elizabeth's reign, when the established weavers of this same area were trying to protect their position by a campaign against unqualified craftsmen and illegal apprenticeship contracts, the hundred jury took part by presentments for the latter offense as well as for illegal looms. The grand jury approved the cloth-searchers' charges against eight of the offenders by making them a part of its own presentment at one quarter sessions.[45] The concern of the jurors over competition which evidently was thought a menace to stable employment in the district may have been greater here than in areas of lesser concentration in the woolen industry because so many workers were involved and because Wiltshire textile workers were dependent on their wages. This may explain the unusual step taken in 1605 either by the grand jury or a hundred jury, probably that of Westbury again, in presenting some forty-three clothiers for not paying their weavers the assessed rates of wages.[46]

Unemployment and the burden of poor relief perhaps occasioned in 1608 the presentments already described of unapprenticed weavers and tuckers by the jury for the borough of Taunton and a neighboring hundred in Somerset.[47] Detection in this instance seems to have been almost immediate, for the offenders were charged with using their crafts only one month. The description of four of them as "grooms," a term that in other contexts appears to have been the Somerset equivalent of the Essex "single man," suggests that the hundred jury was impelled by the same concern that has been observed in constables' presentments to prevent young bachelors from competing with householders, especially if the offenders were newcomers to a parish. An association of hundred juries' presentments for lack of apprenticeship with the policy of protecting the married

[44] Wiltshire MS. Sessions Minute Books, V, Trin. 20 Jas. I, presentment of eight offenders.

[45] Wiltshire MS. Sessions Minute Books, II, Trin. 44 Eliz., hundred jury presentments of two weavers for taking apprentices who were sons of husbandmen (contrary to Sect. 21 of 5 Eliz., c. 4), of a husbandman taking an apprentice in weaving though not himself qualified, a widow retaining an unapprenticed journeyman, and eight or nine weavers for keeping too many looms (under the Act of 1555). *Ibid.*, Epiph. 45 Eliz., for the Grand Jury adoption of the cloth-searchers' presentments.

[46] Wiltshire MS. Sessions Rolls, No. 3, Trin. 3 Jas. I.

[47] See above, Chap. V, n. 124, the contemporary complaint there quoted of increased poor relief.

householder from (by the standard of the time) unfair competition, can be seen also in some of the Essex presentments of Elizabeth's reign, although in the seventeenth century in this county none of the hundred juries' presentments against single men out of service are linked with apprenticeship prosecutions.[48]

The tendency of so many of the presentments by public agencies to fall within periods of at least local economic stress shows that their main concern was not with the enforcement of apprenticeship for its own sake, but was part of their recurrent struggle with the problems of vagrancy and poor relief. Constables and juries gave even these problems only intermittent attention. In Wiltshire, for instance, as early as July 1603, when the weavers' difficulties had probably already been referred to the justices for solution, the hundred jury blandly pronounced that "all is good and fair," though the cloth-searchers were still bringing in some prosecutions.[49]

The hundred juries must have overlooked many more offenders against the apprenticeship regulations than they presented. Perhaps most of the known apprenticeship prosecutions by informers and private individuals occurred within hundreds whose juries were making regular presentments of other offenses to quarter sessions. In Essex, the distribution of Westminster professional informations within the various hundreds of the county compares as follows with that of statute sessions:

	Apprenticeship informations at Westminster[50]		Extant statute sessions returns in same hundreds
Year	*Occupation*	*Hundred*	
1571	Mercer	Chelmsford	2 Chelmsford
1579	2 Grocers	Chelmsford	2 Chelmsford
1580	Linendraper	Chelmsford	3 Chelmsford
1582	Clothier	Lexden	1 Lexden
	Baker	Waltham	1 Waltham
1583	Woolendraper	Lexden	1 Lexden
1585	Woolendraper	Uttlesford	1 Uttlesford
1586	1 Woolendraper 2 Linendrapers	Dunmow	1 Dunmow
1602	Miller	Freshwell	1 Freshwell

48 Cal. Q.S., IV, 228, S.R. 44/40 (the seasonal tilemaker-and-tailor of 1573); *ibid.*, XIV, 181, S.R. 105/34 (July 1588, a bachelor as an unapprenticed painter); *ibid.*, XVII, 164, S.R. 150/37 (July 1600, two single men "for using the science of a blacksmith contrary to the laws" — perhaps a case of being out of service rather than a charge of lack of apprenticeship).

49 MS. Sessions Rolls, No. 1, presentment by Westbury hundred, Trin. 1 Jas. I. The justices' orders regulating apprenticeship for weavers of the district were issued at the October sessions, see next chapter.

50 Exchequer Q.R.M.R. and Q.B.C.R. Informations against residents of cor-

It can be no accident that the known presentments by public agencies (in contrast to the professional informations, particularly in Essex) include none for unapprenticed retailing; though many of these documents are lost, those preserved must be a random sample, and it appears likely that the evasion of the apprenticeship regulations in retailing was not regarded as an offense requiring public presentment. In Essex itself, in 1572, in a year of increased emphasis on the statute sessions' responsibilities,[51] retailers in Chelmsford and Brentwood petitioned the justices of the peace to take steps against competitors from outside, who had set up retail shops as "mercers, haberdashers, and grocers" in these two places; yet in that year at least three statute sessions were held for the hundred of Chelmsford, with presentments from the town of Chelmsford for service offenses, but none for apprenticeship.[52]

It would not be reasonable, however, to argue from this that the public agencies would not have taken action against offenders, however great the volume of evasion of the apprenticeship law. The enforcement of apprenticeship, like that of regulations for particular industries and of the rules against usury, seems in general to have been considered as not among the responsibilities of local officers or of community juries. But, unlike offenses under the laws just named, evasions of the requirement of apprenticeship for entry into an occupation, or breaches of the clause limiting the number of apprentices of a master, could not have increased considerably in any one community over short periods without pressure on the livelihood of the established residents. Their relative neglect by local authority tends to confirm the concept of a society in which apprenticeship was the habitual pattern of life for the adolescent hoping to earn his

porate jurisdictions (beyond the authority of the statute session of the hundred) have been omitted. None of the few informations in the Essex quarter sessions (from 1591 on) involved hundreds for which contemporary statute sessions returns are extant.

[51] From 1569 to 1574 in Essex, there appears to have been improved control of service contracts through the statute sessions. From 1569 the Privy Council had been exhorting local authorities to suppress vagrancy, and from 1571 to 1573 the Essex statute sessions record an increased number of presentments of masterless men and women. In 1572, the justices of the peace were giving special attention to the regular holding of the statute sessions (Cal. Q.S., IV, 74–75, S.R. 40/1).

[52] Cal. Q.S., IV, 48, S.R. 39/25; 129–130, S.R. 41/30; 131–133, S.R. 41/31; 142, S.R. 41/41.

living wholly or partly in a craft. This was a society also in which industrial growth for the average community was gradual or non-existent. Where it occurred, industrial expansion was probably dispersed through the district, so that illegal concomitants in any one township would normally be too few to excite inquiry by local officers or jurors.

The local authorities upon whom lay the duty of overseeing the public order and welfare of the county as a whole, of holding the balance among the often conflicting restrictive policies of the individual communities, were the justices of the peace. Their relation to the enforcement of apprenticeship must now be examined.

IX

JUSTICES IN AND OUT OF SESSIONS

Regulation of apprenticeship by local officers implied two duties: to prevent entry into occupations without the due service of the statutory term of apprenticeship, and to ensure full performance of contracts of apprenticeship once made. Both forms of control when exercised by the justices of the peace have left some record in orders issued by them in quarter sessions. Supervision of contracts, however, was carried on chiefly by individual justices, acting singly at home, holding private sessions with one or two colleagues, or attending the high constables' statute sessions. Most of the justices' work in enforcing apprenticeship was such as to leave little written trace, and it is therefore likely to be underestimated. Their various duties under the Act of 1563 have already been outlined. Their fulfillment of them will be discussed under two heads: what they may have done individually and in private sessions, and how they treated problems of apprenticeship in quarter sessions.

An initial step either to secure the proper performance of contracts by masters and apprentices or equally to bar the unqualified use of a craft or trade would have been to compile local registers of indentures. But the justices of the peace were not assigned by the Act any responsibility or authority for the registration of apprentices, and there is no evidence that they assumed either. The certificates of parents' estates which three justices of the peace were supposed to sign, for apprenticeship in certain occupations, were to be enrolled by officials of the city or town where the master lived, or in the rural parish for apprentices to country weavers, though here the agency was not prescribed.[1] Applicants for patents made use of the gap thus left in the mechanism of enforcement to urge the establishment of

[1] 5 Eliz., c. 4, §§20, 22, 25 (see App. I).

local or national registries. A partial closing of the gap by the work of high constables' statute sessions has been suggested in the preceding chapter. The informal organizations of crafts in small towns and villages, about which so little is known, may here and there have provided the means and the supervision for enrolling indentures of their own apprentices, though in Wiltshire registration of weavers' apprentices had to be enforced by special order at quarter sessions.[2]

The actual work of an individual justice can be known only from the problems he had to refer to quarter sessions, from diaries, or from the occasional documents relating to official business which are preserved in family muniments because a justice or his clerk failed to file them with the clerk of the peace.[3] The richest of these yet available are the well-known papers of Sir Nathaniel Bacon of Stiffkey, Norfolk, a man eminent and influential as a magistrate and busy commissioner in this county in the late sixteenth and early seventeenth centuries. The printed selections from among these relics of Bacon's long life as an active justice of the peace cannot indicate the share of his time that a justice might have to spend on questions of apprenticeship, and the numerous warrants Bacon granted and recognizances he took do not record their subject matter.[4] But his papers suggest that the role of a justice of the peace in settling disputes between master and apprentice may have been only a small part of his very considerable service as a mediator in private quarrels, as an authority who could take bonds from the differing parties to observe agreements, or could arbitrate an out-of-court settlement of lawsuits already begun. Often the contribution of the justice of the

[2] See below. No certificates signed by justices have come to the notice of the present writer. If any survive, they are probably to be found in borough archives or parish chests.

[3] Few justice-of-the-peace diaries are known. The Mosley diary, kept by successive generations of justices, is available in MS. in the John Rylands library of Manchester (the first seven years have been printed as *Manchester Sessions*). The Webbs cite this and MS. Wiltshire diaries of the eighteenth century (*Parish and County*, 388–389 and n.). The Letter Books of Suffolk justices of the peace in Hist. MSS. Comm. 13th Report, App. 4, *MSS. of E. R. Wodehouse, Esq.*, are compilations of sessions documents. There are three diaries for the seventeenth century: *Diary of Walter Yonge, Esq.*, ed. G. Roberts, Camden Society XLI, of the early seventeenth century but nothing about sessions work; *The Diary of Edmund Bohun, Esq.*, with Introductory Memoir by S. W. Rix, of the later century; *Diary of Henry Townshend . . .*, ed. J. W. W. Bund, for the middle part of the century.

[4] Some 25 or 26 recognizances on the average were issued by Bacon each year between 1584 and 1591.

peace must have consisted in the weight of his local prestige (a composite of his personal character, his family repute, his connections and estates) and in his common sense and patience in dealing with lesser neighbors, tenants, and acquaintances. In matters of apprenticeship, his word must have been authoritative many times merely as that of a familiar employer. No doubt this was the relationship of Sir Nathaniel Bacon to the mason for whom he smoothed out a difference with an apprentice over conditions of employment.[5] In other cases, a complaint was made to the justice whose residence was nearest: when in Charles I's reign, a fuller of Coggeshall failed to get the release of his son from the Braintree barber to whom he had been apprenticed over seven years before, he complained to Sir Thomas Wiseman, whose manor of Rivenhall lay within four or five miles of the town, and Wiseman granted a warrant to the constable of Braintree to bring the grasping master before the quarter sessions at Chelmsford.[6] Minor as such cases were, nevertheless the contribution a justice of the peace thus made to the satisfactory working of the apprenticeship system was direct and considerable, though not of a kind that can be estimated. His influence, and his availability to all comers, were therefore important in relation to the enforcement of legal apprenticeship, as they were in maintaining the peace of the county. A brief glance, however, at the competitors for a justice's time for individual arbitration shows that due attention to neighborhood problems cannot have been easy. Justices of the peace in quarter sessions often delegated to one or more of their colleagues the preliminary inquiry into and sometimes the determination of matters before the whole bench. In apprenticeship itself, these might include such disputes over the contract as had come before Bacon or Wiseman, or perhaps complaints of ill usage; in other county business,

[5] *Supplementary Stiffkey Papers*, ed. F. W. Brooks, Camden Society, 3rd Series, Miscellany XVI, 21. The terms of the agreement are fairly typical of the more liberal contracts: the apprentice is to continue in service till the following Michaelmas (apparently the dispute concerned the term of indenture), his master to pay him then the 10/– provided for in the indentures, to furnish one suit for work days and one for holidays, and tools for his craft, consisting of hammer, square, plumb rule, and trowel.

[6] Essex Cal. Q.S., XX, 116, S.R. 257/70, Easter 3 Chas. I. On Sir Thomas Wiseman, see Morant, *History of Essex*, II, 559. The order settling the dispute was signed by Sir Thomas, and by Sir William Maxey of Bradwell near Coggeshall. (On Maxey, see Morant, II, 156; *Visitations of Essex*, ed. W. C. Metcalfe, Harleian Society, XIII, Visitation of 1634.)

the inspection of a high constable's accounts or of the necessary repairs of a bridge.[7] The Privy Council regularly referred local difficulties and complaints to one or a few justices. In March 1589, Thomas Fanshawe was to settle a disputed title at Barking. In August he, Robert Wroth, and Thomas Powle were to be responsible for special watches on account of wandering bands of soldiers near London. Each of these three men had duties outside Essex: Thomas Fanshawe was the Queen's Remembrancer of the Exchequer and a justice of the peace not only in Essex but in Hertfordshire and Middlesex; Robert Wroth, heir to widespread estates, had recently filled the sheriff's office in Essex and was a Middlesex justice of the peace; Thomas Powle had been since 1562 one of the Six Clerks in the Chancery Office.[8] In February 1589 Sir Thomas Mildmay and Robert Clarke, Esq., of the same county and the latter a baron of the Exchequer, were to examine suspects in a robbery; in April Mildmay, with two colleagues, Sir John Petre and Edmund Pirton, were to settle a testamentary wrangle over the estate of a deceased fellow-justice; in May, Pirton was directed to act with two other Essex justices of the peace and three from Suffolk in compounding the claims of creditors of a Colchester merchant bankrupt in the Fleet prison. To another baron of the Exchequer and Essex justice of the peace, Thomas Gent, Esq., was referred in December 1589 the problem of "decay of trade" in the town of Halstead after the migration of the Dutch baymakers there to Colchester.[9]

Four justices were required to dissolve a contract of apprentice-

[7] Somerset MS. Sessions Minute Books, IV, Recognizances, Easter 6 Chas. I, example of dispute over apprenticeship contract referred from quarter sessions. Illustrations of reference from Q.S. to one justice are not as frequent for apprenticeship as for the other activities mentioned above, for which no specific citation is given here; the reader can find instances at random in printed sessions records.

[8] See note 9 for the Privy Council letters. For Fanshawe see the *D.N.B.*; Commissions of the Peace as listed in the Bibliography show him serving on the Hertfordshire bench from at least 1577 and in February 1591 he was addressed in a Privy Council letter as a Middlesex justice of the peace (*Acts P.C.*, Eliz., XX, 312). For Wroth, see Morant, *History of Essex*, I, 162–163, and Commissions of the Peace as above. For Powle, Morant, I, 3, 10; *Calendar of Patent Rolls*, Eliz., II, 227.

[9] Similar illustrations could be taken at random as these were, from any few pages of the Privy Council Register; for these, see *Acts P.C.*, Eliz., XVII, 107, 81, 143, 157; XVIII, 56, 276. Clarke and Gent are mentioned in these letters by their office, and see also Foss, *Biographia Juridica*, 166, 294. For Mildmay and Petre, see above, Chap. VII and n. 70.

ship, and this responsibility has left its traces in the sessions records more often than any other apprenticeship question with which the justices had to deal, perhaps because the legal points which might arise not only called for one of these four justices to be of the quorum [10] but made it preferable to have the authority of the general sessions of the peace behind their decisions. Sometimes this authority was essential to enforce an order: in Cheshire a widow complained to quarter sessions that her son, apprenticed to a Nantwich dyer at a premium of £8, had been turned off by his master, who then refused to obey the order of the "justices of the hundred" that he should repay half this sum.[11] In a case of discharge, there were usually questions to be settled about the return of personal belongings to the apprentice and sometimes as to a sizable premium, or the master who had forfeited an apprentice might bring suit to recover him.[12] The function of the quarter sessions as a board of appeal for both masters and apprentices in so far as it achieved some sort of rough justice — harsh it would generally be — served the same end as the work of an individual justice.

Indenturing for a shorter term than the statutory seven years was rarely a cause for discharge of an apprentice's indenture.[13] Apprenticeship contracts probably tended in fact to run for the seven-year term, at least until a much later period. Countless incidental refer-

[10] These were the smaller number of the whole commission of the peace who were named in the commission as necessary for the conduct of the judicial business of the county; in the reign of Elizabeth this list gradually enlarged, from one clearly of those justices qualified by legal training or experience (or reliability) to one including more and more of the commission; by the seventeenth century the justices of quorum are nearly all the commission, except (often) the most recently appointed or (sometimes) those with least estate.

[11] MS. Sessions Recognizance Books, Vol. 1619–1640, Epiphany 3 Chas. I.

[12] The history of the premium remains unexplored, so far as the present writer is aware; payment of one by those responsible for placing the apprentice was common from at least the early seventeenth century, varying in amount with the place and trade. A case in the Warwickshire records illustrates the possibility of suit by a discontented former master, who in this instance, on forfeiting his apprentice by order of quarter sessions, sued the apprentice's father for enticing and detaining the boy. (*Sessions Order Books*, I, 77).

[13] An example is to be found in Lancashire, *Quarter Sessions Records*, 256, Easter 1605, at Ormskirk, apprentice discharged because bound for three years only. A few cases elsewhere have been seen but not noted. Indictments or informations for the offense involved occur, though not frequently; but like the offense of nonregistration, some may be concealed under the general charge of apprenticing "contrary to the statute."

ences to apprenticeship agreements show that the normal term was the legal one, or longer. But such violations as occurred lacked a complainant to bring them to notice, unless craft organizations or local authorities did so. There seems to have been an increasing tendency, consistent with all that is known of the immense growth of poor-law business in the work of quarter sessions, for questions of parochial apprenticeship to outnumber by far the nonparochial.[14] In general, the absorption of the justices in the judicial and administrative problems of poor relief, even before the settlement law of the Restoration added its intricacies to their burdens, must have been to the detriment of such attention as they might have given to the enforcement of industrial regulation. The development of regular meetings of the justices additional to quarter sessions and the efforts made by both the central government and, in some counties, by the justices themselves to improve their supervision of county affairs were almost wholly due to the growth of poor law business; to the increase of licensing; and in some part also to the enforcement of service contracts under the Act of 1563. Before considering whether the additional procedures contributed to the enforcement of apprenticeship, a digression is necessary to distinguish the different types of sessions held by the justices.[15]

The most informal of these additional meetings grew out of the work that any two justices were competent to do "out of sessions," that is, without a jury of presentment. Two justices together had a considerable criminal jurisdiction, including many offenses under the vagrancy and game laws and the service clauses of the Act of 1563, and many administrative powers. There is no question from the later sixteenth century of the use in a number of counties[16] of

[14] This is suggested in the proportion of orders issued at quarter sessions, and can be traced, for example, in successive volumes of the Warwickshire *Order Books*.

[15] The description which follows is based not only on the contemporary works of Lambard and Dalton, and on modern authorities (the Webbs, Holdsworth, the introductions to printed series of quarter sessions records), but on observed practice in the sessions themselves. It is not possible to accept the description given by the Webbs of "petty sessions" as identical in the early seventeenth century with divisional special sessions (*Parish and County*, 400ff); the two kinds of meeting were already distinct, though contemporary terminology is confusing.

[16] Counties in which some kind of justices' petty sessions are known to have been meeting included Essex where, however, in Elizabeth's reign the sittings of two or more justices seem to have been primarily to license alehouses and super-

the term "petty sessions" for meetings of justices; but their nature in the different shires where they are encountered is not so certain, that is, whether in particular instances they were justices "in sessions" or "out of sessions." The latter seems to be the more probable, in that while in several counties there is record of presentments at petty sessions (for hundreds or other units), these are by high and petty constables, and there is no known mention of the attendance of a jury. Nevertheless, the source of many of the presentments is unidentified.

The relation of the petty sessions, which probably met each quarter,[17] to the justices' monthly meetings established in some counties by the early seventeenth century and perhaps before, is obscure.[18] Both may have developed from recurrent duties performed by justices out of sessions. The growth of justices' petty sessions seems in Essex to be associated with sittings of two or more justices to license alehouses; in Somerset and no doubt elsewhere, two

---

vise statute sessions (Cal. Q.S., *passim*); in Staffordshire, petty and privy sessions are mentioned by 1591 and may go back much earlier (*Q.S. Rolls*, III, xxii-xxiii; the editor traces them to 1537; they were attended by a presenting jury and they seem to have been of the nature of special sessions, see below); in Cheshire, a privy sessions is referred to in 1592, and in 1628 justices were dealing with service and apprenticeship contracts in meetings within the hundreds (MS. Sess. Recognizance Books, Vol. 1576–1592, Epiph. 34 Eliz.; Vol. 1593–1608, Epiph. 45 Eliz.; Vol. 1619–1640, Epiph. 3 Chas. I; see above, n. 11); in Wiltshire in 1591, some weavers were ordered by quarter sessions to appear at a petty sessions for a hearing on an unrecorded charge (*Minutes of Proceedings*, 143), but there is an earlier mention of presentments at petty sessions in 1580 (*ibid.*, 58). In Somerset, the earliest extant reference seems to be in the opening years of James I's reign; among other matters, high constables were presenting men out of service or idle (MS. Sess. Indictment Rolls, No. 23, 9 Jas. I, Item 71; see also for other mention, Som. Rec. Soc., XXIII, 36, 78, 344).

[17] In Warwickshire, the justices' "sittings" in the various hundreds, a practice in being when the records begin in 1625, are assumed by the editors of the sessions books to have been quarterly meetings; no jury seems to have attended. (*Order Books*, I, 5, 12, 74, 120; xxix). In Leicestershire, the accounts of petty constables in one parish show them in 1616–1621 attending "privy sessions" of the justices at dates between quarter sessions (*Market Harborough Parish Records, 1531–1837*, ed. J. E. Stocks and W. B. Bragg, 69–74, 85, 105).

[18] In Cheshire, the January quarter sessions of 1603 ordered that negligent constables were to appear before the justices of the peace "at their monthly meeting" (*Q. Sess. Recs.*, 51). In Lancashire in early 1630 the quarter sessions asked the justices of the peace of one hundred, a very large one, to arrange several places "for the three weeks meeting for suppressing of wanderers and other occasions" (MS. Sess. Order Books, No. 7, Epiph. 6 Chas. I, at Preston). The North Riding apparently also knew such meetings (N.R.R.S., I, 190n).

justices were periodically available to certify the enrolment of deeds.[19] Sir Francis Walsingham described in 1574 the informal meetings of justices in one Norfolk division, every three weeks or monthly, to inspect the Bridewell at Acle, this business being followed (after dinner at the inn, he explains) by reports from the high constables of misdemeanors which were within the competence of justices out of sessions, or by the settling of disputes between neighbors which used to fill the hundred court.[20] Reports and disputes alike, be it noted, might have included questions of apprenticeship contracts. In Northamptonshire, the holding of "three weeks' sessions" was said in 1630 to be an ancient practice approved by the justices of assize; the justices of the peace met divisionally "for the better execution of certain laws." This description may have initiated the inquiry sent in November of 1630 by the Earl of Manchester to his brother Lord Montagu as to the "articles" of inquiry used at these sessions. A copy was sent him, and in January he told Montagu that the "books" then being distributed to the counties were based on the Northamptonshire practice — these were copies of the well-known Book of Orders of 1631, prescribing monthly meetings of justices of the peace to execute the poor law.[21] The temporary success of the Privy Council's directive [22] may have been due as much to the fact that what it enjoined was already an accepted institution in at least certain districts as to the force of conciliar government at this period.

The three weeks' sessions or monthly meetings and the "petty sessions" appear to have been identical in composition and function. Both were intended to give continuity of control by the justices over the business which any two could handle, and they served also to collect from the constables reports of other matters for the quarter sessions. There were in existence, however, though it is not possible to determine how widely used or how active, more formal sessions with a larger competence. These were the "special sessions" constituted, like the quarter sessions, whenever two justices sat, one

[19] For Essex, various references suggesting a combination of other business with the licensing sessions (Cal. Q.S., *passim*); for Somerset, see *Somerset Enrolled Deeds*, passim.

[20] R. H. Mason, *The History of Norfolk*, II, 17, citing a letter of Walsingham to Burghley.

[21] *Quarter Sessions Records*, 91; Hist. MSS. Comm., *Buccleuch*, I, 271.

[22] Leonard, *English Poor Relief*, 158–159; see above, Chap. V, n. 131.

of whom was of the quorum, at a time and place regularly appointed. They were most often used for inquiry into and disposal if possible of particular business under one or more statutes; the two illustrations given by Lambard are those under Section 30 of the Act of 1563, and under the Act of 1572 for vagrancy, to both of which a jury of presentment would be summoned. The presence of this jury was one feature by which special sessions are to be distinguished from mere sittings of any two or more justices.[23] Both quarter sessions and special sessions might be divisional in form, that is, attended only by justices, jurors, and officers from the nearest areas of the county, for geographical convenience. Thus the special sessions, appointed by the Act of 1563 to be held for inquiry, was to be divisional, the justices "within their limits."

The Elizabethan device of special sessions of inquiry, held by the justices of the peace to hear and determine presentments by juries, had a precedent in the earlier sixteenth century. In 1541–42 a statute prescribing what came to be called the "Six-Weeks' Sessions," to be held in each hundred or equivalent division, had attempted to make these special sessions a permanent method of supervising the enforcement of specific laws. But it was soon repealed because the burden of jury attendance so often during a year was too great.[24] Nevertheless one of the first steps taken by William Cecil at the beginning of Elizabeth's reign to put into effect measures for strengthening the realm was to order the justices of the peace in each county to hold particular assemblies for inquiry into the execution of his program.[25]

[23] Lambard, *Eirenarcha*, 3rd ed., 617–621. The problem in each instance of knowing the type of meeting mentioned in a document arises both from frequent lack of occasion to mention the jury, and from the varying usage of the terms "special" and "petty." Thus in Essex is found a petition for a "petty sessions" to be called to inquire into a riot (Cal. Q.S., IV, 222–223, S.R. 44/28, Easter 15 Eliz.); this Lambard calls a "special service" (1st ed., 287), not a sessions at all. Even the high constables' statute or petty sessions were sometimes called "special sessions."

[24] 33 Hen. VIII, c. 10, cited by Holdsworth, IV, 146. Repealed by 37 Hen. VIII, c. 7. The statute directed that special sessions be held at least six weeks before each quarter sessions. On the cause for repeal, see Holdsworth, IV, 146; *Oxfordshire Justices of the Peace in the Seventeenth Century*, by M. S. Gretton, Oxfordshire Record Society Series, XVI, lxxxiii. In spite of it, divisional special sessions were thereafter recommended on occasion by the central government to carry out directives, as for example in May 1554, to Norfolk justices of the peace to suppress rumor-mongers (J. Strype, *Ecclesiastical Memorials,* III, Pt. II, 214, letter of 23 May, 1 Ma.).

[25] *Tudor and Stuart Proclamations*, I, No. 565, May 1562, referring to first

Resort to divisional assemblies by the central government was chiefly in periods of intensified concern over vagrancy or scarcity. The practice was required of the justices in the campaign to suppress vagrants in 1569–1571, by the original Book of Orders for control of the grain supply issued in January 1587, and by its reissues in the next decade; but these are only the most striking episodes in a gradual and apparently spontaneous organization of local government by convenient smaller areas within most of the counties, not only for special inquiries but for regular administrative and military needs.[26] Thus instructions sent by the Privy Council in June 1605 for divisional assemblies of the justices of the peace in every county were novel only in their intention to make these a part of normal operation in the execution of the statutes catalogued in the orders, and even this intention had been anticipated generations earlier. Like the special sessions of the Act of 1541, the assemblies to be held according to the orders of June 1605 were catch-alls — they were to inquire into the execution of several laws at once.[27]

The surviving record in some counties of divisional meetings ordered by the justices themselves suggests that local initiative may have widely adopted this device for particular purposes. The earliest illustrations, as it happens, concern the enforcement of portions of the Act of 1563, though it is not clear whether presentment juries were expected to attend. In Devon, for example, the quarter sessions in 1601 ordered the division of the county into six districts, each under four to six justices to whose meetings the high constables were to report cases of giving or taking excessive wages.[28] In Wiltshire, a few months before the Privy Council's orders, the January Quarter

---

order in the preceding year; *Tudor Economic Documents*, I, 325–330. See also Putnam, "Northamptonshire Wage Assessments." See Introduction above.

[26] For 1569–1571, Leonard, *English Poor Relief*, 80–81; for the Book of Orders and its reissues, *ibid.*, 84f., and Gras, *The English Corn Market*, 236. The use of the "divisions" can be followed in the State Papers and Privy Council Register. It is paralleled by the regular practice by the Council of referring matters to the nearest justices, an informal sectioning-up which must have made for better use of local knowledge, as well as widened the circle of justices of the peace called upon for frequent, direct service to the central government.

[27] A full transcript of the orders is printed in Gretton, *Oxfordshire Justices*, xxv. The assemblies were to be held each quarter between the dates of the quarter sessions, and constables were to attend with presentments and offenders. See below, Chap. X, for the situation which evoked these orders.

[28] MS. Sessions Books, II, Mich. 43 Eliz. This was in connection with a wage assessment of the previous spring.

Sessions of 1605 arranged for divisional meetings of the justices to consult on enforcing the Act of 1563.[29] The continued use in the early seventeenth century of the nickname to which the Act of 1541–42 gave rise, for intersessional meetings in at least one county, the North Riding, suggests a continuity of some kind during the intervening generations, and not merely a new procedure begun by the conciliar orders. Here, although the earliest reference to the "Six-Weeks' Sessions" is in 1606, the whole procedure, as revealed in the surviving records, suggests old habit. The sessions met for areas covering one or two wapentakes, once every quarter between the quarter sessions, presentments being made by juries and by constables of both ranks. The subject matter, however, appears to be identical with the Council's directive. Though the sessions were held with considerable regularity during most of James's reign, perhaps especially so after 1610, there is little if any trace of them after 1631 and in 1635 a distinct suggestion that the practice had lapsed.[30] But losses of the records of such special sessions, like those of petty sessions, may have been especially heavy: in the North Riding, there are references in the quarter sessions documents to entries once made in the "rolls" of various special sessions, rolls no longer extant, possibly because they were in the custody of a justice of the peace or of his clerk living near the usual meeting place.[31]

In sum, before the Act of 1563 was passed the justices of the peace were accustomed to use other means than their quarterly general sessions to perform their duties. Periodic informal sittings of two or more justices for recurring duties may have developed before or in the early seventeenth century into quarterly or monthly meetings attended by constables with their presentments for a general inspection of a defined range of business both judicial and administrative. Systematized to some degree by the initially effective enforcement in 1631 of the Book of Orders, they continued well into the eighteenth century. The special sessions meeting divisionally, the

[29] MS. Sessions Rolls, No. 2, Epiphany 2 Jas. I. Similar orders were issued a year later.

[30] This was a quarter sessions order that the divisional justices of the peace should hold an annual sessions "if they see cause" to inquire into abuses committed by parish officers (N.R.R.S., IV, 32). The first mention in 1606, *ibid.*, I, 30; for the series of sessions, I and II, *passim*.

[31] *Ibid.*, I, 17n., 24n.

justices "in sessions" with presentment juries in attendance, inquiring and sometimes determining either under one or more particular statutes or with almost as wide a range as quarter sessions itself, were known also before 1563. But in spite of the Council's efforts early in James's reign and their apparent use in certain counties for a number of years thereafter, these sessions seem to have lapsed. Their history has never been traced, but it can be suggested that the seventeenth century like the earlier sixteenth found difficulty in bringing together adequate juries of presentment for such interim sessions. It was hard enough to get the quarterly jury service performed, and a decline in the value of the juries of the hundreds as presentment agencies to the quarter sessions becomes evident long before that of the constables.[32]

It will be clear that the justices in their private or petty sessions could do no more for the enforcement of apprenticeship than was within the powers of any one to four justices in settling complaints, compelling due service from apprentices, and certifying to indentures, which has been described on earlier pages. Much of their work of this kind has been lost to sight for lack of record at the time as well as from losses of documents since. An Essex justice of the peace, supervising a statute sessions in the hundred of Harlow, explained to the clerk of the peace the absence of a report from this hundred on the ground that there were only "small matters" presented "whereof I have taken order." [33] Even where these sittings of two or more justices helped to enjoin on the constables a conscientious presentment of offenses, it has been seen how rarely apprenticeship was among the subjects they presented. Any further contribution by the justices of the peace to the execution of the apprenticeship provisions through the additional sessions must be looked for in the work of special sessions, including those sessions of inquiry prescribed by the Act of 1563 itself.

[32] Yet divisional special sessions were being held in Essex in the Restoration period (MS. Sessions Rolls, No. 420, Trin. 21 Chas. II). The generalizations in the text for the period after 1642 are based on examination by the writer of sessions records of the same group of counties as that included in the present study, and with the same qualification, that the purpose of the search was primarily to trace apprenticeship enforcement.

[33] Cal. Q.S., VI, 193, S.R. 55/37, Mich. 17 Eliz., letter from James Altham, Esq. Two years later, he is reported as having dealt with some "singlemen out of covenant" who had been presented to the high constables' petty sessions, VII, 106, S.R. 61/13.

The special sessions directed to be held in the emergencies of 1569–1571, 1587, 1594, and 1597 naturally concerned the problems created by the emergency, not the everyday operation of normal apprenticeship regulation, although the vagrancy measures of 1569–1571 included the enforcement of compulsory service for masterless men and may therefore have touched the unapprenticed worker in individual cases. But the comprehensive instructions from the Privy Council in 1605 did include "the statute concerning artificers" among those which the divisional assemblies were "to enquire of and see the due execution." [34] An occasional presentment, however, in the North Riding series of special sessions, for offenses under the wages or service clauses of the Act of 1563, and the few apprenticeship cases brought in the same court, are the sole evidence of active execution of "statutes of artificers" by such divisional assemblies.[35] Yet otherwise the subject matter in this series and in the few recorded special sessions of 1606 in Essex conform to the council's order.[36] In the West Riding in 1604, justices meeting for two wapentakes (whether "in" or "out" of sessions is not clear) complained to the constables of "the unskilful persons that daily set up trades and mysteries in those things wherein they were never lawful apprentices." [37] When divisional assemblies were utilized in Wiltshire in 1616 to effect orders made at a quarter sessions, they were concerned only with enforcing the service contract and parish apprenticeship and with improving constables' presentments to quarter sessions.[38]

Almost no trace has been found of the special sessions of inquiry to

[34] Gretton, *Oxfordshire Justices*, xxvii.

[35] The majority of North Riding cases of hiring for less than a year or without the required certificate of discharge from a former employer, of taking or paying wages over the assessed rates, and of refusing to record servants' wages, seem to have been brought before the quarter sessions rather than the special sessions (N.R.R.S., I and II, *passim*).

[36] Cal. Q.S., XVIII, 175, S.R. 178/69, 176, S.R. 178/73, "Sessions of the Peace" held before three or more justices, with a jury presenting masterless men, unlicensed victualers, sellers of beer above the assize, householders taking "inmates." Two such sessions are recorded for different hundreds, in October and November 1606, the hundred which had its sessions in late November having had a previous one in August.

[37] Heaton, *Yorkshire Industries*, 106. Nothing is known of the circumstances inducing this concern, presumably exceptional, or of subsequent steps taken by the justices.

[38] MS. Sessions Minute Books, III, Epiphany 13 Jas. I; IV, Easter 14 Jas. I. The form of the order for the assemblies indicates their accepted operation.

be held under the terms of the Act of 1563. Those in Devon in 1601 and in Wiltshire in 1605 obviously were not the twice-yearly sessions under the Act, but extraordinary meetings ordered for a particular need, and their implication is that the sessions which should have been in routine operation were not at that time normal procedure. This is expressly stated in the North Riding a few years later: the justices in quarter sessions, referring to complaints they had received that the "statute of laborers and apprentices" was not observed and the sessions "appointed by that law" not held, ordered in 1610 that thenceforward these special sessions were to be kept by the justices in their several divisions, but they were to use them also as occasions for inquiry into the execution of the statutes "for alehouses, rogues, vagabonds, etc." [39] Thus they apparently were merged into the "Six Weeks' Sessions" already discussed whose subject matter corresponded so closely to that prescribed by the Privy Council in 1605. Yet wherever such sessions were held, in the North Riding or elsewhere, they may have exercised a supervision of the statute sessions and its enrolment of servants which could have amounted to supervising apprenticeship contracts as well.[40] The Wiltshire special sessions of 1605 were to consider the "Statute 5 Eliz.: for laborers touching the [hiring?] departing wages and ordering of apprentices and servants in husbandry and all other trades mentioned in that statute." [41]

In only one county and in one year has a clear record been seen of the statutory special sessions. This was in Wiltshire in 1577: in January and June of that year, at Trowbridge and at Warminster, "Sessions upon the Statute of 5 Elizabeth" were held, the first before three justices of the peace, the second before two. But even at these there is no actual record of inquiry into the Act of 1563 (though this may have been the carelessness of the clerk); like the North Riding sessions, they were conveniently taking care of whatever needed doing. At the January sessions recognizances were granted to weavers accused of felony and to alehousekeepers for their ap-

[39] N.R.R.S., I, 204. Possibly this order was a cause of the increased regularity of the "Six Weeks' Sessions" after 1610.

[40] Reference has been made above (n. 33), to a justice of the peace in Essex having been present at statute sessions. One or two justices attended them in several hundreds, in Elizabeth's reign, but whether sporadically or regularly cannot be traced.

[41] MS. Sessions Rolls, No. 2, Epiphany 2 Jas. I.

pearance at the next quarter sessions. At the June sessions the only record of business was a recognizance to keep the peace.[42]

The records of special sessions were subject to the same accidents as those of the petty sessions or the monthly meetings: careless filing and failure to record business summarily dispatched. Either or both may account in part for apparent neglect of the duty enjoined by the Act of 1563. But any widespread and regular holding of the prescribed sessions of inquiry could hardly have failed to leave its mark in cases certified to quarter sessions for further action, even though the records of the special sessions did not survive. Nothing like this can be found even in the relatively well-preserved Essex series.[43] On the evidence it must be allowed that only rarely can the justices of peace have been taking, by means of any variety of the special sessions, positive steps to enforce the apprenticeship regulations of the Statute of Artificers. What can be said of the justices of peace in quarter sessions?

The core of quarter sessions procedure was the presentment by the jury or juries according to the charge delivered to them by the justices of the peace; it was only thus that the justices could carry out the function of hearing and determining vested in them by their general commission and by statute.[44] Technically not essential to procedure at the quarter sessions, but as much a part of actual business there as the juries' presentments, were the reports of high and petty constables, based on the same or a similar charge. In an important sense, the justices of the peace were doubly passive in the work of law enforcement. First, the charge, which emphasized the matters most needing inquiry, came to them from above, and very little is known of the justices' discretionary powers or their practice

[42] *Minutes of Proceedings*, 24, 29. The present writer may have overlooked rare entries of such special sessions in some sixteenth-century records, as this one in Wiltshire was overlooked until made evident by the printed page. But there are none in the long Essex series.

[43] Examination of sessions bundles in various counties for writs summoning jurors and constables to make their presentments might reveal more systematic meetings of special sessions than the present writer has been able to trace. Such writs have sometimes survived where little else remains of Elizabethan sessions business, as in Devon and Norfolk. Writs dating from before and after 1563 repose in the Norfolk and Essex files summoning high constables to bring their returns from statute sessions and jurors to attend to present offenses against "the statutes of laborers," but these writs appear to be all for the quarter sessions.

[44] Holdsworth, *English Law*, IV, 142.

in altering it. In theory their initiative cannot have been large; the central government expected compliance, at least in James's reign. When Lord Chancellor Bacon addressed the judges in the Star Chamber before they went on circuit in February 1618, he advised justices of the peace to obey commandments and not to dispute them.[45] But in one example of a charge delivered to the high constables at quarter sessions by the spokesman for the justices of the peace, there was noticeable variation from that delivered by the judges on circuit to the same officers at the assizes.[46] At the beginning of Elizabeth's reign, the typical charge by a justice of the peace seems not to have been at all selective; in fact until Lambard's systematization [47] the justice delivering the charge at quarter sessions and attempting to model himself on the manuals published for his guidance must have read out a mere catalogue of statutes with no principle of arrangement. There is no indication that the selective charge with its typical "articles" for special inquiry was expected from the justices of the peace at quarter sessions.

The second sense in which they were only passive agents of law enforcement was expressed by that justice who never sat upon the bench, Adam Overdoo: "what can we know? we hear but with other men's ears; we see with other men's eyes; a foolish constable, or a sleepy watchman, is all our information . . . This we are subject to, that live in high place, all our intelligence is idle, and most of our intelligencers, knaves . . . I Adam Overdoo, am resolved therefore . . . to make mine own discoveries." [48] He was in this of one mind with the framers of the Act of 1597 prohibiting the use of tenters to stretch cloth, the one instance in which the justices of the peace were called upon to add to their multiform office that of inspector.[49] The narrow limits to the justices' powers of enforcing efficient presentment on the constables have been already suggested. In Essex, following their order to the high constables in 1572 to hold the statute sessions regularly, their success seems to have been considerable, but this was

[45] *Works*, XIII, 305.

[46] Staffordshire MS. Sessions Rolls, No. 100, Easter 7 Chas. I.

[47] But Lambard's scheme was not based on the comparative importance of enforcing various laws, and so was entirely unlike the charges delivered by the justices of assize in a later generation.

[48] Ben Jonson, *Bartholomew Fayre*, Act II, Scene I.

[49] Except in relation to the presentment of highways, and their administrative duties in regard to the work of repair on these and county bridges.

at a time when migrant workers in the county were evidently numerous, and the high constables themselves must have been anxious to reduce the number of masterless in their communities.[50] This is the only occasion in which the result of the justices' orders can be traced. In Jacobean Wiltshire, for example, the evidence, if any, has disappeared of the effectiveness of an order in 1616 that the constables were to make written and signed presentments upon oath at every sessions "in such sort as they do at the assizes"; in the years before and after 1616 only a few constables' presentments are in the files. Presentments of negligent constables, though frequent in several counties, yet are low in proportion to the number of constables in each county and their opportunities for negligence. But reassuring presentments of "all well" occur suspiciously often in all counties in the seventeenth century and among the presentments in Elizabethan Essex to the statute sessions. Moreover, the justices could probably expect little if any initiative from the high or petty constables in departing from the letter of the charge to take notice of other offenses of which they might know fully as much.[51] If the system of presentment operated as it seems to have done, no doubt the justices did not expect such initiative, any more than they themselves may have gone beyond what was delivered them from higher authority.

This attitude throughout local government perhaps explains the by-passing of the justices of the peace which was in effect suggested by one of them to Burghley in 1597 for better enforcement of legislation then pending. Anthony Cope of Oxfordshire, writing out what he had intended to say in the Commons on the bill for depopulation, urged Burghley to use his influence to add to the bill a clause providing for inquiry into its execution by the justices of assize; they were to act by presentments from juries of "the better sort." This suggestion is made, Cope explains, because "all men without express limitation are unwilling to press the execution of penal statutes"; evidently he did not trust the justices of the peace at all in this matter and the justices of assize only if the statute itself prescribed their action.[52]

Even for the set articles of inquiry received by the justices of

[50] See above, Chap. VIII, n. 51.

[51] See the next chapter for an illustration. On the other hand, an example of apparent administrative initiative by high constables in connection with Essex unemployment in 1572 has been cited (Chap. VII, n. 78); see also preceding note.

[52] *Tudor Economic Documents*, I, 87–88.

the peace in charge from the judges on circuit, their positive response in or out of sessions must frequently have been that which evoked in 1601 one of the Privy Council's many rebukes. In a series of exhortations for enforcing the Act of 1597 against cloth-stretching, the council reproved the Middlesex justices for their practice of issuing their writs to the constables "without taking further accompt"; "in which case," added the letter, "it were a shorter course for us to send our warrants immediately unto them." [53]

Direct enforcement of the seven-year term of apprenticeship appears to have been confined to the general competence of the justices of the peace in quarter sessions to hear and determine on indictment, presentment, and information before them, and to issue administrative orders. For the Elizabethan period few orders by quarter sessions on this or any other subject have survived. Besides, quarter sessions in Elizabeth's reign, especially in its earlier years, probably remained a relatively simple affair in which there was little occasion for sessions orders. In the seventeenth century the bulk of the administrative business, and the residue of the judicial which expressed itself in orders rather than judgments, concerned poor relief, communications, and the collection and expenditure of county funds. None of these matters had acquired important dimensions in the earlier years of Elizabeth.[54] In Essex, certainly not an isolated shire, orders made at the quarter sessions either were few or imperfectly recorded, or both. Incomplete recording is suggested by the absence of any orders for wage assessments, either new ratings or renewals — surprising in a county where the statute sessions were so regularly kept.[55] But in any event, no Elizabethan orders for apprenticeship are extant in this county, or in the available sessions records of other counties in the selected list.[56]

[53] *Acts P.C.*, Eliz., XXXII, 164.

[54] Determining who were the poor chargeable to a given parish consumed increasing time at quarter sessions after the first act establishing a compulsory poor rate, in 1572 (14 Eliz., c. 5).

[55] The existence of an assessment in 1598 is referred to in a petition cast in a novel form, filed at the April Sessions of 1599: "We present ourselves to be offenders against the rate made [17 April, 40 Eliz.] for servants wages, and desire the favor of the court"; the petitioners represent that the rates for the top grade of servants in husbandry, and for laborers, are too low and suggest the correct amounts. This looks like a variant of the statutory "advice" which the justices of the peace were to take when about to assess wages. (Cal. Q.S., XVII, 116, S.R. 145/58.)

[56] See Bibliography for the extant sixteenth-century records of orders. In

The earliest orders for apprenticeship are those issued by the Wiltshire justices of the peace at the Michaelmas Sessions of 1603 for the cloth-weaving industry of the county. Their intervention was undoubtedly associated with the campaign already described to protect the established weavers against intruders, working as master-craftsmen or as apprentices and journeymen.[57] The orders not only reaffirmed existing apprenticeship regulations, but in effect made new law — an interesting illustration at this date of the "provincial legislature" in action.[58] Those of most interest for the present discussion concern registration of apprentices, the age for release from indentures, the companies of weavers, and the toleration of the unapprenticed. The first provided for registration of "all such as are now allowed to be apprentices" and for the future oversight of apprenticeship contracts by the appointed overseers of the occupation.[59] The provision for release of the apprentice set twenty-four as the age for finishing the term, "to avoid young marriages and the increase of poor people." The order recognizing companies of weavers in corporate towns, boroughs, and market towns granted them a three-mile radius of (apparently voluntary) membership and supervision. Virtually new law was the order covering the existing situation, according to which those who had entered the trade contrary to the statute within two years and all intruders (without limitation to two years) who had "other things to live upon," might be expelled; all unapprenticed men "as are now permitted to be master weavers" were prohibited from taking apprentices, or keeping more than one loom.

The significance of these orders for estimating the attitude of

---

general, the Elizabethan practice seems to have been to keep merely brief notes in the sessions rolls or minute books except of the most important orders, and it seems possible that no entry at all was made except for matters continuing from session to session. Separate order books are a development of the later seventeenth century, usually not till the second quarter or later, and this itself testifies to the larger and more complex volume of business.

[57] See above, Chap. V, and n. 120.

[58] S. and B. Webb, *Parish and County*, 533. Ignorance of the Act of 1563 is shown in the order that no weaver shall keep more looms "than the statute 5 Eliz. alloweth"; there is no provision concerning looms in this act. The new restrictions limited the number of looms and apprentices more rigidly than existing statute law (the Act of 1555). The orders are printed in Hist. MSS. Comm., *Various Collections*, I, The Records of the County of Wiltshire, 74–75.

[59] Overseers or searchers were, by the Act of 1601, to be appointed by justices of the peace or town officials for the cloth industry in all parts of England.

justices of the peace toward enforcement of apprenticeship lies both in their occasion and in their obvious concern for the problem of poverty. The two are interrelated: the justices were ready, like the hundred jury of Westbury, to intervene to protect the established employment of the area at a point of unusual pressure,[60] but not at the expense of creating another employment difficulty in its place. They temporized, to avoid the problem of relief for those thrown out of work by a sudden enforcement of laws which clearly had not been strictly applied over prior years. Some of the unapprenticed would be allowed to continue in the occupation, under restrictions; and the future was to be cared for by improved oversight, registration, and avoidance of early marriage on the part of workers who gained independence too young. Their compromise seems at least to have established a set of rules for the Westbury district which were claimed forty-four years later as in effect until "these disordered times" of 1647, when some "ancient weavers" complained of the young apprentices under twenty-four years of age who refused to serve out their terms and, instead, married and set up looms for themselves.[61] Certainly during this whole interval the very few recorded apprenticeship prosecutions against Wiltshire weavers were not in the Westbury area. But the question has already been raised how far the absence of cases indicated positive enforcement or mere lack of pressure to violate apprenticeship restrictions in a static period of the broadcloth industry.[62]

The 1603 orders were thus not primarily an enforcement of the apprenticeship laws for an industrial or even an economic purpose. They were to stabilize a troubled district especially vulnerable to the gusty winds of economic fortune,[63] and to remove a potential source of social and political disturbance. The measure of the justices' concern for the apprenticeship law in itself is supplied in their order of only three years before, when they put informations for apprenticeship at the mercy of individual justices of the peace.[64]

[60] There is nothing to show for what area the orders of 1603 were intended, i.e., whether for the Westbury district only or the whole county.

[61] Hist. MSS. Comm., *Various*, I, 114. This is the petition mentioned in Chap. V, n. 122.

[62] See above, Chap. V.

[63] In 1603, when the plague was in Westbury, special contributions were ordered for its relief, the inhabitants of the town being chiefly weavers and spinners (Hist. MSS. Comm., *Various*, I, 74).

[64] See above, Chap. I, and n. 18.

Local communities linked their problems of poor relief to failure to exclude the unapprenticed worker. The officials of Cambridge appealed in 1631 to the Privy Council to support the town's effort to prohibit illegal cottages and lodges, and the exercise of trades without apprenticeship. They attributed the poverty of the town to the increase of poor residents, the "mingling of trades, multiplying of tradesmen, retaining of apprentices." [65] The sensitiveness of local authorities to the dangers of unemployment is illustrated more than once in James I's reign. In Wiltshire unemployed weavers of Bradford, who in July 1607 said they numbered twenty, complained to the justices of the peace against their employers the clothiers who had discharged them. The complaint was carried to the judges of assize probably by the weavers, who thought redress was slow, and the judges returned the problem to the justices of the peace to solve in their divisions.[66] That apparently so few unemployed could attract this much attention suggests that competition from the unapprenticed in the Westbury area or elsewhere need have been on only a modest scale to alarm the justices of the peace.

But the authorities' efforts to maintain employment might conflict with enforcing the seven-year term of apprenticeship as often as they contributed to it. When the drapers of Preston in Lancashire tried in 1634 to suppress allegedly unapprenticed competitors in the adjacent country villages by prosecuting about a dozen offenders,[67] the judges of assize referred the Preston company's complaint to three justices of the peace. Their report was later confirmed by three more, who agreed in subordinating enforcement of apprenticeship to the maintenance of employment in the district: "The several trades are rather to be continued . . . than suppressed, for that many [68] thereby purchase relief for themselves and families where otherwise they would live very poorly or be cast on the country." Moreover, the village dealers, handling a variety of merchandise,

[65] *Cal. S.P.D.*, Chas. I, 1631–1633, 63.

[66] MS. Sessions Rolls, No. 5, Trin. 5 Jas. I; since the Easter sessions roll is missing and no entry was observed in the minute book, it is not certain when the complaint was originally entered. The direction of the justices of assize seems adapted to a larger area of unemployment, but the terms of the petition are quite clear, that it came only from the twenty weavers of Bradford. Other petitions may have been received from other centers.

[67] See above, Chap. V, and n. 130.

[68] The drapers' company had claimed that fifty or more country dealers were operating.

were distributors of flax, and this the justices thought of great benefit to "the poorer sort of people who live by spinning and weaving linen cloths . . . and not being able to travel to market . . . will be forced to beg for their relief and a means to increase our poor to abundance." [69]

The attitude of the justices of the peace in some of the individual apprenticeship prosecutions brought before quarter sessions demonstrates again their willingness to put employment before insistence on the letter of the law. When a complaint was entered against a fustian-maker, at Essex quarter sessions, the justices ordered that it must be exhibited as an information and tried "in course of law," since the trade "appeared to the Court to be much profitable for the setting the poor on work, and doubtful if [it] were any offense against the statute." [70] A desire to temper the results of a conviction to allow the offender to continue earning a livelihood may have prompted an unusual order by the Wiltshire quarter sessions. A weaver in a village of the northern textile district was informed against, in 1613, apparently by a trade competitor, for setting up shop as a grocer during two years past. The jury found him guilty for half that time; but before judgment, on the agreement of both parties, the "ending" of the case was referred to Sir Henry Poole, the offender meanwhile desisting from the trade.[71]

In a Lancashire case, the motive of poor relief is unmistakable. In 1630, several men were indicted at the Manchester October Sessions for exercising the trade of shearman, among them an Abraham Carneshaw, described as a laborer; at the next Sessions his father petitioned that "he and his family are only maintained by the labor . . . of his son Abraham," who had served a five years' apprenticeship to a shearman and "now works in the trade very well."

[69] Wadsworth and Mann, *The Cotton Trade*, 59.

[70] Cal. Q.S., XVII, 256A, S.R. 158/39, memorandum of June 1602 by William Wiseman, Esq., J.P. The complainants apparently did not press the charge at quarter sessions.

[71] MS. Sessions Minute Books, III, Epiphany 10 Jas. I, information against Moses Seaborne (described as a husbandman in one entry); Mich. 11 Jas. I, Appearances and Orders. Note the reduction of the term of offense by the jury's verdict, an example of a tendency already mentioned; see above, Chap. VI. Sir Henry Poole had been on the Wiltshire commission of the peace since at least early 1590, and probably before, serving continuously (except perhaps for an interval about 1608) to his death in 1632; his estates lay in Oxfordshire (where he was also a justice of the peace) and Gloucestershire as well as in Wiltshire.

The order was noted on the petition, "to use the trade according to law." [72] A similar appeal was recorded in Staffordshire, from a baker who in his youth had been apprenticed by Lady Paget — wife to the then representative of a family nearly a century old in the county [73] — and had served most of his term when he was "translated" to Lord Paget for the remainder, and thereafter continued to serve him as his baker for eighteen years; during ten years afterward he had carried on his trade in the parish of Bromley Paget for his neighbors, "baking only brown bread." Now, his petition continued, he was molested for using his trade, but as an enclosed certificate from the overseers of the poor testified, he and his family would be a charge on the parish "if he is suppressed from baking"; a certificate also from Lord Paget's brewer confirmed the history of his apprenticeship.[74] No order on this appeal is recorded, but perhaps the absence of any indictment in the roll may suggest that it was quashed.

John Leake observed in the sixteenth century, in connection with abuses in clothmaking, that the justices of the peace favored employment as compared with law enforcement: "the magistrates perceiving what multitudes of poor do hang upon them [the clothiers] have much favored the matter"; that is, they had failed to execute the laws against cloth-stretching, false weights and lengths, and the rest.[75] This was a natural emphasis. In so doing, as Heckscher said of the usefulness of the justices of the peace in administering the poor law and regulating agricultural labor, "they acted largely in their own interests as land and property owners." [76] Were they, however, neglecting not only their statutory responsibility in regard to industrial regulation, but also the injunctions of the central government? Were the local authorities, from justice of the peace down to constable, failing to fulfill a role as "agents of unified industrial regulation" [77] in which they had been cast by the central executive as well as apparently by Parliament? It remains to examine the attitude of the central government toward enforcing the seven-year term of apprenticeship, with a glance by the way at evidences of its attention to industrial controls generally.

[72] MS. Indictment Rolls, Bundle 7, Mich. 6 Chas. I; Order Books, No. 7, Epiph. 6 Chas. I; Petitions, Recognizance Bundles, 6 Chas. I.

[73] Rowse, *The England of Elizabeth*, 243.

[74] MS. Sessions Rolls, Mich. 15 Chas. I.

[75] *Tudor Economic Documents*, III, 220–221.

[76] Heckscher, *Mercantilism*, I, 246.

[77] *Mercantilism*, I, 246, in reference to the justices of the peace.

X

THE CENTRAL GOVERNMENT

In matters which engaged the attention of the central government, lack of care and diligence by the justices of the peace was likely to bring upon them from the Privy Council a stern or a petulant rebuke, an inconvenient summons to attend its pleasure in London, or even dismissal. The council kept watch upon the local authorities, sometimes by means of local complaints, and recurrently through reports by the lords lieutenant (when and where these officers were appointed), the bishops, and the judges of assize.[1] The central government thus possessed ways of securing reasonably reliable information on local performance of duty. How effectively it could enforce the execution of its orders is another question and one largely irrelevant to the present study, as will be seen. But the prevailing continuity of service on the commissions of the peace indicates that the most powerful penalty, actual dismissal from office, may have been com-

[1] Two sets of reports from the bishops illustrate the central government's supervision: in 1564 when the main question was to know which among the justices of the peace supported the religious settlement (*Letters from the Bishops to the Privy Council . . . 1564*, Camden Miscellany, IX); and in October 1587 when the bishops were to answer a series of questions on dismissing or replacing members of the commissions of the peace on various grounds (some of their reports in Strype, *Annals*, III, Pt. II, App., Bk. II, 449ff). Their frank and often vivid comments are exemplified in the report cited in Rowse, *The England of Elizabeth*, 359, as by the judges of assize for Devon and Cornwall in 1587, but which resembles the reports of the bishops in this year; it may be that of the Bishop of Exeter (B.M. Lansdowne MS. 53, f. 83, dated October 1587). The judges of assize were consulted, probably late in 1561, on changes in the commission of the peace (B.M. Lansdowne MS. 1218, f. 64f, dated 16 February 4 Eliz. but many of their recommendations are in effect in the commission entered on the Patent Roll 11 February 1562, see *Calendar Patent Rolls*, Eliz., II, 433–447). The lords lieutenant appear to have been consulted rather on individuals than for reports on the entire commission for their counties.

paratively rare.[2] The mere threat of it was nearly as potent, since it endangered the sensitive spider-web of family influence. Even this may not have been often employed as a means of control. The tone of helpless exasperation which occasionally sounds through the reproving, exhorting, and insistent letters from council to justices, and the recognizable instances in which the latter's quiet unresponsiveness defeated the council's intentions, suggest no very sure command of central over local government. Much more effective undoubtedly was the hidden persuasiveness on individual justices of the peace of so deft and informed a governor as William Cecil.[3] Does not the shrillness of the council's scoldings increase after his death, it may be asked.

There were two principal means by which the central government instructed local authorities on the matters to which they were to give special care. One was the charge delivered by a high officer of state to the judges of assize at the beginning of each term of the law-courts for their guidance in their circuits. The other was the direct route of orders and suggestions from the Privy Council to the collective commissions of the peace or to individual members. A third source from which the professional lawyers and the studious amateurs among the justices of the peace could learn how to apply statute regulations was the series of decisions by the central courts interpreting the law. How much place did the enforcement of apprenticeship have in these three vehicles of communication?

The charge to the judges of assize was normally accompanied by articles for presentment, a list of the subjects on which presentments by juries and local officers were particularly important.[4] These were transmitted in each circuit to the grand jury. A part or all of the same

[2] Recommendations for dismissal made in the reports mentioned in the preceding footnote were not necessarily adopted, to judge from some Libri Pacis subsequent to them. Dismissals might be merely the result of the accession of a new lord keeper, not to penalize the dismissed but to make room for his own nominees. Discharge from the commission could not always be enforced promptly, see Willcox, *Gloucestershire*, 59.

[3] Rowse, *The England of Elizabeth*, 281, referring to Burghley's intimate knowledge of family connections.

[4] Perhaps more correctly, the articles were given "in charge," as in medieval procedure (Holdsworth, I, 269, IV, 143). But at least by the seventeenth century, the "charge" seems to have developed into an address detached from the specific articles. These in turn appear to have undergone within Elizabeth's reign a transformation from a comprehensive catalogue of matters for presentment to a selective guide, as suggested in the text above.

charge might be addressed to the justices of the peace of the shires within the circuit. In turn, the justices delivered a charge to the jurors attending quarter sessions and the same charge or a variant of it to the high constables. The articles for which petty constables were responsible were transmitted to them. Step by step each agency of law-enforcement and of administration was thus educated in what was required of it.

Complete series of the articles of presentment of any one period are rare, but a comparison of representative lists of various dates will indicate the emphases and the omissions sufficiently to show the central government's preoccupations and their translation into local terms.

An example of the articles as they were initially delivered to the judges of assize by one of Elizabeth's high officers of state cannot be given, but it is possible to see what subjects were being emphasized in the latter part of James's reign. Lord Chancellor Bacon's speech to the judges in June 1618, besides dwelling on the dangers of recusancy, urged care to employ the poor and to put out poor children as parish apprentices, to "cherish manufactures, old and new, especially draperies," to regulate alehouses and correct laxity by clerks of the peace and of the market in seeing to the assizes of beer and bread, and to mend highways.[5] The month before, articles had been sent from the chief justice of the King's Bench to justices of the peace in which first priority was given to "that part of the statute of 5 Eliz. which appoints the wages of servants and manual laborers to be rated" and compels service. Stress was laid also on the Act of 1601 concerning alehouses, the Act of 1589 on cottages and lodgers, the Act of 1555 on highway maintenance.[6] One version of directions given the West Riding justices of the peace by the assize judges in 1618 follows more closely the order and substance of Bacon's speech.[7] Of about the same period must be the model offered by Michael Dalton of a charge from the judges of assize to the justices of the peace, differing in arrangement and contents from those already described.[8] Its articles: (1) alehouses, unlicensed or

[5] *Works*, XIII, 302–306.

[6] Hist. MSS. Comm., *Buccleuch*, III, Montagu Papers VI, 2nd ser., 203, April 16, 1618, the articles as sent by Sir Henry Montagu to the Middlesex justices of the peace according to the charge.

[7] *Sessions Records*, II, 397.

[8] Dalton, *The Country Justice*, 2nd ed., 315. His headings have been freely

disorderly; (2) roads and bridges needing repair; (3) observance of the duty of hue and cry; (4) laborers compelled to go into service; (5) parish relief of the poor by apprenticing children and providing work; (6) recusants; (7) rogues and vagabonds arrested and punished; (8) house of correction maintained; (9) performance of watch and ward; (10) weights and measures inspected.

With these examples of the first stages in transmitting from central to local government the urgencies of the moment may be compared a few of the lists of articles as they were given to high constables for presentment. The earliest representative is the memorandum of 1566 already mentioned, probably based on a set of articles.[9] The earliest surviving official form seems to be that attributed to Sir Edward Coke, probably delivered by him at the first assizes after his promotion to the chief justiceship.[10] An abstract follows:

"Articles which the constables of each hundred are to observe and answer unto at the beginning of every assize." [11]

1. Felonies since the last assizes and pursuit of them.
2. Vagrants apprehended, how the watches have been kept.
3. Recusants not coming to church.
4. Decay of houses of husbandry.
5. Lands within twelve years turned from tillage to pasture.
6. Alehouses licensed and the unlicensed punished.
7. Observance of regulations by licensed alehouses.
8. Engrossing, forestalling and regrating.
9. Maltsters making malt without license.
10. Vagabonds punished and the impotent poor provided for.
11. Sufficiency of estates and discretion of petty constables; none to be admitted but subsidy men of good understanding.

---

expanded in the text above. The West Riding charge included, in a different order, Dalton's first, fifth, and sixth articles.

[9] See above, Chap. VIII, and see n. 8 for doubt as to the sessions for which such a set of articles would have been intended.

[10] See Article 5 in the text above: the Act of 1597 (39 Eliz., c. 2), for the maintenance of tillage, referred to conversions since 1593 (the repeal of earlier laws); twelve years from this date would bring the date of these articles to 1605 or 1606. Coke's appointment as chief justice of the Common Pleas was June 30, 1606. His first assizes would have been the midsummer circuit, that on which at Norwich he urged the grand jury to reform informers.

[11] S.P.D. Eliz., CCLXXVI, No. 72, printed almost in full in *Cal. S.P.D.*, Eliz., 1598–1601, 519. It is itself undoubtedly an abstract, made as notes for or from the actual charge as delivered at the assizes. In the text above the quotation is not word-for-word, but no effort has been made to standardize the original's varying form of statement from article to article. The apparent partial duplication of Nos. 2 and 10 suggests that two different statutes were in mind.

12. All masters to be presented that retain their servants out of the general petty sessions, or give greater wages than shall be set down by the justices of the peace; whether petty sessions be kept at times accustomed, so that men be retained but in petty sessions . . . and the retainer be made known to the chief constables and entered into their books.

13. No new cottages to be allowed to be built, but the justices of the peace to suppress such.

14. Any lord or freeholder erecting a cottage with less than four acres to maintain the poor inhabiting it. . . .

15. All unlawful games, drunkenness, whoredom, and incontinency in private families to be reported, as on their good government the commonwealth depends.

16. To inquire into and present masters who turn away servants before the time for which retained, "for that thereby many become rogues and idle persons."

17. To inquire after poulterers and purveyors selling victuals at unreasonable prices.

18. To inquire into dove houses kept by other than lords of the manor and parsons of the town.

This list was of course not a complete departure from its predecessors so far as these may be judged by the notes of 1566: the Elizabethan articles included the substance of Coke's second, sixth, and eighth articles and a part of his twelfth and thirteenth; the three additional articles not appearing on the 1606 list did not concern economic regulations. The presentments by the high constables of a Somerset hundred at Taunton assizes in 1616 show either some changes in the official articles or local adaptation in arrangement and subject: recusants; absence from church; breaking the assize of beer; drunkenness; hue and cry; watch and ward; roads and bridges; cottages; vagrants punished and passed; masterless men.[12] Two years later the articles at Lancaster assizes "whereof the high constables are to enquire" agreed with those of 1606 more closely: the first ten were identical, but the subjects of Coke's eleventh through fourteenth articles are lacking, being replaced only by a virtual repetition of the second article and by a twelfth concerning provision for relief of the poor.[13]

By the reign of Charles I, the basic list had become "the fourteen articles." With local variations such as occurred in earlier times, these lived on as guides for the high and petty constables' present-

[12] MS. Sessions Indictment Rolls, No. 33, Part I, Item 70.

[13] *Manchester Sessions*, I, ed. E. Axon, The Record Society [of] Lancashire and Cheshire, XLII, 54–55.

ments at assizes and quarter sessions until well into the eighteenth century.[14] No standard form has been seen, but the return from a Norfolk high constable in 1642, when combined with that of the grand jury, supplies an approximate list of the articles given in charge by the justices of the peace: recusants; absence from church; disturbers of divine service; riots; watch and ward; condition of the house of correction; extortioners; unlicensed alehouses; rogues and vagabonds; relief of the poor; roads; the good conduct of constables and bailiffs. One article on which no reports were received from the petty constables is not mentioned by subject.[15]

The local variations may in part have arisen from minor changes made by the justices of the peace to suit local needs, but probably were chiefly the result of the far from rigid construction which the high and petty constables put upon their duties. A conscious effort to depart from the directions is unlikely. High constables in a Somerset hundred, to excuse their lack of presentments at the Taunton assizes of 1616, said that they had conferred with their predecessors but that these claimed they had had no articles given them in charge at the last assizes and could therefore give the new incumbents no advice.[16] Here the high constables were obviously unwilling to take the responsibility of acting on their own motion to report offenses.

In view of this no doubt characteristic inertia on the part of local officers,[17] and of the absence in all the known sets of articles before

[14] The earliest reference noted to the "fourteen articles" was in 1626, when the grand jury at the July Assizes for Essex presented returns from high constables to "the 14 articles" (MS. Assizes Records, S.E. Circuit, Indictments, Bdle. 68.)

[15] MS. Sessions Rolls, 18 Chas. I, return from hundred of Northerpingham; grand jury presentment, April Sessions at Lynn. There seem to have been only thirteen articles in all. Typical examples of presentments by petty constables in 1634 are printed in the Worcestershire *Calendar of Quarter Sessions Papers*, pp. 563ff. These appear to be also answering only thirteen articles, though one return refers to the "14." Their substance is similar to the Norfolk returns, but they include certain substitute matters, i.e., the number of vintners and common bakers, and unlawful gaming. Petty constables' returns in Essex of the same period include reports as to common brewers, weights and measures in the market if any, and forestalling, regrating or engrossing. (Cal. Q.S., XX, 265, S.R. 271/27.)

[16] MS. Sessions Indictment Rolls, No. 33, Part 3, Item 138.

[17] A high constable in Essex, when submitting the reports of his petty constables to quarter sessions in 1630, excused having nothing himself to present on the ground that "the articles came so lately to my hands" (Cal. Q.S., XX, 268, S.R. 271/42).

1643[18] of any mention of enforcing the apprenticeship provisions of the Statute of Artificers, the rarity of presentments for such offenses by high or petty constables is hardly surprising. The few that were made must be considered astonishing displays of initiative. Must the more numerous presentments by hundred juries of apprenticeship offenses be regarded in the same light? It is impossible to say, for in none of the available lists of articles is there an indication whether they were for the guidance of hundred juries as well as constables, and actual presentments by hundred juries tend to be even less complete than those of the local officers — they present offenders under certain heads only, without mention of other matters omitted or satisfactory. Their wider range of subject, however, as in Elizabethan Essex, has already been noted, and may indicate the habit and exercise of a greater discretionary power in selecting subjects for presentment. Nevertheless, references in general terms in their returns to the articles given them in charge occur in the Elizabethan and Stuart periods alike, and there is no reason to suppose that these lists differed substantially from the others reviewed.

The concern of the central government, so far as it can be revealed in these discontinuous samples of the instructions to local authorities, is thus seen to be primarily with the same problems as that of local government itself — poverty, employment, conditions of service, public order, and transport.[19] Enforcement in the food trades of the available controls on commodity distribution was emphasized by the Privy Council in periods of dearth, primarily as a measure to prevent disorder. But actual presentment of illegal middlemen, even in food supplies, was sporadic, although lists of articles for presentment often included this subject. Still less attention was given by presenting juries or local officers to illegal dealing in industrial commodities such as wool and hides.[20] Three classes of industrial regulation in the period 1563–1642 seem never to have been included in the articles, whether these were as they originated or as they were

[18] By 1670, petty constables' presentments to quarter sessions in Northamptonshire include with some regularity, as No. 8 or No. 9 of eleven to fifteen articles, offenders who exercise occupations without having been apprenticed for seven years (MS. Sessions Rolls, various).

[19] The problem of religious conformity, which takes a leading place in several of the lists of articles, is left out of account in this enumeration.

[20] This impression derives from casual observation of presentments by local agencies to quarter sessions, but instances may have been overlooked.

locally adapted: the apprenticeship law in its various clauses established by the Act of 1563; usury laws; and laws governing particular industries. With the first two classes, local officers and juries sometimes went beyond their explicit directions, presenting violators of the seven-year term and on rare occasions offenders against the clauses regulating the number and qualifications of apprentices; very exceptionally, they took notice of usurers.[21]

The regulation of apprenticeship was recognized to a slight degree in the second channel of communication between central and local government, that of letters from Privy Council to justices of the peace. This recognition, however, was given only on rare occasions, and generally at the instance of petitioners to the council, not as a matter to which importance was attached by the central government of its own motion. Four examples of the council's intervention are no doubt typical, and may be comprehensive.[22] The first was in March 1586, when the council directed the justices of assize and the justices of the peace of Devon and Cornwall to examine complaints from kersey weavers and to enforce compulsory apprenticeship on their behalf against intruders.[23] The season was uneasy, with export trades disrupted by the Spanish embargo of 1585, English retaliation, war in the Netherlands; there were reports during the winter of grain scarcities. A second occasion was in 1605, when the winter had brought such a menace of scarcity that the earl of Dorset, then lord treasurer, wrote urgently to justices of the peace that "the poor

[21] The extent of enforcement of the usury laws, like that of most mercantilist regulation, has never been studied. It has been said that administering the usury law of 1571 "was part of the regular routine of the justices of the peace." It appears to have been so only in the same degree to which enforcement of the seven-year apprenticeship was, i.e., as one of the offenses which they might hear and determine; or they might be called upon to intervene between debtor and creditor in individual cases of hardship. But the "presentments before quarter sessions" which have been mentioned by one authority seem with few exceptions to have been indictments or informations by private persons; for example, despite the North Riding's unusually active system of presentment by public agencies, only one case occurred between 1605 and 1639 of a probable presentment for usury (N.R.R.S., I, 46). Observation in other counties agrees with this. The quoted phrases are from Tawney's Introduction to Wilson's *Discourse*, 163.

[22] Exclusive of occasional council recommendations for leniency toward individuals prosecuted for violating the requirement of the seven-year term of apprenticeship (see above, Chap. VI).

[23] *Acts P.C.*, Eliz., XIV, 21, 27. Apprenticeship was required by the Acts of 1555 and 1557 in weaving and clothmaking, as well as by the Act of 1563.

people were ready to mutiny." In June, the council sent the orders previously described for the organization of divisional assemblies to take measures against popular unrest, among them to enforce the Statute of Artificers.[24] A third instance came in the next reign, the appeal in May 1631 from the town of Cambridge for the Privy Council's help in enforcing the seven-year term of apprenticeship against intruders, as a means of protecting the town's employment and lessening its poor rate at a time of pressure on both.[25] Suitable orders were issued by the council. But within two months it had given special permission to a qualified chandler in Cambridge to trade as a draper though he had never been apprenticed to the latter occupation.[26]

The recurrent dilemma in apprenticeship enforcement, illustrated in this Cambridge sequence, is apparent also in the fourth example of the council's intervention to uphold the apprenticeship law. This was the campaign already mentioned of craft groups in several northern towns to suppress unapprenticed rural competitors.[27] When brought to the council's attention, their effort received official support. The Company of Shoemakers of Chester had petitioned the two assize judges of the circuit for aid against unapprenticed intruders, "living near the city"; the judges consulted the Privy Council, who directed them to see that the fees of the prosecutors were moderated, since the petitioners were very poor and their object was "to the general good." The same order was issued simultaneously on behalf of the Chester Company of Glovers, whose petition had been accompanied by a certificate from the justices of the peace of the harm done to the trade by the intruders.[28] But three years later, after receiving a petition from the "Shoemakers of Cheshire" against the

[24] Essex Cal. Q.S., XVIII, 82, S.R. 171/57, Easter 3 Jas. I, copy of letter of 22 February 1604/05; for the June orders, see above, Chap. IX, n. 27. The council's list of statutes to be enforced in the interests of public order included those concerning "Laborers," "alehouses and tipplers," "the assize of bread and drink," "rogues and vagabonds," "setting of the poor on work and to bind children prentices," "artificers." The distinction thus made in 1605 between the statutes "of laborers" and "concerning artificers" is consistent with a sixteenth- and seventeenth-century practice of applying the pre-1563 title to questions of wages or of service contracts.

[25] See the preceding chapter.

[26] E. M. Hampson, *The Treatment of Poverty in Cambridgeshire, 1597–1834*, 23 and n. 3.

[27] See above, Chap. V, and n. 130, 131.

[28] Privy Council Register, Chas. I, XLI, 373, January 31, 1631/32.

Company of Shoemakers of Chester, the council wrote to the lord lieutenant of the county, the earl of Derby, to arrange a compromise between the two groups, so that neither would offenders against the apprenticeship laws be encouraged "nor the Company suffered to use any rigor against those who are known to be sufficient workmen and have continued long in the trade." [29]

The series of complaints to the council had started with that of the Chester feltmakers in 1628, and was at its peak in 1633–1635 with petitions from various Lancashire trades — the skinners and glovers, the shoemakers, the glasiers, and in a jurisdictional dispute the dyers. The council on the whole showed itself favorable to "the orderly government of cities and corporations," referring the petitioners to special hearings before the justices of assize backed by the threat to the offenders of summons before the council. For the Lancashire shoemakers in 1633, the same special order was added as for this craft at Chester in the preceding year, but no other intruders except the Cheshire shoemakers seem to have applied to the council for relief from prosecution.[30] The setting for these events was, so far as is yet known, one of fairly general good business,[31] and the council intervention in these cases was apparently only a manifestation of the favorable policy toward corporations which was characteristic at this period of Stuart government.[32] Despite activity in other counties than Lancashire and Cheshire in prosecuting the unapprenticed during the late 1620's and early 1630's, there has been observed no evidence elsewhere of Privy Council support or particular encouragement from government.[33]

[29] XLIV, 292, 19 December, 1634.

[30] XXXVIII, 230, 501; XXXIX, 385, 397; XLII, 478; XXXVIII, 230, June 1628, reply to petition from the Chester feltmakers; XLIII, 28, 25 May 1633: i.e., that the fees payable by the prosecutors should be reduced.

[31] See reference in n. 27 above.

[32] On the motives of Stuart policy toward industrial corporations, see Unwin, *Industrial Organization*, 143; Heaton, *Yorkshire Industries*, 218–219ff. The appeal from one Chester company ran in terms designed to interest the government: the Glovers, Felmongers, and Leathersellers in 1630/31 complained to the council of untrained intruders, by whose competition the petitioners were disabled from contributing to subsidies (P.C.R., Chas. I, XL, 332).

[33] Strict regulation of the cloth industry and of apprenticeship has been attributed to the earl of Strafford when beginning his service as president of the Council of the North in 1629. See C. V. Wedgwood, *Strafford, 1593–1641*, 106–107, referring to Reid, *The King's Council in the North*, 412. The source quoted by the latter is only the general statement by Cunningham (*Growth of English*

The course of apprenticeship prosecution in these years of Charles I's reign, within the period often characterized as that of "really efficient central government,"[34] throws into sharp relief the lack of effort by the central government to chart a consistent policy or to set objectives for the local authorities in enforcing apprenticeship. In the eight years 1627–1634, the apprenticeship prosecutions (on the seven-year clause) from all sources in the quarter sessions of the selected counties totaled from 547 to 621. The majority of these were by professional informers. Only six or seven were presentments brought by public agencies. In the Lancashire records there is no trace of measures taken by county authorities, by presentments or by orders, to check the unapprenticed competitors of the townsmen to whom the Privy Council had given its blessing, and whose probable agent Thomas Pilkington was then occupied in haling the offenders into court.[35]

The third means of guiding from above the application of statute law in the local courts was through the influence of the decisions and opinions of the high courts at Westminster. The developing case law on the question of regulation versus restraint of trade has commonly been regarded as an important factor in the decline of compulsory apprenticeship. If within the period 1563–1642, the central courts were interpreting the limits of regulation in a sense unfavorable to the apprenticeship provisions of the Act of 1563, this influence might help to account for the indifference of local authorities. For the later seventeenth and the eighteenth centuries, it would be necessary to determine the practical effect on the cases in assizes and quarter sessions of interpretations at Westminster, a number of which were by then hostile to the apprenticeship law, although one modern view holds that judicial interpretation even in the later periods was "far from being so uniformly unfavorable as has been supposed."[36] Be-

Industry and Commerce, II, 311) of his own view of industrial regulation during the period 1629–1640. The present writer is ignorant of any other foundation for it.

[34] Heckscher, *Mercantilism*, I, 256.

[35] Pilkington, a skinner, is named as the prosecutor in one after another of the petitions from the town companies in the Lancashire campaign. He is the informer in cases brought before quarter sessions in 1633–34, two dozen or more prosecutions of skinners alleged to be unqualified. He may have been hired by the various craft organizations.

[36] Derry, "The Enforcement of Apprenticeship," 10–11. Investigation by the

fore 1642 no adverse opinion had crystallized in the central courts, nor is it possible to see in the reported cases "evidence of aversion to the Statute of Artificers,"[37] with one exception which apparently had no influence. This was a case of 1591 in which the court reportedly held that apprenticeship to any trade named in the Act of 1563 was sufficient qualification for all. It was referred to by Lord Mansfield in 1756 as not then good law; but it does not appear to have been used even in its own time as a precedent, so far as citations in the law reports suggest.[38]

The issues which arose in apprenticeship cases, according to the few prior to the Restoration which are dealt with in the various Law Reports, can be summarized as: (a) inaccuracies in wording; (b) the effect of the Act of 1589 on the venue; (c) the interpretation of trades as within the meaning of the Act of 1563; (d) applications of the custom of London; (e) the relation of guild ordinances to the Act.

Dismissals of prosecutions of all types for very minor verbal inaccuracies in the indictment were frequent in the Tudor and Stuart periods, so that their occurrence in cases of apprenticeship need not in itself suggest any bias in the courts against enforcement.[39] Recorded cases in the Law Reports in general belong to the later seventeenth century, when a frequent inaccuracy was to omit to state whether the occupation involved was "used" in 1563. The Elizabethan and early Stuart entries in the Westminster courts' rolls and in the sessions records sometimes record that a prosecution has been dismissed for insufficiency, but without detail.[40]

The trend of decisions in the cases involving the Act of 1589 has been mentioned in an earlier chapter.[41] On the next point, that of

---

present writer of apprenticeship cases in sessions and assizes records of the post-Restoration period indicates little if any relation between decisions and opinions handed down at Westminster and the actual course of apprenticeship prosecution.

[37] Heckscher (I, 291) finds this in the case of the Tailors of Ipswich, discussed later in the present chapter.

[38] J. Burrow, *Reports of Cases . . . in the . . . King's Bench*, Pt. IV, I, 2: Mansfield in *Raynard v. Chace*, citing Leonard's *Reports*.

[39] Holdsworth, *English Law*, IV, 531; IX, 260–261.

[40] The sole entry, if any, of the cause of dismissal usually is "for error" or "for insufficiency." One apprenticeship case of 1613 illustrates the kind of technical inaccuracy adequate for dismissal: "because it wanteth voluntarie," i.e., the Latin indictment lacked the statement that the illegal occupation had been voluntarily exercised. (Essex Cal. Q.S., XIX, 105, S.R. 202/32.)

[41] See above, Chap. III, n. 14.

construing occupations to be outside the application of the Act of 1563, in two decisions occupations were excluded because they involved only buying and selling. The first was a judgment in the Exchequer in 1580 in an information against a clothier, that the statutory "exercising a trade" was not applicable to the buying of unfinished cloth and its later sale by the buyer after being put out for finishing. In the second, in 1600, the occupation of costermonger was said to be exempt. The earlier judgment seems never to have been reported, and mention of the later has been seen only in a nearly contemporary case.[42] Cases were also argued before 1642 on the ground that a given trade was not one requiring skill, or, in one against a brewer, that "nine out of ten were not apprentices." But only two decisions construed the occupation in question unfavorably. The first, Tolley's Case in 1613 in which Chief Justice Coke presided, involved the trade of upholsterer, which appears in only four prosecutions in the Exchequer and Queen's Bench during Elizabeth's reign and none from the selected counties in any courts before 1642.[43] The reported judgment included a gratuitous exemption of several other occupations from the Act of 1563 on the ground that they required no skill. But apprenticeship prosecutions continued for some generations to be brought against offenders in these occupations, and there is no evidence that even the central courts were influenced by the suggested exclusions.[44] The second such case occurred in 1638, when the King's Bench is reported to have agreed that the occupation of hempdresser was "no such trade as is within that statute" because it demanded little learning or skill. The judgment

[42] Exch. Q.R.M.R., Hil. 22 Eliz., m. 65; *Tudor Economic Documents*, I, 382. Prosecutions of clothiers were infrequent both before and after 1580, and none against costermongers or other hucksters was observed.

[43] The phrase about the brewer's trade is that quoted from Coke's opinion in the upholsterer's case, and probably refers to *Shoile v. Taylor*, in 1606 or 1608, reported by Coke and by Croke ([E. Coke], *The Reports of . . .*, VII, Pt. 13, 12–13; [Croke], *The Reports of . . .*, 4th ed., II, 178). Tolley's Case ([E. Bulstrode], *The Reports of . . . in King's Bench*, 186), was reversed in 1668 as bad law and was then said to have been poorly reported (J. Keble, *Reports in . . . King's Bench*, Rex v. Sellers).

[44] This (Tolley's Case) was discussed by Heckscher, *Mercantilism*, I, 292–293, with perhaps more significance than it deserves, although he recognized that it had no immediate effect as a precedent. It seems possible, in the present writer's view, that the late seventeenth-century reporting of it confused counsel's argument with judges' opinion, though the phrase is used "it was agreed and resolved . . ."

can hardly have narrowed seriously the application of the Act of 1563.[45]

Arguments and decisions in cases concerning the custom of London would not have affected prosecutions before county quarter sessions. As to the final class of issues, involving the relation of the Act of 1563 to guild ordinances, the best known case is that of the Tailors of Ipswich, in 1613, in which a guild ordinance was condemned as more restrictive than the apprenticeship regulation of the Act of 1563, the latter being upheld by implication.[46] The decision which invalidated the guild requirement that its permission be obtained to exercise a trade after serving an apprenticeship has been viewed as showing Chief Justice Coke's "aversion" to the Act of 1563, on the ground that the guild's allowance was the only effective means of enforcing the statute.[47] But at the time of the decision evidence of the enrolment of apprenticeship indentures in the freemen's register of a corporate town or borough was still a reasonably well-enforced prerequisite for admission by apprenticeship to the freedom of any corporation. Nothing more should perhaps be read into the decision than its obvious intent to prevent the growth of restrictive guild by-laws.

Another case of James I's reign involving a guild ordinance has been quoted by a modern writer as a decision in favor of the common law and against statutory apprenticeship.[48] This is putting more of a load on it than it can carry. The Newbury weavers' guild had attempted to enforce an ordinance requiring, for admission to the company, apprenticeship within the town and the exercise there of weaving for the five years previous to the ordinance. The issue was stated by Sir Henry Hobart in his report of the case as "between the particular privileges of towns and the general liberties of the people"; according to Hutton's report, the judges in conference agreed, without giving an opinion on this general issue, that the ordinance was absurdly restrictive, and judgment was given against the guild. But in his reported argument, Hobart recognized the principle of the

[45] [Croke], *The Reports of . . .*, (1683), III, 499, *Rex v. Fredland*, 14 Chas. I. No prosecutions have been seen for using the occupation of hempdresser.

[46] [Coke], *The Reports of . . .*, VI, 53; also known as the Clothworkers of Ipswich.

[47] Heckscher, I, 291.

[48] Kramer, *The English Craft Gilds*, 161.

Act of 1563 that the place where apprenticeship was served was immaterial, quoting in support the case of the Tailors of Ipswich.[49]

In sum, hostility in the central courts to the regulation of apprenticeship can be found before 1642, if at all, only in isolated judgments or opinions, and was not therefore a cause of the failure of central and local government to take more positive steps to enforce it.[50]

[49] [Hobart], *The Reports of . . .*, 5th ed., 210–211, case of *Norris v. Staps*, 1616; *The Reports of Sir Richard Hutton . . .*, 2nd ed., 5.

[50] Even in the case of *Jennings v. Pitman*, in 1621–1623, in which the question was whether an apprenticeship contract was void without the certificate of three justices of the peace to the parents' estate. Though the comment was made that these certificates had not been used, it was said that they were essential; but no decision on the case is reported. (Hutton, 63; the case was brought as an action of covenant in the Common Pleas.)

XI

EFFECTIVENESS OF PUBLIC AGENCIES

The starting point for an estimate of the weakness and strength of public agencies in the enforcement of the seven-year term of apprenticeship is the number of presentments under this provision of the Act of 1563. They were very few and the majority were without result. In the period 1563–1642, such presentments by local juries and constables were only some 50 to 65 in the quarter sessions of the selected counties, exclusive of Norfolk where all record of results is lacking.[1] Of these, to adopt the classifications used in a previous chapter,[2] about four-fifths were "inconclusive," appearing to have been dropped without record of the issue of process. From one-ninth to one-seventh were "ineffective": one was an acquittal after jury trial; six were dismissals, with three specified as insufficient of which one, ironically, was a grand jury presentment.[3] Only two, one-twenty-fifth or less of the total, had a recorded "effective" result: in one case, the offender was allowed a mitigated fine of 3/4 on a charge of illegally exercising the occupation of baker for seven months; in the other, the fine on an illegal joiner was 20/–, a sum perhaps arrived at by a reduced verdict of half a month though the term of the original charge is unknown.[4] As with indictments, the inconclusive presentments were probably equivalent to the ineffective. A presentment by a Wiltshire hundred jury in 1622 of a widow for unapprenticed

[1] Only five or six presentments for apprenticeship were observed in the Norfolk sessions records.

[2] See above, Chap. VI.

[3] For the last-named case, Wiltshire MS. Sessions Rolls, Trin. 13 Jas. I, presentment against Roger Monday, and MS. Minute Books, III, Trin. 13 Jas. I and Mich. 15 Jas. I. One of the six dismissals was in Elizabeth's reign, the others and the one acquittal in the next.

[4] Essex Cal. Q.S., XVI, 53, S.R. 116/34, Easter 33 Eliz.; N.R.R.S., III, 155, Special Sessions for Pickering and Whitby, October 1622.

baking was apparently dropped without proceedings, and in 1627 she was again presented as having exercised the trade illegally for four years.[5]

Two weaknesses in the dependence of local justice on the unpaid and often unassisted parish constable may be the chief causes of the characteristic predominance of inconclusive presentments in Tudor and Stuart quarter sessions. One of these must have affected equally all other types of prosecution. This was the difficulty the constable encountered in performing one of his most important duties, that of executing the warrants issued by the justices of the peace to bring offenders and witnesses into court. The typical entry of writ after writ issued as normal sessions routine, and the frequent lag of several quarter sessions between indictment and first appearance, demonstrate an obvious defect in local law-enforcement, jeopardizing not only the maintenance of public order but the whole apparatus of mercantilist regulation. As the Restoration justices in the North Riding complained, failure of accused persons to appear in court "tends to the smothering of offenses." [6] In theory of course the constables were assisted, at their need, by any able-bodied resident on whom they called for aid; and in the larger parishes there were subconstables or the head-boroughs, third-boroughs, or tithingmen.[7] But volunteer or amateur help was subject to weaknesses of its own, as in the Somerset case when three neighbors of a constable allowed an offender to escape "whilst the constable was pulling on his boots." [8] Other excuses offered by unsuccessful Dogberrys reveal their frequent helplessness, and illustrations of the physical hazards and actual violence suffered by parish officers are

[5] Wiltshire MS. Sessions Minute Books, V, Trin. 20 Jas. I, presentments by Westbury hundred jury; VI, Trin. 3 Chas. I, by same.

[6] N.R.R.S., VI, 117. Yet the printed Order Books for Somerset and Warwickshire in the seventeenth century contain relatively few references to negligent constables, while in the North Riding the numbers vary: in the two decades 1606–1615 and 1661–1670 there was the largest quantity of cases of failure to execute warrants (20 in each).

[7] See S. and B. Webb, *Parish and County*, 27n., and their reference to the contemporary treatment, by writers of legal manuals such as Lambard and Dalton, of these officers as synonymous with the constable. A variety of instances in sessions records shows them in the capacity of assistants, thus corroborating in the earlier period the Webbs' findings for the later seventeenth century and the eighteenth.

[8] MS. Sessions Minute Books of Recognizances and Orders, I, 1613–1620, July 1620, list of warrants.

not wanting in sessions records; yet the number is astonishingly small for so turbulent an age.

The second weakness in local enforcement affecting the quantity of inconclusive prosecutions, and the one which was perhaps the most important single cause of dropped presentments by public agencies, was the lack of recognition that the expenses of a prosecution which was initiated by a public agency should be met from public funds. Scant attention has been given in modern studies of mercantilism to the problem of how costs of prosecution were handled. Scattered evidence from the apprenticeship indictments of the later seventeenth and eighteenth centuries testifies to the practice of charging the defendant with his own costs even in the event of acquittal or dismissal, except when the prosecutor was a common informer.[9] But in any period it is hard to find who bore the costs of the prosecution when this was based on presentment by constable or jury. In one recorded conviction of an apprenticeship offender, presented by a hundred jury, he paid only his fine and his own fees.[10] Presumably, proceedings on a jury presentment had to await either a court order that county funds should bear the expenses of the charge or the willingness of some member of the jury or other private individual to assume the costs.[11] When the presentment was made by a constable, though proceedings could perhaps have rested with anyone to take at private expense or with the county if the justices so ordered, in practice he sometimes undertook prosecution himself, at least for offenses in which he had a personal interest. A Warwick-

[9] For example, in Worcestershire, the marginal note on a constable's presentment of an unapprenticed baker, which had been quashed for insufficiency, was "remains 5s. to be paid." (MS. Sessions Minute Books II, January 1723, presentments by the constable of Blockley against John Broadway.) There is also the incident of the vengeful tanners of Rochdale who intended to ruin a competing currier by the cost of the suits they would bring against him (see above, Pt. I, Introduction, n. 5).

[10] Northamptonshire MS. Sessions Files, Trin. 21 Chas. II, list of Fines, John Killingworth for trading as a mercer. Entries in other apprenticeship cases of the same years suggest that though convicted offenders paid their fines, they may have escaped payment of fees (*ibid.*, Mich. 21 Chas. II, Fines, Edward Harper; Epiph. 23 Chas. II, Fines, William Henfrey).

[11] According to the Webbs, *Parish and County*, 466, the presentment of a constable might, if accepted by the grand jury, "become the basis of an indictment which any person who chose to pay the necessary fees could prefer. In those cases in which the justices so ordered, the clerk of the peace would prefer the indictment at the expense of the county."

shire constable, who claimed expenses of 26/6 in prosecuting for a refusal to contribute to the rate levied to reimburse the constable for previous outlays, was awarded by the justices in quarter sessions the sum of 13/4, payable however by the offender, not by the county; [12] but perhaps the officer considered himself lucky to have secured even a contingent refund of half his costs. No court orders assessing costs of prosecution against offenders or from the public funds have been seen in connection with constable or jury presentments for apprenticeship offenses.

The deterrent effect of such risks of substantial disbursements from the constable's private purse may be appreciated even better when they are viewed as only one class of expense for which he was liable and the most easily avoided by a policy of masterly inactivity. A set of constables' accounts [13] exemplifies some of the minor items: "for making our bill before the justices," at a petty sessions, 2d.; "for charges going to the justices," 4d., 8d. or 12d.; "for a horse hire to a privy sessions . . . with other charges," 2/–; recurrent small sums which could mount to a formidable total for these small farmers and tradespeople even without the heavier outlays so often quoted in descriptions of parish life, for carrying vagrants into another parish, and the like. Sums expended by petty constables in Warwickshire during the first half of the seventeenth century ranged, according to their claims for repayment, from £1 to £85 in the course of a year's term in office.[14] These financial obstacles to effective enforcement probably were more decisive than the more obvious weaknesses of service by paid substitutes or of such peculation in office as there may have been. If the latter defect had been characteristic, there would have been a larger volume of complaint against the constable, and a smaller volume of protest from the constable against the burdensomeness of the office.[15] The most frequent charges brought

[12] *Sessions Order Book*, II, 200, Easter 1648.

[13] *Market Harborough Parish Records*, 69–74 (items mostly in 1616).

[14] *Sessions Order Books*, passim.

[15] The extent of either practice is impossible to estimate. References to the hiring of substitutes are sufficiently scattered to suggest that it was a widespread method of escaping service distasteful to the well-to-do (numerous complaints in Lancs. MS. Sessions records; and see Somerset Record Society, XXVIII, 160). There are also occasional prosecutions against corrupt constables: one in Essex made a good thing out of office by embezzling public funds raised in the parish toward purveyance, the provision of gunpowder, and the like (Cal. Q.S., XIX, 436–437, S.R. 233/132, Midsummer 19 Jas. I). But the present writer has

against petty constables were those from their superiors in station, the high constables, for negligence in executing warrants and in making presentments.

Before reviewing the major defects in the system of making presentments, the possibility should be mentioned that a cause for the dropping of presentments once made might have been a lack of method in ensuring the grand jury's approval of them. The status of hundred jury and constable presentments as independent initiators of prosecution is not clear. In the Elizabethan and early Stuart periods there were variations in county practice. Procedure in quarter sessions, furthermore, differed from statements in legal manuals on the question whether such presentments must be passed upon by the grand jury as if they had no greater independent force than the accusations of private persons.[16]

The inadequacies which created the principal obstacles to thorough returns from constables and juries can be summarized, not necessarily in the order of their importance, as: the large number of matters to be watched over and reported, and for high and petty constables, the lack of sufficient time to execute their varied duties; an unwillingness of jurors and constables to make trouble, for themselves, their neighbors, or their social superiors; a membership of hundred juries not sufficiently representative of all areas within the hundred or of all classes, and possibly, as time went on, drawn from a narrowing range of individuals; and a lack of control by higher authority over the whole system, more especially over the hundred juries' performance of duty.

Previous chapters have sketched the burden and variety of work committed to high and petty constables who were at the same time working farmers, small businessmen, or, if gentlemen, men busy with management of their own small estates and perhaps the stewardship

---

not observed any such "interminable series" of complaints against constables as the Webbs record for the eighteenth century (p. 69) and retains the impression that performance of the obligation and duties of service was on the average surprisingly conscientious.

[16] This paragraph is based on observation of sessions records in the selected counties and on the *dicta* of legal writers of the period, for whom the reader is referred to the Bibliography. The most unequivocal of the latter, on the independent force of presentments by public officers including constables, is W. Sheppard, *The Whole Office of the Country Justice of Peace*, 2nd ed., 104. The Webbs assume that a constable's presentment must be approved by the grand jury (see n. 11 above).

of greater properties. Members of presentment juries, even though free of the interim duties of the constables, found attendance at quarterly sessions sufficiently onerous to evade it if possible by compounding with bailiffs for exemption — by 1606 the right to collect such compositions had been granted to patentees [17] — or by private arrangements with the clerk of the peace.[18]

The close intimacy of country life, if it made for better knowledge of one's immediate neighbors, must have tended to turn the business of presenting their misdeeds into personal problems of strained relations, petty grudges, even a threat to security of livelihood for an unlucky juror or constable. Dalton's summary of the perennial dilemma in appointing constables was anticipated by an Elizabethan jury: from the petty sessions held for one Essex hundred by the high constables, the jury itself sent the justices of the peace a request that they order the constables to return from every parish a sufficient number of jurors possessed of at least £3 in goods, "forasmuch as . . . the petty constables do most commonly return a very small number, and that such poor and unskilful persons, to appear at the petty sessions, as either cannot or dare not present any disorders." [19] Complaints recur of an insufficient number or quality of jurors, throughout the different levels of jury service at assizes and quarter sessions.[20] To secure adequate representation of all parts of the

[17] *Parliamentary Diary of Robert Bowyer, 1606–7*, 92, 25 March 1606; and a reference to a renewal of the same patent or patents or to issue of new, *Cal. S.P.D.*, Jas. I, 1603–1610, 409.

[18] *Cal. S.P.D.*, Addenda, 1625–1649, 85–86, a letter attributed to 1625, from a Devonshire man to the Duke of Buckingham stating a series of grievances of which one was the burden on the poorer men of jury service because gentlemen and the "best yeomen," men worth £100 a year, induce the clerk of the assizes and the clerk of the peace, "for a fee," to record them as if they had appeared for jury service though in fact they "think it base to attend at sessions."

[19] Cal. Q.S., IX, 68, S.R. 73/72, petty sessions for Chafford hundred, 4 Jan., 22 Eliz. The minimum estate suggested was a modest one even for the period: in Leicestershire in 1570–71, out of a sample of 102 farmers' inventories only seven left personal estates of less than £10 (Hoskins, *Essays*, 135). In Essex, two generations later, a mason left a personal estate appraised at about £6½, a husbandman one of about £10 to £12 (*Farm and Cottage Inventories*, ed. F. W. Steer, 71–72).

[20] For example, N.R.R.S., I, 263 (1612), a bailiff fined for an insufficient return of jurors, and 268 (1612), a general comment on the negligence of the bailiffs in this respect; Huntington Library, Stowe MS., Letters, Oversize, Item 41 (Notes of Edwin F. Gay), a letter from the Privy Council to the sheriff and justices of the peace of Buckinghamshire, against the continued sparing of gentlemen and "most able freeholders" from jury lists; and see preceding note.

hundred or the county was another difficulty, to which presentments empty of reports from certain districts bear witness.[21] From whatever complex of causes, a tendency also is apparent, already in some counties in the Elizabethan period, for the same individuals to be called upon for jury service sessions after sessions.[22] This might have introduced into the system of presentment a useful element of experience, but more probably contributed to its decline into a routine formality.

Out of the catalogue of imperfections from which the system suffered, perhaps only three had a directly adverse influence on the enforcement of apprenticeship — the constables' lack of adequate time and assistance, the juries' lack of full representation of all districts, and the reluctance of both to stir up trouble. The overaweing of local officers and jurors by their more powerful neighbors, landlords, or patrons might deter them from presenting offenders of considerable local standing and influence, but hardly the craftsman or shopkeeper who was their near-equal. Nevertheless, a habit of convenient blindness, cultivated for some matters and persons, would decrease the general watchfulness which was the foundation of community responsibility in law-enforcement. The habit is reflected in the prevalence at every stage of presentment and in every generation of the comprehensive "all is well," or its equivalent in a well-intentioned if unsuccessful Latinity, "omney beney." Occasionally, and especially in the Elizabethan and early Stuart periods, this may have been justified by the duplication of presentments in surviving private jurisdictions: an Essex petty constable in 1571 explained his blank report by prior presentment at "court and leet [held] twice in [each] year." [23] But a stereotyped "all well" becomes

[21] For example, a presentment from the hundred of Dunmow in Essex in 1580, for one parish "we know nothing by reason there is none of the jury" (Cal. Q.S., IX, 100, S.R. 74/50, Easter 22 Eliz.); from the half hundred of Witham, "we can say no further . . . for that we have none of our jury of [eight parishes or hamlets enumerated]" (XIV, 179, S.R. 105/31, Midsummer, 30 Eliz.).

[22] This is obvious in Essex in the 1560's, the only interval which the present writer sampled on this point (Cal. Q.S., *passim*); in Staffordshire the grand jury in 1589 included men who were on it two and four years before (*Q.S. Rolls*, I); in the West and North Ridings in the late sixteenth and early seventeenth centuries the same jurors often reappear, some of them repeatedly (*W.R.S.R.*, I, II; N.R.R.S., I-III).

[23] Cal. Q.S., III, 233, S.R. 36/36, Midsummer, 13 Eliz., return from High Ongar to the petty sessions for the hundred of Ongar. A similar return in 1631

common long before the eighteenth century though not till then was the extreme of absurdity reached in forms printed with negative answers to the "fourteen articles" for constables' presentments.[24] The virtual disappearance before the eighteenth century of presentments by hundred juries, while the constables' returns were still being made with some regularity in several counties, may have been partly owing to the absence in all periods of effective control over the hundred juries as well as to the gradual decay of the institution; constables were held by penalties for nonpresentment to some duty of reporting however perfunctory.

The strength of local government, even in regard to the enforcement of statutory apprenticeship which received so little attention in presentments, resided in the intimacy of its operation in village and manor. Inefficient as the police organization of the township was because of its amateur character, its voluntary nature was itself of incalculable weight in law-enforcement, through all it implied of acceptance by the community of traditional regulations and duties. The pressure to conform which this exerted was reinforced by the difficulty of escaping neighborhood knowledge of private affairs; immunity for an offense could not be counted upon even when it was often preserved. In matters of apprenticeship, regulation of contracts within a rural community was certainly in some areas and perhaps more generally than can now be traced a part of the supervision of conditions of employment on farm and in craft. Attested apprenticeship, moreover, conferred a greater security against being drafted into farm or domestic service; it was evidence of "belonging" in the parish where it was served and so constituted a claim for parish relief in misfortune or old age; and for the newcomer who had served as apprentice elsewhere it might be a valuable entry permit to settled residence.

(Cal. Q.S., XX, 284, S.R. 273/35, Epiph. 6 Chas. I). See above, Chap. VIII, n. 4, for the overlapping of jurisdictions. Sometimes presentments in tourn or leet were reported to the quarter sessions, for example, in 1568 a list of amercements "of the sheriff's tourns and leets" in the hundred of Hinckford was filed in the Essex Sessions Rolls (III, 9, S.R. 26/18); in Cheshire in 1594, presentments taken in the sheriff's tourns in three hundreds were said to have been certified at quarter sessions "according to the statute" (MS. Sessions Recognizance Books, III, 1593–1608, Jan., 36 Eliz.).

[24] Examples occur in the Norfolk quarter sessions from the 1740's onward. The earliest of these observed was in MS. Sessions Roll, Various, 1734–1757, dated in 1743.

Obviously, in addition to these indirect and direct influences favoring observance of the apprenticeship requirement, local government provided the framework within which the private interests already discussed made their involuntary contributions to upholding the law. It cannot be said, however, that local authorities in general gave much more positive help than was inseparable from their functioning at all: the practices of mitigating or perhaps even of refunding penalties have been described, as well as the tendency of jury verdicts to reduce the charge, and, in the relatively few conclusive cases, the outnumbering of recorded convictions or submissions by dismissals and acquittals or by rejection of the original bills. Yet, although comparative figures are not to be had for prosecutions on other statutes, the apprenticeship cases may well be typical of results in the majority of suits for offenses against economic regulations. Certainly the overwhelming share, among apprenticeship cases in most counties in the eighteenth century, of rejections by grand juries and acquittals by petty juries makes the Elizabethan and Stuart periods seem by contrast eras of considerable enforcement.[25]

At this earlier time, the system of local government, ill adapted though it was to carry out the detailed regulation and administration necessary in the ideal mercantilist state and seemingly required by the statutes if these are taken at their face value, nevertheless possessed a vigor of operation surprising for a system without strong internal disciplinary powers. Toward the objectives set by the needs and wishes of its own officers and communities and by higher authority, it could and did put forth much, if discontinuous, effort. But the enforcement of the statutory seven-year term of apprenticeship was not among these objectives, except when it provided a weapon for the perennial struggle to maintain the contemporary standard of "full employment" in the local labor market by expelling "intruders."

Why was it not? The answer depends on the view taken of the nature of English mercantilism in the sixteenth and early seventeenth centuries. In this connection, there is significance in the lack of interest shown by local and central government alike in enforcing the more strictly economic-industrial regulations, those with the least direct relation to social stability and public order. Evidence of the

[25] Apprenticeship cases into the later eighteenth century have been compiled for selected counties, and their results analyzed, by the present writer.

lack has already been noted in the omission from both the central government's directives and the local authorities' presentments of the statutes regulating specific industries and the use of capital.[26] Two instances from Elizabeth's reign will serve to illustrate possible motives for the government's rare interventions to enforce industrial legislation. In each of these, the standards for clothmaking were the issue, in years when export markets had declined and the government was under pressure from merchant interests, but also when slackened employment was to be feared. One was in 1577, when the Privy Council instructed the justices of the peace in Suffolk and Essex to see that the statutory standards were modified in the making of these counties' specialty of colored cloth.[27] The second, often described, was the irate correspondence of the council with the Yorkshire and Lancashire justices in 1600–1601 over their virtual refusal to enforce the prohibition of 1597 on the use of tenters in clothfinishing.[28] In neither instance did the council imply that the justices had neglected to fulfill a normal responsibility for enforcing this type of regulation. In the second incident, the council itself displayed an unusual concern for an objective primarily economic and not directly associated with crises of popular complaint or possible tumult. There was, however, a secondary association of this kind. Though the initial appeals to the council in the matter of tenters came from merchants trading to France, where English sales were affected by seizures of stretched cloth, the social consequences of a lack of "vent over sea" were always to be dreaded, especially at a time when the drain of men and money into Ireland, and into the Continent for the Spanish war, was being resisted in the counties.

An exception to a habitual government inattention to industrial regulation might appear to be the short-lived plan for county corporations to control the manufacture of new draperies. Proposals were urged on the Privy Council in the second decade of James I's reign and in the early twenties for corporations within the "clothing counties" in which leading officers and members would be the lord lieutenant of the county, the justices of the peace, and "other gentlemen of the best rank and quality," and at length one or two of

[26] The lord chancellor's exhortation in 1618 to the judges to cherish manufactures can hardly count as an exception to the statement in the text. It does not appear to have been implemented in the judges' charges to local authorities.

[27] *Acts P.C.*, Eliz., IX, 385.

[28] XXX, 602–603; XXXI, 78, 111; Heaton, *Yorkshire Industries*, 141–143.

these ambitious organizations were incorporated, although none actually functioned. But a modern student of these schemes regards them as designed primarily "to establish and expand" new textile enterprises, not merely to regulate the existing industry. The standard provisions for control of quality and types of cloth were embodied in the charters, but these were incidental to the main object. However, public authorities would have administered the regulations only in the capacity of officials of these county-wide "gilds."[29] The form in which the proposed incorporations came near to realization in 1624–25 was developed from a union of the dreams of their original promoter Walter Morrell with the "remedies" for the textile depression proposed by the special committee of 1622 on the decay of trade. One of the committee's suggested cures was the establishment of a corporation in each county, made up from the "most able and sufficient men," to regulate the existing cloth manufactures. The context of this proposal does not indicate that by this phrase the committee intended the local authorities, rather that they envisaged self-government by the industry. Such an omission of the county government is consistent with prevailing attitude and practice.

Industrial regulation, including the enforcement of apprenticeship according to the Statute of Artificers, thus seems to have occupied a consistently peripheral position in the sphere of central and local government concern with mercantilist policy throughout the period 1563–1642. If this interpretation is correct, it destroys in respect to a large segment of economic controls the contrast usually assumed to have prevailed between the period of "personal government" in the 1630's and a preceding laxity. It suggests moreover that not all the ingredients in English mercantilism of the sixteenth and seventeenth centuries which derived from earlier municipal practices continued equally to determine its emphasis, and that this emphasis for Tudor and Stuart government was not primarily on the regulation of industry for economic objectives.

[29] F. J. Fisher, "Some Experiments in Company Organization," *The Economic History Review*, IV, No. 2, 190–193; and on the place of Morrell's schemes in Stuart policy, 186–187, where they are interpreted as sincerely intended constructive proposals which were given correspondingly sincere support by the government. The quotation in the text is from one of the earlier projects of Morrell's, about 1615, for the new draperies of Hertfordshire and Devon (S.P.D., Jas. I, XCVI, No. 40). The incorporations of the mid-1620's were also to apply to the new draperies; an article in the *D.N.B.* on Walter's relative

Tudor and Stuart mercantilism represented the concepts and habits of a village and manorial economy quite as much if not more than those of a town economy. The operation of local government turned upon the system of presentment by local officers and juries; it continued to hinge on this for longer than the period under consideration here, despite the increased powers of justices out of sessions. Much of the substance of the presentments, even when clothed by Tudor or Stuart statute in a modern dress, was as familiar to local authorities as an inherited coat, and much was being watched over and reported, merely from the acceptance of long habit, to the surviving instruments of old jurisdictions, the manorial courts and those which had once been the king's. The customary and the natural preoccupation of these courts was with the problems which might affect the peace and livelihood of the local community; and this same preoccupation is evident in the problems presented to the quarter sessions, which for the petty constable or even the high constable was perhaps in this age a less important arena than the leet, the tourn, or the statute sessions. Most of the justices of the peace were as closely bound in to the local network of land tenure and family alliance as the lesser men. Their dominant concern whether as lords of manors or as representatives of the crown was the preservation of order and status. The essence of the relation of the justices of the peace to industrial regulation can be illustrated by two incidents. When in 1592 the bay-makers at Halstead in Essex annoyed those of Colchester by using the same seal for their bays, the decision as to a trademark was referred by the Privy Council to Sir William Waldegrave and Sir Thomas Lucas as the nearest justices, to the former of whom, the council letter explained, the town of Halstead appertained. When in 1618 an attempt was made to collect customs on the overlength of Devon kerseys measuring more than the statute standard, four Devon justices represented the case of the industry to the council, explaining that there was no sale in the usual export market, Rouen, for cloths any shorter, the merchants were not buying because of the customs, and the weavers, spinsters, and fullers lacked work.[30]

Thus a threat to the livelihood of their manorial tenants or unem-

---

Hugh Morrell mentions the grant of charters for Hertfordshire and Devon in 1624 and 1626.

[30] *Acts P.C.*, Eliz., XXII, 444, Jas. I, III, 212; S.P.D., Jas. I, XCVII, No. 85.

ployment within the jurisdiction of their commissions belonged to the normal concern of the justices of the peace, since both jeopardized social stability. But otherwise conditions affecting the producer were apparently considered to be outside its scope, except for wages and the contract of service which were of prime importance to the land. The service contract, moreover, became even more intimately associated with community problems after the enactment of compulsory poor rates, in its possible effects on the liability of a parish to pay relief; it had always had a close connection with the universal and understandable fear of vagrancy. If the known sets of articles for presentment, and the known charges by the officers of state to judges of assize and justices of the peace, can be accepted as expressing the objectives ordinarily proposed by the central government to local authorities, then it may be concluded that industrial regulation was not conceived, either at the center or at the circumferences, as a normal part of the duties of local government.

Even if industrial regulation had taken a greater place in the concept of local government's functions, one of the original motives for a considerable part of sixteenth-century industrial legislation was no longer important. This part comprised the provisions of various statutes designed to prevent the spread of industry into the countryside and thus to call a halt to the industrialization of England. The vain hope of checking the economic tides inspired much of the legislation in the middle years of the sixteenth century, not the least of which were the apprenticeship clauses of the Statute of Artificers.[31] Like so many laws, these were formulated as a solution to problems of a past age rather than with foresight of new needs, and they reflect the forebodings of the difficult middle decade. But within a quarter century, despite the recurrent slumps in the export of textiles and fluctuations in domestic prosperity, the viewpoint toward the spread of industry may have altered. Is it fanciful to see in two apparently unrelated enactments of 1576 the bond of a common outlook? These were the first national provision by statute for regular means of employing the poor, and the repeal of the restriction on country clothmaking for the three chief broadcloth counties of the southwest.[32] There may already have been occurring that change in the dominant economic creed from distrust to acceptance and en-

[31] See Introduction above.

[32] 18 Eliz., c. 3, and Leonard, *English Poor Relief*, 72; 18 Eliz., c. 16.

couragement of industry which is typified by the contrast between William Cecil's memorandum of 1564 and Bacon's exhortation of 1618, and which has been regarded as marking the early seventeenth century.[33] If this shift took place earlier, its effect on the enforcement of apprenticeship may have been felt in the otherwise somewhat puzzling inclusion of informations on the seven-year requirement in the Act of 1589. The sponsors of the act may of course have pursued single-mindedly the associated purposes of lessening the depredations of informers and relieving the dockets of the Westminster courts. But if the control of apprenticeship had occupied the central position in economic and social policy that it appears to have done at the outset of the reign, would such an estimate of its importance as seems implicit in this statute have found a place in any legislation? In 1589 it is evidently ranked as of local rather than national interest.

Yet alone of the regulations intended as barriers to industrial growth, the institution of the compulsory seven-year apprenticeship lived on because it was more than a mere negation; without benefit of statute it had acquired positive values suited to the social structure as much as or more than to the economic life of the period. It fitted also into the framework of the agrarian mercantilism which was the characteristic objective of government regulation in Tudor and Stuart England, but because of the inherent vitality of apprenticeship it presented even in this setting few problems demanding government attention. A still deeper cause than the nonindustrial nature of earlier English mercantilism, or than the disappearance of one of the originating motives for a national apprenticeship law, or than the continuing usefulness and meaning of apprenticeship, was perhaps a concept of statute law as the expression of a standard which could be approached but never — or not safely — realized. When London distributors of dairy products complained in 1616 to the Privy Council that they were harassed by informers (under the sixty-year old statutes), the council forbade the prosecutions, on the ground that while the regulations were "good" they would stop a necessary trade if strictly enforced. And how revealing that remark of a Jacobean member of Parliament, already quoted, that if penal statutes were enforced to the utmost it would be "unsufferable." In this light, the dominating role of private persons and private interest

[33] This suggestion as to the "economic gospel" of the Stuart period, in Fisher's "Some Experiments in Company Organization," 185.

in the enforcement of mercantilist policy must not be regarded as the result of the inefficiency of public authorities who failed in a prescribed duty or of the early influence of legal doctrines opposed to restraint of trade. Elements of *laissez faire* and of self-government were as essential components of English mercantilism as they were of the whole fabric of English life.

CONCLUSION

Upon the extent to which the seven-year term of apprenticeship prescribed by the Statute of Artificers was enforced depends its importance as a factor in the economic development of Elizabethan and Stuart England. Yet the dominant role of private interests in enforcing it meant from the outset that it was never directed by conscious policy toward economic or social ends. Had it been firmly applied and with intention, it might have hampered the extension of industry and trade outside the towns, restricted the growth of the putting-out system, and tended both to immobilize shifts of occupation and to make rigid the demarcation of crafts and trades. To what degree were there at least accidental effects which might have altered direction or pace of change in these respects?

The distribution of apprenticeship cases among occupations and areas, though varying between town and country, shows that the seven-year term was enforced outside the corporate towns to which its enforcement has sometimes been assumed to have been limited. Professional informers prosecuted country as well as town offenders; and they were presumably no more and no less successful in the country than in the town, except possibly where an offender's greater ignorance of the law or remoteness from the seat of justice might have been an added inducement to composition. Informers working for organized trade groups of the towns, and other townsmen warring individually on country competitors, provide some of the recorded cases, but can only occasionally be identified. Attempts to control competition within the market area of the corporate or unincorporated town may often be suspected from the tendency of the places named in prosecutions (as the offender's place of illegal business) to bunch around a larger center, but without intensive local search no proof is available. Instances in which a town versus country fight is clearly visible are the Crediton weavers in 1599 and 1605, the Essex retailers in 1571, or the trade groups in the Lancashire and Cheshire towns in Charles I's reign. Usually, however, such a conflict can only be inferred, as when a Salisbury baker sued a man professing the same occupation at the adjacent village of Fisherton Anger.[1] The nuisance value of prosecutions for country clothmaking is indicated by the wish of clothing villages like those of Essex in Elizabeth's reign to get exemption from the statutory prohibition, and by the protests of Wiltshire and east Somerset clothiers which led to the Act of 1576. Apprenticeship prosecutions must have had a similar effect, but they cannot have been governing factors in the rate of dispersion of economic activity through the countryside.

To the closely associated question, whether the apprenticeship requirement affected the growth of the putting-out system, the same argument may be applied. There was no conscious use of prosecution either to restrict the territorial spread of putting-out or the number of putting-out employers. Here again, the private interests engaged in prosecuting violators were influenced by the same economic conditions as those which helped to determine the degree of observance or evasion of the law. This may be illustrated from the textile industry, the most important in which the putting-out organization was established. The weavers, in all clothing districts of the country, considerably outnumbered the clothmakers. The proportion of clothiers to weavers varied with the scale of the particular branch of the industry. The larger Leeds clothiers in 1629 were said to be employing about forty persons apiece, or a proportion of about seven weavers to every substantial clothier; but for the West Riding, as a whole, especially in the kersey-making district of Halifax, many clothiers employed only their own families and were their own weavers.[2] This must have been true of many if not most of the Devon clothier-weavers. At the other extreme were the clothiers of Wiltshire, where in 1621 seven were said to employ at least 1500 persons, or presumably some 30 weavers each. The large Suffolk clothier was computed in 1618 to employ at least 500 persons [perhaps 70 to 80 weavers] weekly.[3]

The apprenticeship prosecutions were over three times as numerous against weavers as against clothiers. In Elizabethan Devon there were none against clothiers under the Act of 1563 and fewer against cloth-

[1] Q.B.C.R., Pasch. 24 Eliz., m. 83.
[2] Heaton, *Yorkshire Industries*, 99, 96.
[3] S.P.D., Chas. I, CXCI, No. 41; Unwin, *Studies*, 280.

makers under the Cloth Acts than against weavers. In Somerset and Wiltshire cases involving clothiers and clothmakers were somewhat more numerous, especially under the Act of 1557.

The terms "clothmaker," "clothier," and "weaver" were used almost interchangeably at times, just as in actual practice the occupations in some districts merged into one another, but on the whole the variations in amount of prosecution are what might be expected from the differences in organization in these three counties. Clothiers in Devon who were dealers and middlemen rather than employers would be beyond the range of the apprenticeship requirement, for the complete absence of any apprenticeship prosecutions against middlemen who were not shopkeepers indicates a general assumption that the Act did not apply to them. The issue was tested for the middleman-clothiers by the judgment in 1580, in an information against a Devon clothier, that the "putting-out" for finishing of cloth bought unfinished did not bring its buyer within the meaning of the Act of 1563 — though whether this case had influence as a precedent may be doubted.[4] In the broadcloth district of the southwest, where the typical clothier was an employer, and generally responsible himself for some of the processes of manufacture under his own roof, the period of rapid expansion had preceded the enactment of the Statute of Artificers and the rate of entry of "intruders" was probably slow. In Elizabethan and Stuart Wiltshire the custom of apprenticeship seems to have prevailed for the clothiers, then and for some generations later, because otherwise a writer of the early eighteenth century could hardly have complained of the lack of apprenticeship among "a third part of the clothiers" of Gloucester, Somerset, and Wiltshire.[5]

Nevertheless, in the woolen industry one of the weakest points in the enforcement of apprenticeship must have been the entry into clothmaking of the wholesaler or retailer, an "exercise of the art" easily concealed by private arrangements with the craftsmen working for him. Instances of such entry occur in apprenticeship prosecutions, but others may be concealed behind the status term so often used to characterize the defendant. In Reading, home of kerseys and

[4] See above, Chap. X, where also is mentioned the opinion in the case of the costermonger, which seems not to have been a narrowing of the scope of the Act by interpretation so much as a mere statement of fact.

[5] Ramsay, *The Wiltshire Woollen Industry*, 60–61; J. Haynes, *A View of the Present State of the Clothing Trade in England*, 83.

colored broadcloth, a mercer secured a dispensation from the apprenticeship requirement in order "to make woolen cloth and kerseys and put the same to weaving and sale." Another of Braintree in Essex was sued by a weaver of Bocking for detaining his wages.[6]

To move from merchandising into clothmaking was one easy breach in the barrier set up by apprenticeship between occupations. A second was entry into the finishing crafts of the textile industry from related occupations. For retailers, the step must have been natural from selling the fabrics to control of their final stages in production. A hint of how this could be done without detection is provided by a Lancashire case of the seventeenth century: three drapers on the outskirts of the town of Rochdale had been prosecuted by shearmen of the town for using their craft without having been apprenticed to it. The case was settled by an agreement before the justices of the peace that none of the defendants would exercise the shearman's craft, hire servants in it, or bargain with any shearmen to work in it, but that they might let a house or shop to a shearman if "without fraud."[7] Identifiable cases among apprenticeship prosecutions, however, are rare. The line between the finishing crafts themselves must have been overstepped, too, more often than is revealed by the observed apprenticeship prosecutions, and so also that between the finishing crafts and clothmaking. When the dyers of Reading complained in 1589 of men who used two or three crafts together without an apprenticeship, a complaint illustrating the defensive interest of the craftsmen in enforcing the law at times of poor business, the Privy Council discovered that these were the clothiers. The council ordered that they should be allowed to continue dyeing so long as they dyed only the wools they themselves converted and no cloth in the piece.[8]

The Act of 1563, if rigidly enforced, might have achieved its implied aim of keeping related crafts and trades apart. Even under the

[6] Palmer's MS. Indexes to the Patent Rolls, XI, entry in 1568 of a license to the mercer (and entries of two other such licenses in 1577 and 1580); the phrasing indicates that the statute involved was that of 1557. For the Essex mercer, Cal. Q.S. XIX, 89, S.R. 200/59 (1612).

[7] MS. Sessions Order Books, 2nd Series, Jan. Sess. at Manchester, 5 Chas. I.

[8] *Acts P.C.*, Eliz., XVIII, 208, 253, 260. Reading cloth was commonly exported to regions lacking expert craftsmen in cloth-finishing and so was locally dyed and dressed before shipment (Friis, *Aldermen Cockayne's Project*, 59); when the dyers' complaint was made, they were probably feeling the loss of the Spanish and Portuguese markets.

haphazard conditions of its enforcement, there is little actual evidence in the apprenticeship cases that the barriers were often crossed, as for example among retailing trades and in food processing. In these two groups of occupations, as within the textile industry, differentiation might be expected to have broken down readily. Yet comparatively few instances have been found, and these chiefly within the little-differentiated retail trades of mercer, draper, and grocer. A partial explanation has already been suggested, other than the imperfect case-records: that the part-time or seasonal nature of many employments made it easy to shift from one to another for short periods without detection, all the more because the professional prosecutor was not concerned to nip offenses in the bud but rather to let them come to full bloom. This in-and-out use of crafts and trades where little or no capital or connections were required must have opened one of the largest holes in the dike of apprenticeship control, difficult to close by any kind of enforcement.

But it does not afford an explanation for the striking lack of prosecutions, associated with the class structure of industry, for the illegal employment of journeymen who had not served an apprenticeship. The requirement of the seven-year term was applied by Section 24 of the Act to all who "used or exercised" a craft or trade. Yet in all periods and occupations, the offender in virtually all the apprenticeship cases appears to be an independent craftsman. How many, especially in the textile occupations or in the Staffordshire group of nailmakers, were in fact employed within the putting-out system is of course not shown in the case-entries. But prosecutions of unapprenticed journeymen are very infrequent: in the two Westminster courts throughout the entire period 1563–1642, not one such case was observed from any county outside London, and in the quarter sessions the record is equally bare. When workers were hired who had not served an apprenticeship, the offending employer was brought to book, not the employee. It is not perhaps surprising that unapprenticed journeymen themselves were not prosecuted, because the chance of collecting composition or penalty from the master was better and because Section 24 is so worded that the penalty would appear to run only against the employer. But even prosecutions of employers are few. There was an absence of professional informing, despite the law's equal inducements to prosecute for employing the unapprenticed and for exercising the occupation as a "master." There also were lacking prosecutions by working craftsmen, even when they were active in attacking illegal retainers of apprentices. Thus the Wiltshire weavers at the beginning of the seventeenth century, although they sued a number of weavers and clothiers for keeping excessive numbers of apprentices or looms, found only five who were hiring unapprenticed journeymen. Yet enforcement of apprenticeship for journeymen was embodied in their rules.[9] In Essex, on two occasions when clothiers and weavers at Coggeshall or Bocking were prosecuted for keeping apprentices illegally, no unapprenticed journeymen were reported.[10]

This uniformity of behavior by prosecutors with such different interests in bringing suit as the professional informer and the working weaver suggests that there was in fact little cause for prosecution, a phenomenon possibly explicable by the indicated conditions in Gloucestershire, itself home of a large-scale textile industry. There the returns of 1608 point to an economic organization in which the "one-man business" was typical, in the textile industry and still more in other industrial and trading occupations, with the hired servant playing a small part outside agriculture and the life of the gentry.[11] The records of hiring sessions in Essex, so far as they go, confirm the Gloucestershire picture in this respect. The majority appear to concern only agricultural or household servants, and craftsmen generally hired one servant at a time, although occasionally two to four. Some even of these hirings may have been for work on the farm, since the return rarely shows whether the servant was to work in the craft of the employer.

If the economic society of Elizabethan and Stuart England was

[9] Journeymen were to show a certificate of their seven-year apprenticeship before being hired (see above, Chap. IX, and n. 58). In two of the five cases the masters were prosecuted as themselves unapprenticed. In the same county, the only other cases of this kind were two in 1639 of fullers for employing unapprenticed journeymen. (MS. Minute Books, Trin. 44 Eliz., presentments by Westbury Hundred Jury; Sessions Rolls, Jan., 45 Eliz., presentments by searchers of cloth, Trin. 3 Jas. I, information by Richard Bond, October, 4 Jas. I, indictment of Thomas Weeke. In 1639, MS. Minute Books, Epiph. Chas. I, indictments of William Crowch and Leonard Boney.)

[10] Cal. Q.S., XIX, 361, S.R. 226/6–12, Mich. 17 Jas. I; 492, S.R. 239/49, Epiph. 20 Jas. I.

[11] Tawneys, "An Occupational Census," 53–57. Among the drapers of Shrewsbury it was apparently usual in the Elizabethan and Stuart periods to observe the company's rule of only two apprentices to each master, and to keep servants but no journeymen (Mendenhall, *The Shrewsbury Drapers*, 101).

predominantly that of the small unit, the craftsman or tradesman working by himself with only family help or at most that of one or two apprentices and one journeyman or none, the absence of prosecutions specifically for the unapprenticed exercise of the function of employing is explained. A London case discloses perhaps a further reason: an information for exercising the trade of a whitster [bleacher] was dismissed by the court because the defendant only employed servants to bleach linen cloth without himself using any manual occupation.[12]

To conclude, however, that the force of the Act of 1563 was directed only against the independent small master would misrepresent the industrial relationships of the period. No evidence exists to show which offenders, among those recorded in all the courts, were working for themselves as independent craftsmen, or which to the order of a putting-out "employer," or which did both; nor are the "employers" among them identifiable, except in duplicated prosecutions under the Cloth Acts and the Act of 1563 when the offender is charged both with unapprenticed putting-out and with unapprenticed weaving, or in the rare instances when he can be identified as a substantial clothier.

One widespread industry has been neglected in the present study, that of leather-processing, subject not only to the regulations of the Statute of Artificers but also to the "Leather Acts." This legislation may explain the infrequency in the leather crafts of apprenticeship cases on the Statute of Artificers within the period 1563–1642. Another explanation may be that leather-processing, measured by the number of craftsmen engaged, was a minor industry outside the largest centers.[13]

In general there is no marked lack of prosecutions, in any major occupation to which the Statute of Artificers applied, for which a reasonable correspondence with economic conditions cannot be found with fair uniformity for all counties studied, until 1589 when the professional informer was restricted in his choice of jurisdictions. The apprenticeship requirement appears to have given way most

[12] Exch. Q.R., Decrees and Orders, Series I, IX, 204d., Pasch., 27 Eliz., information of Mich. 26 Eliz.

[13] As in Gloucestershire (Tawneys, "An Occupational Census," 36). Occasional instances were noted of unapprenticed entry into clothmaking by leather-workers — the two industries being linked through their raw materials — but little evidence of movement in the reverse direction.

often, as might be expected, in periods of expansion, which enforcement by private interests probably did little to check. The professional did not wish to do so since he profited by it; trade competitors, it would seem from the timing of prosecutions, often ignored or were ignorant of the violations until the pressure of leaner years put them on the defensive. How far a systematic enforcement of the Act could have ironed out business fluctuations may be questioned, for the same reason that it would have been difficult to prevent the penetration of occupational barriers — the prevalence of the short-run use of crafts or trades. The Act would have been most effective where it was least needed, in the occupations for which the advantages of possessing capital, trade connections, or skill and experience, made a short-run use least possible. In these the institution of apprenticeship tended to enforce itself by its business and social values. In all occupations, it had the attraction of offering opportunities for greater security of status. The point has already been labored that apprenticeship in Elizabethan and Stuart England was the rule and not the exception in economic and social life except in certain well-defined employments at both ends of the industrial scale: those using unskilled labor in mining, quarrying, or transport; and at the other end, those in which the place of the independent master craftsman was taken by the entrepreneur managing the investment of capital. In "occupations" not existing in 1563 and therefore exempt from the Act but otherwise similar in organization to those under it — the new textiles are the chief example — any comparative advantage accruing to them by this exemption was lessened in two ways. One was the tendency of apprenticeship to spread into them without legal requirement; the other was the way in which the seven-year term was enforced. It was neglected by central and local government, with rare exception, throughout the eighty years before the Civil War, and the majority of prosecutions by all but professional informers were apparently ineffective; while the latter imposed compositions equivalent to a burdensome but presumably not ruinous tax.

This is not to deny the initial importance of the enactment of an apprenticeship requirement applicable to the crafts and trades of the country as a whole without distinction of place. Although the uniformity which obtained under it could not have been achieved unless it had rested on a practice already widely accepted, the Act provided a standard for the regulation of trade which may have helped to check the more extreme restrictive attempts of particular corporations. (Its application in this way can be seen in the case of the Tailors of Ipswich.) Without it, there might not have been free entry into occupations in a period in which the claims of private privilege were so strong, but very possibly either a growth of monopoly licensing or the spread of corporate controls.

The decline of the institution was gradual, piecemeal, and much later than the era here considered. Whenever and wherever the process of decay occurred, it can hardly have been attributable to the direct effects of a decline in the theory or practice of public regulation, which had contributed so little directly to the long-continued life of apprenticeship. In the eighteenth century, the disuse of common informing and an apparent change in the character of county government played some part, but these belong to a later story.

APPENDIXES

BIBLIOGRAPHY

INDEX

APPENDIX I

The Provisions of the Statute of Artificers Relating to Apprenticeship and Its Enforcement

For the convenience of the reader, those sections of the Act of 1563 ("An Act touching divers orders for artificers, laborers, servants of husbandry and apprentices") which deal with the subject of apprenticeship and with the agencies empowered by the act to enforce the apprenticeship regulations are transcribed here.

XIX. . . . Every person being an householder and 24 years old at the least, dwelling . . . in any city or town corporate and . . . exercising any art, mystery or manual occupation there . . . may . . . retain the son of any freeman not occupying husbandry nor being a laborer and inhabiting in the same or in any other city or town . . . incorporate, to serve and be bound as an apprentice after the custom and order of the city of London for seven years at the least so as the term and years of such apprentice do not expire . . . afore such apprentice shall be of the age of 24 years at the least.

XX. Provided . . . that it shall not be lawful to any person dwelling in any city or town corporate . . . exercising any of the mysteries or crafts of a merchant trafficking . . . beyond the sea, mercer, draper, goldsmith, ironmonger, embroiderer, or clothier, that doth or shall put cloth to making and sale, to take any apprentice or servant to be instructed . . . in any of the arts . . . which they . . . do use or exercise, except such servant or apprentice be his son or else that the father or mother of such apprentice or servant shall have at the time . . . lands, tenements or other hereditaments of the clear yearly value of 40/– of one estate of inheritance or freehold at the least to be certified under the hands and seals of three justices of the peace of the shires or shire where the said lands . . . do . . . lie to the . . . head officers of such city or town corporate and to be enrolled among the records there.

XXI. . . . It shall be lawful to every person being an householder and 24 years old at the least and not occupying husbandry nor being a laborer dwelling . . . in any town not being incorporate that . . . is . . . a market town . . . and . . . exercising any art, mystery or manual occupation . . . to have in like manner to apprentice or apprentices the child or children of any other artificer . . . not occupying husbandry nor being a laborer which . . . shall inhabit . . . in the same or in any other such market town within the same shire, to serve as apprentice . . . as is aforesaid to any such art . . . as hath been usually exercised in any such market town where such apprentice shall be bound . . .

XXII. Provided . . . that it shall not be lawful to any person dwelling . . . in any such market town . . . exercising the . . . art of a merchant [etc., as in XX] . . . to take any apprentice or in any wise to . . . instruct any persons in the arts . . . recited, except such servant or apprentice shall be his son or else that the father or mother of such apprentice shall have lands [etc., as in XX] . . . of the clear yearly value of £3 of one estate of inheritance or freehold at the least, to be certified [etc., as in XX] . . . , to the head officers . . . of such market town where such apprentice or servant shall be taken, there to be enrolled . . .

XXIII. . . . It shall be lawful to any persons . . . exercising the art or occupation of a smith, wheelwright, plowwright, millwright, carpenter, rough mason, plasterer, sawyer, limeburner, brickmaker, bricklayer, tiler, slater, hellier, tilemaker, linenweaver, turner, cooper, millers, earthen potters, woolen weaver weaving housewives' or household cloth only and none other cloth, fuller, otherwise called tucker or walker, burner of ore and wood ashes, thatcher or shingler, wheresoever he . . . shall dwell . . . to have . . . the son of any person as apprentice in manner and form aforesaid to be . . . instructed in these occupations only . . . albeit the father or mother of any such apprentice have not any lands, tenements nor hereditaments.

XXIV. . . . It shall not be lawful to any . . . persons other than such as now do lawfully . . . exercise any art, mystery or manual occupation to set up . . . or exercise any craft, mystery or occupation now used . . . within the realm of England or Wales, except he shall have been brought up therein seven years at the least as apprentice in manner and form abovesaid, nor to set any person on work in such mystery, art or occupation being not a workman at this day, except he shall have been apprentice as is aforesaid or else having served as an apprentice as is aforesaid shall or will become a journeyman or be hired by the year, upon pain that every person willingly offending . . . shall forfeit . . . for every default 40/– for every month.

XXV. Provided . . . that no . . . persons . . . exercising the art . . . of a woolen cloth weaver, other than such as be inhabiting within the counties of Cumberland, Westmoreland, Lancaster, and Wales, weaving friezes, cottons, or housewives' cloth only, making and weaving woolen cloth commonly sold . . . by any clothman or clothier, shall take . . . any apprentice or shall . . . instruct any person . . . in the . . . art of weaving aforesaid in any village, town or place (cities, towns corporate and market towns only except) unless such person be his son or else that the father or mother of such apprentice or servant shall at the time . . . have lands and tenements or other hereditaments to the clear yearly value of £3 at the least of an estate of inheritance or freehold to be certified [etc., as in XX] . . . , the effect of the indenture to be registered within three months in the parish, where such master shall dwell . . . , upon pain of forfeiture of 20/– for every month that any person shall otherwise take any apprentice or set any such person on work contrary to the meaning of this article.

XXVI. . . . Every person . . . that shall have three apprentices in any of the said crafts . . . of a clothmaker, fuller, shearman, weaver, tailor, or shoemaker, shall retain . . . one journeyman, and for every other apprentice above the number of the said three apprentices one other journeyman, upon pain for every default therein £10.

XXVII. Provided . . . that this act . . . shall not extend to prejudice . . . any liberties heretofore granted . . . to . . . the company . . . of worsted-makers and worsted weavers within the city of Norwich and . . . county of Norfolk. . .

[XXVIII. Provision for compulsory apprenticeship to husbandry or to another occupation on the requirement of a householder with half a plowland in tillage; provision against the abuse of apprentice by master; and for failure of apprentice to "do his duty."]

XXIX. Provided . . . that no person shall by force . . . of this statute be bounden to enter into any apprenticeship other than such as be under the age of 21 years.

XXX. And to the end that this statute may . . . be . . . put in good execution . . . Be it enacted . . . that the justices of peace of every county dividing themselves into several limits, and likewise every mayor and head officer of any city or town corporate shall yearly between the feast of St. Michael . . . and the Nativity . . . , and between the feasts of the Annunciation . . . and . . . of the nativity of St. John Baptist . . . make a special and diligent inquiry of the branches and articles of this statute and of the good execution of the same, and where they shall find any defaults to see the same severely . . . punished. . .

[XXXI. Provision for payment of justices of the peace, etc., of 5/– a day for each day's sitting in execution of the statute, from the forfeitures due by force of the statute, but for not more than three days at one time.]

XXXII. . . . The one half of all forfeitures and penalties . . . mentioned in this statute other than such as are . . . otherwise appointed, shall be to our sovereign lady, the Queen's Majesty, . . . and the other moiety to him or them that shall sue for the same in any of the . . . Courts of Record or before any of the Justices of Oyer and Terminer or before any other justices or president and Council before remembered [i.e. of the North and of the Marches of Wales], by action of debt, information, bill of complaint or otherwise . . . , and that the said justices or two of them whereof one to be of the quorum, and the said presidents and Council as is aforesaid, and the said mayors or other head officers of cities or towns corporate shall have full power and authority to hear and determine all . . . offenses . . . against this statute . . . , as well upon indictment to be taken before them in the sessions of the peace as upon information, action of debt, or bill of complaint to be sued or exhibited by any person, and shall and may . . . make process against the defendant and award execution as in any other case they lawfully may . . .

XXXIII. Provided . . . that this act . . . shall not be prejudicial . . . to the cities of London and Norwich or to the lawful . . . customs . . . of the same . . . for . . . taking of any . . . apprentices. . .

[XXXIV. Contracts of apprenticeship contrary to this statute to be void, penalty of £10.]

[XXXV. Contracts of apprenticeship good even though made while apprentice under age.]

[XXXVI. Proviso for apprentices in Godalming, Surrey.]

[XXXIX. Provision for recapture of runaway apprentices and servants.]

XL. Provided . . . that it shall be lawful to the high constables of hundreds in every shire to hold . . . and continue petty sessions otherwise called statute sessions within the limits of their authorities in all shires wherein such sessions have been used to be kept in such manner and form as heretofore hath been . . . accustomed, so as nothing be by them done therein contrary or repugnant to this present Act.

The above transcription has been made from a photograph of the Parliament Roll (Parl. Roll 127), a copy of which the writer owes to the kindness of Professor N. S. B. Gras.

APPENDIX II

Table I

Prosecutions in Two Westminster Courts and Quarter Sessions for Seven-Year Term, Act of 1563
1563–1603 [1]
By Selected Counties and in Aggregate

County	Professional prosecutions	Other private prosecutions	All prosecutions by private agencies	Prosecutions by public agencies [7]	Total prosecutions
Devonshire	91 or 94	6 or 9	100	0	100
Somersetshire	39	20	59	3	62
Wiltshire	35	22 to 32	57 to 67	0	57 to 67
Worcestershire	23	13	36	2	38
Essex	76 to 81	34 to 39	115	8 to 10	123 to 125
Norfolk	107 to 113	10 to 16	123	1	124
West Riding [2]	5 to 7	8 to 10	15	0	15
North Riding [3]	—	—	—	—	—
Lancashire [4]	17	9	26	—	26
Cheshire	6 or 7	0 or 1	7	0	7
Staffordshire	45	3	48	0	48
Warwickshire	23	5	28	—	28
Nottinghamshire	2	3	5	—	5
Northamptonshire	12 or 15	3 or 6	18	—	18
Leicestershire	7	4	11	—	11
	488 to 508 [5]	140 to 170 [6]	648 to 658	14 to 16	662 to 674

(1) Exchequer Queen's Remembrancer 1563–1603; Queen's Bench Coram Rege 1563–1588; Quarter Sessions as extant, see Bibliography.
(2) Cases from the West Riding in the Exchequer, if any, were not noted.
(3) Cases from the North Riding in the Westminster courts, if any, were not noted.
(4) Cases from Lancashire in the Queen's Bench, if any, were not noted.
(5) Includes 32 to 37 from Quarter Sessions.
(6) Includes 63 to 79 from Quarter Sessions.
(7) All are from extant Quarter Sessions; none occur in the Westminster courts.

Table II

Prosecutions in Two Westminster Courts, Assizes,[1] and Quarter Sessions, for Seven-Year Term, Act of 1563 1603–1625 [2]

By Selected Counties and in Aggregate

County	Professional prosecutions	Other private prosecutions	All prosecutions by private agencies	Prosecutions by public agencies	Total prosecutions
Devonshire	3 or 4	7 or 8	10 or 11	0	10 or 11
Somersetshire	46	113 to 115	159 or 161	11	170 to 172
Wiltshire	6	66	72	11	83
Worcestershire	0	9	9	0	9
Essex	38 to 47	66 to 77	113 to 115	3	116 to 118
Norfolk	177 to 180	22 to 25	202	4	206
West Riding [3]	0	4	4	—	4
North Riding [4]	19 or 42	41 to 77	83 to 96	4 to 17	100
Lancashire [5]	2	4	6	0	6
Cheshire	2	1	3	0	3
Staffordshire	4 or 6	4 or 6	10	0	10
Warwickshire	0	1 or 2	1 or 2	—	1 or 2
Nottinghamshire	1 to 4	4 or 5	6 to 8	0	6 to 8
Northamptonshire	2	2	4	—	4
Leicestershire	4	4	8	—	8
	304 to 345 [6]	348 to 405 [7]	690 to 711	33 to 46	735 to 744

(1) Assizes records only for Essex: 13 nonprofessional prosecutions.
(2) K. B. sampled only for years Easter 1603 to Hilary 1607 inclusive, Easter 1616 to Hilary 1617 inclusive.
(3) Cases from the West Riding in the Exchequer, if any, were not noted.
(4) Cases from the North Riding in the Westminster courts, if any, were not noted.
(5) Cases from Lancashire in the King's Bench, if any, were not noted.
(6) Includes 55 to 60 cases in Westminster courts, the remainder in Quarter Sessions.
(7) Includes 51 to 55 in Westminster courts, 13 in Assizes, the remainder in Quarter Sessions.

Table III

Prosecutions in Two Westminster Courts, Assizes,[1] and Quarter Sessions, for Seven-Year Term, Act of 1563
1625–1642 [2]

By Selected Counties and in Aggregate

County	Professional prosecutions	Other private prosecutions	All prosecutions by private agencies	Prosecutions by public agencies	Total prosecutions
Devonshire	5	5	5	0	5
Somersetshire	122 to 169 [6]	59 to 62	184 to 228	0	184 to 228
Wiltshire	9 to 13	48 to 52	61	2	63
Worcestershire	0	4	4	0	4
Essex	33 to 36	49 to 57	85 to 90	6	91 to 96
Norfolk	296 to 299 [7]	7 to 10	310 to 329	0 or 1	310 to 330
West Riding [3]	0	8	9	0	9
North Riding [4]	37 to 45	12 to 21	57 or 58	0	57 or 58
Lancashire [5]	0	52 to 54	52 to 54	0	52 to 54
Cheshire	0	1	1	0	1
Staffordshire	0 or 1	0 or 1	1	0	1
Warwickshire	0 to 2	2 to 5	4 or 5	0	4 or 5
Nottinghamshire	55 or 56	3 to 4	59	0	59
Northamptonshire	—	1 [9]	1	—	1
Leicestershire	—	—	—	—	—
	552 to 621 [8]	251 to 285 [10]	833 to 905 [11]	8 or 9	841 to 914

(1) Assizes records for Essex only.
(2) King's Bench sampled only, for years Easter 1625 to Mich. 1627 inclusive, Easter 1634 to Hilary 1637 inclusive.
(3) Cases from the West Riding in the Exchequer, if any, were not noted.
(4) Cases from the North Riding in the Westminster courts, if any, were not noted.
(5) Cases from Lancashire in the King's Bench, if any, were not noted.
(6) In Somerset, 36 to 38 cases may not be for apprenticeship; 2 may be nonprofessional.
(7) Includes 21 repeats of same offenders in later years. Actual number of *informations* is larger than this by about 70 repeats of same offenders within same year.
(8) Includes 3 in Westminster courts; 28 to 30 in Essex Assizes.
(9) No quarter sessions records extant except in one year, no apprenticeship cases. This entry is recorded in King's Bench as removed from Quarter Sessions by certiorari.
(10) Includes 1 to 3 in Essex Assizes.
(11) To this total should be added 5 ex officio informations in the King's Bench, from Norfolk, West Riding, Northamptonshire, all probably professional.

APPENDIX III

I. "Ancient Fees . . . taken by Clerks being Attorneys in the office of his highness Remembrancer of the Exchequer" *

Attorney's fee of every client every term . . .	3/4
Warrant of attorney . . .	/8
Making of every ordinary information . . .	3/4
Inrolling it . . .	3/4
Writs . . . (each)	2/–
Drawing all informations, pleadings, verdicts, orders, decrees, compositions, per sheet . . .	1/–
Entering rule for day to plead or answer . . .	4/–
Entering every continuance of term upon record . . .	4/–
Inrolments of every Roll . . .	6/8
Entering judgment on record . . .	3/4
For writ of certiorari . . .	3/4
For making a license for the informer to compound and for entering same in the book whereby to draw the defendant to make a fine with the King . . .	3/–
Attorney's fee for reading client's evidences at day of trial or hearing, [etc.] . . .	3/4

Two additional items payable by a defendant were for the entry of his appearance (fee of 4d.) and for "making the Attorney General's confession for discharge of any . . . information" (fee of 2/–).

II. A second statement of charges made in the Exchequer, the King's Bench and the Common Pleas suggests in more detail how costs could mount up during the progress of a suit. †

In the Exchequer:

Fees for writs, entries, [etc.] on every action . . .	2/–
Attorney's fee in K. R. office . . .	3/4
Making ordinary information . . .	3/4

* Lansdowne 168, f. 94–95.

† *An Exact Table of Fees of All the Courts at Westminster.* London, 1694.

Inrolling information . . .	3/4
Sheet drawn, of information [etc.] . . .	1/–
copy . . .	8d.
Ingrossing warrant for a composition . . .	6/8

In the King's Bench; Fees of Crown Office:

For everyone indicted on any offense, for plea of not guilty . . .	2/–
On information for like plea . . .	2/–
For continuance after issue joined, every term . . .	2/–
For special pleas to indictment or information, [etc.] . . .	13/4
"and for Gloves" . . .	13/4
For fine on information, for King's part, where informer has compounded . . .	11/–
For exhibiting information *qui tam* . . .	3/4
For appearance on information *qui tam* . . .	2/10
For copy of information or pleas, party pays for every sheet . . .	8d.
For every certiorari . . .	4/-
For entering and making a license to the informer to compound . . .	1/-
Clerk of Rules hath for copying of every license for informer to compound . . .	4d.

In Common Pleas:

Judges' fees —	
Granting license to compound on a penal law . . .	2/-
Assessing King's part of forfeiture on a penal statute after composition with the informer . . .	2/–
To the Judges' Clerk —	
For entering in his book license to compound on a penal law . . .	6d.
For entering King's part . . .	6d.
Fees of Protonotaries —	
For declaration in actions of debt, [etc.] . . .	2/–
for every sheet over three . . .	8d.
Entry of information on penal law . . .	2/–
for every sheet over three . . .	8d.
Entry of license of Court to compound on penal statutes . . .	2/–
Entry of writs, continuance, [etc.] . . .	2/–
Fees of Protonotaries and their Clerks, touching informations only —	
Entry of information and signing of subpoena only . . .	2/8
Signing of any other process . . .	1/4
Ingrossing every information, to clerk . . .	8d.
Copy of information if of five sheets of paper or more, to clerk . . .	3/4
if over five sheets, per sh. . . .	8d.
Making of copies for fine on an information . . .	6d.

Entering general issue on the roll where the information was first entered, to clerk . . .	8d.
Registering license to compound in office-book, to clerk . . .	4d.
Fees to Filazers —	
For every capias, alias, [etc.] . . .	1/-
Attorneys' fees —	
Per cause per term. . . .	6/8

Many more fees appear than are included in this summary, all those being omitted which do not expressly relate to suits on penal statutes. A large number, however, of those left out, fees due to the under-officers of the courts, must have been payable by the parties in penal statute cases.

This part of the statement is described as "the Ancient Fees, according to the best information we can get," and three names are subscribed, with the date of December 1689. It is not clear, therefore, what fees — all or none — correspond to those levied in the later seventeenth century, or how indicative of current practice are the references to the fines for the King after composition, etc. Apprenticeship cases, except by certiorari and a few actions of debt, had long since vanished from the two Westminster courts examined.

BIBLIOGRAPHY

No attempt has been made to bring together here a comprehensive bibliography of all sources and works utilized in the making of the book. The list is more inclusive for some sections than for others: for example, it records every class of manuscript source investigated though a few proved of little value for the immediate inquiry. The itemization of utilized lists of justices of the peace and of printed county records is also complete. The purpose in these parts of the bibliography has been to collect and classify types of material essential to a study of mercantilism in practice, for the possible benefit of other students. Printed source material otherwise, and the secondary books and articles, are only a selection of the total consulted, though including most of those cited in the book.

PRIMARY SOURCES

MANUSCRIPTS

PUBLIC RECORD OFFICE

Assizes Records, Southeastern Circuit, Indictments Bundles, Rolls for the county of Essex.

The only surviving series before the second half of the seventeenth century. Eleven years are missing, at scattered dates from 1578 to 1637; others are defective. At this period the bundles should contain rolls for Norfolk, but none are extant before 1692.

Exchequer King's (Queen's) Remembrancer: Agenda Books.

A fairly complete contemporary index to the Memoranda Rolls by county, name of defendant, and class of offense.

—— Barons' Depositions, No. 284.

—— Entry Books of Decrees and Orders, Series I and II.

A valuable supplement to the Memoranda Rolls.

—— Informations, Bundle No. 2.

Examined in search for informers' licenses to compound; none found, and none appear to have survived as a group.

—— Memoranda Rolls.

Indispensable for any study of the operation of mercantilist regulations.

—— Miscellanea, Parliamentary and Council Proceedings, Nos. 25, 27.

Supplementary to the collection of state papers, domestic.

—— Proceedings, Bundle 70.

—— Repertory Rolls.

Occasionally useful in supplementing Agenda Books.

King's (Queen's) Bench: Controlment Rolls.

Entries of writs and pleas only.

—— Coram Rege Rolls.

As essential to use for prosecutions under penal statutes as the Exchequer Memoranda Rolls; but the lack of an index to type of offense makes the search time-consuming.

Palmer's MS. Indexes to Chancery Patent Rolls.

Patent Roll, 2 Eliz., Part 3, m. 7.

Privy Council Registers: Vols. 32 seq.

Used as continuation of the printed volumes.

State Papers Domestic: Elizabeth, James I, Charles I.

Used by individual reference from the *Calendars*.

BRITISH MUSEUM

Additional MSS. 21611.2, f. 11–16

—— 34324, f. 8, 9, 15, 19

—— 34324.30, f. 145

Harleian MSS. 589, f. 310–315

—— 1603, f. 3

—— 2104, f. 464, 469, 471

Lansdowne MSS. 22, f. 37–38, 85

—— 60, f. 23

—— 114, f. 5

—— 152.8, f. 132

—— 160, f. 332

—— 167, f. 10, 16, 18, 23, 24, 27, 40, 45, 94, 101, 123, 138, 140, 144

—— 168, f. 70, 72, 94–95, 344

—— 168.2, f. 40

—— 168.3, f. 44

—— 171, f. 407, 436

—— 172, f. 241

LOCAL ARCHIVES: COUNTY QUARTER SESSIONS *

Cheshire (at Chester): MS. Indictment Books, fragments 1559–1561, earliest complete 1565–1592, continuous thereafter, with some gaps after 1668.

A full record of prosecutions except for bills rejected by the grand jury. Entries of presentments from 1592.

—— Recognizance Books, earliest 1559–1571, continuous from 1576, with some gaps after 1650.

These volumes also contain minutes of orders.

—— Rolls, earliest 1569, a defective but almost continuous series.

Abstracts from these records have been printed, see below.

Devon (at Exeter): MS. Order Books, earliest 1592–1600; sampled.

Brief entries of recognizances, verdicts, and orders.

—— Sessions Rolls, earliest 1592, imperfect series to 1631 and after 1655.

The printed volume contains extracts only.

Essex (at Chelmsford): MS. Sessions Rolls, earliest 1556. An unusually complete and continuous series, though with some gaps, especially from 1557 through the 1560's; occasional rolls missing thereafter.

Invaluable.

—— Sessions Books, earliest 1631, incomplete series of Minute Books of Recognizances and Traverses.

Contain some continuing orders for wage assessments.

—— Typescript Calendar of Quarter Sessions Rolls, 1556–1660. Essex Record Office, Chelmsford, 22v.

A complete transcript, with full index for earlier volumes, index of place-names for remainder.

Lancashire (at Preston): MS. Indictment Rolls, earliest 1606, extant for only three other years before 1628, continuous thereafter with a few gaps.

—— Order Books, 1st Series, earliest 1619–1622, serious gaps. This series is in fact one of Minute Books of Recognizances and Traverses.

—— Order Books, 2nd Series, earliest 1627, continuous through 1642 and after 1645 but with gaps.

Useful for lists of attendance of justices of the peace at sessions as well as for record of orders.

* Except as indicated, the following sessions records were examined throughout, to varying dates in the middle or later eighteenth century, in the preparation of the present study and its intended continuation. Except when cited in the present study, MS. records not extant before 1642 are not listed here.

—— Petitions Bundles, earliest 1626, only three others before 1642, excellent series after 1647.

Valuable.

—— Recognizances Bundles, earliest 1605/6; sampled.

—— Sessions Rolls, earliest 1589–90; fragmentary to James I, defective and with some years missing thereafter.

From 1627, a continuous series of records of prosecutions can be compiled from these Rolls plus the Indictment Rolls and Order Books 1st Series. The earliest rolls, through 1606, have been printed, as well as extracts from sessions papers for the years 1616–1623. See below.

—— "Notes of Proceedings before Oswald Mosley and Others." Transcript by E. Axon, various dates, in John Rylands Reference Library, Manchester. See below.

Norfolk (at Norwich): MS. Minute Books of Sessions Proceedings, earliest 1562–1568, two others of the sixteenth century; next not till 1639–1644, scattered periods thereafter.

Surviving volumes useful for lists of attendance of justices of the peace at sessions, county officials, licenses, minutes of orders.

—— Sessions Rolls, earliest temp. Hen. VIII (sampled), scattered years only to 1554; thereafter seriously defective in individual extant rolls and with serious gaps (e.g., 1574–1580, 1582–1587, etc.).

Throughout there is hardly any five-year period, from the sixteenth through the eighteenth century, which is not seriously broken.

Northamptonshire (at Northampton): MS. Minute Books, earliest October 1669–January 1679, continuous thereafter.

Contain recognizances, licenses, minutes of orders.

—— Sessions Rolls, earliest 1630 (printed), continuous from Oct. 1657 (printed) with occasional sessions missing, especially in 1680's and 1690's.

Exceptionally full series of constables' presentments.

Nottinghamshire (at Nottingham): MS. Minute Books, earliest 1604–1607, continuous through 1642.

Full record except for lack of entry of origin of indictments.

Somersetshire (at Taunton): MS. Indictment Rolls, earliest 1571; a few scattered years in 1590's; continuous 1602 to 1645 with some gaps; numerous gaps 1651–1668; continuous thereafter with very few gaps.

Very valuable series for the early Stuart period.

—— Registers (Minute Books), bundle of pages from scattered sessions temp. Eliz.

—— Minute Books of Recognizances and Orders (Registers), earliest 1613–1620; this series printed, with supplements from the Indictment Rolls, see below under Printed Sessions Records. Duplicate vols. in draft.

—— Sessions Rolls, fragments temp. Eliz.; sampled 1607 on.

Staffordshire (at Stafford): MS. Sessions Rolls, earliest 1581 (printed through 1609, see below); sampled only, 1632 seq.

Warwickshire (at Warwick): MS. Indictment Books, earliest 1631 (printed, see below).

—— Order Books, earliest 1625 (printed, see below).

West Riding of Yorkshire (at Wakefield): MS. Minute Books of Indictments, earliest 1637–1642 (printed, see below). Next 1647–1649; continuous thereafter, except for four sessions in 1660, 1665, 1689, at least into 1776.

—— Sessions Rolls, earliest 1598–1602 (printed, see below). None extant 1602–1662. Thereafter the Minute Books can be partially supplemented from the Rolls (as for ignoramus bills, not recorded in the Books).

Wiltshire (at Devizes): MS. Minute Books, earliest 1575–1592, next 1597–1603, continuous from 1609–1665. (First volume printed with some entries of 1563 and 1574; see below.)

The first volume contains entries of recognizances, traverses, and fines, in which the offense is often unidentified.

—— Sessions Rolls, earliest 1602 but incomplete; fairly continuous thereafter but with some bad gaps (e.g., 1612–1614, 1616–1621 inclusive, and others).

The fuller entries in the Minute Books at this time compensate to some extent, but do not include a record of ignoramus bills or of orders. Sessions Rolls not examined except by sampling from 1624 through 1646, 1648–1673; from 1673 to 1745 they are the sole record of prosecutions in the absence of further Minute Books during this period. (Extracts from the Sessions Rolls are printed in Hist. MSS. Comm., (*Various*, see below.)

—— Order Books, earliest 1641–1654, continuous thereafter.

Worcestershire (at Worcester): MS. Sessions Rolls, earliest 1591, a defective and incomplete series (printed through extant rolls of 1643, see below); occasional in 1650's to 1662; continuous from

1665 to 1711 and fairly complete. Eighteenth-century rolls have serious gaps.

LOCAL ARCHIVES: MUNICIPAL RECORDS

Chester: MS. Apprentice Indentures, vol. 1550–1650.

Exeter: MS. City Sessions Rolls, earliest 1557/8, series incomplete.

—— City Sessions Books, earliest 1618–1621.

Great Grimsby: MS. Court Books, earliest 1539–1548; loose pages temp. Ed. VI; vol. 1562–1575; loose pages temp. Eliz. and Jas. I.

One of the rare series of entries of statute sessions.

Northampton: MS. Assembly Books, I, 1547–1627.

—— Book of Apprentice Indentures, 1561–1721.

Norwich: MS. Minute Books of Sessions Proceedings, IV (1561–1570); V (1571–1581); VI (1581–1591); VII (1591–1602).

—— Book of Depositions, 1563–1572.

—— Books of Chamberlains' Accounts, vols. 1553–1567, 1580–1589, 1589–1602.

Thetford: MS. Hall Books, vols. 1570–1622, 1620–1623, 1624–1639

—— Register of Proceedings, vol. 1578–1586.

—— Sessions, Court of Record, and Freemen's Register Book, 1610–1756.

—— Town Book, 1598–1622.

Records of some sixteenth-century statute sessions in the Hall Books, and some of the eighteenth century in the Sessions Book.

Worcester: MS. Liber Recordum, vols. 1564–1566, 1575–1576, 1582–1583, 1615–1616, 1625–1626.

LIBRI PACIS AND OTHER LISTS OF JUSTICES OF THE PEACE *

1558/59: British Museum Lansdowne MS. 1218, f. 1–44b. (Basic lists for some counties may have antedated Elizabeth's accession, in others probably were after January 22, 1559; compilation in general is between December 1558 and January 1559, with later corrections.)

* Arranged chronologically and including both MS. and printed sources. All but four of these MSS. (1558/9, 1569, October 1587, 1604) are catalogued by Professor B. H. Putnam, "Justices of the Peace from 1558 to 1688," *Bulletin of the Institute of Historical Research,* IV (1926–27), 144–156. The suggested dates, however, differ occasionally from Professor Putnam's ascriptions. There is a range of uncertainty in dating many of these *Libri*, some of which appear to be compiled from lists of varying dates for the several counties.

1558/59: State Papers Domestic, Eliz., II, f. 17 seq. (In some counties identical with Lansdowne list, in others show evidence of being later; several later corrections.)

1561?: B.M. Lansdowne MS. 1218, f. 52–92. (Probably earlier than October 1561, according to evidence of omissions of the sheriffs in several counties who were on commissions of the peace again in February 1562.)

F. 64 is a report by the judges of assize recommending a few names in various counties for appointment or dismissal. Dated "16 Feb. 4 Eliz.," but some of their recommendations had already taken effect in the commissions entered on the Patent Rolls February 11 and February 18, 1562.

1562: *Calendar Patent Rolls*, Eliz., II, 1560–63, February 11 and 18, 1562. (In some counties these lists give effect to recommendations made by the judges of assize probably in late 1561 or early 1562.)

1564: *A Collection of Original Letters from the Bishops to the Privy Council, 1564, with Returns of the Justices of the Peace . . .*, ed. Mary Bateson. The Camden Miscellany, IX, London, 1895.

A classification of the justices of the peace according to their religious convictions, with occasional comment on their other qualifications.

1569: S.P.D., Eliz., LIX, Nos. 48, 50, 67; and Northts., (no No.); LX, Nos. 1, 21, 30, 30.I, 39, 39.I, 39.II, 53, 53.I, 53.II, 63.I; LXVII, Nos. 21.I, 24.

Signatures of justices of the peace, November 1569 and later, to the Declaration for the Act of Uniformity; above references are for the selected counties only (no return for Staffordshire or West Riding).

1573/74: B.M. Egerton MS. 2345, f. 1–48. (A contemporary endorsement as 16 Eliz., but probably based on lists earlier than October 1573 with later corrections.)

1573/74: S.P.D., Eliz., XCIII, No. 9. (Contemporary endorsement as 16 Eliz.; in some counties identical with Egerton 2345, in others apparently later. Probably end 1573 or early 1574 for most counties but for Cheshire basic list prior to October 1573; for Somerset, corrected after August 1574.)

1575: S.P.D., Eliz., CIV. (Lists compiled from returns in June 1575 of the resident justices of the peace and their administrative divisions.)

1577: S.P.D., Eliz., CXXI. (In general, lists appear to be of date between May and midsummer 1577, but in Wiltshire basic list may antedate later 1576 and certainly is before March 1577.)

1579/80: S.P.D., Eliz., CXLV. (Probably late autumn 1579, in some counties basic list apparently before October 1579; in several counties later corrections.)

1582: B.M. Lansdowne MS. 35, f. 130–140b. (Incomplete lists, omitting in most counties the names of the officers of state and, in many, all justices of the peace above the rank of esquire. Difficult to date: in some counties basic list might be of 1581, but in others between May and August 1582; in one apparently after September 1582.)

1583/84: B.M. Harleian MS. 474, f. 1–97. (This contains a Liber Pacis and also various commissions for special purposes. Dates vary considerably. The lists of justices of the peace in most counties appear to date in the second half of 1584; in some, however, basic lists may be of 1583; many are corrected as of late 1585 or after February 1586.)

1584/85: B.M. Lansdowne MS. 737, f. 132–183. (In most counties basic lists apparently between May and October 1584; in a few, may be early 1584 or even 1583. Most are corrected in later 1585.)

1587: Strype, J., *Annals of the Reformation* . . . (Oxford, 1824), III, Pt. 2, App., Book II, 449–466.

Reports from the bishops of certain dioceses to a questionnaire from the Privy Council on the justices of the peace dated October 1587.

B.M. Lansdowne MS. 53, f. 83, dated October 1587.

A report on the justices of the peace of Devon and Cornwall, probably from the Bishop of Exeter.

1596: S.P.D., Eliz., Case F, No. 11. (Assignable in most counties to about June or July, but in one, basic list belongs to 1595.)

1604: B.M. Additional MS. 38139, f. 108–178. (Endorsed with regnal year "2 and 38 Jas. I" but despite this ascription to a date later than July 24, 1604, basic lists in some counties apparently are of 1603 and in one perhaps late 1602. No corrections.)

1608: S.P.D., Jas. I, XXXIII. (Contemporary endorsement of the list of the judges of assize with date "20 May 1608"; but in all counties the lists of justices of the peace in the section containing names of officers of state antedate 19 April, and in several counties the local sections of list belong to 1607; in two this basic list may be of 1606. All lists are corrected in official section after April 28, 1608; other corrections for a few counties can be dated as late as 1611–1614.)

1621/22: Crown Office, Chancery, XIII, Book I (S.P. 193/13). (Official sections of lists date between July 16 and September 30, 1621, and in several counties before August 29; in some counties local section is based on a list of early 1621, in one apparently on a list of early 1620; in another possibly one of 1619. All lists are corrected after September 17, 1622, some as late as November–December 1622.)

1625/26: B.M. Harleian MS. 1622. (Official sections later than 1 November 1625; local sections in certain counties appear to be earlier and in one even of late 1624, while in others the local sections are of December 1625 or later.)

1631/2: S.P.D., Chas. I, CCXII. (Endorsed with date "February 1631," old style. In most counties no evidence against this date; but in one the local section is earlier than December 1631; in another may be late 1629 or early 1630.)

1636/7: S.P.D., Chas. I, CCCCV. (Endorsed "December 1638," but in some counties basic list in local section belongs to 1636, May or later, and in others the first quarter of 1637.)

Public Record Office, *Lists and Indexes*, IX (1898): list of sheriffs of England and Wales.

PRINTED WORKS

PARLIAMENTARY PROCEEDINGS AND STATE PAPERS

Acts of the Privy Council of England, N. S., 1542–1604, ed. J. R. Dasent. 32 v. London, 1890–1907.

Acts of the Privy Council of England, 1613–. London, 1921–[38.] (In progress.)

A Booke Containing All Such Proclamations as were published during the Reign of . . . Queen Elizabeth, collected by H. Dyson. London, 1618.

Calendar of State Papers Domestic: 1547–1625, ed. R. Lemon and M. A. E. Green. 12 v. London, 1856–1872.

—— 1625–1649, ed. J. Bruce, W. D. Hamilton, and S. C. Lomas. 23 v. London, 1858–1897.

Calendar of State Papers Foreign, Elizabeth, ed. J. Stevenson and others. London, 1863–[1950.] (In progress.)

Useful for the present study only for occasional comment on economic conditions.

Calendar of State Papers Venetian, Vols. VII–IX, 1558–1603, ed. R. Brown, G. Cavendish Bentinck, and H. Brown. London, 1864–1897.

See preceding item.

A Collection of the Substance of Certain Necessary Statutes . . . London, 1561.

Commons Debates, 1621, ed. W. Notestein, F. H. Relf, and H. Simpson, 7 v. New Haven, 1935.

Journals of the House of Commons, London, 1803.

Journals of the House of Lords. n. p., n. d.

Parliamentary Debates in 1610, ed. S. R. Gardiner. Camden Society, LXXXI. n. p., 1862.

The Parliamentary Diary of Robert Bowyer, 1606–1607, ed. D. H. Willson. Minneapolis, 1931.

Statutes of the Realm. 9 v. Record Commission, 1810–1828.

Tudor and Stuart Proclamations, ed. R. Steele. 2 v. Oxford, 1910.

LOCAL PUBLIC ARCHIVES: COUNTY RECORDS

(This list includes some volumes for periods after 1642)

Cheshire: *Quarter Sessions Records*, ed. J. H. E. Bennett and J. C. Dewhurst. The Record Society [of] Lancashire and Cheshire, XCIV. n. p., 1940.

Lancashire: *Lancashire Quarter Sessions Records*, ed. J. Tait. Chetham Society, New Series, LXXVII. London and Manchester, 1917.

—— *Manchester Sessions*, I, ed. E. Axon. The Record Society [of] Lancashire and Cheshire, XLII, n. p., 1901.

Lincolnshire: *Minutes of Proceedings in Quarter Sessions Held for the Parts of Kesteven in the County of Lincoln*, ed. S. A. Peyton. Lincoln Record Society, 2 v. Lincoln, 1931.

A helpful introduction; full transcripts.

Middlesex: *Middlesex County Records*, ed. J. C. Jeaffreson. 4 v. London, n.d.–1892.

This older series is selective and thereby loses in value as compared to a full calendar.

—— *Middlesex Sessions Records,* New Series, ed. W. Le Hardy. 4 v. London, 1935–1941.

Norfolk: *The Musters Returns for Divers Hundreds in the County of Norfolk . . . ,* ed. H. L. Bradfer-Lawrence. Norfolk Record Society, VI n. p., 1935.

Northamptonshire: *Quarter Sessions Records of the County of Northampton,* ed. J. Wake. Northamptonshire Record Society, I. Hereford, 1924.

An informative introduction by S. A. Peyton. Full transcripts. Appendix gives a list of resident justices of the peace for 1631 (not included in section above).

—— *The Montagu Musters Book,* ed. J. Wake. Northamptonshire Record Society, VII. Peterborough, 1935.

Nottinghamshire: *Nottinghamshire County Records,* ed. H. H. Copnall. Nottingham, 1915.

Short selections from the sessions records compiled to illustrate the character of sessions business.

Somersetshire: *Quarter Sessions Records for the County of Somerset,* ed. E. H. B. Harbin. Somerset Record Society. 4 v. n. p., 1907–1919.

—— *Somerset Enrolled Deeds,* ed. S. W. B. Harbin. Somerset Record Society, LI. n.p., 1936.

Staffordshire: *The Staffordshire Quarter Sessions Rolls*: I–IV, ed. S. A. H. Burne. Collections for a History of Staffordshire, William Salt Archaeological Society. Kendal, 1931–1936; V, ed. S. A. H. Burne. The Staffordshire Record Society. Kendal, 1940.

—— [VI], ed. D. H. G. Salt. The Staffordshire Record Society. Kendal, 1950.

Warwickshire: *Quarter Sessions Order Books,* ed. S. C. Ratcliff and H. C. Johnson. Warwick County Records, I–IV. Warwick, 1935–1938.

—— *Orders Made at Quarter Sessions,* ed. S. C. Ratcliff and H. C. Johnson. Warwick County Records, V. Warwick, 1939.

—— *Quarter Sessions Indictment Book,* ed. S. C. Ratcliff and H. C. Johnson. Warwick County Records, VI. Warwick, 1941.

Wiltshire: Historical Manuscripts Commission, *Various Collections,* I, The Records of the County of Wilts. (1901), 67–176.

—— Merriman, R. W., "Extracts from the Records of the Wiltshire

Quarter Sessions," *Wiltshire Archaeological and Natural History Magazine*, XX (Devizes, 1882), 322–341.

—— *Minutes of Proceedings in Sessions, 1563 and 1574 to 1592*, ed. H. C. Johnson. Wiltshire County Records, IV. Devizes, 1949.

Worcestershire: *Calendar of the Quarter Sessions Papers, 1591–1643*, ed. J. W. Willis Bund. Worcestershire County Records. Worcester, 1900.

Useful introduction, especially for activity of justices of the peace in and out of sessions; provides two commissions of the peace for the county, 1601 and 1620, not included in section above.

Yorkshire: North Riding: *Quarter Sessions Records*, ed. J. C. Atkinson. The North Riding Record Society. 9 v. London, 1884–1892.

In the later volumes the transcripts are not as complete as in the first. Their lack of full entries of names, places, and occupations seriously limits their usefulness.

Yorkshire: West Riding: *West Riding Sessions Rolls, 1598–1602*, ed. J. Lister. Yorkshire Archaeological Society Record Series, III. n.p., 1888.

—— *West Riding Sessions Records*, II, ed. J. Lister. Yorkshire Archaeological Society Record Series, LIV. n.p., 1915.

This volume contains Orders 1611–1642 and Indictments 1637–1642.

LOCAL PUBLIC ARCHIVES: MUNICIPAL AND PARISH RECORDS

The Little Red Book of Bristol, ed. F. B. Bickley. 2 v. Bristol and London, 1900.

Market Harborough Parish Records, 1531–1837, ed. J. E. Stocks and W. B. Bragg. London, 1926.

Minutes of the Norwich Court of Mayoralty, 1630–1631 . . . , ed. W. L. Sachse. Norfolk Record Society, XV. Norwich, 1942.

The Records of the City of Norwich, ed. W. Hudson and J. C. Tingey. 2 v. Norwich and London [1906–1910].

The Register of the Freemen of Norwich, 1548–1713, ed. P. Millican. Norwich, 1934.

Records of the Borough of Nottingham, ed. W. H. Stevenson and others. 7 v. Nottingham, 1882–1947.

Minutes and Accounts of the Corporation of Stratford-upon-Avon, ed. R. Savage and E. I. Fripp. Publications of the Dugdale Society. 4 v. London, 1921–1929.

LEGAL WRITINGS

Bacon, F., *Works*, ed. J. Spedding, R. L. Ellis, and D. D. Heath. 14 v. London, 1857–1874.

Brown, W., *The Practice of His Majesty's Court of Exchequer* . . . 2nd ed. London, 1699.

[Bulstrode, E.], *The Reports of Edward Bulstrode . . . in . . . King's Bench*. 3 pt. London, 1657–1659.

Burrow, J., *Reports of Cases . . . in the . . . King's Bench*, Pt. IV. 5 v. 2nd ed. London, 1771–1780.

[Coke, E.], *The Lord Coke His Speech and Charge*. London, 1607.

—— *The Reports of Sir Edward Coke* . . . revised . . . by G. Wilson. 7 v. London, 1777.

[Croke, G.], *The Second Part of the Reports of Sir George Croke . . . of . . . cases in the King's Bench and Common Pleas* . . . 2 v. London, 1683.

—— *The Second Part of the Reports of Sir George Croke . . . of . . . cases in the King's Bench and Common Pleas* . . . 2 v. 4th ed. London, 1791.

Dalton, M., *The Country Justice*. London, 1618; 1619; 1626; 1630; 1635; 1655; 1666; 1682.

Successive editions of such manuals occasionally reveal changes in emphasis.

Dyer, J., *Reports of Cases in the Reigns of Henry VIII, Edward VI, Mary, and Elizabeth*. 3 pt. London, 1794.

Fitzherbert, A., *L'Office et authoritie de justices de peace* . . . enlarge per R. Crompton. London, 1583.

Hawarde, J., *Les Reportes del Cases in Camera Stellata, 1593 to 1609*, ed. W. P. Baildon. London, 1894.

[Hobart, H.], *The Reports of Sir H. Hobart* . . . 5th ed. London, 1724.

[Hutton, R.], *The Reports of Sir Richard Hutton . . . Containing . . . Many Choice Cases . . . in the . . . Reigns of King James and King Charles*. 2nd ed. London, 1682.

Keble, J., *Reports in the Court of King's Bench* . . . 3 pt. London, 1685.

Lambard, W., *Eirenarcha*: or, *of the Office of the Justices of Peace* . . . London, 1581; 1582; 1588; 1594; 1599; 1602; 1610.

See under Dalton. Lambard's handbook for justices of the peace was the basis for all its successors.

Select Cases Before the King's Council in the Star Chamber, 1477-1544, ed. I. S. Leadam. 2 v. Selden Society, XVI, XXV. London, 1903, 1911.

Sheppard, W., *The Whole Office of the Country Justice of Peace.* 2nd ed. 2 pt. London, 1652.

GENERAL

The Acts and Ordinances of the Eastland Company. By M. Sellers. Camden Society, 3rd Series, XI. n. p., 1906.

Aubrey, J., *Collections for the Natural and Topographical History of Wiltshire,* ed. J. Britton. London, 1847.

The Diary and Autobiography of Edmund Bohun, Esq., . . . With an introductory memoir . . . by S. W. Rix. Beccles, 1853.

Diary of Henry Townshend of Elmley Lovett, 1640–1663, ed. J. W. Willis Bund. Worcestershire Historical Society. London, 1920.

Diary of Walter Yonge, Esq. . . . , ed. G. Roberts. Camden Society, XLI. London, 1848.

Farm and Cottage Inventories of Mid-Essex, 1635–1749, ed. F. W. Steer. Chelmsford, 1950.

Gerard, T., *The Particular Description of the County of Somerset.* Somerset Record Society, XV. n. p., 1900.

Contemporary, useful for manorial descents.

Habington, T., *A Survey of Worcestershire.* By John Amphlett. Worcestershire Historical Society. 3 v. Oxford, 1895–1899.

Local families and estates described by a contemporary of Catholic connections.

[Hales, John], *A Discourse of the Common Weal of This Realm of England* [1549], ed. E. Lamond. Cambridge, 1893.

The problems of his time as viewed by the best economic writer of the period.

Harrison, W., *Description of Britaine and England,* 2nd and 3rd Books, Part I, The Second Book, ed. F. J. Furnivall. The New Shakspere Society. London, 1877.

The classic description of Elizabethan England.

Historical Manuscripts Commission, Reports: *Buccleuch and Queensberry, Duke of,* MSS. at Montagu House, 3 v. 1899–1926.

—— *Hatfield House MSS.* (Salisbury, Marquess of). 18 v. (In progress.)

Essential source material to examine, but with relatively little of direct bearing on the present study.

—— *Various Collections*, 8 v. 1901–1914.

—— *Wodehouse, E. R., Esq.*, MSS., 13th Report, App. 4.

Latimer, H., *Works*, ed. G. E. Corrie. Parker Society. 2 v. Cambridge, 1844–45.

[Leland, J.], *The Itinerary of John Leland*, ed. L. T. Smith. 5 v. London, 1907–1910.

Indispensable source for local conditions in the pre-Elizabethan generation.

Norden, J., *Speculi Britanniae Pars* . . . By Sir Henry Ellis. Camden Society, IX. London, 1840.

Contemporary description of Essex by the noted topographer.

The Official Papers of Sir Nathaniel Bacon of Stiffkey, Norfolk, ed. H. W. Saunders. Camden Society, 3rd Series, XXVI. London, 1915.

A unique collection, outside sessions records, in its variety and fullness; the supplementary volume should also be consulted. Provides two commissions of the peace for the county, 1614 and 1616, not included in section above.

Prices and Wages in England, ed. Sir William Beveridge. London, 1939.

Supplementary Stiffkey Papers, ed. F. W. Brooks. Camden Society 3rd Series, LII, Miscellany XVI. London, 1936.

Trevelyan Papers, Part III, ed. Sir W. C. Trevelyan and Sir C. E. Trevelyan. Camden Society, CV. n. p., 1872.

Tudor Economic Documents, ed. R. H. Tawney and E. Power. 3 v. London, 1924.

An easily accessible collection of essential source material.

The Visitations of Essex, ed. W. C. Metcalfe. Harleian Society, XIII–XIV. 2 v. London, 1878–1879.

The Visitation of Somerset in 1623, ed. F. T. Colby. Harleian Society, XI. London, 1876.

Westcote, T. *A View of Devonshire in 1630*, ed. G. Oliver and P. Jones. Exeter, 1845.

Unusual among county descriptions for its detail on social and economic classes and on local industry and trade. Useful also for family connections.

Wilson, T., *A Discourse upon Usury* [1572]. With an Historical Introduction by R. H. Tawney. London, 1925.

SECONDARY WORKS

General histories and works of reference are not included unless directly cited in the text.

BOOKS

Baldwin, F. E., *Sumptuary Legislation and Personal Regulation in England*. Baltimore, 1926.

Beaven, A. B., *The Aldermen of the City of London*. 2 v. London, 1908.

Blomefield, F., and C. Parkin, *An Essay towards a Topographical History of the County of Norfolk*. 11 v. 2nd ed. London, 1805–1810.

Boyne, W., *Tokens Issued in the Seventeenth Century . . .* London, 1858.

Campbell, M., *The English Yeoman*. New Haven, 1942.

Chanter, J. R., and T. Wainwright, *Barnstaple Records*. 2 v. Barnstaple, 1900.

Cheyney, E. P., *A History of England from the Defeat of the Armada to the Death of Elizabeth*. 2 v. New York, 1926.

Collinson, J., *The History and Antiquities of the County of Somerset . . .* 3 v. Bath, 1791.

Useful for its detail on the number of houses per parish.

Cotton, W., *An Elizabethan Guild of the City of Exeter*. Exeter, 1873.

The only account of one of the important local organizations of the Merchant Adventurers.

Court, W. H. B., *The Rise of the Midland Industries 1600–1838*. London, 1938.

The only special study of the metalworking industries of the midland counties in the sixteenth and seventeenth centuries, although chief attention is given to the later seventeenth and the eighteenth centuries.

Cunningham, W., *The Growth of English Industry and Commerce*. 6th ed. 3 v. Cambridge, 1919.

Dunlop, O. J., and R. D. Denman, *English Apprenticeship and Child Labour*, New York, 1912.

The only special study in the field. Based on guild and municipal records rather than on those of county quarter sessions. Records of the central courts not utilized. Chief attention is given to the period beginning with the Civil War, and to conditions of apprenticeship and the apprentices' training.

Ehrenberg, R., *Hamburg und England im Zeitalter der Königin Elisabeth.* Jena, 1896.

Still an important source for information not available elsewhere outside archives.

Epstein, M., *The Early History of the Levant Company.* London, 1908.

Largely superseded by A. C. Wood's fuller study.

Foss, E., *Biographia Juridica.* London, 1870.

Friis, A., *Alderman Cockayne's Project and the Cloth Trade.* Copenhagen and London, 1927.

Valuable for information on markets for different types of English woolens as well as for its detailed accounts of policy.

Gras, N. S. B., *The Evolution of the English Corn Market.* Cambridge, Mass., 1915.

The standard work on the subject; indispensable.

Hall, H., *Society in the Elizabethan Age.* 3rd ed. London, 1892.

Contains transcripts of illustrative source material.

Hamilton, A. H. A., *Quarter Sessions from Queen Elizabeth to Queen Anne* . . . London, 1878.

A description of material in the Devonshire quarter sessions records, but with illustrative extracts only. Contains a commission of the peace for the county, 1592, not included in section above.

Hamilton, E. J., *American Treasure and the Price Revolution in Spain, 1501–1650.* Cambridge, Mass., 1934.

Hampson, E. M., *The Treatment of Poverty in Cambridgeshire, 1597–1834.* Cambridge, 1934.

Heaton, H., *The Yorkshire Woollen and Worsted Industries.* Oxford 1920.

A valuable regional study, but with chief emphasis on the later seventeenth and the eighteenth centuries.

Heckscher, E. F., *Mercantilism,* tr. Mendel Shapiro. 2 v. London 1935.

Already a classic, and indispensable for any study of economic policy in the sixteenth to the eighteenth centuries.

An Historical Geography of England, ed. H. C. Darby. Cambridge, 1936.

Hoare, R. C., and others, *The History of Modern Wiltshire.* 6 v London, 1822–1844.

Holdsworth, W. S., *A History of English Law.* 9 v. Boston, 1924–1931

Hoskins, W. G., *Essays in Leicestershire History.* Liverpool, 1950

—— *Midland England.* London, 1949.

Kelsall, R. K., *Wage Regulation under the Statute of Artificers.* London, 1938.

Kramer, S., *The English Craft Gilds.* New York, 1927.

Latimer, J., *The Annals of Bristol in the Seventeenth Century.* Bristol, 1900.

—— *Sixteenth-Century Bristol.* Bristol, 1908.

Leonard, E. M., *The Early History of English Poor Relief.* Cambridge, 1900.

Lipson, E., *The Economic History of England.* 3 v. I, Fifth Edition, New York and London, 1929; II and III, London, 1931.

—— *The History of the Woollen and Worsted Industries.* London, 1921.

Mason, R. H., *The History of Norfolk . . .* 2 v. London, 1884–85.

Maxwell, P. B., *The Interpretation of Statutes.* London, 1946.

Mendenhall, T. C., *The Shrewsbury Drapers and the Welsh Wool Trade in the 16th and 17th Centuries.* Oxford Historical Series, No. 23. London, 1953.

Moens, W. J. C., *The Walloons and Their Church at Norwich . . .* Publications of the Huguenot Society of London. 2 v. in 1. London, 1887–88.

Morant, P., *The History and Antiquities of the County of Essex . . .* 2 v. London, 1768.

Useful for manorial descents and occasionally for comment on the location of industries.

Morris, R. H., *Chester in the Plantagenet and Tudor Reigns.* [Chester, 1893].

Neale, J. E., *The Elizabethan House of Commons.* London, 1949.

Nef, J. U., *The Rise of the British Coal Industry.* 2 v. London, 1932.

Price, W. H., *The English Patents of Monopoly.* Cambridge, Mass., 1913.

A standard in its field but with less direct bearing on the present study than its title would suggest, since its chief emphasis is on industrial patents.

Ramsay, G. D., *The Wiltshire Woollen Industry in the Sixteenth and Seventeenth Centuries.* London, 1943.

The only special study in print of this important regional industry.

Read, C., *Mr. Secretary Walsingham and the Policy of Queen Elizabeth.* 3 v. Cambridge, Mass., 1925.

Reid, R. R., *The King's Council in the North.* London, 1921.

Rowse, A. L., *The England of Elizabeth.* London, 1950.

—— *Tudor Cornwall.* London, 1941.

Scott, W. R., *The Constitution and Finance of English, Scottish and Irish Joint-Stock Companies to 1720.* 3 v. Cambridge, 1912.

Skeel, C. A. J., *The Council in the Marches of Wales.* London, 1904.

Strype, J., *Annals of the Reformation and Establishment of Religion* . . . 4 v. Oxford, 1824.

—— *Ecclesiastical Memorials* . . . 3 v. Oxford, 1822.

Appendices in both these works contain valuable primary sources.

Tawney, R. H., *The Agrarian Problem in the Sixteenth Century.* London, 1912.

Trevor-Roper, H. R., *The Gentry 1540–1640,* The Economic History Review Supplements 1. London and New York, n. d. [1953].

Unwin, G., *Industrial Organization in the Sixteenth and Seventeenth Centuries.* Oxford, 1904.

—— *Studies in Economic History.* London, 1927.

Victoria History of the Counties of England, ed. William Page and others. Westminster, 1900– (In progress.)

Wadsworth, A. P., and J. De L. Mann, *The Cotton Trade and Industrial Lancashire, 1600–1780.* Manchester, 1931.

The chief emphasis is on the later seventeenth and the eighteenth centuries.

Webb, S., and B. Webb, *English Local Government: The Parish and the County.* London, 1906.

Indispensable for any work involving knowledge of local government, even though dealing primarily with developments after the Revolution.

—— *English Local Government: English Poor Law History: Part I, The Old Poor Law.* London, 1927.

Of less immediate relevance to the present study.

Wedgwood, C. V., *Strafford, 1593–1641.* London, 1935.

Willan, T. S., *The English Coasting Trade, 1600–1750.* Manchester, 1938.

Willcox, W. B., *Gloucestershire, A Study in Local Government, 1590–1640.* New Haven, 1940.

ARTICLES

Cozens-Hardy, B., "The Maritime Trade of the Port of Blakeney, Norfolk, 1587–1590," *Norfolk Record Society,* VIII (n.p., 1936), 17–37.

Deardorff, N. R., "English Trade in the Baltic during the Reign of

Elizabeth," *Studies in the History of English Commerce in the Tudor Period* (New York, 1912), 219–328.

Derry, T. K., "The Enforcement of a Seven Years' Apprenticeship under the Statute of Artificers," *Abstracts of Dissertations for the Degree of Doctor of Philosophy*, Oxford University, IV (Oxford, 1931), 9–17.

Dickin, E. P., "Notes on the Coast, Shipping, and Sea-borne Trade of Essex, from 1565 to 1577," *Transactions of the Essex Archaeological Society*, XVII, New Series (Colchester, 1926), 153–164.

Elton, G. R., "Informing for Profit: A Sidelight on Tudor Methods of Law-Enforcement," *The Cambridge Historical Journal*, XI, No. 2 (1954), 149–167.

Fisher, F. J., "Commercial Trends and Policy in Sixteenth-Century England," *The Economic History Review*, X, No. 2 (November 1940), 95–117.

Valuable for the statistics on cloth exports, with however much qualification they must be used.

—— "The Development of the London Food Market, 1540–1640," *The Economic History Review*, V, No. 2 (April 1935), 46–64.

—— "Some Experiments in Company Organization," *The Economic History Review*, IV, No. 2 (April 1933), 177–194.

Gay, E. F., "The Rise of an English Country Family," *The Huntington Library Quarterly*, I, No. 4 (July 1938), 367–390.

Gay, M. R., "Aspects of Elizabethan Apprenticeship," *Facts and Factors in Economic History* (Cambridge, Mass., 1932), 134–163.

Hill, C., "Professor Lavrovsky's Study of a Seventeenth-Century Manor," *The Economic History Review*, XVI, No. 2 (1946), 125–129.

Kerridge, E., "The Movement of Rent, 1540–1640," *The Economic History Review*, Second Series, VI, No. 1 (August 1953), 16–34.

Peyton, S. A., "The Village Population in the Tudor Lay Subsidy Rolls," *The English Historical Review*, XXX, No. 118 (April 1915), 234–250.

Putnam, B. H., "Northamptonshire Wage Assessments of 1560 and 1667," *The Economic History Review*, I, No. 1 (January 1927), 124–134.

Reynolds, B., "Elizabethan Traders in Normandy," *The Journal of Modern History*, IX, No. 3 (September 1937), 289–303.

Rich, E. E., "The Population of Elizabethan England," *The Economic History Review*, Second Series, II, No. 3 (1950), 247–265.

Simpson, H. B., "The Office of Constable," *The English Historical Review*, X, No. XL (October 1895), 625–641.

Tawney, A. J., and R. H. Tawney, "An Occupational Census of the Seventeenth Century," *The Economic History Review*, V, No. 1 (October 1934), 25–64.

A unique and important yardstick for various local studies.

Tawney, R. H., "The Rise of the Gentry, 1558–1640," *The Economic History Review*, XI (1941), 1–38.

—— "The Rise of the Gentry: a Postscript," *The Economic History Review*, Second Series, VII, No. 1 (August 1954), 91–97.

Thrupp, S., "The Grocers of London," *Studies in English Trade in the Fifteenth Century*, ed. E. Power and M. M. Postan (London, 1933), 247–292.

INDEX